Studies in Romance Languages : 1

The Literary Mind
of Medieval &
Renaissance Spain

Essays by Otis H. Green

Introduction by John E. Keller

The University Press of Kentucky

Lexington 1970

Standard Book Number 8131-1204-4
Library of Congress Catalog Card Number 74-111510
Copyright © 1970 by The University Press of Kentucky
A statewide cooperative scholarly publishing agency serving Berea College,
Centre College of Kentucky, Eastern Kentucky University, Kentucky State
College, Morehead State University, Murray State University, University of
Kentucky, University of Louisville, and Western Kentucky University
Editorial and Sales Offices: Lexington, Kentucky 40506

Contents

Preface

In this brief introductory study no attempt has been made to present anything like a complete treatment of the life and works of Otis H. Green. Nor can we offer here the complete listing of his copious bibliography. Dr. Green's friend and colleague at the University of Pennsylvania, Arnold Reichenberger, has written of these matters and one may read and refer to both in the January 1969 *Hispanic Review*, an issue enlarged beyond the journal's normal size so as to honor Dr. Green with articles written by a small number of his friends in the field of Hispanic studies.

For the sake of a somewhat greater sense of completeness, however, and for those unable to consult the honorary number of *Hispanic Review*, we reprint a "vignette" from *PMLA*, LXXVI, no. 5 (December 1961), iv, written by George Winchester Stone to honor Green as outgoing first vice president of the association. Dr. Stone wrote: "Otis Howard Green (OHG to his friends), retiring First Vice President of the Association, first joined the MLA in 1924, shortly after he had received his Master's degree from Pennsylvania State College. He came there from his undergraduate work at Colgate, and continued for his Doctor's degree in Spanish at the University of Pennsylvania (1927). He is a broadly travelled man of wide school experience, as attested by the fact that he was born in Monroe, Michigan, educated in New York and Pennsylvania, studied in Madrid, taught in secondary school in Hightstown, New Jersey, and has taught (to date) at the University of Pennsylvania for thirty-eight years, with summer school variation for five years at the University of Colorado. From 1938 to 1945 he served his turn as Chairman of the Department of Romance Languages at Penn. He is on the Advisory Council for the Department of Modern Languages, Princeton, and has taken active interest in many professional organizations such as the Committee on Renaissance Studies of the ACLS, the Renaissance Society of America, the

Medieval Academy of America, the Modern Humanities Research Association, the Instituto Internacional de Literatura Iberoamericana, and the American Association of Teachers of Spanish and Portuguese. He has long been co-editor of the *Hispanic Review*, having been associated with that scholarly publication since its beginning in 1933. As every Hispanist knows, he has contributed widely to the learned journals in his field of primary interest—the ideological background of the Spanish Renaissance. He has published over seventeen articles and books in the last nine years. His first book was the *Life and Works of Lupercio Leonardo de Argensola* (1927), the Renaissance Spanish poet and dramatist. In 1952 he published *Courtly Love in Quevedo* (with a Spanish translation in 1955). In 1944 he had edited *Una Excursión a los Indios Ranqueles*, by Lucio V. Mansilla. He is a loyal and devoted friend to persons and to scholarship, as attested by his transcribing, editing, and completing the late Joseph Eugene Gillet's fourth volume of his monumental edition of *Torres Naharro and the Drama of the Renaissance.*

"OHG has a unique way of arranging his time. One of the very few people who has a key to College Hall, he arrives at his office any time between half past five and seven in the morning, just to get a leg up on his work, has a second breakfast between eight and nine, while the mail is being distributed, and carries on from there. His extracurricular passion is for camping, hiking, and the quiet of the Adirondacks, the Rockies, and the Canadian mountains. Amid the solitude of nature he composes verses from time to time, or writes of things far removed from the Spanish Golden Age, such as "Adirondack Sea Serpent," and for *The General Magazine and Historical Chronicle* of the Pennsylvania alumni. His son is a teacher of biology at Penn, and his three grandchildren enjoy life as grandchildren do.

"OHG has been a member of the MLA Committee on Research Activities and the Committee on Book Publications. As a member of this last committee we came to know his quiet nature, solid commentary, and high set of standards for scholarly achievement. Since we have often seen eye to eye with him on MLA committee problems we are more than ever inclined to praise his perspicuity as a committeeman. His motto is *hic et nunc,* so every letter, inquiry, set of proof, and the like is handled by him with the greatest possible speed and dispatch, commensurate with thoughtful judgment on the particular problems involved."

Thanks to this succinct and excellently presented vignette which would be equally pertinent to Otis Green's career as he leaves the presidency of the Modern Language Association in 1969, we can now turn to the prefatory remarks necessary to the presentation of the articles we have selected from his copious publication.

From 1937 or so onward Otis Green in studies and even in book reviews began consistently to serve notice on the scholarly world of Hispanism that he was then attempting and would continue to attempt through his lifetime to replace the generalities so frequently, carelessly, and even stubbornly made about the Middle Ages, the Renaissance, and the Baroque. He planned to accomplish these aims by marshaling plain but pertinent facts to show just how inane, and therefore how incorrect and unsatisfying, such generalities are. In this flight from what he calls "notional beliefs" handed down across the ages, Green sought to build upon a solid ground of actual evidence, rather than upon the shaky ground of opinion. The articles printed herein, not only those which appeared before the publication of his magnum opus, *Spain and the Western Tradition: The Castilian Mind in Literature from El Cid to Calderón*, but also those drawn directly from that great four-volume work, will reveal some of this foundation of solid ground composed of evidence assembled from the actual thought and ideas with which medieval and Renaissance men colored their writings. We should be grateful to Otis Green for taking the time and for exercising the care necessary to study and assimilate so much of the available and vast corpus of literary material which provided this evidence.

Not many scholars have the daring, sheer grit, and determination, plus, of course, the knowledge required to begin and to carry through such an undertaking. And almost none would have emerged from such fertile and versatile research and publication with a masterwork like his.

But Otis Green's daring is proverbial and has manifested itself from as early as 1908 when he realized the inadequacy of Spanish scholarship dedicated to the influence of certain areas of medieval literature upon the Spanish Renaissance. It was in this stage of

Green's scholarly investigation that he discovered even Menéndez y Pelayo to be unaware of some of these influences, a matter to be discussed in the Introduction to this collection of essays.

Green's scholarship, since he began to publish the results of his research and since he began to teach and otherwise make known his beliefs and findings, has made a definitely strong impact upon Hispanic studies everywhere. By the time he began to publish *Spain and the Western Tradition* the volume and quality of his thinking was well known and his scholarship was unquestioned. It seems no more than natural and to be expected that he should interpret in his longest work the flowering, and the withering, too, of five whole centuries of Spanish literary culture as manifested in the basic ideas of Spain's great medieval and Renaissance authors and thinkers.

Our volume of articles selected from Otis Green's writings does not pretend to offer anything resembling a detailed coverage of his thinking on these matters. Instead, it presents only a modest number of the many important aspects of his lifelong effort. Some of the essays offered herein have come directly from his magnum opus, while others—in fact the majority—are drawn from materials printed elsewhere, some in out-of-date and difficult-to-obtain or out-of-print journals. The arrangement of the articles we present is not chronological according to their publication. They are chronological, however, in another sense, for their order has been determined, insofar as is possible, by the periods and the authors which they discuss. For this reason the essays on medieval subjects precede those on matters pertaining to the Renaissance. All, however, develop some important aspect or aspects of the thinking of men in the Middle Ages and in the Renaissance, and all play an important role in Otis Green's own thought about Spanish literature in these two significant periods.

I am persuaded to believe that a mélange of Green's ideas, such as that making up the present volume, can be more satisfactory to the general public than Green's attempt to encompass all his ideas in his four-volume work, since it can be argued that in disparate essays the reader would not have to encounter and consider the vast sweep and depth which of necessity would exist in a more definitive work, and people of a wide variety of interests might dip into their own and related areas without having to absorb the vast totality of Green's thought in his opus. Indeed, Alexander Parker has pointed out in his article "Recent Scholarship in Spanish Literature," *Renaissance Quarterly*, XXI, no. 1 (Spring 1968), 118–24, that no one, not even Otis Green, can present a complete set of ideas about so vast a matter, leading him to say with reference to *Spain and the Western Tradition,* that "It is not quite as systematic as it might have been," (p. 122) and that "vast though the work is there are even gaps that one would like to see filled: nonetheless the general argument [that it is no longer possible to segment the cultural history of Spain into clearly distinguished 'epochs'] is a convincing one" (p. 123). It certainly is convincing. This and other scholarly excellencies of the book caused the careful Parker to write also that Otis Green's *Spain and the Western Tradition* "is the most important single contribution in the last few years to the study of Spanish literature and its intellectual background in the Renaissance and the Baroque periods" (p. 122).

Ideas such as the segmenting of Spain's cultural history into distinguishable "epochs," is a good example of what Otis Green abhors. This and other ideas not acceptable to him have led to the articles we publish in this volume. As one unravels Green's thinking, it becomes clear that he is not trying to impose his views upon his colleagues; he has no ax to grind; and he does not set out to be controversial. Nor does he stubbornly cleave to one view, even if by refusing to do so, he sometimes weakens his own arguments. His plan is to collect evidence that should have been collected by earlier scholars, but which they overlooked, and with this evidence to help his students and his colleagues to see some of the errors perpetrated across the years and to prevent such errors from appearing in their own thinking and from rendering their own studies erroneous.

John E. Keller

Introduction

The first essay we offer is Chapter I in Volume I of *Spain and the Western Tradition*. Its title is "The Medieval Tradition: *Sic et Non*." In this essay the reader will find the kind of *mesura* so lauded by the sages of the Middle Ages as they indulged in the double standard accepted by the inhabitants of that distant period. This selection has already proved to be of exceptional interest to medievalists everywhere. Permit me to cite here some previously published ideas of my own, touching this particular point, which appeared in a review for *Speculum*, XL (1965), 349. "Chapter I explores the oft-accepted, yet not fully understood, contradictory character of the Hebrew-Graeco-Roman-Medieval-Renaissance cultural synthesis. Professor Green's knowedge of the relationship of these problems to medieval Spanish life and letters is deep. Seldom, if ever, has this reviewer found a clearer treatment, or one as fresh in approach, or as bright with new light thrown upon the results of the scholarship of the last few years, or so panoramic in an over-all ingathering of facts from the major areas of medieval research."

Alexander Parker in his own review of Volume I of *Spain and the Western Tradition* (*Hispanic Review*, XXXIII [1965], 66) writes convincingly of Green's impact and of the importance of his work, and, at the same time, shows clearly that he, and by implication other scholars, though not in complete agreement with Green, are nonetheless influenced by his thought. "This first volume deals with the themes of chivalry and love: Its great merit is that it demonstrates the essential continuity between Middle Ages, Renaissance and Baroque. There is, of course, development, but above a persisting tradition which is that of the concepts, attitudes and imagery of courtly love. This is not contradicted but 'modified and ennobled' by the Renaissance Neoplatonism of Italy. The former had been in its own way, an attempt to affirm the nobility rather than the depravity of human love; the latter had the same aim but gave it a different direction." Parker, careful to tell his readers that Green's assertions are sound and plausible, goes on to make it clear what scholars should question. "While I do not think that Professor Green's argument can be contradicted, there remains (as is inevitable in the case of every pioneer study) room for further discussion and clarification of definitions. This is likely to concern the framework or setting in which the first and last chapters place this historical exposition of the love theme—in what Professor Green calls the *Sic et Non* of medieval civilization, the attempt of the Classical-Hebrew-Christian tradition to harmonize the claims of the Human and the claims of the Divine. Professor Green, while realizing that without this there could have been no literature, finds in Spanish writers of the Golden Age a remarkable indulgence in 'sinning,' and this he calls 'truancy.' By looking at the matter in this light he is virtually a pioneer breaking through the frontiers of conventional literary history and criticism. The questions he hereby opens up I myself find fascinating. He is right to see the theme of love within the context of the reconciliation of human glory and spiritual duty, but whether one sees this reconciliation achieved in particular cases will depend on where one places the reconciling mean between the extremes of 'humanism' and 'puritanism'; over the centuries the standards aspired to, even within Christianity, have tended to differ, sometimes widely."

Professor Parker pursues the *sic et non*, so stressed by Otis Green, into subsequent centuries of Spanish literature, as, of course, had Green in his opus. He writes: "Professor Green (and these are most interesting sections of his book) sees the reconciliation succeed in Garcilaso but fail in Herrera. The success of the one and the failure of the other are, I would agree, indisputable (especially if aesthetic values are also allowed their way), but this presupposes a sympathy with Garcilaso's vision of human glory which many of his own countrymen in the generation or two after him would have considered it 'truancy' to feel. It is, of course, impossible to speak of 'reconciliation' (in Professor Green's sense) in the Mystics, but they, or at least the philosophically-minded among them, would not have accepted as true to Plato's philosophy of love any lesser level of fruition than the one reached by them.

This is not to question the rightness of Professor Green's judgements; I wish only to emphasize that his terms of reference are so temptingly wide that he will encourage speculation in many directions."

Since, as Parker points out, Professor Green is virtually a pioneer breaking through the frontiers of conventional literary history and criticism, the time is not ripe for assessing the greatest impact of such exploration upon Hispanic studies: his opus, after all, has so recently been published. Scholarly studies and theories sprout sometimes with maddening slowness, and if they are generally accepted within the lifetime of their creators, they are fortunate, indeed, and exceptional. Even so, Otis Green's influence is being felt strongly and there is reason to believe that a work as thought-provoking as *Spain and the Western Tradition* has made a contribution of consequence.

Edward Glaser, whose scholarship deserves great respect, sees Volumes I and II as remarkable additions to modern thinking on literary matters. He writes in a review of Green's first two volumes for *Modern Philology*, LXIII, no. 4 (May 1966), 349–50: "The two volumes under discussion, a partial realization of an ambitious plan, present a thematic organization that is entirely original. Furthermore, they show that the study of literature may not be detached from that of the culture which produced it; and they make a convincing case for the claim that sustained attention to European trends will be repaid by fresh insights into the Iberian literary genius. One final observation: While an undertaking of such magnitude is bound to displease some critics in some places, it is beyond dispute that *Spain and the Western Tradition* will remain for years to come a work unique in its kind."

To Manuel Durán the impact to be made by *Spain and the Western Tradition* will be great indeed. In a review in *Hispania*, I (1967), 1018, he sums up his opinions: "The dominant feeling for this reader at the end of the entire series is one of admiration. Prof. Green has included so many facts, so many ideas, so many interpretations in these four massive volumes that no review, no matter how long, can do full justice to them and enumerate all the points that these volumes include. Let us add that they are being translated into Spanish and are to appear shortly in Spain, published by

Editorial Gredos. Prof. Green's thesis is carefully expounded and documented. It is basically one of *identity* – of Spain and the Western cultural tradition – and *continuity* – of Renaissance and post-Renaissance Spain with the Medieval tradition. This thesis needed to be restated. Implicit in the works of a Menéndez y Pelayo, for instance, it has been obscured or challenged by some contemporary scholars. It was time to reexamine the whole panorama of Spanish culture. At times we cannot help but feel that Prof. Green has 'overcompensated,' that is, that he underlines too much the continuity and the identity that did exist, that did play certainly a crucial role in shaping Spanish culture. This is probably unavoidable. No scholar operates in a vacuum. There is always a polemical background that makes him underline certain ideas more than others. This is his way of making his attitude clear and explicit, of telling us what he thinks we may have forgotten. As for this reader, although I disagree occasionally with Prof. Green's emphasis and believe that some of the motivations for the facts Prof. Green so aptly describes should be sought elsewhere, I think we have in *Spain and the Western Tradition* a unique tool, one which shall prove indispensable to several generations of Hispanists. I intend to keep it on my desk and consult it frequently. I think most Hispanists, here, in Spain or elsewhere, whether they agree with Prof. Green's thesis or not, will do the same."

In general, then, reviewers see *Spain and the Western Tradition* as a major work of present-day interpretation and criticism and believe that its scholarly impact will continue and expand.

In 1958 Otis Green's article "On Juan Ruiz's Parody of the Canonical Hours" appeared in *Hispanic Review*, XXVI (1958), 12–34. It was still another learned approach to the why and the wherefore of the *Libro de Buen Amor* of Juan Ruiz, Archpriest of Hita, and it made sense with Green's convincing documentation and arguments as to what Bruce Wardropper has happily described as "the innocent Goliardic nature of the parody of the Canonical Hours" (*Modern Literature*, Vol. II [Englewood Cliffs, N.J., Prentice-Hall, 1968], 80). Those scholars and especially those students interested in the famous *Libro*, who had been floundering in somewhat stunned confusion in the sea of theory and learned controversy over what Juan Ruiz wanted to tell his audiences –

whether they were readers or hearers—were relieved at Green's simple, straightforward, and acceptable explanation. To them it makes no difference that not all scholars have accepted his beliefs, for even though Green differs, often radically, from such luminaries as Leo Spitzer, the late and lamented María Rosa Lida de Malkiel, and Américo Castro, to name only three, his ideas are well documented and indicate that he has assembled a strong arsenal of scholarship, ranging from medieval latinity, for the most part clerical, to the most up-to-date modern trends exemplified in the anthropological concept of the culture pattern à la Ruth Benedict.

One is tempted here to turn aside and to discuss Green's interpretation of Juan Ruiz's famous prose Prologue to his *Libro de Buen Amor,* for here again is Green at his best in debunking many of the complex and often not very plausible ideas put forward by scholars of this century and the last. This, however, is a long, though interesting, story and it can be read in detail in *Spain and the Western Tradition,* Chapter II, entitled "Medieval Laughter: the *Book of Good Love.*" I mention this treatment of the Prologue, because it, like the essay "Juan Ruiz's Parody of the Canonical Hours," demonstrates the depth of Green's thought and scholarly research in the preparation of ideas to be presented to the public. Both reveal that Green does not theorize without the necessary investigations of background, no matter how complex and difficult that background may be. One is led to speculate, as he reads Green's works, on the failure of previous scholars, especially of those deeply grounded in medieval [scholastic] philosophy, allegory, and satire, to unravel the clearly obvious meanings of the archpriest in his famous parody.

Readers can pursue, in Chapter II of Green's opus, some of his other ideas as to the fourteenth-century mind, as represented by the thought of the Archpriest of Hita. Green certainly maintains a constant plea for a down-to-earth *raison d'être.* To him the *Libro* is an art of love, about several pairs of lovers, and is one of the most prolonged and uproarious parodies ever written about any human society. He sees, as I have stated in a review for *Speculum,* Juan Ruiz as a preacher, but not one of the usual kind. He sees Juan Ruiz attempt "to solve the preaching dilemma by two principal concessions: (1) the claim made by him that his worldly wicked book has a deep allegorical significance; and (2) the use of the palinode or recantation in which the truant literary artist returns to the religious fold with all sincerity" (from a review by John E. Keller, *Speculum*, XL [1965], 350).

Juan Ruiz, then, like Chaucer his contemporary, illustrates a phase of the *sic et non* treated in the first essay of our mélange of Otis Green, a phase of a thought pattern, of an acceptance of right and wrong, of a dichotomy perforce recognized by writers throughout the Middle Ages. Whether Otis Green had an ax to grind or not—and most theorists indeed must grind axes—he has given his readers much food for thought. He has focused light upon some very important facets of the medieval Spanish mind. Green has showed that in the medieval Spaniard's need for pleasure and comic relief from his awe of the sacred, he sought satisfaction in humor.

The third essay lets his reader see the tenacity of the Spaniard in retaining his medieval heritage, a most significant element of Spanish thinking always and even to this day.

The subject matter of this essay, "Courtly Love in the Spanish *Cancioneros*," printed in *PMLA*, LXIV, no. 1 (1949), 247–301, moves the reader chronologically into the fifteenth century and out of the true Middle Ages. Indeed, the fifteenth century, used by Green because this was the century of the *cancioneros*, is but a steppingstone into the sixteenth and seventeenth centuries. Apparently what Green calls the "truancy" concerning love continued in a somewhat, but not a very different form, and this age-old truancy, so much a part of courtly love, lived on and had to be reckoned with far into the seventeenth century.

The essay is especially pertinent and is deeply interesting to any student of literature, indeed to any student of ideas, mores, and human thought. Green wrote it partially because no less a personage than Menéndez y Pelayo himself had greatly disparaged the courtly poetry of the *cancioneros*, which he called "futile verses, verses with no species of passion . . . subtle concepts . . . something which in sum, entertains the ear agreeably without any impression in the soul" (translation mine from *Juan Boscán* [Madrid, 1908], 240). Such disparagement by a person of Menéndez y Pelayo's stature, gravely damaged scholarly interest in an

important area of Spanish literature and discouraged a few generations of students to boot. It was one of those notional ideas so much
abhorred by Green, and it needed to be corrected by evidence to
be found through careful study of the *cancionero* poets.

The reader will observe in this lengthy essay much that is familiar to him, but also much—and this, of course, is all important—
much that is divergent from previous notions about courtly love
and especially about its tenacious hold upon the Spanish mind in
the Renaissance.

The fourth essay, "Symbols of Change," is taken from *Spain and
the Western Tradition* where it appears as Chapter I in Volume III.
Both the second and third volumes lead the reader out of the
Middle Ages and into the Renaissance and the Golden Age, making
Volumes II and III far more diverse in content than Volume I. In
theme and structure, then, Volume II is quite independent of
Volume I, although, to be sure, it is a confirmation of it.

"Symbols of Change" follows Spain's almost sudden emergence
from the inferiority she had felt earlier into the position of a great
world power, replete with proud national traditions and blessed
with intellectuals accepted by the great minds of Europe. In this
essay Green begins with the dates 1380 and 1389, during which
period Spain became fully conscious for the first time of the marvels of Antiquity. He then progresses across the next two centuries
and prepares his reader with the foundations and the backgrounds
of Spain's later greatness which attained its culmination in her
Golden Age. In this important essay we see great figures emerge—
such thinkers, believers, and doers as Juan de Mena, the Marqués de
Santillana, Nebrija, Columbus, Cisneros, Herrera, Luis de León.
Here we see Spain in ferment. Indeed, this chapter from Volume III of *Spain and the Western Tradition* opens the door to the
several areas of Spanish expansion—geographical, cultural, political,
intellectual, and religious.

In the High Renaissance in Spain one would expect the Spanish
mind to occupy itself, as did the European mind in general, with
the place of pagan mythology in the scheme of life. In his essay
" 'Fingen los poetas,' Notes on the Spanish Attitude toward Pagan
Mythology," from *Estudios Dedicados a Menéndez Pidal* (Madrid,
1950), Green shows us the thinking of some poets who opposed

the pagan myths, whether as allegorical interpretations of the Christian ethos or as merely beautiful decorations. We read of Jorge Manrique, Juan de Mena, Don Pedro of Portugal, Juan de Padilla, and Luis Vives in this connection; but then we turn to those Spaniards whose philosophy allowed them to accept the marvels of mythology–Santa Fe, Fray Alonso de Santa Cruz, Encina, and Pedro Calderón. On the one hand, then, stands Encina with his wholesome acceptance of the place of mythology in the scheme of literature, and on the other hand, stand the dissenters against mythology's place in any Christian writing. One could hardly choose a brief essay more indicative of divergent thought patterns and beliefs than this.

In the essay entitled "Se acicalaron los auditorios: An Aspect of the Spanish Literary Baroque," published in *Hispanic Review*, XXVII, no. 4 (1959), 413–22, Green treats the changing tastes of poets, as the Spanish erudite mind turned toward the baroque. These beginnings and this development came at the end of the sixteenth century and the beginning of the seventeenth, for here the Spanish public, for a time at least, turned toward the new elegance and away from simpler and clearer language. The same, we know, prevailed in England, France, Italy, and Germany. Green builds his evidence citing great names in the development of *elegancia y dulces palabras*. He includes Alonso García de Mata-moros, Juan Huarte de San Juan, Fray Diego de Velades, Francisco de Medina, Fray Pedro Malón de Chaide, Diego Pérez de Valdivia, Juan Bonifacio, Pedro Simón Abril, Fray Hortensio Félix de Paravicino, and Fray Diego de Moya, all of whom seem to Green to be fomenters of, for the most part, but to some degree as dissenters against, the new eloquence.

Green shows the desire of some segments of the public for complexity and dramatic action and words, both on the stage and in the pulpit. "It is thus seen," he writes, "that the *comedia* was not the only genre that was–almost–a communal enterprise. In pulpit oratory also, and in prose generally, the nation as a whole deter-mined the character of its culture: *se acicalaron* los ingenios, even among the *vulgo*."

Green's essay "Boscán and *Il Cortegiano*: The *Historia de Lean-dro y Hero*," *Boletín del Instituto Caro y Cuervo*, IV (1948),

3-14, reveals a typical Spanish Renaissance sophisticate's thinking as he planned and wrote his own particular version of the famous classical story of Hero and Leander in a form acceptable to his contemporaries. It is an interesting exercise, for it allows Green's readers to glimpse Boscán at work developing a poem that could satisfactorily metamorphose Musaeus' priestess of Aphrodite into a lady of the Renaissance and cause the passion of the lovers to conform to the code of Platonic love made evident by Castiglione in his *Il Cortegiano*. The essay is a remarkable portrayal of how Renaissance Spaniards and Renaissance Italians–Boscán and Castiglione–could regard as perfectly Christian the suicide of Hero and certain Platonic and Stoic ideas. "Greek and Roman ethics and moral wisdom," writes Green at the end of this article, "were regarded, both by Boscán and by Castiglione, as aids and handmaidens of Christian morality."

One of the most penetrating, thought-provoking, and complex chapters of *Spain and the Western Tradition* is Chapter II, entitled *Desengaño*, in Volume IV (1966), 43-76. Alexander Parker, in his deeply perceptive review for *Hispanic Review*, XXXVI (1968), 59-63, writes of this chapter: "The chapter on *desengaño* is the most valuable in the book. At last students, so many of whom find it difficult in our affluent society to grasp the concept, can be given a very helpful definition, worth quoting here almost in full: '*desengaño* is related to the sort of awakening to the nature of reality that the Prodigal Son must have experienced: "I will arise and go to my father." This waking to true awareness is called *caer en la cuenta:* to have the scales fall from one's eyes, to see things as they are. Such a state of mind is desirable. Disillusionment comes to be viewed, even to be venerated, as a sort of wisdom–the wisdom of the Stoic *sapiens*, or wise man of antiquity, who was fully aware of what constituted the *summum bonum*, the supreme good, and was utterly unenticed by everything else; a wisdom perhaps not unlike what the French mean today in their phrase *n'être pas dupe*, to be nobody's fool' (p. 44). Professor Green, rightly stressing how much we need a historical study of the semantics of the word *desengaño*, questions whether the 'state of mind' it denotes did in fact arise in association with the period of Spain's decline. He quotes an example of this use of *desengaño* from Feliciano de Silva in 1534 and another that may be earlier. All this is a fruitful and illuminating discussion" (p. 61).

In this chapter, then, Green attacks the nonsensical, albeit right, prevalent concept that to late sixteenth- and all seventeenth-century Spaniards the world was a kind of charnel house in which men wait until death claims them. He reveals that even though *desengaño* or disillusionment beset the Renaissance and post-Renaissance Spanish mind it was not the kind of disillusionment that shattered faith and led to dangerous pessimism. Terrible as was this *desengaño* in Christian Europe, when science was making startling inroads upon what men had always believed, *desengaño* was a purifying agent in Spain, even as it was abroad. The crux of the matter might be said to be that the purifying agency in Spain produced a reaction toward tradition rather than movement away from tradition. Green in this chapter reveals how this reaction, this current running counter to the results of *desengaño* abroad, was equally powerful and even equally effective in shaping the mentality of the thinking Spaniard. One can see that *desengaño* was a boon in Spain, for there minds could not willingly accept anything save the patristic and Thomistic world view, which for them had never faded. *Desengaño* was associated with eternal wisdom, for *desengaño* taught Spanish thinkers that disillusionment led straight to understanding of God's intent and man's relationship to His intent. Edward Glaser expresses some of this extremely well in his review of Volume IV in *Renaissance Quarterly*, XXI, 4 (Spring 1968), 60–64. "Chapter II," he states, "establishes that baroque pessimism has been over-emphasized. True enough, the writings of the period reveal a keen awareness of the transience of human endeavors, but they also convey the notion that time presents an opportunity to those who know how to take advantage of it. The baroque creed, Green contends, finds genuine expression in Chapter IV of the *Viaje del Parnaso* in which an as yet unappreciated Cervantes serenely reaffirms his faith in the lasting value of poetic creation. The chapter on *desengaño*, a sequel to the preceding disquisitions, draws an important distinction between disenchantment as such and the awakening to a heightened awareness that it causes. Such a passing from ignorance to knowledge is for the author of the very essence of baroque *desengaño* vividly portrayed in Gracián's Criticón and Cervantes' *Don Quijote*. An 'anthropological optimism' permeates both works, for the trajectory of the respective heroes shows that it is within the possibilities of man to attain the comprehension of truth" (p. 62).

Green, as we have seen from the reviews, focuses upon Gracián and Cervantes; also brought into focus, however, are Quevedo and Calderón, to name only major literary figures. With such thinkers and writers as these he is able to highlight the development of *desengaño* or baroque pessimism for his readers. Of special interest to all are his remarks on Cervantes and the *raison d'être* of Don Quixote's mind, but let the reader peruse these ideas in Green's own words in Chapter II of Volume IV which are reproduced in the selected essays.

Only some half a dozen years before the publication of Otis Green's first volume of *Spain and the Western Tradition* he published in *Hispanic Review*, XXV (1957), 175–93, an article entitled *"El Ingenioso Hidalgo,"* which explains Green's own special ideas as to the more or less unnoticed reason for the use of the controversial adjective *ingenioso*, which had been translated in a wide variety of ways in various European languages. Green had read, before he wrote this essay, the extant material explaining *ingenioso*, which he elucidates for his readers. To these ideas he adds his own and points out that Cervantes' contemporaries "would have followed with clear understanding the course of Alonso Quijano's transition from a country gentleman of *choleric temper* to an *imaginative* and *visionary* monomaniac, and would have interpreted this transformation, as Cervantes had conceived it, in the light of their knowledge of Greek and Arabic physiological and psychological theories regarding the balance and imbalance of the bodily humors." What a provocative subject for any reader! Green more specifically sets out to reveal that Alonso Quijano was a man for the most part *colérico* and was driven to insanity by a passion and by lack of sleep which produced a hypertrophy of his *imaginative faculty*. Green sees that the concepts held by physicians of the sixteenth century were extremely important, and thus, in Quijano's aberration he sees that his madness follows a natural course away from and back to normality, and that his moments of "sanity" were due to periods of rest or to the removal of the causes of this insanity. "In short," writes Green, "it will be shown—if my arguments carry conviction—that Don Quijote's adventures could have happened only to a *colérico*, a man by nature *caliente y seco*, and that such a man was, according to Renaissance psychology, of necessity *ingenioso*" (p. 177).

Some four years ago, and two years before the first volume of Green's great opus was published, his name appeared under an article "El Licenciado Vidriera: Its Relation to the *Viaje del Parnaso* and the *Examen de Ingenios* of Huarte," which Green had written for *Linguistic and Literary Studies in Honor of Helmut Hatzfeld* (Catholic University of America Press, 1964), 213–20.

In this remarkable psychological tale—really a study of human psychosis as displayed in Tomás Rodaja, whose insanity led him to believe that he was made of glass—Cervantes brings to life the medical and psychological doctrines of Juan Huarte de San Juan's *Examen de ingenios para las ciencias*. The article reveals some of the beliefs Spaniards held in the early years of the seventeenth century about the maladies of the mind and relates the unfortunate Tomás Rodaja's unhappiness to Cervantes' own rancor against a society unwilling to reward his better qualities. In *El Licenciado Vidriera* Green sees a new facet of Cervantive greatness—the ability to blend known and accepted medical and psychological tenets with fictional events springing from certain personal aspects in Cervantes' own life and unhappiness. The modern flavor, if one may liken Cervantes' use of the medical science of his day to similar literary usages in our own time, is striking.

The penultimate essay in this florilegio of Otis Green's essays is "Don Quijote and the *Alcahuete*," published in *Estudios Dedicados a James Homer Herriott* (Madison: University of Wisconsin Press, 1966), 109–16. Here Otis Green studies the reason or reasons Cervantes had for spending a considerable amount of space on the eulogy of *alcahuetería*. Rodríguez Marín in his critical edition of the *Quijote* had termed Cervantes' treatment as "festiva." Green, as usual, goes far beyond works of literature and examines religious tracts, civic treatises, and legal documents. He shows Cervantes in a serious frame of mind and not a festive or jocular one, when that great novelist put into the mouth of the Knight of La Mancha his interesting and provocative praise of prostitution.

The final essay, "Lope and Cervantes: Peripeteia and Resolution," was first presented to the public in the Spanish Section of the Kentucky Foreign Language Conference, April 1968. It seems an ideal terminal essay because it marked almost the last public appearance of Otis Green before his retirement from the University of Pennsylvania. This learned paper was presented at the first general session of the South Atlantic Modern Language Association in Jacksonville in 1968. Its title, said Otis Green in its first paragraph, "is highly significant, and might be applied, in theory to nearly all, in practice to a very large portion, of Spanish belles-lettres not only during the Renaissance but also before and after that period." A final reason for the essay's inclusion is the fact that it is exemplary of Otis Green's deepest and most mature thought.

In this perceptive article Green takes time to trace something of the course of that responsibility shared by literary artists of all ages —that of giving instruction and producing pleasure. He then reveals a deeper, though not original, penetration of what Lopean drama might have been. Far more than mere show business, it came almost as close as any literary form could come to satisfying the most deep-seated needs of individuals in Spain as well as the needs of the Spanish nation. The seeking of such aims—unattainable aims in many cases—could have led the Spaniard and his nation toward glorious goals, or goals less glorious. Lope must have believed that a properly motivated play, directed at the proper level of humanity, not a level above humanity's comprehension, could point out both the unattainable and the glorious.

More original is Green's contention that in spite of Cervantes' flexibility and Lope's rigidity there exists a fundamental similarity in the characters and personages of their works. It would be quite undesirable here to state what these unexpected similarities are, for to do so would vitiate for the reader the exciting essence of the essay itself. It can be said, however, without too greatly exposing Green's thesis, that both Lopean and Cervantine characters followed a distinct and yet a related peripeteia—all important in the final assessment of their masterpieces.

It is not an easy task, although it may be a pleasant one, to introduce essays written in such a learned, yet empathic manner, by a person of Otis H. Green's stature. The best that I have been able to do in this Introduction, has been to skim but lightly the surface of the twelve essays and to offer some suggestion of their importance in twentieth-century Hispanic scholarship. The reader is now directed to the essays themselves where he can assimilate to the best of his own personal abilities and interests Professor Green's considerations of the Spanish mind of the Middle Ages and the Renaissance.

I *The Medieval Tradition:* Sic et Non

*Each lived on in his books—Jerome in
his* Letters, *Augustine in his* Confessions, *Abelard in his* Sic et Non, *Aquinas in his* Summa Theologica—*and in
each a question was embodied of the
sort that must be answered anew by
each succeeding generation of Christians . . . : Is it possible to synthesize
Christianity and culture?*[1]

OMNIA SECUNDUM LITEM FIERI[2]

The Middle Ages, like the Renaissance that succeeded them, were
polylithic. Consider, for example, Dante's vivid mosaic portrait of
Rome. In it we find "the Trojan legend of Rome and that of
Aeneas; the antitheses of Rome of the pagan Caesars and Rome of
the martyrs, Rome of the Christian emperors and Rome of the
popes, the pagan and Christian Rome in general; there is, furthermore, Rome as a *civitas sacerdotalis et regalis,* and another Rome
represented by the commune of medieval city Romans; a Rome
compared, as a Holy City, to Jerusalem, and another Rome compared to Babylon, the Great Whore of the Apocalypse; finally, a
universal Rome, the *caput mundi* and mistress of the human race,
and also a Rome that was the capital of Italy."[3] Even more striking
is the evidence that the Age of Faith was torn by conflicts suggestive of the shattering dissensions of the Reformation. At the beginning of the twelfth century Tanchelm proclaimed that he possessed
the Holy Spirit in the same sense and in the same degree as Christ
and that, like Christ, he was God—a claim which was accepted by
his followers, some of whom drank his bath water as a substitute
for the Eucharist. Luther's idea that the Anti-Christ who sets up his
throne in the Temple is the Pope at Rome was a commonplace

among the eschatologically-minded movements of the later Middle Ages, one of whose *prophetae* was burned at Paris in 1209. This same "prophet," long before Savonarola (d. 1498), proclaimed that the French king would reign under the dispensation of the Holy Spirit, after the great purification of the kingdoms of the earth. In 1315 a famine caused the circulation of a prophecy that the poor would overthrow the Church, after which men would be united in exalting one single Cross. Joachim of Fiore (d. 1202) prophesied that a secular king would chastise the worldly Church until in its present form it was utterly destroyed. A Latin manifesto of 1409 (or 1439) proclaimed not only the exaltation of the Germans above all peoples, but the expropriation of the Church of Rome and the killing of all its clergy. In the later Middle Ages the adepts of the Free Spirit inspired the most ambitious essay in social revolution that medieval Europe was ever to witness.[4]

The war—*secundum litem*—of conflicting forces manifests itself even in the realm of artistic theories and attitudes. "The aesthetics of the Middle Ages is the result of a conflict of two opposing tendencies: one characterized by simplicity, measure, logic; the other by imagination, exuberance, unrestrained freedom. . . . We intend to stress the characteristic traits of this strange 'baroque' taste, which is too often forgotten because it is not in harmony with our classical preferences. One must not underestimate its historical importance; to do so is to falsify the facts completely . . . the 'classicists'—Quintilian, Fortunatianus, Cassiodorus, Isidore—proclaim the ideal of clarity; those of the 'baroque' party—Virgil the Grammarian, Hypericus, Abbon de Saint Germain—proclaim the ideal of obscurity."[5]

THE MEDIEVAL MYTH

The Middle Ages, assuredly, had their sign, their myth; the paramount motif was the problem of the relationship between God and man, understood in the light of Augustine's sense of sin and grace.[6] The problem required an intellectual solution. Inevitably, the solutions varied. Tertullian (d. 220), a Stoic materialist, maintained that God is corporeal and the soul, a bodily substance. Ambrose (d. 397) and Augustine (d. 430) brought in Neoplatonism.[7] The latter's theology was "a weaving together with marvelous subtlety, of different strains logically independent, and in most men psychologically incompatible."[8] Sharp conflicts occurred from the eleventh century onward. In the twelfth century Peter Abelard (d. 1142) lined up in his *Sic et Non* eighteen hundred conflicting opinions of the Church Fathers pro and con on one hundred and fifty-eight propositions of theology and ethics as a first step to understanding the conflicts: "by inquiry we discover the truth."[9]

Augustine's Hellenized-Platonized Christianity imposed itself on the barbarian peoples of Western Europe. That it was foreign to them is obvious. Plato called the world of sense half real, as lying midway between being and non-being.[10] He taught that the true life of the soul "can be realized only in the other world, that world of pure forms, colourless, shapeless, intangible, which is the natural nourishment of the intellect."[11] How could such declarations of the unreliability and worthlessness of the world enter into the world view of peoples who were dynamic, possessing an immense and exuberant vitality and an unlimited thirst for power and prosperity: *aumentar sus estados*—to expand the borders of one's estates[12] —in the words of the fourteenth-century Castilian Prince Don Juan Manuel? These barbarian peoples were in love with the world and the flesh, and they were quite willing to risk going to the devil to get them: *e non se parte dende, ca natura lo enriza*—man turns not from his sin, for Nature eggs him on—, according to a contemporary of the Prince just quoted, Juan Ruiz, Archpriest of Hita (d. 1350?), in his *Book of Good Love*. Attracted both to Greek thought and to the Roman philosophy of power, and only half successful in their adaptations of them to their own situation,[13] the peoples of Western Europe resemble the Children of Israel in the Wilderness in their long vacillation between Baal and Jehovah. Paradoxically, both the Children of Israel and the men of Western Europe believed their respective prophets.

DUAL ALLEGIANCE

In accord with the atmosphere of the age in which they lived, and in spite of all paradoxes,[14] the members of the feudal aristocracy of the Middle Ages were intensely devout. With a few possible exceptions,[15] they accepted absolutely the teachings of the Christian Church. They might sin with vigor and enthusiasm, but they repented and atoned with equal thoroughness.[16] Their sinning and repenting were not merely a matter of the inherent human duality of body and spirit—surely a Mohammedan needed to repent less often—but arose, in frequently tragic fashion, from the inescapable fact that these men owed allegiance to a dual and conflicting set of values. "Este mi justo, si no cristiano deseo," says the unfortunate Ruperta in Cervantes' *Persiles y Segismunda* (Book III, Ch. 16) as she spells out her vow to avenge her husband's death. Her determination, both *just* and *un-Christian*, is symptomatic of the dilemma that concerns us in this chapter. As Arthur O. Lovejoy has said: "Most of the religious thought of the West has . . . been profoundly at variance with itself."[17]

The triumph of the Jewish-Greek-Christian self-contradicting synthesis is, in the opinion of Professor Lovejoy, one of the most extraordinary in the history of human thought. It was never a perfect synthesis. In literature contradiction is seldom absent. In most matters, medieval literature accepted and employed the religio-philosophical virtues, vices, and sins; yet the earthly pursuits of love and war brought forth value-systems which, though they adhered to the religio-philosophical code whenever possible, nonetheless contradicted that code when necessary.[18] The quarrel between philosophy and poetry, already known to Plato, was given new form by the founders of the Middle Ages. Cassiodorus (d. 598) and Gregory the Great (d. 604) represent the contending forces. The former would include the culture of the pagan past in his plans for a liberal monasticism; the latter would throw the past away. There will be renewed ups and downs as the Middle Ages progress. There will be different effects from different men and at different moments. Though the effect of the mastermind of Gregory will be especially powerful, the ultimately victorious party will be that of Lactantius (d. 4c.) and Cassiodorus, advocates of a Christian humanism in which the old education is vitally embedded in the new.[19] Yet the victory of *Sic* can never silence *Non*; neither the one nor the other can be eliminated. Professor Rand (*op. cit.*, pp. 64–65) takes as type and symbol a bit of the Eucharistic liturgy preserved in one of its most ancient monuments, the *Missale*

Gothicum. In the *benedictio populi* for the eve of Epiphany, Christ is besought to turn dull hearts to Him, even as at the wedding of Cana He converted water into wine—not just wine, but Falernian. Horace's best! Though stricter souls denounced it and threatened to break it, that jar of old Falernian always reposed in the sanctuary of the Church.

True as this is, it is also true that even when art and piety placed the beauty and charm of earthly life in the service of religion, the artist or lover of art was expected to take care not to surrender to the charms of color and line. Knightly exercises and courteous fashions with their worship of bodily strength and grace; honors and dignities with their vanity and pomp; and especially love with its adoration of the earthly creature—what were they, asks Huizinga (*op. cit.,* pp. 30–31), but pride, envy, avarice, and lust? To be admitted as elements of higher culture all these things had to be ennobled—in principle!—and raised to the rank of virtue. The impossibility of the endeavor will be the subject of our chapter, Truancy and Recantation.

This worship of strength and grace, of vanity and pomp, even succeeds in tainting the general attitude toward the Christian virtues. Our witness, St. Francis de Sales, died in 1622, but the date is unimportant since his statement applies to all the centuries here surveyed. In the eyes of the world, says our Saint, virtues are either abject or honorable. Patience, sweetness, simplicity, and humility are virtues that the worldly man considers vile and abject. On the other hand, he greatly esteems prudence, courage, and liberality. Even in the exercise of a single virtue, some actions are scorned and others honored. To give alms and forgive offenses are both charitable actions. The first is honored by every one; the second, despised by the worldly.[20] Wernher of Elmendorf, a chaplain of the Hohenstaufen period (12–13c.), is all for the worldly, the knightly, virtues. In a didactic poem on morals which he wrote for the benefit of a certain Provost Dietrich, the sources quoted are almost exclusively classical, and the poet gives his reason for citing the classics in preference to King Solomon: "Solomon sets up the ant as a model to us; but if I can learn virtue from a tiny insect, I can even more easily get it from a pagan." Wernher's great concern is for honor and public esteem, and his view never wanders from the knightly circle.[21] Similarly Commines (d. 1511), in his *Mémoires*, characterizes Charles the Bold in four words: *Il desiroit la gloire*. Not that this was necessarily a sin: *appetitus gloriae non est peccatum*, wrote St. Thomas. But the desire for fame involved men in wars, not always just ones. It involved them also "in a courtly sphere whose ideal is not the ecclesiastical ideal and which seeks expression not only in literary forms, but in the refinements of life: banquets, royal or princely entries, processions, festivals, ceremonies of the court."[22]

It is this other world, this "sphere whose ideal is not the ecclesiastical ideal," that will lead us from the general historical considerations of the preceding pages into the world that is to concern us in the remainder of this book: the world of Spanish letters and, to begin with, the world of the medieval Spanish *caballero*.

THE WORLD OF THE SPANISH KNIGHT

The Spanish feudal noble, like his congeners in other parts of Europe, indeed more than they,[23] lived for war, and it was with the greatest difficulty that his passion and lust for competitive armed strife became tempered in its violence, ennobled—in principle!—and raised to the rank of virtue. The elemental and barbarian character of this unchecked passion is seen in the primitive *Cantar de los Infantes de Lara*, which recalls prodigies of valor, acts of supreme betrayal and vengeance, and the sending of eight heads to Almanzor, the Moorish general of Cordova. Yet the softening effect of the institution of chivalry is already perceptible in this barbaric medieval poem. As the father of the Infantes de Lara recognizes the head of each of his seven sons, he pronounces over it a eulogy, and the seven eulogies together summarize the qualities of the perfect knight: loyalty, justice, truth, valor, fidelity, generosity, a fondness for good company.[24]

THREE TYPES OF CHIVALRY

Sidney Painter, in his *French Chivalry* (Baltimore, 1940), analyzes learnedly the three forms of medieval knighthood: the chivalry of the *knights*, that of the *clergy*, and that of the *ladies*. For the moment, we are concerned with the earliest form of this progressively modified ideal, the chivalry of the knights. Curtius has argued (*op. cit.*, Excursus XVIII, 519–37) that earlier attempts of scholars to draw up a "knight's decalogue" or to formulate a consistent code of chivalric virtues led to the same sort of *Sic et Non* that we find elsewhere in medieval life, and that no comprehensive synthesis is possible. As tempered by the idea of chivalry, however, the code of the medieval aristocratic fighting man did require that he strive or at least claim to be brave and loyal, true to his word, faithful to his lord, eager to destroy the enemies of his God or king, magnanimous towards a defeated foe. He must renounce ambush, striking a fallen opponent, deserting his post, or surrendering while there is hope of victory.

Chivalry of the knights

All of these requirements are met in the twelfth-century *Poema de Mio Cid*. Here the fighting is always just—unlike some of the fighting of the historical Cid, Rodrigo Díaz de Bivar, who could take up the sword against a Christian enemy in the service of a Mohammedan ally. The *Poema*, like every true popular epic, is above all a poem of honor[25]: of its loss through no fault of the hero and its reconquest at the expense of the Moors as the hero wins through to a life of full and self-sufficient manhood, reflecting glory and a new dignity on his fellows through the performance of great deeds. Yet this primitive and feudal pursuit of glory is tempered by what Painter calls religious chivalry.[26] Readers of the poem will recall the insistently recurring words *Padre spirital*. Nothing in it is at variance with the "chivalry of the priests," but religious chivalry is still unobtrusive, merely forming part of the poem's orchestration. The poem's theme, its dominant tone, is the pursuit of glory.[27]

Chivalry of the priests

One must move forward to the early years of the fourteenth century to find a genuine example in literature of the chivalry of the priests. It is a rather amorphous yet remarkable work, regarded as the first Spanish novel. Its title establishes one point: *The Book of the Knight of God Whose Name Was Zifar, Who Because of His Exercise of Virtue and Heroic Deeds Became King of Menton.*[28] The hero is "a knight from the [Oriental] Indies, whither St. Bartholomew carried the Gospel, after the death of Our Lord. This knight was given at his baptism the name of Zifar, and later was called Knight of God, because he was ever close to God, and God to him, in all his adventures and deeds, as you shall hear. . . . And therefore this book is called *The Book of the Knight of God,* the said knight being perfect in natural intelligence, in courage, in justice, in good counsel, and in good will." Though cast down by Fortune, "he never despaired of the mercy of God, believing that He could transmute that evil fortune into better, as indeed He did, as you now shall hear." Readers will profit, says the anonymous author, by the heroic deeds, the excellent examples, and the numerous Catholic doctrines of so fine a book.

From now on, the religious note sounds clearly in the best examples of the Spanish romances of chivalry, no matter how obstreperously the other notes—fighting and love, the more worldly chivalry of the knights with its cult of honor and that of the ladies with its excesses of adoration—may dominate the orchestration. What the concept of religious chivalry added specifically was protecting the good and weak, fighting always in a righteous cause, defending the Church and clergy, and constantly warring on the enemies of the Faith.

Chivalry of the ladies

Third in point of time, though certainly not in eventual importance for the growth and popularity of the chivalric romance, was the chivalry of the ladies. With the growth of courtly love, of *Frauendienst* and *Frauenverehrung*—entirely absent from the *Poema de Mio Cid* and the *Caballero Zifar*—, the chivalric knight came to be thought of as one who was ever ready to serve his lady in her slightest whim, even though such service might deprive the knight of his honor. *Le chevalier de la charrette,* by Chrétien de Troyes (d. 1190?), is an excellent example. Its hero not only possesses all the worldly virtues of the perfect knight, he not only will submit to the extremes of suffering and base humiliation for his lady's sake, but as a last measure of devotion he bears her unreasonable displeasure in unquestioning obedience. She on her part tests him to the uttermost, forcing him upward by a series of escalations toward the perfection of courtly love. All this striving is aided by a foreknowing—an un-Christian—Providence, the Providence of love that rules supreme in the realm of the imagination and of poetry.[29] This type of chivalric lover would imperil his soul and defy the anger of the Church for love. The fair name of his lady was his chief concern, and the knight-errant wandered about the country, like Don Quijote, challenging all and sundry to fight or admit that his particular lady was the fairest, gentlest, noblest, and most accomplished in the world. This concept of chivalry dominated the famous courts of love and is reflected in the romances of the Arthurian cycle.[30] The ethical and religious complications of this type of literature—enjoyed, with later regret, by such serious and devout persons as Juan de Valdés, and by such saints as Ignatius de Loyola and Teresa of Avila—will be analyzed in our chapters on courtly love and on truancy. For the present it is sufficient to indicate that the main interest is no longer fighting, nor the mere display of the knightly virtues per se, nor the protection of the weak and the defense of the Faith. These may indeed all be present in large proportion in a single work, as in *Tirant lo Blanc* (1490), whose author, Joanot Martorell, was greatly interested in military strategy and presented his knights as actually eating and drinking, and both sleeping and dictating their wills in bed, as the Curate enthusiastically explains in Part I, Chapter vi of *Don Quijote;* but if the Curate extolls the book as "a treasure house of delight," it is principally because of the love interest of this novel, perhaps the most sensual in Spanish literature: "Here are set forth the stratagems of the damsel Placerdemivida, the love affairs and deceits of the widow Reposada, and the Empress enamored of Hipólito, her squire."[31]

Most typical of the chivalry of the ladies is the anonymous *Amadís de Gaula*, a story already famous at the end of the fourteenth century which was given the form we know at the beginning of the sixteenth. There is still much fighting in this book. There is concern for honor and fame—the business of knights.

Amadís even disappears for a long period, traveling incognito and engaging in adventures in order to recover the honor which he felt to be slipping from him because of the inactivity imposed on him by his lady. But the hero's—and the reader's—interest centers in Oriana and her exquisitely secret, courtly amour with Amadís. The Spanish *caballero* now appears as much more than a fighter; he is also a courtier adorned with all the courtly graces in his contacts with his overlord, with his equals, and with women—especially with women. His complete sentimentalization occurs, however, in another book, Diego de San Pedro's *Cárcel de amor* (1492).

The *Cárcel de amor* is certainly earlier than the known form of the *Amadís* (1508) but the chronology is confused by the fact that we do not know just what Garci Rodríguez de Montalvo found (and retained or altered or rejected) in the materials he worked with as he rewrote and expanded the *Amadís*. It seems safe to regard San Pedro's *Cárcel* as a more extreme, though probably not an earlier, sentimentalizing of the *caballero*. In it, the hero worships that greatest of female characters in the tradition of courtly love, *la belle dame sans merci*, and in it he dies, an *amant désespéré*, from self-imposed hunger because his lady, out of regard for her honor, cannot accept his suit. The only military action is subordinate to the love plot.

The sequels of these knightly and sentimental romances become, in the sixteenth century, a mighty river of printed material, some of it excellent, much of it worthless except as a witness to the ideals— no less than to the taste—of the times. The cycle is completed in *Don Quijote*. In Cervantes' masterpiece these novels find not merely their parody, but their supreme justification and apotheosis, as Cervantes takes over their framework and much of their substance and adapts them to his own purposes as he conceives and creates, in the first modern novel, a supreme instrument for the critical portrayal of the gist of human experience. Don Quijote represents in his person an epitome of the three chivalries: knightly aggressiveness; defense of the weak and oppressed and eagerness to fight the Turks; and unswerving fidelity in moments of glory, humiliation, and defeat to his courtly love for Dulcinea del Toboso. Again it is necessary to look forward to a later chapter for an analysis of the meaning of this great book. Here we need only point out that Cervantes does not let his hero die in his error, but brings him back from his madness to recognize and renounce the *Non* inherent in his career as a knight – the *Non* which, in the presence of the Ultimate Truth to which death leads all men, can no longer enter into combination with the *Sic*, that is to say, the positive and eternal values of Alonso Quijano the Good, values that the dying hero, like Bunyan's Valiant-for-Truth, takes with him across the Shining River. This is the explanation of the renunciation in the infinitely moving deathbed scene that so many have found disquieting.

SIC ET NON: SPANISH AWARENESS

It now remains to gather up the various threads of this chapter and to observe them as they show on the face and on the reverse of the tapestry – the *Sic* and the *Non* of medieval life and ideals, as these are expressed in Spain's early literature of chivalry. We shall not argue in favour of the one or against the other. Each had its place in life and – no matter by what means of rationalization, allegorization, or retractation – each demanded its place in literature.

War

The first thread in our tangled skein, the first *Non* in opposition to the *Sic*, is the mere act of war.[32] Pedro Mexía is keenly aware of the paradox in his much-translated *Silva de varia lección* (1542): "But the art and science of war, the moving against each other of organized military forces, though it have its beginning and origin in sin, and though its means and often its ends be but cruelty and bloodshed and evil, is held in such high regard that men have preferred this art and honor, and the persons wise and skilled therein, to all other arts and abilities, and give it first place and the highest rank in their esteem."[33]

Fortunately for Christian society, which obviously could not exist without military defense, it was possible to rationalize a way out of the categorical imperative: *Thou shalt not kill*. All conceivable latitude seems to be allowed by Dr. Martín de Azpilcueta, el Doctor Navarro, one of the directors of Spain's national conscience in the age of the Counter Reformation, in his *Manual de confesores y penitentes:* "Many times a man kills another without incurring guilt, namely when he does so as an act of public justice, according to St. Thomas . . . and in a just war, and to defend his life. And even when he cannot otherwise defend his property, as (according to Cajetan and others) we proved above . . . , although one should have greater regard for another's life than for his own property if it is merely a case of [financial] need. . . . But he should have greater concern to preserve what is his, for the sustenance of his life and of those dependent on him, than for the life of another . . . according to Saint Thomas. . . . Likewise, when death is inflicted in defense of another."[34]

Honor and vengeance

In our practical world these solutions have at least been widely accepted. It would appear, however, that the clergy, as they struggled with the problem of reforming the excesses of the knights, consumed some of their own spiritual energy and themselves succumbed to the attractiveness, or the attraction and invincibility, of the *Non.* One may even—in the opinion of Azpilcueta—commit homicide in defense of one's honor: "And we hold the same opinion in cases where, by not defending himself with weapons, he would be injured in his honor or person, since (as said above) he may justly kill to defend his property, and honor is more valuable than property; and personal injury exceeds any injury to one's property. Wherefore we concluded above, with Panormitano, that if the man attacked cannot flee without dishonor, he is not obliged to flee; and if he cannot defend himself from being struck by the hand, or from a wound of some other sort, without killing his adversary, he may kill. . . . We add however (because we are told that we should) one clear thing, namely: that the husband who kills or wishes to kill his wife having found her in adultery, sins mortally, although by law he receive no punishment therefor" (*loc. cit.*).

Was the matter really as simple as this?[35] Quite evidently, it was not. Antonio de Torquemada, in his *Coloquios satíricos* (1553),

after expounding the Christian doctrine of honor, causes the inter-
locutor Antonio to confess: "And what I have said here between
us, as between friends, I would not dare to say in public, because
some would refuse to listen to me, others would think I was crazy,
others would say that these things were rank heresy against the
good order of the state, and other things no less foolish."[36] The
view thus privately expressed but prudently kept under wraps
appears a few pages earlier (*ed. cit.*, p. 533ab) in the same *Coloquio: "Antonio.—* . . . according to that definition we must consider honor in one of two ways. One of these ways is *as Christians*
[italics mine], and if we are as good Christians as we should be, we
have a greater obligation to our faith than to our honor. *Jerónimo.*
—That is a thing that no one can deny. *Antonio.*—That being so,
what is there today in the world so contrary to the true Christian
faith as honor, considered not as philosophers define it, but as we
feel in regard to it? . . . This holy faith of ours is founded on true
Christian humility, and honor, as I have said, is a vain and proud
presumption, and is thus irreconcilable, because all those who desire and strive for honor follow a road which is not the road of the
Christian."[37]

Of such voices there are many. Venegas, in his *Agonía del
tránsito de la muerte* (preliminaries dated 1537), declares that a
distorted sense of honor is one of the vices peculiar to Spain: "The
third vice [of the Spaniards] arises from pride of lineage, which,
though it appears to be common to all nations, in this sense is
characteristic of Spain only, that the newness of one's family is
considered a dishonor—unless one's family has its roots . . . in the
region . . . whence came the Goths" (*ed. cit.*, p. 174a). The same
author, in his *Differencias de libros que ay en el vniuerso* (1540),
makes no concession at all to how Spaniards "feel about honor":
"Finally, all those who, in order to preserve their honor have no
regard for the honor of God, are heading toward the abyss of
perdition, which is a broad path that leads to Hell."[38] And one year
later Francisco de Osuna, the mystic whose writings were of such
great help to Saint Teresa in her search for understanding, says
bluntly: "Every noble lineage has had its origin in tyranny."[39] The
tension can be traced throughout the Spanish Golden Age and it is

unnecessary to multiply texts. José de Valdivielso (d. 1638) pours contempt on the honor concept in his allegorical plays on the Eucharist.[40]

Another manifestation of *Non* is vengeance, an offshoot of the honor code. "Vengeance is mine; I will repay, saith the Lord."[41] Who, in 1492, could doubt that these were the words of the Holy Ghost? Yet in the *Cárcel de amor* the King expresses the belief that vengeance is as important in matters of honor as Christian forgiveness is in other matters. Such separation of a man's social conduct into two compartments by virtue of an ethical "double truth" might be—indeed was—allowed a king in his public acts. In the individual conscience the problem could not be so simple, as Pedro Malón de Chaide makes clear in *La conversión de la Magdalena* (1588): "Tell me, you who make sport of Christianity, you firebrands of Hell, vessels of the anger and wrath of God, how is it possible for you to preach a gospel and proclaim a doctrine and observe the teachings of a book contrary to the Book of Christ? Read in the [Book] of God and you will see that, if you pardon not, there is no Heaven for you; read in your book and you will see that if you do not avenge yourselves, there is no honor for you."[42] There are even those, he says, who make a display of the vengeance taken, who are puffed up because they have humiliated another. "In these there is little evidence that they are predestined to salvation. I do not say that they are not, for this is God's secret; but I say that if they are, they give little sign thereof" (*ibid.*, p. 166).

Vengeance is simply forbidden.[43] Azpilcueta in his *Manual de confesores* (*ed. cit.*) leaves no room for doubt: "One should therefore greatly pity those who go to confession or take communion while harboring the intention of taking personal vengeance on one who may have slapped, wounded or beaten them, or called them traitor, faithless, thief, bad woman, Jew, Moor, heretic, or by some other injurious term. . . . Indeed one should pity them and beg them with tears of compassion to note that they are in the diabolical state of eternal damnation . . ." (p. 99). It is mortal sin for one to allow another to take vengeance for him: "if, having received some injury and knowing that his relatives or friends wish to avenge him, he did not expressly forbid them to do so" (p. 155). Even more: a man mortally wounded may not, without mortal sin, slay a withdrawing enemy with one last dagger thrust or pistol shot: "one who is mortally wounded, or whose assailant has left him and is now fleeing, may not without sin kill him, because such an act would now be vengeance and passes the limits of self-defense" (p. 149).

Duels and tourneys

A direct offshoot of the spirit of honor and the desire for vengeance (if not of a merely vainglorious urge to acquire fame) is the duel, either in single man-to-man encounter, or in a tourney. "The clergy and the knights disagreed in the matter of tournaments; to the clergy they were sinful and wasteful shows, while to the knights they were a noble sport where a man could best show his prowess and daring" (La Monte, *op. cit.*, p. 383). Sometimes the warning of their sinfulness was sounded, not by a priest but by a member of the knightly class indirectly taking part in a joust. Chapter lvi of Book I of the *Tirant lo Blanc* bears the heading: "Concerning the Allocution Which the Earl Marshall, as Judge of the Battle, Delivered to the Two Knights," and in it this official of the field of honor says: "I am judge by the power which you have invested in me, and by reason of my position it is my duty to warn and to beg you . . . to be pleased not to enter into such a dangerous pass as this, and to look to God, and not willfully to seek your destruction by an act of suicide, because you well know that the man who seeks his own death will in all justice not be forgiven by Our Lord." "No more of that," he is told, "since each of us knows his own worth and what he is able to do, both in temporal and in spiritual things." A strange indulgence, and an inconsistent scruple, appear in Chapter lxii of Book I. As two knights prepare for a duel, two friars, "by order of the judges," actually confess them, "and they took communion, using an ordinary piece of bread, because in a situation like that they could not be given the body of Jesus Christ" (*Libros de caballerías españoles*, ed. cit., pp. 1131, 1163).

Fray Hernando de Talavera (d. 1507), confessor to Isabella the Catholic, in his *Breve forma de confesar* condemns tourneys and extends the guilt even to those who grant ecclesiastical burial to those killed therein: "No less guilty of sin are those who allow

burial in sacred ground of those who die as heretics, or excommunicated . . . or of those who die in tourneys and similar war-like
jousts, or of those who die of the wounds received in them"
(*NBAE, XVI,* 27a, 20ab). Don Francisco Quevedo Villegas (d.
1645), who perhaps admired nothing so much as a soldier, is
eloquent in his condemnation of duels: "This bloody folly, this
criminal rage, this fury contrary to every law human and divine,
that is called the *Book of the Duel,* is tainted by the infamy of its
descent, which is as ancient as the world."[44] The Jesuit Juan Euse-
bio Nieremberg (d. 1658) is no less eloquent: "It is likewise a thing
scarcely to be endured by Christian patience, against ecclesiastical
obedience and against religion, since the guilty man chooses to die
in sacrilege and excommunicated."[45] Earlier in the *Epistolario* he is
more specific: "I suppose you are pleased that you were successful
in your duel; but I think that you have lost instead of winning, and
that you have brought honor only to the devil, since in his service
you offered a sacrifice of your life and your soul. . . . It is a great
shame . . . that a law of the devil should be kept by Christians. . . .
The rigor of their observance is such that they hold meetings to
determine if there was the slightest deviation and to endeavor to
carry it out most strictly . . . and he who fails therein they regard
as infamous—a practice not to be found among the Moors. . . .
How are there so many that fall down before the idol of honor?
. . . For this point of honor, among Christians, is—in accordance
with the law of the duel—totally opposed to Christ and to the
gentleness of his Gospel, to the great ruin and destruction of
Christians" (pp. 69–70). In 1625 Father Agustín de Herrera condemned the law of the duel as it was utilized by the dramatists in
their plots: "There is another doctrine found in our comedies,
more suitable to be wept over . . . than recorded. This is the cruel,
bloody, barbarous and heathen doctrine of the so-called law of the
duel. This idol of vengeance, called point of honor . . . , is wor-
shipped in our comedies . . . , a sacrilegious fragment from the
ruins of paganism, since it is directly opposed to the laws of
Christianity. The same ink that inscribes the points of the duel
erases the Gospel of Christ. This idol, overthrown by the preaching of the spreaders of the Gospel . . . , now is restored in our
comedies to a place on the fantastic altars of honor."[46]

The religion of love

Honor and the duel had to do with the chivalry of the knights. There is also a peculiar contradiction involved in the chivalry of the ladies. It is what C. S. Lewis calls the "religion of love"[47] and it amounts to the apotheosis, the deification of the beloved:

> When [Lancelot] comes before the bed where she lies, he kneels and adores her . . . , there is no *corseynt* in whom he has greater faith. When he leaves . . . he makes a genuflexion as if he were before a shrine. The irreligion of the religion of love could hardly go further. . . . Where it is not a parody of the Church [this religion of love] may be, in a sense, her rival—a temporary escape, a truancy from the ardours of a religion that was believed into the delights of a religion that was merely imagined. . . . It is as if some lover's metaphor when he said "Here is my heaven" in a moment of passionate abandonment were taken up and expanded into a system. Even while he speaks he knows that "here" is not his real heaven; and yet it is a delightful audacity to develop the idea a little further. If you go on to add to that lover's "heaven" its natural accessories, a god and saints and a list of commandments, and if you picture the lover praying, sinning, repenting, and finally admitted to bliss, you will find yourself in the precarious dream-world of medieval love poetry.

Such excessive adoration of the beloved is the sin of Amadís of Gaul. As he moves forward to fight the dragon (Bk. III, Ch. 73), the latter comes forth "much more fierce and strong then he ever was before—a circumstance caused by the fact that the devils, seeing that this knight placed more hope in his beloved Oriana than in God, were enabled to enter more powerfully into the beast and make him fiercer." The abuse was not limited to the world of books. The anonymous author of the fifteenth-century *Libro de la consolación de España* speaks of real men in the world about him:

> in these days we regard vices and sins as virtues . . . for we give the name of love and attachment to lust of the flesh and to adultery; we apply the great name of love to a thing so vile and take from it its own proper designation; and we esteem most

highly the man who is most involved in these love affairs, and he is most honored as a result thereof, and most praised, and even he becomes arrogant about his acts of folly. And he who has no such love affairs has no consideration at all and is regarded as a fool. God has no part at all in the young men and women, because they put blinders on their consciences and offend Him in a thousand ways in this evil commerce, saying that they love their friends—male or female—more than they do Him; and those who hear these things take delight therein, with a special desire to acquire a reputation as lovers themselves. . . . The male sinners are more numerous than the female, but in general all are guilty.[48]

This writer complains also that, on the eve of battle, knights trust more in the protecting love of their ladies than in the loving Providence of God: "It is not customary nowadays for men to go to confession and make reparation for their sins before a battle, since such a procedure is not in fashion, nor do their captains tell them to do so in their harangues, for they would never get ahead by doing so; on the contrary they ask the men how they are making out with their girl friends, and then admonish them to fight bravely for the love of their ladies. And the poor devils say that with the favor of those females they go into battle, for the grace of God and his favor are not necessary to them in their sad and willful plight, nor do they have a single care for good thoughts or good works" (ibid., pp. 250–51).

Books of the Amadís type affected also the aspirations, and, through them, the conduct, of feminine readers, of ladies in real life. The effect was widely regarded as deleterious. Martín de Riquer has studied the attacks on the novels of chivalry and finds that the readers of these books were believed to be "incited to sensuality and vice."[49] Fray Luis de Granada wrote in 1582:

I should now like to ask those who read false and mendacious romances of knighthood why they do this. They will reply that among all the works of man that can be seen by our bodily vision, the most admirable are courage and feats of daring. . . . Hence it is that people flock to see tourneys and bullfights and duels, and things of that sort—the admiration for which is always

accompanied by feelings of delight and pleasure. For this reason
also escutcheons and coats of arms of families have their origin
in great deeds of prowess, and in no other virtue. This admiration is so common that it manifests itself not only in true achievements, but also in deeds that are imaginary, fabulous, and false,
and this is the cause of the great vogue of those books of
imagined deeds of chivalry . . . , those vain exploits, accompanied many times by an outright licentiousness that turns the
heads of women readers, causing them to believe that they
themselves deserve to be the objects of the *service d'amour* no
less than the fine ladies for whose sake so many exploits and such
noteworthy feats of arms were accomplished.[50]

In a manuscript *Diálogo entre christianos* (1539) by Fray Juan de
Villagarcía the charge is made that the female reader identifies
herself with the heroines of these novels: "perchance wishing to be
another Oriana, served by another Amadís."[51] In *Don Quijote*
(Part I, Ch. 32) the scullery maid Maritornes, no moralist, admits
making exactly such identifications: "on my word, I too like to
hear about those things, they're just plain lovely; most of all when
they tell about some lady in her knight's arms under the orange
trees, while the duenna stands guard, half dead with envy and
fearing at every moment they'll be caught. Believe me, all that is as
sweet as honey."

Suicide

The religion of love-of-women can lead to the greatest sin of all:
suicide. In the *Cárcel de amor*, Leriano permits himself to die of
hunger because of his disappointment in love. We shall treat of
death and suicide in a later chapter, but full understanding of our
present problem of *Sic* and *Non* requires a mention of suicide here.
Despairing lovers talk of it continually, especially in lyric poetry.
Actual cases of it are few. Very enlightening is a comparison
between Cervantes' condemnation of suicide in his serious religious
play *El Rufián dichoso* and his presentation of it in *Don Quijote*
(Part I, Chs. 13–14). Here in the episode of Marcela and Grisós-
tomo, in a scene that is touchingly and tragically romantic, Cervantes expresses neither praise nor blame.[52]

SYNTHESIS AND SEPARATION

To understand a period one should understand its illusions, its fancies, its errors, its success in muddling through. Starting with the earliest medieval texts, we have seen how the medieval background is, in many respects, the background also of the Golden Age, to its very end. Somehow, the contradiction-ridden synthesis of *Sic* and *Non* worked, and under it men were able to live in a way—and with beliefs—generally satisfactory to themselves. As for the workability of the synthesis in real life, we have the testimony of Antonio López de Vega, in his *Paradoxas racionales* (1635): "One does not lose in the eyes of men his standing as a Christian and as a man who knows what is fitting when he takes part in a duel. This is a contravention of Divine law, to be sure; but without losing our standing as Christians we break that law frequently, every day. That does not mean that we would hesitate for an instant to risk our lives a thousand times over for the truth of our faith, nor could anyone who sees us take part in duels doubt for a minute that we would do what I have said, should the occasion arise."[53] As for the success of the synthesis in the dream world of literature-as-entertainment, we have, over against the outcries of the moralists, the fact that the novels of chivalry multiplied and were read, as were the other novels, poems, and plays that gave expression to the ideals of combat, honor, glory, and courtly love.[54] The romances of chivalry formed the favorite reading, for recreative purposes, of all ranks for the space of half a century. The Franciscan Miguel de Medina placed the *Amadís* on a level with Xenophon, Euripides, Sophocles, Plautus, and Terence.[55] We may be disinclined to take this seriously, but we must give more heed to the poet Luis de Góngora, ordained priest and chaplain to the King, when he declares that *Palmerín de Inglaterra* deserves to be commemorated in bronze (*ibid.*, p. 117). There was simply a general division between *las cosa de tejas arriba* and *las cosas de tejas abajo*—between things human and things divine.[56] Cervantes' friend advises him, in the Prologue to Part I of *Don Quijote*, to keep these two worlds separate. There is no need, he says, to cite Aristotle or St. Paul or Cicero, "all the more since . . . you are not . . . obligated to preach to anybody, mixing things human and divine, which is a kind of mixture wherein no sensible Christian should become involved." The same spirit of separation is reflected in the request of Jorge de Montemayor, author of the pastoral novel *Diana* (1561), to Fray Bartolomé Ponce, author of a *contra-factum* of the *Diana* entitled *Clara Diana a lo divino* (1582): "Father Ponce, you friars should do penance for all of us, since gentlemen of rank have no other profession than arms and love." Father Ponce replied: "I assure you, Señor Montemayor, that with my crude and rustic style I will compose another *Diana*, who will take after yours, wielding a sturdy club."[57] All this was said with much laughter, whereupon "the banquet came to an end, and each went his way."

2   On Juan Ruiz's Parody
of the Canonical Hours

That *coplas* 372 to 387 of the *Libro de buen amor* contain a parody of portions of the liturgy, and that this parody is intended to be funny, not sacrilegious, is well known.[1] My purpose in the present article is to look more deeply into the humorous use of "accommodated" Biblical or liturgical texts in Europe, to show the existence of similar practices in other cultures, to examine the human basis of the phenomenon of religious parody, and to offer what I hope may be accepted as well-conjectured, perhaps even well-reasoned interpretations of the Latin phrases used by Juan Ruiz in order that we may have a more exact understanding[2] of these sixteen *coplas*—as close an approximation as we can get to what Juan Ruiz's audience or readers must have understood, appreciated, and laughed at. The result may well throw light on the *Libro de buen amor* as a whole. May we not think of *all* its parts as sharing in the purpose of the portion here studied, that is to say, as constituting pleasurable and comic relief from the awe that surrounds revered mores and rites? "Tetrica sunt amoenanda jocularibus," wrote the fifth-century bishop Sidonius Apollinaris (*Ep.* i. 19). "Aliquando plus delectare solent seriis admixta ludicra," declared Hugh of Saint Victor more than six centuries later,[3] and Diego Sánchez de Badajoz—much later still—put the same thought into the *Introito* of his *Farsa teologal:* "Que entre reir y reir/ bueno es la verdad decir,/ y por esto soy venido."

Gay yet respectful parody of sacred ceremonies, persons, or texts is a human phenomenon so diffused through many cultures that any given instance of it seems to have its justification in human nature. The greater the esteem in which certain mores are held, the more pleasurable is the comic relief which the act of parody provides. "The blasphemy is not intended to move ironical smiles, nor the indecency to move prurient titters; what both want from the audience is a hearty guffaw."[4]

Knud Rasmussen reports the following, which he observed among the Netsilik Eskimos:

> A curious game, a particular favorite among the children was [the spirit game], in which they imitated and parodied shaman seances and the general fear of evil spirits with a capital sense of humor. They held complete and true shaman seances, fought with imaginary enemies just as grown-ups do; in fact, they even used the same formulas that they had heard their parents utter when really in fear and danger. Although this game was absolute blasphemy, the grown-up audience writhed with laughter, just as if they took a certain satisfaction in seeing the evil and inexorable gravity of life made the subject of farcical burlesque. Some hours later it might happen that an attack of illness, or perhaps a bad dream, would rally the grown-ups to a seance during which they desperately sought to defend themselves against hidden enemies, with exactly the same means as the children had mocked in play. When I mentioned this remarkable circumstance to my friend Kuvdluitssoq, and enquired of him whether it was really prudent to mock the spirits, he answered with the greatest astonishment pictured in his face that the spirits really understood a joke.[5]

Julian H. Steward studies this phenomenon in an article entitled "The Ceremonial Buffoon of the American Indian," bringing together data from what would appear to be a complete survey of the literature on the problem at the time he wrote – 1930.[6] The American Indian actually introduced into his most sacred ceremonies a comedian whose primary business it was to delight the spectators. One main category of the buffoon's activity was the ridicule or burlesque – even the defiling – of sacred and vitally important ceremonies, persons, or customs. The very act of transgression was a potent source of comedy, and in direct proportion to the seriousness of the infringement of normal rules of behavior – parody tends to be most obscene in areas where ecological conditions give greatest importance to fertility rites. The practice is world wide.[7] In Samoa a jester's dance provides relief to the dance of the sacred *taupo*. The African Masai dances had a similar frivolity. The primitive Kouds of India actually permitted ridicule of the goddess to whom sacrifice had been made. The Latin Middle Ages are rich in humor of this sort. Monastery humor was permissible in very early times. Mico of St. Riquier sketches a scene of nudification. Egbert, teacher at the cathedral school at Liège, included in his *Fecunda ratis*, written for schoolboys, a story *De Waltero monacho bracas defendente.*[8] The poetry of the goliards went farther: *Verbum bonum et suave* easily became *Vinum bonum et suave.*[9] In France, Feasts of Asses, Feasts of Fools—with sermon, Host, and all—profaned cathedrals in the most extraordinary manner.[10] The medieval "sermons joyeux," we are told by Émile Picot, "débutaient d'ordinaire par une citation latine." The Biblical texts were "travestis de la façon la plus grotesque." The sign of the Cross and the *Ave Maria* "subissaient eux-mêmes des transformations bouffonnes."[11] When we find, therefore, that Juan Ruiz prefaces his *Libro de buen amor* with such a "sermon joyeux,"[12] and includes in his poem an interlude of considerable length whose sole interest is its humorous parody of the sacred, we must not be scandalized by his "profanation." He was doing what others had done before him and would continue to do for centuries.[13]

I see no special significance in the fact that before Juan Ruiz "a nadie se le ocurrió . . . tomar como tema de parodia el rezo de las horas canónicas," nor do I follow Professor Castro in his affirmation that "procediendo así satisface el autor su ansia de expresión vital, puesto que tales rezos dibujan la vida del clérigo desde el alba hasta la noche, y son símbolo de la concreta humanidad de una persona."[14] I do not see in Juan Ruiz's treatment of the liturgy in the *coplas* here studied any *necessary* consequence of the dwelling together on Spanish soil, throughout the Middle Ages, of "cristianos, moros y judíos." Yet it is true that the Mohammedans also farced their sacred texts. Angel González Palencia tells us that Abu Zayd, the protagonist of the *Maqamat* of El Hariri (1053–1122), was a "cincelador de versos curiosos, de enigmas, de charadas, de frases ingeniosas, de parodias irreverentes de temas sagrados," and that in the latter Abu Zayd "pone a prueba todos los artificios y sutilezas de la lengua árabe," *without*, however, losing his sense of "los altos principios de la religión."[15] We have here but one more example of a tendency which knows no limits of geography or of culture.[16] Juan Ruiz[17] could have conceived his parody as he conceived it, and could have given it the form that he gave it, anywhere in Christian Europe.[18]

The tracing of the history of the "accommodated" sacred text in Spanish literature would take us far afield. No attentive reader of the medieval *cancioneros* can fail to have been struck by the popularity of this device. María Rosa Lida passes in review the essential texts on p. 319 of her study of Juan Rodríguez del Padrón,[19] and in another article, "El romance de la misa de amor,"[20] makes clear the sacred character of this type of parody: "La enunciación de cada palabra de la misa cobra tanto valor como el recitado . . . de un conjuro, al punto que la . . . devoción medieval creó un diablillo, Tittivillus, encargado únicamente de recoger las palabras omitidas o farfulladas durante el oficio,[21] y pensó . . . que el Enemigo debía tener por su más exquisito triunfo la alteración que introdujeran sus víctimas en . . . las palabras del santo ritual. En la mente de un fino poeta aquel antiguo temor vino a asociarse con el gesto de maravilla del tañedor, y, al encarecer con una leve aura de hechicería la belleza de la devota, gustó . . . porque introducía en un *juego poético*, decididamente alejado de la realidad, las *representaciones más altas y más caras* del pueblo que lo contaba."

Long before the Council of Trent (1545–1563), Fray Hernando de Talavera, Isabella the Catholic's confessor (d. 1507) raised a protest against a practice related to, but the direct opposite of, the phenomenon studied here, i.e., the playing or singing of "canciones o cantos seglares" as an interpolated part of the divine service.[22] The stern moralist Juan Luis Vives (d. 1540) makes his condemnation much more sweeping: "Así, digo que es contra la religión burlarse el hombre con las cosas sagradas, o tomarlas y traerlas en la boca, aplicándolas en cosa de burla o fuera de propósito, o en cuentos o fábulas fingidas, o en dichos maldicientes, que es como derramar cieno en la medicina que os había de dar salud; mas aplicarlas a cosas sucias, esto ya es cosa maldita e intolerable."[23] Martín de Azpilcueta, "el Doctor Navarro," one of the "principales artesanos de la reforma católica," in 1545 spoke out against the "irrupción en el santuario de regocijos profanos."[24] He did so again in 1567 in his *Manual de confesores y penitentes*, with the following extenuating remarks: "Mortal. Por quanto se haze injuria

al culto ecclesiastico, y a Dios, segun Caietano, al qual alibi segui-
mos, alegando para ello el concilio de Basilea [1431–1449]. Lo qual
mesmo ordenó agora el Concilio Tridentino.²⁵ Y con el añadimos,
que si algunos con simplicidad pensando que esto es licito, *para
recreacion, porque veen que se acostumbra comunmente*, y si supiessen que lo tal era pecado mortal no lo harian, serian escusados
de tanto, mas no de todo. Agora empero dezimos, que *no parece
pecado mortal*, sino quando la cancion es torpe, y suzia, o vana y
prophana *cantada durante el officio diuino*, por los que son auisados
que no son licitos. Lo mesmo dezimos de los que la noche de
Nauidad dizen pullas, o maldiciones a los que piden la bendicion,
para dezir las leciones, como lo diximos alibi."²⁶

This leniency, sanctioned by the Council of Trent—"con él
añadimos"—seems far removed from the rigorism which we should
expect in these matters, yet it exists to this day: this type of
sacrilege is venial if the sacred words are employed for joking
utterances which, otherwise, are honorable. In the Noldin-Schmitt
Summa Theologiae Moralis, we read: "Sacrilegium grave commit-
titur si verba [scripturae] ad inhonesta et vana adhibentur; veniale
esset, si ad iocos de cetero honestos adhibentur; quod si verba s.
scripturae non ad meros iocos adhibentur, sed ad propria sensa
verbis s. scripturae exprimenda, etiam omnis irreventiae culpa abesse
potest, praesertim si non usurpentur verba ipsius Christi Domini
neve saepius ac veluti ex consuetudine id fiat. Cavendum tamen, ne
sensus iocosus subiciatur verbis s. scripturae, quae in missa et officio
divino occurrunt, ne detur ansa distractionibus inter orandum ori-
turis."²⁷

Azpilcueta, in his *Manual* of the year 1567, remarks that unseemly accommodation of sacred texts "se acostumbra comunmente." The custom, though tempered, was to persist well into the
next century. I shall provide examples from the Renaissance and
late-Renaissance periods, in order that Juan Ruiz's *coplas*, with
their obscene parody of the canonical hours, may be understood in
the light, not only of what preceded them, but also of what followed.

Rodrigo de Reinosa (still living in 1524?) composed a "letanía
con santos profanos," one of them being Tarquin, the ravisher of
Lucretia.²⁸ In the *Farsa dos fisicos* of Gil Vicente (d. 1536?), the

clérigo-amador recognizes Cupid as his overlord and begs him to cure his sufferings: *"In te speravi* [Ps. 7. 1.] e espero."[29] A burlesque Paternoster was recited by the Spanish troops ranged beneath the windows of the imprisoned Pope during the sack of Rome (1527).[30] Dr. Andrés Laguna (d. 1560), a layman "capaz de dar lecciones al teólogo de oficio" and at the same time a sort of Spanish Rabelais[31] whose *Viaje de Turquía* "respira fe robusta en Cristo Salvador, en el Dios de los Evangelios y de San Pablo,"[32] includes therein the following parody of the *Benedictio Peregrinorum*[33] and the *Ordo Commendationis Animae*[34]: "Con el corazón abierto y las entrañas, daba un arcabuzazo en el cielo que me parecía que penetraba hasta donde Dios estaba; que decía en dos palabras: Tú, Señor, que guiastes los tres reyes de Lebante en Belén y libraste a S. Susana del falso testimonio, y a S. Pedro de las prisiones y a los tres muchachos del horno de fuego ardiendo, ten por bien llevarme en este viaje en salvamento *ad laudem et gloriam omnipotentis nominis tui,* y con esto algún pater noster. . . ."[35]

The *Viaje de Turquía* was not printed in the sixteenth century and it is possible that if it had been, the passage here quoted might have caused difficulties with the Inquisition, which omitted from the corrected edition of Torres Naharro's *Propalladia* (1573) the whole of the theologically argumentative *Diálogo del Nacimiento* together with the *Adición del Diálogo,* which ends with a burlesque of the *Ave Maris Stella.*[36] But other works *were* printed and allowed to circulate[37] in which sacred parody is unblushingly indulged in. Capmany, in his *Teatro histórico-crítico de la elocuencia española,* brought together the parodies of the Bible and of the language of theology which he had culled from the works of Quevedo, principally the *Buscón.*[38] It is, of course, a fact that when, in 1639, Quevedo fell from grace and lost the support of Olivares, "alle Schriften, die der gebrochene Quevedo verleugnet hat,"[39] among them the *Buscón,* were forbidden. The *Buscón,* "etwas geändert," received in 1644 "die bischöfliche Genehmigung" and was reprinted. In these maneuvers there was more politics than religion.[40] All of this is of minor interest for us; what *is* of importance is that the 1626 edition of the *Buscón* was issued with the authorization of the Vicario General of the Archbishopric of Zaragoza.[41]

On October 8, 1621, another work, by the Mercedarian friar
Gabriel Téllez, received from Fray Miguel Sánchez the customary
ecclesiastical approbation, with the usual words of praise: the *Cigarrales de Toledo*. Although Tirso, like Quevedo, suffered persecution at the hands of zealots,[42] I have been unable to find his name
listed in any Index of forbidden books published in the seventeenth
century. Apparently objection was never made to the following
example of "the medieval taste for humorous blasphemy"[43] from
Tirso's *Cigarrales*—an example all the more noteworthy in that it
involves the Passion and makes direct reference to El Justo.[44] A
caballero and his servant Carrillo have been driven from an inn by
an attacking band of highwaymen. Carrillo laments:

> Bien le decía yo a V. md. que, aunque perdiéssemos media
> jornada . . . , no hiziéssemos noche en ventas, donde cada día
> representan la passión de Cristo. Porque en aquélla vendió un
> calabrés a su Maestro por treinta dineros; fué una vez sola; pero
> aquí cada día se venden inocentes passageros. Y hasta el nombre
> lo dize, pues no en valde se llaman ventas en España las hosterías,
> y sus dueños, venteros, que es lo mismo que vendedores. El
> prendimiento se verifica en el que acabamos de ver y huir. El
> grasiento huésped . . . bien puede passar plaça, en la barriga y
> corpulencia, de Anás, si en la espesura y autoridad de barbas, de
> Pilatos. Aquí açotan—si no en la coluna, sobre un banco—las
> bolsas. Y ya que no niegue San Pedro, reniegan al hazer de la
> cuenta . . . unos con otros, cantando a media noche gallos, que
> no dexan pegar los ojos en toda ella. No faltan moças tentadoras,
> que a fuer de la de Pilatos desantinan a los passageros. Sobre
> nuestros vestidos y hazienda echarán agora suertes los sayones
> vandoleros. Allí huvo dos ladrones, y el uno fué bueno; aquí
> infinitos, y todos son malos. Salvóse allí Barrabás, porque pade-
> ciese el Justo, y aquí el ventero, peor que él, quedará libre,
> pagando nosotros. Sólo falta que se ahorque Judas, que es el
> huésped, que nos vendió, y oxalá lo haga, resucitando nosotros
> desta desdicha a la restauración de nuestros coxines y portaman-
> teos. ¡Amén Jesús!
>
> No bastaron cuyadados para que no me riyese de la acomodada
> alegoría de mi desnudo impaciente.[45]

Of special interest, for our purposes, is the final comment, with
its reference to the "acomodada alegoría," which is none other than

the "accommodated text," the history of which we have been tracing.

I shall quote yet another passage by Tirso de Molina, from the comedia, *Cómo han de ser los amigos*. Don Manrique, smitten by "the lovers' maladye of *Hereos*,"[46] cries out in despair: "Por mi culpa, por mi culpa." Tamayo, the *gracioso* in this play, interrupts him: "Y por tanto, pido y ruego/ a Dios y a Santa María,/ a San Miguel y a San Pedro. . . ." His master asks in amazement, "¿Qué dices?" and Tamayo replies: "La confesión. . . ." Don Manrique continues to rave, claiming that—since his heart has left his breast to inhabit that of Armesinda—he is *dead*, and he asks for burial. His servant follows his humor and announces the arrival at the funeral, first of the deceased's relatives, then of the "niños de la doctrina," various mendicant orders and religious brotherhoods, the "pobres," the priest and his acolyte, and the beadle. "¡Ea! que el Responso cantan./ ¿Quieres que sea el *Memento*,/ o el *Peccatem* [*sic*] *me quotidie*,/ responso de majaderos?" Don Manrique gives the command "Canta," and Tamayo begins. "Ya va: *quia in inferno . . ./ nulla est redemtio. . . .*" The litany follows: *Sante Petre, ora pro eo;/ Kyrie eleyson; Christi eleyson;/ Kyrie eleyson. . . .*" After which Don Manrique ends the scene with the words: "¡Ay, confusos devaneos!/ Dejadme morir, pues ya dejo/ de mi firme amistad al mundo ejemplo."[47]

Such a scene must have been regarded as "seemly" in the seventeenth century. And the end is not yet. When the people of Mexico were striving in the 1840's to protect their territory from the forces of American expansion, an unknown spokesman of the *pueblo*, quite possibly an embattled priest, had recourse to the age-old tradition of the accommodated text and composed a burlesque Paternoster to arouse the spirit of resistance. Sacred parody has here lost its guffaw, but it retains the element of ridicule:

> El anciano y vil Scott,
> Como en maldades tan diestro,
> Sin más ley que su ambición
> Quiere ser el *Padre nuestro*.
>
> . . . .
>
> Y tú, General Santa Ana,
> De la Patria héroe inmortal,

Líbranos destos malvados
Y *mas líbranos del mal.*[48]

With the *Amén* that ends this Mexican *corrido* I turn from an historical survey of the accommodated text in Spain to my specific task of interpreting, with a rigor heretofore not undertaken, the difficult *coplas* of Juan Ruiz.[49] The task will be delicate. We must realize, as C. S. Lewis warns in his discussion of late medieval literature in Scotland, that in reading comic works of this kind we have to make a readjustment. "We must think ourselves back," he tells us, "into a world where great . . . poets lavished their skill on humours now confined to the preparatory school or the barrack room." In Juan Ruiz's poem, just as in Dunbar's *The Twa Mariit Wemen and the Wedo*, "the almost unparalleled grossness" is there for the sake of fun, and the fun "lies in its sheer preposterousness and in the virtuosity with which the poet goes piling audacity on audacity." Lewis makes his warning even more specific: "If you cannot relish a romp you had best leave this extravaganza alone."[50] Not that we are here engaged in a "romp." If we would understand the Archpriest's masterpiece—and the Archpriest himself—we cannot "leave alone" this component of his art.

To the reader or hearer familiar with the Bible and the liturgy—and the hearers or readers in this case were ecclesiastics—each Latin phrase suggests an association of ideas. Any individual association, like the sentences we once studied in school, may be simple, complex, or compound. When simple, it is direct, without *arrière pensée:* the words quoted need the words left unsaid to make complete sense. This is seldom the case. More often than not, the reader (or hearer) will find himself making complex associational bridges, involving meanings far removed from that of the words left unsaid, and it is here that the humor, and the blasphemy, come in. There are other cases, which I shall call "compound," where a two-level bridge is built across the gap: the surface meaning involves a clear and direct, as against a distorted, association, while a quite different and far from edifying meaning hovers in the background, the whole constituting a sort of equivocal double play. With this explanation I shall proceed *copla* by *copla;* each example of accommodation will be readily recognized as belonging to one or another of the categories indicated.

In *copla* 372[51] the author returns to his "pelea" with Don Amor, after having told the story of the "pleito" between the wolf and the fox, with Don Ximio as judge. Don Amor, like the wolf in the story, is a hypocrite: he inveighs against types of indulgence to which he himself is prone. He has no thought for the corporal works of mercy: the persons he visits are not the sick, "synon solteros, sanos, mancebos e valyentes," and if he encounters "loçanas" he addresses them "entre dientes." With *copla* 374 the parody is announced: "Reças muy bien *las horas* con garçones folguines,/ *Cum his qui oderunt paçem*, fasta que el *salterio* afines." The Latin is from Psalm 119, 6 (Vulgate numeration), but it is of no help to study the phrase in its Biblical setting, as we shall see in many other cases. The humor consists in the *deviation* from the normal association and its intensity is proportional to the violence of the deviation. This first *copla* of our parody is a preamble. The *clérigo enamorado* is with *mancebos*, his cronies in the tavern, loud roisterers *qui oderunt pacem*, hale fellows with whom it is pleasant –*bonum*–to enjoy the cup of fellowship: *Ecce quam bonum (habitare fratres in unum*–Ps. 132, 1). In this case the bridge is "simple." It is necessary to supply the full Biblical text in order to catch the sense. Then comes line *d: In noctibus extollite (manus vestras in sancta*–Ps. 133, 2). The words *manus vestras in sancta* help us not at all; the bridge is "complex." I interpret as follows: the *buenos bebedores* are invited to *empinar el codo (extollite)* at this decidedly late cocktail hour, to lift up the winecup for one last drink. The words *in noctibus* determine the time; they are from the last psalm of compline, the last prayer of the *day*, sung in the early evening. The last words of line *d* thus come in naturally: "*despues vas a matynes*." The meaning is that it is midnight. The *clérigo*, having finished compline–the last of his daytime duties–and feeling the blood-warming glow of the wine, now goes off to his *nightly* "prayers," his *work* of the night, or, to imitate the Archpriest's humorously blasphemous language, his "nightly devotions." Matins constitute the first prayer of the *new* day, although daylight is a long way off; prime, the second of the canonical hours begins at 6 A.M.[52]

Stanza 375 begins with the line "Do tu amiga mora comienças a leuantar." It is unrealistic to assume, with Professor Castro, that "el rezo en alta voz se confunde con el ruidoso amanecer de quien, al levantarse, saca también de su reposo a los instrumentos de música. . . . Para entender las coplas 375 y 376 hay que suponer que el clérigo y su amiga moran en las misma casa."[53] The lover is not *rising* from a night of love; that night is just *beginning*, and the dawn is some six hours off. Properly to interpret *leuantar* we must be prepared to face the scabrous. Erich Auerbach, in the chapter of his *Mimesis* entitled "Frate Alberto," refers to Boccaccio's blasphemous phrase *la resurrezion della carne* as being "part and parcel of the medieval repertoire of farce" and explains Rabelais' *ad te levavi* (Ps. 24, 1) as signifying sexual erection.[54] Although in Spanish the normal verb for this meaning is *alzar*,[55] *levantar* was also used, as in Quevedo's rendering of Martial's epigram *In Galliam:* "que un frailazo omnipotente/ hará mucho en levantar."[56] The next line begins *Domine labia mea (aperies et os meum anuntiabit laudem tuam*–Ps. 50, 17). Song appears to be present here ("en voz alta a cantar"), and the "simple" bridge suggests praise of the beloved. There is also, probably, an additional "complex" bridge, in which case the image is osculatory. Lines *c–d* continue: "*Primo dierum omnium*, los estormentos tocar,/ *nostras preçes ut audiat*, e faceslos despertar." The meaning is on two levels. The simple and obvious one tells of waking the musical instruments to sound and waking the beloved with a serenade *muy de madrugada. Primo dierum omnium* (from St. Gregory's hymn for matins) cannot mean "on the first day of creation," but suggests the early hour (cf. Latin *prima nocte*). "Los estormentos tocar," on the simple level refers to the actual playing of music to induce the beloved to lend ear (*ut audiat*–from the same hymn) to the lover's entreaties. But there is another bridge, as this *copla* looks forward to and anticipates *copla* 384. Both *tocar* and *estormentos* have a scatological meaning well known to Chaucer's Wife of Bath (in her Prologue). Godefroy[57] defines *instrument* as "parties honteuses" and cites this example: "Avant qu'il ne peust toucher a l'instrument naturelle d'elle."[58] *Faceslos despertar*, the last words of this *copla*, can refer only to the *estormentos*–there is no manuscript authority for the reading *fázesla* (Cejador). The meaning is again double: the *instrumentos* awaken to sound and to other sensations.

Desque sientes a ella, the first words of 376, have the same double sense: *sientes* is a verb of sense perception, and can refer to both hearing and touch. The lover's heart expands. We now pass from matins to lauds, usually sung with matins, a sort of "apéndice de los Maitines." The lover is instructed—and here Juan Ruiz forgets his *pelea* with Don Amor and falls back into the familiar framework of his *ars amandi*—to sing praises—*Cantate* (*Domino canticum novum* —Ps. 150, 1)—in the dawning light—*aurora lucis* (from an Easter hymn)—and to beg her to yield grace by entoning the *Miserere,* wherewith "mucho te le engraçias."

In 377 the sun has risen; it is the hour of prime, or six A.M. The lover appeals to his Trotaconventos—*Deus in nomine tuo* (*salvum me fac*—Ps. 53, 3)—to arrange a tryst by leading the beloved to the fountain or river to fetch water. The identity of the *amiga* appears to have changed. The concrete situations of 375–376, where no go-between was necessary, are replaced by vagueness ("sy es tal; sy es dueña"—378, 379), and distance is interpolated until we come to 381, where the *amiga,* thanks to the *vieja,* is *presta* and again assumes individuality—but this disappears again in 385 ("dizes a la que viene") and in 386, where the singular *amiga* becomes plural and generalized ("quier blancas, quier prietas"). Such shifts are typical of Juan Ruiz, and recall the succession of his *own amigas*— now a *panadera,* now a *dueña cerrada,* now an *otra non sancta,* etc.

In 378 the Archpriest continues his discourse in his customary Ovidian vein. If the beloved belong to a stratum of society that makes it unseemly for her to play the role of *moza de cántaro,* the *vieja* may take her to the garden to "coger rosas bermejas." This is a normal expedient, a "simple" bridge. The garden tryst is one of the oldest of literary motifs. But there is an added "complexity." "Coger rosas," i.e., "das Röslein brechen," is a euphemism for defloration,[59] and the force of this image carries over into the second half of the *copla.* If in her naiveté the beloved is taken in by love's protestations, "*quod Eva tristis* trae de *quicumque vult* re-druejas." *Quod Eva tristis* (*abstulit*) is from the hymn sung at lauds, *quicumque vult* (*salvus esse*) from the Athanasian creed. I interpret: if the young woman allows herself to be deceived she will harvest from the garden of folly, i.e., from listening to *Who*

will come with me and be my love (*quicumque vult*)?, a fruit no
less bitter in its consequences than *quod Eva tristis abstulit* as her
reward for listening to the serpent. She will harvest *redruejas*,
flowers that blossom and wither, that shrivel without giving fruit.
    Copla 379 introduces yet another alternative. If the lady's re-
serve is so great that the measures previously suggested could not
be effective, it will be necessary to overcome her resistance with
sweet music, in which case—the poet enjoins—the lover should lay
siege to her mind and lips and tongue: "*os, lynga, mens* la enuade,"
whereupon she will throw caution to the winds and love will have
its way: "Va la dueña a tercia, caridat *legem pone*" (Ps. 118, 33).
Os, lingua, mens, (*sensus, vigor*) is from the hymn of terce, sung at
9 A.M.; *legem pone* (*mihi, Domine*) is from the fragment of Psalm
118 "qui occupe l'heure de tierce."[60]
    Copla 380 contains no Latin phrases. The first two lines require
no explanation. The *misa de novios* of *c*, desired by the lover, is, I
believe, a very special and personal type of "mass": "sin gloria y sin
son," that is to say, an entirely private affair between him and her,
not merely a *misa de amor* but a *misa de amantes*. Line *d* is
obscure: "coxqueas al dar ofrenda, byen trotas al comendon." The
obvious meaning, arrived at by inference, is that the lover is a
selfish *goloso:* "cojo para la ofrenda; para pedir, trotón," according
to the modern rendering of María Brey Mariño. *Comendón* is a
difficult word and at best we are thrown back on conjecture. If it
means, as Américo Castro suggests, the "encomienda del alma de
los difuntos," a semantic stretch of the imagination makes it possible for us to interpret: "you are halt and lame when it comes to
giving but you are quick to *encomendarte* to the mercy of your
amiga." I regard as altogether too literal—and hence far removed
from the spirit of this parody—the full interpretation offered by
Castro.[61] Could *comendón*, as here used, be related in meaning to
commenda, defined by Du Cange as *depositum?* The poet's intention would then be scatological: *depositum seminis*. The offering as
symbolized by the almsbox is repugnant, but an *offrande*—a delivery—of quite another sort is made with all eagerness: *trotas*.
    At this point the plot thickens. After *tercia* comes *sesta:* it is sext,
or 12 noon. The first three words of 381c are "Comienças: *In*

verbum tuum" (*supersperavi*–Ps. 118, 81). The simple and direct Biblical association is perfectly applicable: "I have trusted in thy word." The lover then says to his *amiga*, "*factus sum sicut uter*" (*in pruina*–Ps. 118, 83) and here the association becomes complex. We are not to think of the psalm in question ("mine eyes fail . . . I am become like a bottle in the smoke"), but of the scatological implications of the word *uter*, 'odre.' This *uter* is not a wineskin being cured over a smoking fire; it is the container of a liquid, and this container–*les coilles* of the *Roman de la Rose* (6966)–is uncomfortably full. The clérigo's *necesidad* is the same as that of Rocinante before his sad encounter with the *desalmados yangüeses* (I, 15). This situation leads up to the "grand misa de fiesta" (381d) which the beloved's *misericordia* is about to make possible.

In 382 the lover says "*quomodo dilexi*" (*legem tuam, Domine*– Ps. 118, 97). The *legem tuam* has become "vuestra fabla," and *Domine*, "varona." The bridge of association is essentially simple: "how I have loved your words." Not so in the scabrous distortion that follows. In *suscipe me secundum* (*eloquium tuum et vivam*– Ps. 118, 116), the word *suscipe* is to be taken in all its suggestive literalness. The poet might have said of the *amiga*, as Sempronio does of Elicia in the *Celestina*[62]: "¡O desventurada e qué carga espera!" The *clérigo* next swears by his tonsure that the *amiga* is a lamp unto his feet: *Lucerna pedibus meis* (Ps. 118, 105) and she replies *quam dulcia* (*faucibus meis eloquia tua*–Ps. 118, 103), "how sweet your words!" None the less, she puts him off, bidding him return at nones, or 3 P.M.

So they go to nones together (383). *Mirabilia* (*testimonia tua*– Ps. 118, 129) he says, referring, not to the testimonies of the Lord, but to his own bright prospects and great expectations. The next words, "dizes de aquesta plana," refer to the *page* of the Psalter or book of hours. *Gressus meos dirige* (*secundum eloquium tuum*–Ps. 118, 133), replies the willing dame: "direct my steps to your room," and she then adds: *justus es, Domine* (Ps. 118, 137), "confío en ti, mi bien." Thereupon "tañe a nona la campana."

Kane makes this *copla* more suggestive than it actually is.[63] Bell and clapper, like hammer and anvil in Alanus de Insulis' *De Planctu Naturae* and in the *Roman de la Rose*, are images that represent the organs of generation[64]; but *gressus meos dirige*, spoken by the *lady*, can have only literal meaning, and *justus* does not mean literally upright in Latin.

Copla 384 reads:

> Nunca vi sancristan que a visperas mejor tanga:
> todos los instrumentos toca con chica manga;
> la que viene a tus biesperas, por byen que se arremanga,
> con *virgam virtutis tue* fazes que ay rremanga.

We have passed from nones to vespers, at the hour of twilight. "Con chica manga" means easily; "por byen que se arremanga," in spite of token resistance; *virgam* (Ps. 109, 2), *verga* (quite literally); *virtutis* means *potentiae*. "Todos los instrumentos" are Jean de Meun's "tous les autres estrumenz/ qui sont pilers e argumenz/ a soutenir nature humaine."[65]

This is the climax. Hereafter the concrete gives way to the abstract as the *clérigo* seeks new partners. In 385a he says *sede a destris meis* to the feminine passer-by, quoting from Psalm 109, 1–the first psalm sung at vespers. If she is prevailed upon to linger, he sings *Laetatus sum* (*in his quae dicta sunt mihi*–Ps. 121, 1): "what joy!" If any *curioso impertinente* stops to see the fun ("qualquier qu' ally se atiene," i.e., "se arrima") he is straightway informed that "they all went that-a-way," or "the fire's up the street": *illuc enim ascenderunt* (*tribus, tribus Domini*–Ps. 121, 4), "thither the tribes went up." And the hour of vespers passes like a "fiesta de seis capas."

To José María Aguado, "la profanación de las coplas 386–387 no tiene nombre." He shudders at the disrespect for the "hondo sabor místico" of compline, the last *rezo diurno*, and abstains from specifying the nature of the desecration.[66] The first of these *coplas* reads:

> nunca vy cura de almas que tan byen diga conpletas:
> vengan fermosas o feas, quier blancas, quier prietas,
> digante *Conuerte nos:* de grado abres las puertas;
> despues: *custodi nos*, te rruegan las encubiertas.

I suggest that *Converte nos* (*Deus salutaris noster*–Ps. 84, 5) means "conviértenos de doncellas en ex-doncellas" and that *custodi nos*

(*Domine, ut pupillam oculi*—from the preliminary prayer for compline) is to be interpreted as an urgent request that the *clérigo*, about to kiss, tell not. *Abres las puertas* scarcely needs comment. The Latin phrases in 387 are all from the *Nunc dimittis* (Luke ii.29–32), the Song of Saint Simeon as he held the Infant Jesus in his arms, or from the *Salve, Regina*, the prayer wherewith "se cierran, como con broche de oro, las preces y los párpados del ministro del Señor"[67]:

> Ffasta el *quod parasti* non las quieres dexar;
> *ante faciem omnium* sabeslas alexar;
> ado *gloriam plebis tue* fazeslas abaxar;
> *Salve, regina*, dizes, sy de ty s'an de quexar.

The words *quod parasti* merely signify *end*, since St. Simeon's song is sung at the end of compline. *Ante faciem omnium* (*populorum*) is another reference to the *secrecy* necessary for what is implied in line c: i.e., each complacent *amiga* is led away from the view of all eyes, except two. Line *c* contains the real "profanación." Where, indeed, does the *gloria* of men of the lover's ilk, of his *ralea*, of his *plebs*, have its center, except in "the instruments of love's war"?[68] It is to that *centrum gloriae* that the *amigas* "se abaxan." One may compare the words of Guzmán de Alfarache: "¿Quién ve un deshonesto, que con aquel torpe apetito adora lo que más presto aborrece y allí busca su *gloria* donde conoce su apetito?"[69] In line *d* we have the "broche de oro" of Juan Ruiz's parody: if, in his haste and through inconsiderateness, the *clérigo* should arouse protest, the formula of mollification is ready to hand: *Salve, regina.*

With this we have come to our own *quod parasti*. Professor Castro, in his study of the *Libro de buen amor*,[70] has rightly stressed what he calls "el tema de la alegría": "vamos acercándonos a la realidad de un Cancionero cuyo tema es presentar proyectos de vida alegre y placentera, y a la vez restringir moralmente las perspectives seductoras que iba abriendo al público castellano."[71] It is as *alegría* that the preceding *profanaciones* are to be understood; the *restringir* appears elsewhere in the poem. William A. Madden, in a thoughtful article entitled "Chaucer's Retraction and the Medieval Canons of Seemliness,"[72] has shown that, in Chaucer's time, habits and attitudes were determined by *social* standards of the

"seemly" rather than by ecclesiastical authority; that both pious
and scatological tales appealed to mixed interests in the hearers.
Swearing, for example, was theoretically condemned, and Chaucer's Parson so reminds the pilgrims; yet swearing, even for a
Prioress, seems to have been common practice, and a reading of the
Canterbury Tales renders its oaths as innocuous as they were to the
pilgrims themselves (pp. 176–177). Juan Ruiz, in his poem as a
whole, consciously shared Chaucer's problem: whether to let his
art act autonomously or to order it by prudence, yet in this parody
of the canonical hours prudence appears to have had no part. Even
the fact that the parody is interpolated in a lengthy section on the
capital sins is not an indication of seriousness—the Archpriest, for
all his *pelea* with Don Amor, finally enlists under his banner. The
gap in medieval art between what was morally and what was
socially acceptable is not, in these *coplas* of the parody, a matter of
concern to Juan Ruiz, though elsewhere that gap is clearly in his
mind. Juan Ruiz could have said, like Alfonso Alvarez de Villasandino:

> Lo que escrivo al rrey leed,
> e averedes que reyr
> de mi nescio argüyr
> en Quaresma con la seed,[73]

or like Juan Alfonso de Baena:

> Señor, con triaca e flor de açusena
> conpus estos metros por arte gayosa,
> a ffyn que rryades, e mas otra cosa
> que se vos mienbre de mi el de Baena.[74]

The necessity, if not the legitimacy of *regocijo* was recognized
by Azpilcueta in his *Manual de confesores y penitentes*, published,
as we have seen, with full awareness of the reforms proclaimed by
the Council of Trent. It is mortal sin, Azpilcueta declares, if a
person impersonates a member of a religious order "para vituperio
de la religión," or to perform, under that disguise, "cosas feas, con
mascaras o sin ellas." But the sin is venial if it is committed "por
liuiandad, o *por regozijar*, sin mal fin, y sin que se sigua [*sic*]

vituperio notable a la religión."[75] The need for pleasurable and comic relief from the awe of the sacred is thus acknowledged by an eminent director of the Spanish national conscience in the *siglo de oro*. In the light of this necessity—a universal phenomenon—the *Libro de buen amor* acquires a new perspective. Its sacrilegious parody is akin to that of Torres Naharro in the *Adición del Diálogo*[76] and to that of the "spirit game" of the Netsilik Eskimos.

3 Courtly Love in the Spanish Cancioneros

I. THE PROBLEM

The unfortunate pronouncements of Menéndez y Pelayo have condemned the poetry of the early Spanish *cancioneros* to undeserved neglect.[1] A revision is in order, for the subject has importance for both Spanish and comparative literature. This poetry is not a mere jumble of far-fetched superficialities. Progressively purged of license and adapted to Christian courtship and marriage, it yet preserves in fairly definite shape the traditional pattern of courtly love. It is necessary to apply to Spanish *cancionero* poetry concepts that have been worked out for other European literatures.

The doctrine of courtly love, as it appears in fifteenth-century Spain, owes much to mediæval ideas on medicine and psychology, on the soul and its passions, and, in general, to mediæval moral philosophy and theology; but its ultimate source is to be found in the love poetry of the troubadours which spread to all the courts of Europe. Ausias March wrote in his *Cants de Amor:*

> Envers alguns aço miracle par,
> mas si'ns membram d'En Arnau Daniel
> e de aquells que la terra'ls es vel
> sabrem Amor vers nos que pot donar.[2]

We have to do with a complex phenomenon: a troubadouresque tradition[3] entangled with the pre-existing Ovidian tradition—though it was forced to modify and even to misunderstand that tradition[4] —and with the later Arthurian stories,[5] and altered through the centuries in the process of its adaptation to Spanish ideals and conditions of life.[6] The present analysis aims to provide the most essential data for an understanding of what might be called the inherited elements in the treatment of love by *siglo de oro poets.*

II. MENA'S DEFINITION

Juan de Mena's definition of love contains most, but by no means all, of the elements which constitute courtly love:

> El qual est tal *medio de dos coraçones*
> que la voluntad que estaua no junta
> la su dulcedumbre *concorda e ayunta*
> faziéndoles vna sus dos opiniones,
> o dando tal parte de sus afeçiones
> *a los amadores sin gozo cadena,*
> e *a los amados deleyte sin pena,*
> a los *menos méritos más galardones.*[7]

The phrases *medio de dos coraçones* and *concorda e ayunta* have to do with the "unity of wills" and the "desire mutually to please" which A. J. Denomy regards as the foundation of *fin' amors*.[8] The words *sin gozo cadena*, applied only to the *amador*, the lover or suitor, indicate "the delight and ecstasy of true love and its bitter-sweet pangs of desire,"[9] a desire that must ever remain a desire—*sin gozo*—in order that its end may be fulfilled[10]:

> Ni biuo desesperado,
> si bien dexo de os gozar;
> que un bien de bienes sin par
> *basta hauerlo desseado.*[11]

The last two lines, *e a los amados deleyte sin pena* and *a los menos méritos más galardones*, refer to the elements of *humility* and *reward generously given* which concern the lover and the beloved respectively. Each of these elements will require full treatment below. For the present it is necessary to understand that the *lover* is always abject, that he gives silent acquiescence to the beloved's wishes, that, in the feudal sense, he is "her man"[12] and that as a vassal he humbly seeks her mercy.[13] The *pena* is for the lover only. As for the *galardones* which the humble lover (*a menos méritos*) may expect to receive—and complains if he does not—they are an indication of the unity of wills already referred to, and consist, in their purest form, of "the *bels semblans*, the indication that the lover's love is acceptable to the beloved and the sign that he may hope for reward, something tangible to satisfy the yearning of his heart."[14] They too will require further treatment in the pages that follow.

III. THE RELIGION OF LOVE

Beside *humility* as a characteristic of courtly love, C. S. Lewis places what he calls the *religion of love:*

> When [Lancelot] comes before the bed where she lies he kneels and adores her: as Chrétien explicitly tells us, there is no *corseynt* in whom he has greater faith. When he leaves her chamber he makes a genuflexion as if he were before a shrine. The irreligion of the religion of love could hardly go farther.[15] . . . Where it is not a parody of the Church [this religion of love] may be, in a sense, her rival—a temporary escape, a truancy from the ardours of a religion that was believed into the delights of a religion that was merely imagined.[16] . . . It is as if some lover's metaphor when he said 'Here is my heaven' in a moment of passionate abandonment were taken up and expanded into a system. Even while he speaks he knows that 'here' is not his real heaven; and yet it is a delightful audacity to develop the idea a little further. If you go on to add to that lover's 'heaven' its natural accessories, a god and saints and a list of commandments, and if you picture the lover praying, sinning, repenting, and finally admitted to bliss, you will find yourself in the precarious dream-world of medieval love poetry.[17]

"Faser dioses estraños e ydolatrar byen es cabsa el amor," declared the Archpriest of Talavera in his *Corbacho.*[18] It was to combat this religion of love that Fernando de Rojas composed *La Comedia o Tragicomedia de Calisto y Melibea,* "compuesta en reprehensión de los locos enamorados que, vencidos en su desordenado apetito, a sus amigas llaman e dizen ser su Dios. . . ."[19] Fray Iñigo de Mendoza's attack upon it is of special interest because it provides not only an almost complete description of the courtly love of the Spanish *cancioneros* but also a preview of the *comedia de capa y espada:*

> Que hagan las aficiones
> ser tu dios lo que más amas,

bien lo muestran las passyones
que en sus coplas y canciones
llaman dioses a sus damas;
bien lo muestra su seruirlas,
su rauiar por contentarlas,
su temerlas, su sufrirlas,
su continuo requerirlas,
su syempre querer mirarlas.
   Bien lo muestra el grand plazer
que sienten quando las miran;
bien nos lo da a conoscer
el entrañal padescer
que sufren quando sospiran;
bien ofrece a la memoria
la fe de sus coraçones,
su punnar por la victoria,
su tener por muy grand gloria
el sy de sus peticiones.
   Su dançar, su festejar,
sus gastos, justas y galas,
su trobar, su cartear,
su trabajar, su tentar
de noche con las escalas,
su morir noches y días
para ser dellas bien quistos,
sy lo vieses, jurarías
que por el dios de Marcías
venderán mill Jhesus Crhistos.
   Como muchas nuezes vanas
se cubren de casco sano,
como engañosas maçanas
que muestran color de sanas
y tienen dentro gusano,
assy por nuestro dolor,
muchos de nuestras Españas
se dan christiana color
que de dentro el dios de amor
ha roydo las entrañas. [*F-D*, 1, 46–47]

Fray Íñigo speaks here of "el dio de Macías." In this Spanish
branch of the religion of love, Macías, *o Namorado* or *el Enamo-*

rado is hero,[20] idol,[21] martyr[22] and saint.[23] The deity is a dual personality: Cupid-Venus. In Juan Rodríguez de la Cámara's *Siervo libre de amor* we learn that: "Passados de la trabajosa vida a la perpetua gloria que poseen los leales amadores, aquellos que por bien amar son coronados del alto Cupido . . . tyenen las primeras syllas a la diestra de su madre la deessa."[24] It is to this same Cupid, in his quality of *son*, that the lovers address their petitions in Suero de Ribera's *Missa de Amor:*

> Cordero de dios de Venus,
> dezían los desamados,
> tú que pones los cuydados,
> quita los que sean menos,
> pues tienes poder mundano,
> o señor tan soberano,
> *Miserere nobis.* [*F-D*, II, 190][25]

In Santillana's *Triumphete de amor* the poet is led to the throne of Venus:

> Do, por más admiraçión,
> me quiso mostrar Fortuna
> la grand clarificaçión,
> muy más cándida que luna,
> Venus, a quien sola vna
> non vi ser equivalente,
> fermosa, sabia, exçellente,
> dina d'exçelsa tribuna.[26]

And it is to Venus that he prays in *El planto que fiço Pantasilea:*

> Venus, de tanto serviçio
> que te fiçe atribulado
> de oraçión e sacrifiçio,
> ¿qué gualardón he sacado?[27]

This is not the celestial Venus of the Neo-Platonists or even of Dante,[28] but a modification of the Doña Venus of the *Libro de Buen Amor* and the mediæval tradition.[29] Her appearance in the works of unquestionably devout poets was, to be sure, a "truancy" which in due time fell under ecclesiastical censure.[30] Martín de

Azpilcueta, el doctor Navarro, in his *Manual de confesores y penitentes*[31] classifies as mortal sin any admixture of *culto divino* and *cantos seglares*, such as the *Miserere nobis* of Suero de Ribera, quoted above; but he makes a qualification which indicates clearly the wide extent of the practice, even in the sixteenth century:

> . . . añadimos, que si algunos con simplicidad pensando que esto es lícito, para recreación, porque veen que se acostumbra comúnmente, y si supiessen que lo tal era pecado mortal no lo harían, serían escusados de tanto, mas no de todo. Agora empero dezimos, que no parece pecado mortal sino quando la canción es torpe y suzia, o vana y prophana cantada durante el officio diuino, por los que son auisados que no son lícitos.[32]

The case for the poets has been admirably stated by C. S. Lewis:

> For poetry to spread its wings fully, there must be, besides the believed religion, a marvellous that knows itself as myth. For this to come about, the old marvellous, which once was taken as fact, must be stored up somewhere, not wholly dead, but in a winter sleep, waiting its time.[33] . . . The decline of the gods, from deity to hypostasis and from hypostasis to decoration, was not, for them nor for us, a history of sheer loss. For decoration may let romance in. The poet is free to invent, beyond the limits of the possible, regions of strangeness and beauty for their own sake.[34]

This religion of love had its decalogue, *Los diez mandamientos de Amor* of Juan Rodríguez de la Cámara (or del Padrón)[35]; its monastic orders,[36] its pilgrimages,[37] its general councils.[38] One of its very curious documents is the *Sermón ordenado por Diego de Sant Pedro porque dixeron vnas señoras que le desseauan oyr predicar:*

> . . . pero porque sin gracia ninguna obra se puede començar, ni medrar, ni acabar, roguemos al Amor (en cuya obediencia biuimos) que ponga en mi lengua dolor; porque manifieste en el sentir lo que fallesciere en el razonar. E porque esta gloria nos sea otorgada, pongamos por medianera entre Amor e nosotros la Fe que tenemos en los coraçones. E para más le obligar, ofrecerle hemos sendos sospiros porque nos alcance gracia; a

mí para dezir, e a vosotras, señoras, para escuchar; e a todos finalmente para bien amar.
Dice el lhema: *In patientia vestra sustinete dolores vestros.*

The sermon ends: "Ad quam gloriam nos perducat.—Amen."[39]
With these facts before us, we shall not be scandalized, as Menendéz y Pelayo was,[40] by the blasphemies of the *cancioneros.*

IV. COURTESY

The treatment of love as a religion, or rather the introduction of religious elements into the *service d'amour,* is in keeping with that characteristic of courtly love which C. S. Lewis calls *courtesy,* and which Myrrha Lot-Borodine defines more accurately as *l'amour vertu:* "une valeur inherente au sentiment."[41] "Only the courteous can love," says Lewis (p. 2), "but it is love which makes them courteous." "It is only the noblest hearts which love deigns to enslave, and a man should prize himself the more if he is selected for such service."[42] This doctrine may seem natural to a modern reader, but it was new and revolutionary when introduced by the troubadours, and it is so foreign to Christian theological and moral conceptions that it is necessary to anticipate here in some slight degree our consideration of its "amorality."[43] Had there been no Fall, says Gregory the Great, the act of generation would have been *sine carnis incentivo.*[44] Passionate love was wicked, even if its object were one's wife: *omnis ardentior amator propriae uxoris adulter est,* wrote Peter Lombard.[45] In the teaching of Albertus Magnus, *if desire comes first,* the conjugal act is a mortal sin.[46] St. Thomas is less severe: "the evil in the sexual act is neither the desire nor the pleasure, but the submergence of the rational faculty which accompanies them, and this submergence . . . is not a sin, though it is an evil, a result of the Fall."[47] "St. Thomas has no conception of a 'passion' which works a chemical change upon appetite and affection and turns them into a thing differing from either."[48] Thus, as far as official teaching was concerned, the mediæval mind had no choice but to regard the passionate and exalted devotion of courtly love as more or less wicked. This cleavage between Church and

Court appears to Lewis as the most striking feature of mediæval sentiment.[49] A. J. Denomy,[50] without showing the actual means of transmission, regards this cleavage as of Arabic origin, finding the possible source of courtly love in a treatise of Avicenna. With that problem we are not concerned here. Our poets of the *siglo quince* are aware of a *poetic*, not a philosophic, tradition; and the "chemistry" of passion whereby *deseo* was ennobled was for them an article of *poetic* faith.

That faith is set forth in the *Sermón* of Diego de San Pedro already quoted:

> Conuiene a todo enamorado ser virtuoso, en tal manera, que la bondad rija el esfuerço, aconpañe la franqueça; e la franqueça adorne la tenplança, e la tenplança afeyte la conuersación, e la conuersación ate la buena criança, por vía que las vnas virtudes de las otras se alumbren, que de semejantes passos se suele hazer el escalera por do suben los tristes a aquella bienaventurada esperança que todos desseamos.[51]

The question naturally arises as to whether this love may be called Platonic. Lewis's answer is a firm negative:

> Those who call themselves Platonists at the Renaissance may imagine a love which reaches the divine without abandoning the human and becomes spiritual while remaining also carnal; but they do not find this in Plato. If they read it into him, this is because they are living, like ourselves, in the tradition which began in the eleventh century.[52]

Ausias March, thinking no doubt of Dante,[53] whose name appears in this same composition, says in Estramp III of his *Cants de Amor:*

> Alguns elets, *en molt espocat nombre,*
> qui solament d'amor d'esperit amen,
> d'aquest' amor participen ab l'Angel
> e tal voler en per null temps se cança.
> Los qui amor ab cos e arma senten,
> amant lo cos e més la part de l'arma,
> grau de amor homenivol atenyen,
> sobre dos colls lo jou d'amor aporten.[54]

March, like the early troubadours, eliminates intercourse[55] and insists on the excellence of unfulfilled desire:

> No sia entes present deshonest acte,
> car fin amor d'altr'amor se contenta,
> si no l'ateny viu de'sperança sola. . . .[56]

In spite of concessions made to the body, March believes

> los fets del mon ser ombra
> d'aquell Sol clar qui tot llur cor escalfa.[57]

He is aware of the contradictions involved, and exclaims to Love:

> O tu, Amor, de qui mort no triumpha,
> segons lo Dant historial recompta,
> e ningun seny presumir no s'ocupe
> contra tu fort victoria consegre;
> e cossos dos ab un'arma governes
> la vida llur en un esperit penja,
> cell qui de tu lo terme pensa'tenyer
> no sab de tu ignorança deixible.[58]

Mario Equicola, writing at the height of the Italian Renaissance (first edition, 1525), and fully aware of the "triplice bellezza Platonica" (fol. 142ᵛ) as well as of all the literature on the subject of love which had preceded him, including the love poems of the *Cancionero General,* still thinks in terms of a *bodily* desire restrained by *continentia, temperantia, vergogna,* and *honestade:*

> Per la qual cosa qualunche dice in bella e saggia donna amare solamente lo animo, lontano dal sentiero della verità si troua; qualunche dice io amo in bella donna e saggia, solamente il corpo et la bellezza di quello, totalmente dal vero si parte. Concludamo qualunche se sia che veramente ama, amar l'animo e corpo insieme, dico amar necessariamente e per vigor naturale l'uno e l'altro, e affermo che l'uno dall'altro in tal amore non pate separatione: li sensi dell' amante dall' amato corpo recercan voluptà sensuale como suo fine; lo animo de vero amante dell'amato animo amor richiede, e esser reamato. Dall' animo dunque vuol amor lo amante: dal corpo vol dell'amor il frutto.

Me serà reparo continentia, in repellere tutti libidinosi disii:
Temperantia me darà arme e scuto in refrenar ogni lasciuia:
Vergogna me porgerà spata in domare li dishonesti appetiti.
Honestade me darà l'asta, in vincere ogni sopraueniente con-
cupiescentia.[59]

Of this tradition, with its inconsistencies, paradoxes, and conflicts, the Castilian *cancionero* poets are keenly aware[60]:

> Cesaría de folía
> sy fuesse vuestro syrviente,
> e faría *cortessya*
> a vos, noble, reverente,
> exçelente de talente
> serviría. [*CB*, no. 504]

This *cortesía* was accessible even to members of the clergy, as is
evidenced by the fact that the *cántiga* just quoted was composed
by Fray Diego de Valencia "por amor e loores de una dueña [not
doncella] de quien él era enamorado."[61] Yet in spite of all truancies
all of these poets could say with Carvajales:

> mas amar et ser amado,
> e vivir enamorado
> es muy noble gentilesa. [*CStun*, p. 346][62]

The ideal lover should be a

> Discreto galán polido,
> valiente, diestro y osado,
> virtuoso, bien medido,
> de los onbres muy querido,
> de las damas más amado,
> por todas mucho loado
> en público e escondido.[63]

He is further defined, with special consideration given to age
limits, by Hernando de Ludueña:

> El galán ha de tener
> lo primero tal hedad
> que de treynta y seys no passe;

no tan moço que el saber
destruya con liuiandad,
porque no se despompasse.
Si con gentil condición
tuuiere disposicion,
es cierto que ganará;
mas todo le faltará
si le falta discreción. [*F-D*, ii, 719]

Musical and poetic accomplishments are a necessary part of his equipment, as shown in the "Ley que fizo Suero de Ribera, qué tales deuen ser los que dessean ser amados":

Deuen ser mucho discretos,
bien calçados, bien vestidos,
donosos e ardidos,
cuerdos, francos e secretos;
muy onestos e corteses,
de gentiles inuenciones,
buenas coplas e canciones,
discretos mucho en arneses. [*F-D*, ii, 191]

The ideal lady, says Fray Diego de Valencia in a "desir a manera de discor [que] fiso ordenó a una dueña, que era su ennamorada en León,"

Es natura angelical,
criatura muy polida,
gesto rreal nunca vi tal,
de todos bienes conplida,
nobleçida e guarnida,
de bondades sin egual. [*CB*, no. 506]

Her picture is given in greater detail by Fernando de la Torre:

De nueuo soy amador
y amado segund creo,
de dona de grand aseo,
digna de mucho loor.

Y digna de ser amada,
segund su mucha veldad,

y digna de ser loada
sobre todas en verdad:
désta que so seruidor
no dubdes lo que yo creo,
que segund su alto aseo
es digna de grand honor.

Y digna de ser querida
de gentiles amadores,
y digna de ser seruida
su velleza por amores:
ésta yo por su amor
viuo con mucho deseo,
ni dubdes segund su aseo
ques digna de gran honor. [*CFT*, pp. 154–155]

Even Fray Iñigo de Mendoza, in a *débat* between *sensualidad* and *razón* permits the former to claim the power of ennobling life:

¿Quién haze las gentilezas,
quién sojuzga los temores,
quién conuierte las riquezas
en justas, galas, franquezas,
sy no los dulces amores
que ponen tan dulce gloria
en la voluntad humana,
que con sola su memoria
morir o leuar victoria
se delibera su gana? [*F-D*, i, 90–91]

In like manner, when Amor reduced Macías to his service and obedience,

con él venía Mesura
e la noble *Cortesya*,
la poderosa Cordura,
la briosa Loçanía. [*CB*, no. 309][64]

Over and above this concept of *courtesy*, there is a deeper significance in *l'amour vertu* as conceived by certain poets, especially those who had come under the influence of Dante, as the Marqués de Santillana certainly had. In his *Visión* he presents his lady as attended by the cardinal virtues.

A la qual señora mía
las virtudes cardinales
son sirvientes espeçiales,
e la façen compañía;
la moral philosophía
jamás non se parte della,
con otra gentil donçella,
que se llama Fidalguía.[65]

And in his Soneto XIV he compares the sight of her to the vision of Christ's transfiguration shared by the three disciples on Mt. Tabor:

Quando yo so delante aquella donna
a cuyo mando me sojudgó Amor,
cuydo ser uno de los que en Tabor
vieron la grand claror que se raçona.[66]

Such sublime heights were known only to Dante and to his closest followers. *L'amour vertu* is more reasonably expressed by Juan del Encina:

Piadosas en dolerse
de todo ageno dolor
con muy sana fe y amor
sin su fama escurecerse;
ellas nos hazen merced
de nuestros bienes franquezas;
ellas nos hazen poner
a procurar e querer
las virtudes e noblezas.

Ellas nos dan ocasión
que nos hagamos discretos,
esmerados e perfetos
e de mucha presunción:
ellas nos hazen andar
las vestiduras polidas,
los pundonores guardar,
e por honra procurar
tener en poco las vidas.

Ellas nos hazen deuotos,
corteses e bien criados;

de medrosos, esforçados,
muy agudos de muy botos.
Queramos lo que quisieren
de su querer no salgamos;
quanto más pena nos dieren,
quanto más mal nos hizieren,
tanto más bien les hagamos. [*CG*, II, 375]

V. SECRECY

Whether love is sublimated into the realm of symbols, as in the poems of Dantesque tendencies, or whether it is, in a courtly and worldly sense, "espejo con que afeytamos/ lo que nos parece feo," it seems inconsistent that the codes of love should constantly enjoin *secreto*. We are here confronted with what Leo Spitzer calls the *paradoxe amoureux* of all troubadour poetry:

> amour qui ne veut posséder, mais jouir de cet état de non-possession, amour-*Minne* contenant aussi bien le désír sensuel de "toucher" à la femme vraiment "femme" que le chaste éloigne-ment, amour chrétien transposé sur le plan séculier, qui veut "have *and* have not."[67]

The paradox is very real. The *noble gentileza* may bring *infamina*. Diego de San Pedro sounds the warning in his much quoted *Sermón:*

> . . . mas todo se deue suffrir en amor y reuerencia de la fama de la amiga, e guardaos, señores, de vna erronía que en la *ley enamorada* tienen los galanes, començando en la primera letra de los nombres de la que siruen sus inuenciones o cimeras o borda-duras, porque semejante *gentileça* as vn pregón con que se haze justicia de la *infamia* dellas. Ved qué cosa tan errada es mani-festar en la bordadura avn lo que en el pensamiento se deue guardar.[68]

"Le chaste éloignement" might indeed give offense to a husband,[69] as it appears to have done in the case of love's martyr, Macías; but in the case of a *doncella*, the need for secrecy would seem to be much less clear. Yet even damsels who later marry the suitor in question run grave risks in seeking to enjoy the "union of hearts and

minds" which was the essence of courtly love. Thus Oriana, in the
Amadís de Gaula, believing her lover dead, falls in a faint. Mabilia
revives her and demands that she show greater self control: "lo que
vos haréis si de vuestra cuita se sabe, será perderos para siempre."[70]
In the sentimental novel, the heroine invariably replies to the first
advances of the *galán* with an outburst similar to that of Laureola
in the *Cárcel de amor:*

> Así como fueron tus razones temerosas de dezir, assí son graues
> de perdonar. Si como eres de Spaña fueras de Macedonia, tu
> razonamiento y tu vida acabaran a vn tiempo, assí que por ser
> estraño no recebirás la pena que merecías, y no menos por la
> piedad que de mí juzgaste, como quiera que en casos semeiantes
> tan devida es la iusticia como la clemencia, la qual en ti secutada
> pudiera causar dos bienes: el vno, que otros escarmentaran, y el
> otro que las altas mugeres fueran estimadas y tenidas segund
> merecen.[71]

The reason for the outburst is made clear by Belisena's reply to
Flamiano in the *Questión de amor:*

> Muchos días ha, Flamiano, que conozco en tus meneos lo que el
> desuarío de tu pensamiento te ha puesto en la voluntad; e no
> creas que muchas vezes dello no haya recebido enojo, a algunas
> han sido que me han puesto en voluntad de dártelo a entender,
> sino que mi *reputación* e honestidad me han apartado dello. . . .
> Mas pues que tu atrevimiento en tal estremo te ha traydo, que en
> mi presencia tu fantasía hayas osado publicar, forçado me será
> responderte. . . .[72]

Undoubtedly, the existence of this attitude and the corresponding insistence on *secreto* in the code were connected with the
existence of persons incapable of understanding the niceties of *fin'
amors:*

> Porque hable vna donzella
> en la quadra o en la sala
> con quien tuuiere afición,
> luego se entiende que aquélla
> a causa de aquello es mala,
> sin fuzia de redempción.

Nunca fué tan gran error,
menos puede ser mayor,
e la ley lo determina;
que el de condición maligna
siempre piensa lo peor.[73]

Hernando de Ludeña insists that there are countless women in Castile who maintain perfect virtue in spite of courtly customs:

Porque ay cien mil mugeres
festejadas, palancianas,
en esta nuestra Castilla
que salen de mil plazeres
sanas como las manzanas,
sin punçada e sin manzilla:
e a las tales condenar
o dexallas de loar,
son malicias infernales,
pues que son tantas e tales
que no se pondrán contar. [F-D, II, 731]

But *cuando el rio suena, agua lleva.* A passage in the *Amadis* links with the courtly word *servir — service d'amour —* another word, *codiciar,* which indicates that the reward or *galardón* sought was at times more than the "unity of wills" and the "desire to please mutually" of the "pure" love of the troubadours:

Mi buena señora, dijo él, no tengáis en nada las palabras que os dije, que a los caballeros conviene servir y *codiciar* a las donce-llas, y querellas por señoras y amigas, y [a] ellas guardar fe de errar, como vos lo queréis hacer; porque como quiera que al comienzo en mucho tenemos haber alcanzado lo que de ellas deseamos, mucho más son de nosotros preciadas y estimadas cuando con discreción y bondad *se defienden,* resistiendo nuestros malos apetitos, guardando aquello que perdiéndolo nunguna cosa les quedaría que de loar fuese.[74]

Diego de San Pedro, in his *Sermón,* lays down the rules:

Pues luego conuiene que lo que edificare el desseo en el coraçon catiuo, sea sobre cimiento de *secreto,* si quisiera su labor sostener e acabar sin peligro de *vergüenza.* Donde . . . paresce que

todo amador deue antes perder la vida, que escurecer la fama de
la que quisiere, auiendo mejor recebir la muerte callando su pena,
que merecerla, trayendo su cuydado a publicación. Pues para
remedio deste peligro . . . deue traer en las palabras mesura, y en
el meneo honestidad, y en los actos cordura, y en los desseos
tenplança, y en las pláticas dissimulación, y en los mouimientos
mansedumbre. E lo que más deue proueer, es que . . . no yerre
con priessa . . . que le hará passar muchas vezes por donde no
cunple, a buscar mensajeros que no le conuienen, y embiar cartas
que le dañen, e bordar inuenciones que lo publiquen.[75]

These are repeated by the poets:

> Mucho en los amores gana
> quien por la senda secreta
> se sabe muy bien bordar;
> maña es, e bien galana,
> de persona bien discreta,
> callando manifestar.[76]

In spite of the difficulties which it imposes, the *silencio prudente* is
fundamental:

> Para fyn de tanto duelo,
> bien sería rasgar el velo
> de la guardada honestad,
> e mis vozes con verdad
> podían bien llegar al cielo;
> mas Virtud, que non consiente
> vn tal caso ser patente,
> por me dar mayor corona,
> ha sellado mi persona
> con silencio de prudente.[77]

Most lovers declare their willing adherence to the doctrine. Juan de
Mena, in his oath of profession in the Orden de Enamorado, is
unequivocal: "prometo de ser secreto."[78] Likewise Jorge Manrique:

> prometo de ser secreto
> y esto todo que prometo
> guardallo será mi oficio. [*F-D*, ii, 238]

Yet how can one love in silence? It was a question of *callendo manifestar*.[79] Santillana addresses his tongue:

> ¿De qué temedes? ca yo non entiendo
> morir callendo sea grand sçiençia.[80]

Some lovers find it impossible not to speak, and Perálvarez de Ayllón exclaims:

> y si ya muy claramente
> muestro el mal qu' ell' alma siente,
> dolor no sufre secreto,
> aunque sea bien discreto
> el que lo siente. [*CG*, II, 116]

Others regard unpublished favors as of no esteem: "Nin fallesçen otros que . . . se visten de tales colores, que la verdat se puede por ellos bien comprehender, ningund plazer nin gloria less paresçiendo sentir, si los resçibidos bienes deuiesen callar."[81] In one way or another, the secrets did become known. Antonio de Velasco compoposes *coplas* to a lady known to have *six* admirers: "Otras suyas a vna dama de la reyna, porque teniendo seys seruidores, en vnas justas que hizieron no salió ninguno dellos a justar" (*F-D*, II, 622).

VI. HUMILITY

What was the nature of the *gloria* of these *resçibidos bienes* which must not be—yet often were—published abroad? Before addressing ourselves to that question it is necessary to examine yet another fundamental characteristic of courtly love, called by C. S. Lewis *humility* and by Myrrha Lot-Borodine "la supériorité de l'objet aimé sur l'amant, ou la suprématie de la *dame*." "The love which is to be the source of all that is beautiful in life and manners," writes Lewis (p. 36), "must be the reward freely given by the lady, and only our superiors can reward." "On ne brûle l'encens que dans un temple," writes Lot-Borodine (p. 228). The lover, in theory, had no thought but for the will, the slightest desire, of his lady: "¡O, amador! si tu amiga quisiere que penes, pena; e si quisiera que mueras, muere; e si quisiera condenarte, vete al infierno en cuerpo y en ánima."[82] The whole gamut of woman's superiority is expressed in Suárez's *coplas* "en satisfación de las quexas que las mugeres tienen de sus seruidores," in the section in which the author "pone las preminencias que sobre nosotros tienen" (*CG*, I, 329). The promise of complete humility is made by Juan de Mena in the oath of profession in the Orden de Enamorado, already quoted:

> Prometo de ser sujebto
> al amor y su serviçio [*F-D*, I, 204]

in words which are later copied by Gómez Manrique (*F-D*, II, 238).

In theory, and with due allowance for the *paradoxe amoureux*, this is a loyalty unto death:

> que en pensar que soys seruida
>   en que muero,
> me plaze, pues tanto os quiero.
> . . . .
>
> pues os quiero de mi grado,
>   tanbién quiero
> lo que quereys, avnque muero.[83]

In practice, many a *belle dame sans merci* interpreted her rights of dominion with a rigor which moved to exasperation, as we shall see, yet many a lover declared that he accepted the code with utter selflessness:

> ca de cuerpo e coraçón
> me soy dado por serviente
> a quien creo non siente
> mi cuydado e perdiçión.[84]

"Qué más quereys de vuestras amigas," asks Diego de San Pedro in his *Sermón*, "sino que con sus penas esperimenteys vusetra fortaleça?" (*Origs.* II, 39a).[85]

Without this concept of love as *experimentarse en fortaleza*, we should be at a loss to understand the excessive duration of the *service d'amour* without *guerredon*.[86] Fernando de la Torre has so served during ten years:

Señor, ha diez años que so enamorado
de dama muy bella que tiene mi vida,
en todos aquellos jamás fue [fuí] llamado
para resçebir merced conoçida. [*CFT*, p. 171]

Of equal duration, and scarcely better rewarded, is the service of
the Conde de Oliva:

Sé que passan ya diez años
que sufres penas crescidas,
en mil angustias y daños,
en dolores muy estraños,
y siempre mal gradescidas. [*CG*, II, 118][87]

In accordance with the doctrine of prolonged desire, the "dolores muy estraños" are a good in themselves. In his "quexa que da
de su amiga ante el dios de Amor" el Comendador Escrivá refuses
Love's offer to relieve him of his suffering:

Amaré pesar, tristura;
será mi vida gemidos;
hasta ver la sepultura
andaré con alaridos
publicando mi ventura. [*CG*, II, 441–442][88]

The joy of suffering is nowhere more exultingly expressed than in
the *Questión de amor* (*Origs.*, II, 73a):

La llaga es muy grande mas es tan ufana
que quanto es más pena mi gloria es mayor.
. . . .
Tan grande es el bien quan grande es el mal,
porque ésta es la ley perfecta de amor.
. . . .
Perdiendo la vida la gloria se gana,
lo uno te hiere, lo otro te sana.

Or in these lines of Luis de Vivero:

Ni me quitan disfavores
que no conozca en su pena
ser tan lindo el mal de amores,

que es mayor bien sus dolores
que sin ellos vida buena:
  pues sus dones
aunque bueltos en passiones,
llenos son de gloria llena. [*F-D*, ii, 715]

In short: " . . . que no ay compañía más amigable que el mal que vos viene de quien tanto quereys, pues ella lo quiere."[89]

VII. THE GALARDÓN

For all this exulting in the pain of suspended desire, the poet is in most cases unwilling *endlessly* to stand and wait. The *gloria*, the *bienes*, the *galardón* are desired, and passionately:

> como no tiene firmeza,
> después viene la amargura.[90]

Moved by this *amargura*, the Condestable de Portugal says in his *Sátira de felice e infelice vida:*

> Mis enoios infinitos
> demandan misericordia,[91]

and Fernando de la Torre loses all patience:

> Reniego de la esprança,
> señora, ques tanto luenga,
> reniego de la tardança
> que mis trabajos aluenga;
> reniego ya de mi vida
> que se puede dezir muerte,
> reniego, ya, mi querida,
> de vuestra crueldad fuerte. [*CFT*, p. 164]

Juan Alvarez Gato demands not merely *misericordia*, but the reward of his service:

> Dama por quien he sufrido,
> a quien dé Dios noches buenas,
> demándote por estrenas
> galardón de lo seruido. [*F-D*, i, 226][92]

The reason is not far to seek: "Todo hombre se enamora / a fin de ser amado."[93] Or, as stated by Fernán Pérez de Guzmán:

> si yo amo a quien me ama
> es vna deuda que pago. [*F-D*, I, 578]

Mario Equicola provides the explanation: "Ma chi in amore mutua beniuolentia cerca, se speranza voluptà li promette, la paura dolore sempre li rapresenta: e perchè è cosa naturale e par facile e giusto, che chi ama sia amato, l'amante non conseguendolo, del cielo, de natura dolersi è costretto."[94] Even Santillana, who in Castile comes closest to Dante's concept of the *donna angelicata*, cries out in Soneto XXIV:

> sacatme
> de tan grand pena, e sentit mi mal:
> e si lo denegades, acabatme.[95]

To have not, and to have. It is this ever-recurring *paradoxe amoureux* that is the origin of the endless succession of lover's plaints in all the *cancioneros*, and that creates the conception of what we might call el *amor tristeza*, which causes Ausias March to exclaim in the first line of his *Cants de amor*, "Qui no es trist de mos dictats no cur," and which is responsible, in no small degree, for the characteristic melancholy of Garcilaso de la Vega: "Sempre è gioioso l'amante franzese, sempre appare miserabile lo spangnuolo . . . . lauda il greco l'amata, donali el tedesco, dilettala il franzese, adora lo spangnuolo: me se da gelosia son tocchi . . . il greco condanna se stesso, ad auaritia il tedesco si muta, in mestitia piange il franzese, muore lo spanguolo."[96] Thus love is sadness:

> Es cosa que nace de la fantasía,
> y pónese en medio de la voluntad,
> su causa primera produze beldad,
> la vista la engendra, el corazón la cría,
> sostiénela viua penosa porfía,
> dale salud dudosa esperança,
> si tal es qual deue no haze mudança,
> ni allí donde está *nunca entra alegría*.[97]

Death is the healer:

> Quien amando es desdichado
> y sin ser querido quiere,
> no viue hasta que muere.
>
> Es vn mal sin tener par
> querer y no ser querido;
> que, viuiendo, no a viuido
> el que ama sin le amar.
> Pues sin remedio a de estar
> quien sin ser querido quiere,
> no viue hasta que muere,

writes Pedro Manuel Ximénez de Urrea in his *Cancionero* (p. 388), and Jorge Manrique seeks the release which comes from the dissolution of earthly ties:

> No tardes, muerte, que muero;
> ven, porque biua contigo;
> quiéreme, pues que te quiero,
> que con tu venida espero
> no tener guerra conmigo. [*CG*, II, 468][98]

True as it may have been "Chè bel fin fa chi ben amando more,"[99] many a lover was unwilling to meet such an end, and wearied of bestowing love "sin que agradecido me sea"[100] and cried out against his *dama*, as did Costana in the *Conjuro de Amor que hizo a su amiga, conjurándola con todas las fuerzas dell amor* (*CG*, I, 316 ff.), in which he expresses the wish that all his sufferings may be hers. Juan Fernández de Heredia writes a poem "en que maldize a su amiga":

> Yo protesto
> aquí de rodillas puesto,
> que si no es justo mi ruego,
> en mí se conuierta luego
> lo que pido a Dios, que es esto:
> . . . .
> . . . aunque os vea
> perdida por mí, no os crea,

> y ansí como soys hermosa,
> para mí, seays la cosa
> de todo el mundo más fea,
> tal que vays
> tan hambrienta que os perdays
> trays ruynes seruidores,
> y os vea morir de amores
> de quantos hombres veays.[101]

The *galardón*, in its purest form, is the *bons semblans*, the *bel accueil* of the courtly tradition, an "indication that the lover's love is acceptable to the beloved"[102]:

> y porque mejor sepays
> qué es la fe de mi cuydado,
> no quiero que me hagays
> más merced que conozcays
> que biuo por vos penado.[103]

Thus Juan Fernández de Heredia asks for nothing beyond the vision of his beloved:

> El galardón es quereros;
> de mis trabajos estraños
> no sólo pagays los daños
> con sólo dexarme veros,
> mas tormentos de mil años.[104]

A thorough reading of the *cancioneros* leaves no doubt that the troubadours' cult of touch as well as of sight, in order that desire might be heightened, was greatly attenuated in Spanish amatory poetry. Yet it is constantly apparent that lovers could not maintain themselves on this ethereal level[105];

> Ya no puedo comportar
> el dolor que me guerrea,
> pues vos plaze que vos vea
> y non vos ose *tocar*.

> El agua dar a la boca
> y que non pueda beuer,

no se puede sostener
tal vida sy non se toca.
. . . .
Bien como la fuerte roca
el fuego suele ronper,
asy mi grand padesçer
mi salud, par Dios, apoca. [*F-D*, ii, 109]

The kiss, on occasion, was requested:

A mí bien me plase, gentil vida mía,
que limpia vivades de todo pecado,
pero una cosa tan sola querría
commo por fruta e buen gasajado:
por que yo bibiese muy ledo e pagado
quando con vos departa en ssolás,
que vos pluguiese que vos diese pas;
e desto sería asas contentado. [*CB*, p. 604]

And a dangerous game was begun:

Sí Dios me consuele, yo leda sería
de vos conplaser, señor, muy de grado,
en lo que mi bien, mi onrra e valía,
pres e onores non fuese menguado;
que mi coraçón seríe conquistado
si vos consyntiesse llegar a mi fas:
tengo que a muchas syn duda el agrás
con tales maneras avedes echado. [*CB*, pp. 604–605][106]

The inevitability of this granting of something more tangible than "mercy" or "pity" was perfectly recognized by the great theoretician of love, Mario Equicola:

Dico adunque che como ogni cosa graue tende al centro, ed ogni cosa leggiera saglie in alto ne mai se ferma se non gliè apposto impedimento fin che non consegua su natural inclinatione, cosí la mente non farà mai fine di appetere se la ragion non l'affrena, fin che non habbia conseguito il disiderato; per ciò che ogni nostra voluptà, ogni respetto al bene, comincia d'amore, corre al desiderio, procede in la speranza, vltimamente ha sua quiete nella voluptà.[107]

VIII. ADULTERY, TRUANCY, RECANTATION

We are thus brought to a consideration of the final distinguishing characteristic of courtly love, designated by C. S. Lewis *adultery* and by Myrrha Lot-Borodine, "le don de soi désintéressé, la gratuité du service, ou *l'amour qui est sa propre fin.*" It has been shown above that *fin' amors* required that the reward be freely given by the lady, and that only our superiors can reward. It is this requirement that the relationship contain no element of obligation or compulsion,[108] together with the belief that marital relations lower the potential of desire which is the *summum bonum*, that eliminates, for the most part, the wife or sweetheart from troubadour love poetry. The elimination is not absolute, even in Provence,[109] and certainly in Spain it was very far from being complete; but the evidence to be adduced will show that the tradition of a strictly *illicit* love was strong enough to give a special character to the love poetry of the *cancioneros*. This special character appears in the constant awareness, on the part of the poet, that his amorous delights constitute a truancy from which, like the prodigal son, he must return, and in the frequent inclusion among a given poet's works of a recantation or palinode.

Where marriage does not depend on the free will of the married, writes Lewis (p. 37), "any theory which takes love for a noble form of experience must be a theory of adultery."[110] It is her awareness of this situation – of the restrictions placed upon the free will of the lovers by the requirements of marriage – that makes perfectly logical Melibea's outcry in the *Celestina:* "más vale ser buena amiga que mala casada."[111] Even when marriage did depend on the free will of the married,[112] the secret and protracted *amour* was a normal expression of youth, beauty, nobility, and desire. Oriana, though her kingly father had promised her free choice of a husband, chose to face the dangers of a secret pregnancy and parturition for the sake of her *fin' amors* (which thereby became *amor mixtus*) and this without "palabra de casamiento" – a device not foreign to the *Amadís*[113] and soon to become customary in the comedia.[114] Her *entrega*, a *favor freely given* – "más por la gracia y comedimiento de Oriana, que por la desenvoltura de Amadís" – rewards the *humility* of her lover: "y cuando así la vío tan hermosa,

y en su poder, habiéndole ella otorgado su voluntad, fué tan tur-
bado de placer y de empacho, que sólo mirar no la osaba."[115]

The theory of true love, incompatible with marriage, is perfectly
expressed by Juan Álvarez Gato under the heading: "Porque le dixo
vna señora que seruía, que se casase con ella":

> Dezís: "Casemos los dos,
> porque deste mal no muera."
> Señora, no plega a Dios,
> siendo mi señora vos,
> cos haga mi compañera,
>
> Que, pues amor verdadero
> no quiere premio ni fuerça,
> avnque me veré que muero,
> nunca querré, ni quiero
> que por mi parte se tuerça.
>
> Amarnos amos a dos
> con vna fe muy entera,
> queramos esto los dos:
> mas no le plega a Dios,
> siendo mi señora vos,
> cos haga mi compañera. [F-D, i, 229]

Juan de Mena, as he professed in the Orden de Enamorado, included in his vow:

> En lugar de castidad
> prometo de ser constante, [F-D, i, 204]

a conceit which is taken up and developed by Gómez Manrique:

> En lugar de castidad
> prometo de ser constante:
> prometo de voluntad
> de guardar toda verdad
> que a de guardar ell amante:
> prometo de ser suiecto
> all amor y a su seruicio;
> prometo de ser discreto,
> y esto todo que prometo
> guardallo será mi officio. [F-D, ii, 238]

Nicolás Núñez, in answer to the query, shall it be *donzella, casada, beata,* or *monja,* declares for the *casada:*

> En la casada, señor,
> quereys exemplo ponerme
> que su victoria es temor;
> el verdadero amador
> nunca tal peligro teme:
> assí que el mal que aquí mora,
> avnque a quien sabe lo digo,
> no es éste el que nos desdora,
> sino ver a la señora
> sierua de nuestro enemigo. [*F-D*, ii, 482]

It was to this sort of truancy, with its concomitant insecurity, that mediæval courtly life owed "half its wilful beauty and pathos."[116] That it was a truancy, an escape, "alike from vulgar common sense and from the ten commandments," that "behind the courtly scale of values rose the unappeasable claims of a totally different and irreconcilable world,"[117] was keenly realized by the Spanish poets.[118] The truancy is taken lightly by Fernán Sánchez Calavera in the *Desir que fiso e ordenó contra una señora de que andava muy enamorado:*

> ¿Pues commo, señora, las vuestra ninnés,
> veldat tan estraña, se podrá sostener
> que un tienpo o otro en alguna ves
> non querrá lo que otras quisyeron saber?
> Por cierto, yo dudo si tal puede ser:
> por ende, segund vuestro tienpo devedes
> usar d'este mundo, que puesto que erredes
> podedes después penitençia faser. [*CB*, p. 604]

This is the attitude of Andreas Capellanus: "Amor iste tantae dignoscitur esse virtutis, quod ex eo totius probitatis origo descendit, et nulla inde procedit iniuria, et *modicam in ipso Deus recognoscit offensam.*"[119] It was widely shared. "Yerros por amores" were, by Christian standards, forgivable; by the rules of courtly love, they needed no forgiveness,[120]

que Dios al buen amador
nunca demanda pecado,

wrote Suero de Ribera (F-D, ii, 194). He finds support in Juan de
Andújar:

> E sy algunos detratores
> con ynorancia iuzgasen
> contra algunos amadores,
> porque lealmente amassen,
> digo que fazen error,
> e non saben que a Cupido
> el mundo es sometido. [*F-D*, ii, 215]

Juan Rodríguez de la Cámara, in a text which throws light not only
on the problem here considered, but also on the problem of the
galardón (see below), questions if such *yerros* may properly be
regarded as such:

> Et si algunas, que son en número pocas, se veen las leyes del casto
> pecho alguna vez traspassar, aquesto auuiene por el engañoso
> amant [*sic*], con falsa lengua e fengidas lágrimas, enbiando fuera
> gemidos sentibles e muy piadosos sospiros, se jura vecino a la
> muerte con fuerça de amor, el dormir se tirando con el manjar
> por algunos días, a fin que ante la constante dama con muerta faz
> paresçiendo, contra sí la pueda mouer a piedat. Onde algunas, de
> aquesta virtud vençidas, del su incorporable [*read:* incompar-
> able] honor . . . se faciendo liberales, por le salvar la vida, son
> vistas errar, *si yerro se deue decir* . . . ¡O ligero yerro aquel del
> qual es prinçipio virtud, e perdonable culpa la que se vee de sola
> humanidat proceder![121]

Others were less complacent. "Amor dexa sanas muy pocas con-
ciencias," declared Juan del Encina in his *Viage y peregrinación a
Jerusalem*,[122] and Fray Iñigo de Mendoza, in his *Vita Christi*, is even
more explicit:

> Non digo que los poetas,
> los presentes y pasados,
> non fagan obras perfectas,
> graçiosas y bien discretas,

en sus renglones trobados;
mas affirmo ser herror
(perdonen si bien non fablo)
en su obra el trobador
inuocar al dios de amor
para seruicio del diablo. [*F-D*, i, 2]¹²³

Yet this was a truancy that even monks permitted themselves: "Esta cántiga fiso e ordenó el dicho Maestro Fray Diego por amore e loores de una *dueña* de quien él era enamorado" (*CB*, no. 504). Fray Diego's loves were plural: "Este desir fiso e ordenó el dicho Maestro Fray Diego por amor e loores de una *donsella* que era muy fermosa e muy resplandeçiente, de la qual era muy enamorado" (*CB*, no. 505).¹²⁴ Nor was the author of these poems a *fraile tabernario:* he was Fray Diego de Valencia de Leon, a Fransciscan,

> maestro en santa theología, . . . muy grant letrado e grant maestro en todas las artes liberales e otrosí era muy grant físico, estrólogo e mecánico, tanto e tan mucho que en su tiempo non se falló omme tan fundado en todas çiençias commo él, e bien se mostró el su saber e çiençia ser mucha e digna de grandes loores en la muy sotil respuesta qu'él dió a Fray Sánches Calavera . . . a la muy alta traçendente quistión de preçitos e predestinados." [*CB*, p. 508].

Even the Cardenal de Valencia requested or hired the poet Vázquez to compose a poem "A la señora doña María Enrríquez, a quien el Cardenal seuría" (*CG*, ii, 504). This was nothing new in the tradition of courtly love. Though Andreas Capellanus eliminates nuns from among the servants of Love, he declares the case of *clerici* to be different: "They are only men, after all, conceived in sin like the rest, and indeed more exposed than others to temptation *propter otia multa et abundantiam ciborum.* Indeed, it is very doubtful whether God seriously meant them to be more chaste than the laity. It is teaching, not practice, that counts."¹²⁵

These Spanish poems, like the poems of the early troubadours, "were written by men who, for the most part, were Catholics and Christians and who had been reared in that faith and in that atmosphere."¹²⁶ There were three possible solutions. One, arrived at by Dante and dimly reflected in one or two poems of Santillana,

was the creation of the symbol, the *"donna angelicata, . . .* de-
venue *Sapience."*[127] A second, favored by the French poets of the
south and of the north (and by Petrarch),[128]

> quittatit résolument les sentiers terrestres et montait droit vers
> les sommets de l'amour divin. Mais cet amour, tout en disant
> adieu aux voluptés du monde, gardait encore entre les plis
> de son manteau d'hermine quelque chose du parfum de l'éternel
> féminin. Seulement à la place du reflet, il adorait le modèle
> lumineux, *l'exemplaire,* comme l'appelait le "réalisme" platoni-
> cien de l'époque: la Dame-Vierge, Mère de toute Beauté et de
> toute Bonté.[129]

This is the solution of Ausais March:

> Mare de Deu, hajes merce de mí
> o fes me'ser de tu enamorat,
> de les amors que so' passïonat
> ja conech cert que so mes que mesquí.[130]

It is also the solution of Alfonso Alvarez de Villasandino, if I
interpret him right, in the *dezir* which he wrote "contra el Amor,
quexándose dél e afeándole e despendiéndose [*sic*] dél":

> Pero non entendades que quero leyxar
> o mundo del todo para me morrer,
> mays quiero, amigos, cantar e tanger,
> leer as estoryas, con aves caçar,
> todas boas mañas seguyr e vssar,
> saluo el trobar que ja non ffarey,
> amar por amores, que nunca amarey
> sy non for aquela [*read* Aquela] que deuo amar. [*F-D,* ii, 387]

It is clearly the solution of Don Francés Carros Pardo:

> Y quando ternés rompido
> el velo de la passión,
> huyd tanta perdición,
> huyd deleite vencido,
> y amad, amad la razón:
> y a la Virgen, Hija y Madre,
> que nos vela de la cumbre,
> siruamos con mansedumbre,

porque quando el vicio ladre,
nos guarde su Hijo y Padre.

The *amadores,* whom he thus addresses, "siguen la voluntad del auctor," saying:

y tú amor, a quien dexamos,
vete, vete, y busca quien
elija tu mal por bien;
que de ti nos alexamos
do virtud manda que vamos. [*CG,* II, 131–132]

It is the solution, in modified form, of the anonymous author of *Coplas de vn gentilhombre las quales se intitulan Remedios de Amores.* Here the Virgin, rather than the object of *servicio* (cf. *siruamos,* above), is the source from which help is sought:

Corramos con deuoción
al ruego de Hijo y Madre,
a la continua oración,
por do alcançemos al Padre.
. . . .
Pensemos el fin mezquino
d'este loco adulterino,
sus deleytes quál nos dexan,
pensemos quántos se quexan
por tan pecador camino,
fuyamos tinta y papel,
su gusto falso de miel
qu'enuenina y enrroña
con açúcar y ponçoña
que se nos conuierte en hiel. [*CG,* II, 27–28]

The third solution is that of the *palinode* pure and simple, without thought of retaining that "quelque chose du parfum de l'éternel féminin" of the songs to the *Vergine bella.* It is the solution of Juan Rodríguez de la Cámara in his *canción, Fuego del diuino rayo:*

Adiós, real resplandor
que yo serví et loé
con lealtat:

adiós, que todo fauor
e cuanto de amor fablé
es uanidat.
Adiós, los que bien amé;
adiós, mundo engañador;
adiós, donas que ensalcé,
famosas, dignas de loor,
orad por mí pecador;[131]

of Villasandino:

Dios castigando castiga
a quien quiere castigar,
ssy castigo e de tomar,
conviene que me desdiga.

Conuiene que me desdiga
para siempre desta vez,
de todo gentil jahez
e de amar ninguna amiga; [*F-D*, II, 403]

of Juan de Mena:

Fuyd o callad, serenas,
que en la mi hedad passada,
tal dulçura enponçoñada
derramastes por mis venas;
mis entrañas, que eran llenas
de peruerso fundamento,
quiera el diuinal aliento
de malas fazer ya buenas.

Venid, lisongeras canas,
que tardays demasiado;
tirad presumpciones vanas
al tiempo tan mal gastado;
faga mi nueuo cuydado
a my biuo entender,
incierto del bien fazer
y del mal certificado.
.   .   .   .

> Aunque muestre ingratitud
> a las dulces poesyas,
> las sus tales niñerías
> vayan con la juuentud;
> remedio de tal salud
> enconada por el vicio,
> es darnos en sacrificio
> nos mismos a la virtud.[132]

It is the solution of Santillana:

> Asy que lo proçessado
> de todo amor me desparte;
> nin sé tal que non s'aparte
> sin non es loco provado, [*Obras*, p. 399]

in spite of his glimmerings, at times, of a *donna angelicata*. It is the solution also of Juan del Encina:

> Can Fe protestando mudar de costumbre,
> dexando de darme a cosas livianas,
> y a componer obras del Mundo ya vanas:
> mas tales, que puedan al ciego dar lumbre,
> y en tales leyendo en gran muchedumbre,
> y en Letras Sagradas de contemplación,
> pues dexa Gerónimo su Cicerón
> que en grande eloqüencia tenía la cumbre.[133]

Of special interest is the palinode of Diego de San Pedro, in the preamble to his *Obra llamada Desprecio de la Fortuna*, where he condemns by title his amatory writings:

> y pues cargó ya la edad
> donde conosco mi yerro,
> afuera la liuiandad,
> pues que ya mi vanidad
> ha cumplido su destierro.
> . . . .
>
> Aquella *Cárcel d'amor*
> . . . .

¡qué dulce para sobor!
¡qué salsa para pecar!

. . . .

¡quán enemigo mortal
fué la lengua para ell alma! [CG, no. 263]

He condemns also his *Sermón*, and of his *Cartas de amores* he asks:

¿qué serán, dezí, señores
sino mis acusadores
para delante de Dios?

And his *coplas, canciones*, and *romances* can only be, he fears,

pertrechos
con que tiren contra mí.

IX. COURTLY LOVE AND MONOGAMY

In spite of this imposing array of recantations, there are many love poems in the *cancioneros* that are concerned with what Lewis calls "the triumphant union of romantic passion with Christian monogamy" (p. 345).[134] In Spain the struggle toward this union—away from the extramarital conception of courtly love[135]—was less protracted than it appears to have been, for example, in England.[136] In fiction, particularly, the heroine is normally unmarried[137]; and in the *cancioneros* the same imagery, the same adoration, the same *supériorité de la dame* that have been documented in the preceding pages of this study are found applied both to the sweetheart-fiancée[138] and to the honored wife.

Examples of the *conquête de la fiancée* are difficult to identify because, in the absence of a heading, it is generally impossible to know whether a given poem falls inside or outside this category. No. 603 of Foulché-Delbosc's *Cancionero castellano del siglo XV* bears this heading: "Esta cántiga fizo el dicho Alfonso Aluarez, por rruego del adelantado Pero Manrryque, quando andaua enamorado desta su muger, fija que es del señor duque de Benauente." There is nothing in its phraseology to distinguish it from its companion pieces in the *Cancionero*, nor is there anything distinctive in no. 636, whose heading reads: "Esta cántiga fyzo el dicho Aluarez, e dizen algunos que la fizo por rruego del conde don Pero Niño quando era desposado con su muger doña Beatriz, e trae en ella como manera de rrequesta e fabla quél e vn rruyseñor tenían vno con otro." In the lines of Stúñiga that follow the words *servicio*, *pesar*, *merecer*, and the expressed determination to remain constant in spite of *días tristes*, are all earmarks of courtly love; but one word, *donzella*, while not proving that the beloved is to become the betrothed, shows clearly that she is not the "femme dans la plénitude de sa maturité" of the *service d'amour*:

> Si servicio merecistes,
> non meresco grand pesar,
> e si vos me conocistes
> para darme días tristes,
> non vos dexo de loar;
> que, par Dios, después de aquella
> devota virgen María,
> de las otras sois estrella:
> nunca nasció tal donzella
> como vos, señora mía. [*F-D*, II, 593–595][139]

And Fernando de la Torre finds *los amores de donzellas* to be not only the source of courtesy and the adornment of life, but also free from those drawbacks which make less acceptable other amorous relationships. In his *Juego de oros, apropiado a los amores de donzellas* he writes:

> Estos son a quien y quales
> todonbre deue seruir,
> y por quien bienes y males
> todos se deuen sufrir;
> éstos son por quien la vida
> se meresce de poner,
> éstos son por quien no oluida
> la gala de se exercer.
> Estos quien fazen fazer
> grandes justas y enbenciones,
> éstos doblan coraçones.
> Estos son los palacianos,
> éstos son los más polidos,
> éstos de quien los humanos

se deuen fallar guarnidos;
éstos son linpios y vellos,
sin algund impedimento,
éstos quien aparte [*read:* ha parte] en ellos
vieu alegre y muy contento,
éstos son por quien abseto
mis trabajos e tormentos. [*CFT,* p. 133]

We are thus already well within the world of gallantry which was to flourish in the *comedia de capa y espada.* The *cancionero* poets go still farther and apply the terminology of *fin' amors,* the *pure* love of the troubadours, to *mixed* love—that which experiences full consummation[140]—and this without the slightest implication that such love "lasts but little and quickly wanes."[141] Thus Gómez Manrique, in his *Estrenas a doña Juana de Mendoça, su muger* (F-D, no. 336):

amada tanto de mí
e más que mi saluación.

So also Jorge Manrique, in *Otras* [*coplas*] *suyas en que puso el nombre de su esposa:*

Vaya la vida passada
que por amores sufrí,
pues me pagastes con sí,
señora, bien empleada:
e tened por verdadera
esta razón que diré,
que siempre ya cantaré
pues que fustes la primera. [*F-D,* II, 244]

Pedro de Mendoza writes in similar vein in *Otra a su muger:*

Como ay toque de oro
donde mejor se apura,
assí soys vos el tesoro
e toque de hermosura.
La que tuuiere mesura
que piense ser singular,
váyase a vos a tocar

e verá si su figura
es oro para dorar. [*CG*, II, 468]

Conventional statements concerning the superficiality of the *can-cionero* poetry must be reconsidered in the light of poems like the *Carta de amores del Conde de Coçentayna para la Condessa, su muger:*

> A la muy linda figura
> en quien mi querer adora,
> Condessa de hermosura,
> de Coçentayna señora.[142]

Far removed from the extravagances of Amadís on the Peña Pobre is the *Canción del Conde de Cifuentes, estando cativo, a su muger:*

> La que tengo no es prisión,
> vos soys prisión verdadera,
> ésta tiene lo de fuera,
> vos, señora, el coraçón.[143]

In Pinar's gloss of the ballad *Rosa fresca, rosa fresca,* the beloved objects to the advances of a lover thought to be married:

> dixo lo que no desdigo,
> que érades casado, amigo,
> allá en tierras de León;

but the lover swears that he was never in Castile or León

> sino quando era pequeño,
> que no sabía de amor. [*F-D*, II, 575]

X. THE NEGATIVE SIDE

Courtly love has thus come full cycle, a development which in England was not accomplished before *The Faerie Queene*.[144] One is tempted to attribute this fact to the native realism of Spain, to the persistence of the tradition of conjugal tenderness and respect which is manifest in the *Poema del Cid*. Whether or not such an explanation is justified, the presence of a realistic current[145] which runs parallel to the idealistic conception of courtly love is well attested in Spain[146]:

> Sabe el vyno a las vegadas
> en copa muy desygual,
> mas amar a las casadas
> a las vezes sabe mal,
> y bien por este tal juego
> do se paga grand portadgo,
> renuncien todos dél luego,
> que yo no menos lo fago.[147]

The falsity of much that is said is admitted, on occasion, even by the lover, as in these lines of Suárez:

> Dezisnos por quexa vuestra
> que mil engaños hazemos;
> mas esta culpa no es nuestra,
> qu'el mismo amor nos muestra
> dezir lo que no sabemos:
> que como con los tormentos
> se condena el malhechor,
> hazemos mil juramentos,
> votos y prometimientos
> con los tormentos d'amor. [CG, I, 330][148]

Similar falsity is attributed to the *dama*:

> . . . en ningund tienpo la creas.
> Porque quanto más segura
> en los tus braços está,
> y diez mill vezes te jura
> que por ty de Dios no cura,
> más te toma que te da;
> y pues que claro te miente,
> porque su cativo seas,
> porque no te desatiente,
> quiérela por açidente,
> y en ningund tienpo la creas.[149]

At other times it was the lady who made sport of those who
claimed to be dying of sweet sorrow: "Aquí comiençan las obras
de Quirós; y esta primera es vna que hizo a vna señora porque se
burlaua de los que dizen que se mueren de amores y que están
muertos; no creyendo que tenga amor tanto poder de matar a
ninguno" (F-D, II, 283). On other occasions it is recognized that
both lady and lover are engaged in a game, as when Puertocarrero's
dama insists that he has no claims on her:

> Que si confessays verdad,
> no aurá culpa ni daño,
> ni vos receleys engaño,
> ni vuestra liberalidad.
> A quitar ociosidad
>   os entrastes;
> pues passatiempo buscastes,
> no finjays necessidad,
> que es tocar en liviandad.
> Pero dexémonos desto.
> ¿Vuestra muger está buena? [F-D, II, 681–682]

In one amazing poem—the *coplas* are simply *desaforadas*—resentment caused a reversal, a turning from white to black, which Juan
Alfonso de Baena included in his *Cancionero* along with things
quintessential, excusing it, seemingly, in the words which I have
underlined:

> Este dezir a manera de diffamaçión fizo e ordenó el dicho Al-
> fonso Alvarez de Villasandino contra una dueña d'este reyno,
> por manera de la afear e deshonrrar, por ruego de vn cavallero
> que *gelo rogó muy afyncadamente*, por quanto la dicha dueña
> non quiso açeptar sus amores del dicho cavallero:

> commo el asno a la borrica
> vos querrya ennamorar.[150]

While constancy was a prime tenet of the courtly code, incon-
stancy, by a variation on the *paradoxe amoureux*, was regarded as
inevitable when absence intervened:

porq' es sabida sentencia
que los peligros de aussencia
son enemigos d'amor,

wrote Perálvarez d'Ayllón (*CG*, pp. 115–116), whose words are confirmed by Jorge Manrique:

Quien no estuuiere en presencia,
no tenga fe en confiança,
pues son oluido y mudança
las condiciones de ausencia. [*F-D*, II, 250]

In the words of Juan Luis Vives: "se desgastan las imágenes graba-das en la memoria."[151] In opposition to the conception of the ideal lady as "la femme vraiment 'femme,' " of "*la femme* dans la pléni-tude de sa maturité," we find in Carvajales an ideal which is the direct opposite. The *service d'amour* is not restful, it is indeed weariness to the flesh:

Amad, amadores, mujer que non sabe,
a quien toda cosa parezca ser nueua,
que quanto más sabe mujer, menos vale,
segund, por exemplo, la hemos de Eua,
que luego comiendo el fruto de vida,
rompiendo el velo de rica ignocencia,
supo su mal e su gloria perdida;
guardaos de mujer que ha platica e sciencia.

Amad, amadores, la tierna edat,
quando el tiempo requiere natura,
questa non tiene ninguna crueldat
nin ofende al amante luenga tristura. [*F-D*, II, 608]

The contradictions of courtly love, its positive and its negative side, are summed up in a *dezir* of Ferrant Sánchez (*CB*, no. 534), in which he sings "maravillándose del Amor e de los nombres que le ponen las gentes, ca los unos le disen bein e los otros le disen mal":

Unos te llaman constante
e perfeto sabidor,
e otros trasechador
e mudable ynorante:

> otros disen que bastante
> eres para rey sagrado,
> otros que de enforcado
> te veen más espetante.

XI. BEAUTY

Denomy, in his definition of *fin' amors* (n. 4, above) speaks of it as "arising from the contemplation of the beauty of the beloved." Long before Bembo, Castiglione, and León Hebreo, beauty was held by Spaniards to be preëminent among the causes of love. This is proclaimed by Juan Rodríguez de la Cámara: "¿Quién negará ser en la *vista* de las donas una oculta diuinidat que, por la diuina mano en su criaçión le seyendo infussa, las partes donde el su rayo alcança en un súbito plazer ençiende, que non paresce de humana, mas de diuina luz descender?"[152] And we read in the *Grisel y Mirabella* of Juan de Flores: "Pues en aquestos comedios assí como su edat crecía, crecían y dublauan las gracias de su beldat en tanto grado que qualquiere hombre dispuesto a amar, así como la mirasse, le era forçado de ser preso de su amor: que por su causa venían a perder las vidas."[153] This conception was Platonic, but it had been adopted at a very early date by Christian theologians: "Pulchro e buono esser il medesmo Thomas afferma: Scoto disse il buono e bello esser vn medesmo. . . . L'uno e l'altro da Augustino la sententia tolse."[154] Typical of its poetical expression are these lines from Gómez Manrique:

> Con la beldad me prendistes,
> con la graçia me robastes,
> con la bondad me feristes
> al punto que me mirastes. [*F-D*, II, 13]

In another poem, the same writer declares:

> Vuestra beldad escogida
> causa que seays así,
> no queriendo, bien querida
> de muchos e más de mí. [*F-D*, II, 21]

His nephew Jorge Manrique is no less explicit:

¡Qué gran aleue hizieron
mis ojos, y qué trayción,
por vna vista que os vieron
venderos mi coraçón! [*F-D*, ii, 240]

So also Soria:

que de la contemplación
ha de nascer la passión. [*F-D*, ii, 261]

And Juan de Dueñas:

Ca sin breuage amoroso
como ya fué don Tristán,
gentil senyora, sabrán
que vuestro gesto hermoso
me conquistó por tal vía,
que Dios nunca me dé bien
si siento en el mundo, quien
más de grado seruiría. [*F-D*, ii, 202]

A similar confession is found in the anonymous *Questión de amor:*

Mis ojos c'an sido la puerta y escala
por do hermosura hirió con sus tiros,
éstos m'an hecho, señora, seruiros.[155]

A dissenting voice is found in the "Canción de Sazedo, diziendo qu'el coraçón tiene la culpa de auerse catiuado, y no los ojos" (*CG*, no. 350). The case may have been similar to that considered by Equicola: "Nondimeno non negamo le non belle con accostumati modi e bei costumi poter se fare amare" (fol. 166).

Still another cause of love is stressed in the *cancioneros:* Fortune, Fate, the influence of the heavenly bodies, which, to be sure, may be indirect causes of love acting through the instrumentality of beauty. This idea also is Platonic: "Platonici dicono," writes Equicola, "esser necessaria cognitione e conuenientia de Idea, Genio e Stella a princio d'amore. . . . Noi non negamo in conseruatione d'amori, similitudine de natura e costumi hauer possanza, ma nelli principii poter solo belleza e gratia" (fol. 124). Fortune and the stars are linked together as co-causes by Lope Stúñiga:

Mis males eran nascidos
ante de mi nasçimiento,
en los signos de sabidos
e planeta de perdidos
fué mi triste fundamiento;
e la rueda de Fortuna,
con el signo más esquiuo,
con la más menguante luna,
me fadaron en la cuna
para ser vuestro captiuo. [F-D, II, 593][156]

"Ordenó mi ventura que me enamorase de Laureola," declares the
lover in the Cárcel de amor (p. 3b). For Amadís, the love of
Oriana had been predetermined, as if it were a knightly quest: "a él
y no a otro era dado de amar persona tan señalada en el mundo" (I,
240). And Juan Rodríguez de la Cámara makes much of the
influence of the stars: "¿Et qué acto más fuerte que resistir, segund
resisten con pura virtud, a la influencia de los cuerpos celestiales, a
las falsas lágrimas e a la fuerça del . . . bien compuesto fablar del
engañoso amante?"[157] Narcís Viñoles personifies these various
forces as Nature:

Tuyo soy, pues que Natura
para ti me hizo ser. [CG, II, 155]

Nature is Natura naturans (as opposed to Natura naturata) of the
Scholastics. This creative power of the universe is the instrument
through which God works his will:

si dizes que soy ageno
niegas lo que hizo Dios.[158]

Similar creative power belongs to Fortune,[159] and Fortuna, like
Ventura, like Natura, is an instrument of the Divine Will.[160]

XII. REASON

Beauty is truth, truth beauty, and beauty is the cause of love.
Fortune and Nature, also operative in love's ups and downs, are
instruments of Providence. We would thus seem to be free from

the *paradoxe amoureux* and love would appear to be the child of the highest faculty of the human soul, reason. In some few cases the poets so represent it. Among these is Juan Álvarez Gato:

> Esta quen virtud sarrea,
> que robó mi coraçón,
> pues en ella bien senplea,
> por ella mi mote sea
> *Sojuzgado por razón*
>
> . . . .
>
> pues quen vos se conformaron
> estas dos desabenidas:
> la beldad y la cordura. [F-D, i, 224]

The same harmony of desire and reason is expressed by Doria:

> Ageno so, no so mío,
>   pues me guío,
>   perdida la libertad,
>   por do va la voluntad,
>   que es de la razón desuío:
>   avnque por vos,
>   tan preciosa os hizo Dios,
>   que el *afición*
>   es conuertida en *razón*
>   y no son dos. [F-D, ii, 257]

Santillana is likewise free from the conflict. He surrenders his free will only to find that it still is free, that *razón* and *afición* are compatible. Here is the last tercet of his Soneto xiv, of Dantesque tendencies:

> El andar suyo es con tal reposo,
> honesto e manso, e su continente,
> que, *libre*, vivo en su *captividad*.[161]

But the paradox returns. Other poets, in overwhelming number, represent love as the child of the appetitive faculty, the *voluntad*, ever at enmity with reason. Tapia writes:

> Es amor vna visión
> que quan presto se figura,

tan presto desaparesce;
afición y no razón,
vn bulto de hermosura
que los ojos entristesce.

Es vn doblado dolor,
es vn senzillo plazer,
nascido del dessear:
éste, señora, es amor,
tan liuiano de perder
quan penoso de ganar. [*F-D*, II, 442]

The contrast between *voluntad* and *razón* is clarified by Gómez
Manrique in his *Regimiento de príncipes:*

Voluntad quiere folgança,
quiere vicios, alegrías,
y fazer noches los días,
posponiendo la tenprança:
no procura grande fama,
menospreçia la salud;
la razón es vna dama
que grandes honores ama
y corre tras la virtud. [*F-D*, II, 121][162]

Don Francisco de Castilla confesses:

y aunque veo que me daña,
dulce voluntad destierra
a la razón. [*CG*, II, 390]

"Menos mal sería morir," writes Carvajales,

que non tal vida vivir,
do rige la voluntad,
sujeta razón e bondad. [*F-D*, II, 619]

Other confessions are not lacking. Gonzalo Carrillo:

El amor lo que procura
contradize la razón,
y lo que el seso assegura
no lo consiente passión;

por donde mis males van
ganando siempre comigo,
pues amor y el seso están
en gran debate consigo. [*CG*, ii, 389]

And Fernán Pérez de Gusmán:

Virtud e delectación
nunca entran so vn techo,
poca participación
han honestad e prouecho;
temprança e ambición
nunca jazen en vn lecho,
la voluntad e razón
no caben en poco trecho. [*F-D*, i, 587]

In this conflict reason may, and on occasion does, have the better part. She comes to the aid of Juan de Mena:

Como en vando quebrantado
con esfuerço más se esmera
quando asoma la vandera
del socorro deseado,
asy fuy yo consolado
quando vi muy derrondón
las señas de la Razón
asomar por el collado.

Voluntad falls back,

ca do mengua la firmeza
temor crece la sospecha;

and

quanto más ella refuye,
más se acerca la Razón. [*F-D*, i, 123]

Yet *voluntad* is a formidable enemy,

Ca no puede ser, notad,
rey señor, esto que digo,

> otro mayor enemigo
> que la mesma voluntad;
> ésta siempre nos guerrea,
> ésta siempre nos conbate
> con deseos que desea,
> nunca cesa su pelea
> nin afloxa el debate.[163]

Hernando de Ludueña admonishes:

> pueda tanto la razón
> que saque la voluntad
> de la sojución del yerro. [F-D, II, 727]

This is in keeping with the doctrine of the freedom of the will:

> Y en dándonos ser humano,
> dió Dios franca libertad
> para elegir mal o sano;
> diónos la sensualidad
> con las riendas en la mano:
> porque en nuestra mano vaya
> si corre tras afectión
> que tropieçe y que no caya,
> y avn más, que se tenga a raya
> con el freno de razón.[164]

Don Francisco de Castilla recognizes his own responsibility in his enslavement to Don Amor:

> Bien sé yo que bien sabría,
> quando de verdad quisiese,
>   defenderme,
> si por la tibieza mía
> mi defensa si no fuesse
>   tan inerme. [CG, II, 291]

But reason may "pander to will," may allow herself, in her encounters with sensuality,[165] to be blinded. Fray Iñigo de Mendoza represents Reason as jousting with *Sensualidad:*

> mas con sus tizones rojos
> y con su saber profundo,

la que biue por antojos
dióle en medio de los ojos
el mayor golpe del mundo.

Con tal fuerça y maestría,
tal rigor y omezillo,
la herió con su profía,
que por los ojos no vía
más que por el colodrillo;
y viendo que el accidente
la cegaua por de dentro
començó en continente
en la manera syguiente
a ferirla con su encuentro. [F-D, I, 89]

Gómez Manrique recognizes a similar situation in his own experience:

No vos loo por amores,
que la ley no lo consiente,
mas porque vuestros valores
son ynmensos çiertamente;
tanto que dan ocasión,
fablando con vos verdad,
a non poder la razón
contrastar la voluntad. [F-D, II, 14-15]

In such cases the lover surrenders his freedom, loses the action of his *libre albedrío*, and is no longer his own master. Costana describes his lady:

Si otras señas agora
quereys por más certidumbre,
es aquella a quien adora
la *libertad* por señora,
y le da su seruidumbre. [CG, I, 326]

As described by Juan de Flores: "el apartarme de amor no sería en mi mano, porque ya en mi voluntad di lugar a mi libertad que ageno senyorío la possea."[166] And by the Condestable de Portugal: "Así que, desesperado, con muy afamada deliberación tuve por conclusión, vista la desesperación que seguía e la crueldat de aquella a quien mi libre alvedrío, seyendo yo libre, me fizo captivo, que alguna causa nin razón poseía de vevir contento de cuanto penando pasaba."[167]

When in this struggle reason is the loser, love becomes:

> Triumpho de los pecados,
> destierro de la razón.[168]

Reason is helpless against love:

> E pues tales mañas tiene
> que do le plaze herir
> ni vale seso ni ciencia.[169]

Don Francés Carros Pardo puts these words in the mouth of the *amadores:*

> De que vencedora queda
> voluntad, que es nuestra guía,
> mató a razón que biuía,
> ni vemos qu'el muerto pueda
> ser biuo como solía. [*CG*, II, 130][170]

Thus love subdues all:

> aquesto sólo sentid:
> que no basta discreçión
> ni coraçón a la lid,
> que desatentó a Dauid
> y enloquesçió a Salomón.[171]

Even Santillana, in whose *Bías contra Fortuna* the *vir sapiens* lives by reason,

> atque metus omnes, et inexorabile Fatum
> subjecit pedibus strepitumque Acherontis avari,

—even Santillana alleges in his favor "la común materia de los fados, ventura, sygnos, e planetas, rreprobada por la Santa Madre Yglesia e por aquellos en que Dios dió sentydo, seso, e juyzio natural, e entendimiento rracional," a doctrine against which the Archpriest of Talavera inveighs in his *Corbacho*, "por quanto algunos quieren dezir, que sy amando pecan, que su fado o ventura ge lo procuraron."[172] In his Soneto VI he asks, "que qué fará él a la ordenança de de arriba; conviene a saber, de los fados, a los quales ninguno de los mortales non puede façer resistencia nin contradeçir":

> Por ventura dirás, ýdola mía,
> que a ti non plaçe del mi perdimiento;
> antes repruebas mi loca profía.
> Di, ¿qué faremos al ordenamiento
> de Amor, que priva toda señoría,
> e rige e manda nuestro entendimiento? [*Obras*, p. 275]

Such confessions of defeat are another form of truancy. Gómez Manrique, in his continuation of Juan de Mena's *Coplas contra los pecados mortales* (*F-D*, I, 147) "aconseja que la razón se siga e no la voluntad":

> Si del luxurioso fuego
> te sentieres acender,
> no le dexes aprender,
> amigo, yo te lo ruego;
> mas luego lo mata, luego,
> con agua de castidad,
> no prouando voluntad
> ni de veras ni de juego. [*F-D*, I, 148][173]

The struggle is difficult:

> muy diffícil, digo yo,
> diga impossible quien osa,
> vencer la muy poderosa
> natura que Dios crió.[174]

Yet victory, through *la gran caridad divina*, is always possible:

> Los deseos sensuales
> en el cuerpo humano son
> montes, setos y zarzales,
> árboles perjudiciales
> que impiden nuestra razón.
> Mas porque éstas[175] muy aína

> nuestra pasión las revesa,[176]
> la gran caridad divina,[177]
> que jamás se desatina,
> es el alano[178] de presa.[179]

Defeat is shameful:

> Jamás los deleytes me parescieron dignos de nobleza, porque
> quanto son mayores y más continuos, tanto más las fuerzas del
> ánimo abaten y suprimen.[180] No es otra cosa deleyte, dize Tulio,
> saluo alegre mouimiento en los sentidos por la suauidat del
> cuerpo; o según los estoycos, soleuanto de ánimo sin razón.[181]
> ¿Puede ser cosa más longe del sumo bien?[182]

XIII. CONCLUSION

In the foregoing pages the conception of *amor-gentileza* has been shown to coincide in its major aspects with the conception of *fin' amors* introduced by the troubadours, a conception which was highly specialized and "thoroughly foreign to human nature in general" and to the religious and moral teachings of Christianity.[183] It was a loftily conceived love of desire. Its moving stimulus was the beauty and virtue of the beloved, yet it was not Platonic. Desire grew in intensity and led from "pure" to "mixed" love, from sight to touch to possession (Oriana). Humility and courtesy were fundamental characteristics. The blasphemous "religion of love" was a normal concomitant. The frequently adulterous character of this love of desire (Macías) and its frequent scorn of marriage (Melibea), though appearing side by side with Christian courtship and marriage and destined to yield place to them, explain the palinodes ("qué salsa para pecar") which numerous poets included among their works. The various types of *paradoxe amoureux—gentileza* as against *secreto*, the *bels semblans* as against the palpable *galardón*, love as the child and as the enemy of reason, love as the source of joy and of despair—are evidences of the contradictions inseparable from such a conception of love. Yet withal it was an *ideal* which governed the lives of generations of men and women and as such it is our duty to understand it. It was indeed often a game, a pastime, a sinful passion, a surrendering of man's dignity, a truancy. It was also a symbol of worldly virtue, a refinement of the emotions, and, in its highest and purest form, it could become an approach, as in some poems of Santillana, to what Equicola calls *amor angelico*. Noble and ignoble, it was a thing to be sought after and to be shunned, a source of inspiration and of *escarmiento*. The extent to which the same concepts and preoccupations carry over into the sixteenth and seventeenth centuries must be left for another study.[184]

4 Symbols of Change

On September 8, 1517, Charles I of Spain—soon to become Charles V of the Holy Roman Empire—set sail from Middelburg in Zeeland on his first visit to his newly inherited Spanish kingdoms. "It was a proud fleet that weighed anchor at five o'clock on Tuesday morning," writes Hayward Keniston in his account of the voyage, "forty ships large and small. The King's ship, the largest of all, was gaily painted green and red, with gold trimmings; the sails, too, bore paintings of the Crucifixion between the columns of Hercules with the device *Plus Oultre*, the Trinity, Our Lady with the Christ Child, and the saints—Santiago, St. Nicholas, St. Christopher with his feet in the sea. To keep the fleet together there was an elaborate set of sailing orders regarding lights and cannon shots."[1]

As we set forth—reader and author—on our own voyage of exploration in search of the differentiating factors that gave to the Spanish Renaissance its special character within the greater European movement, we may well pause to consider the symbols painted on those sails. The emblem of the Pillars of Hercules and the device *Plus Oultre* (the Burgundian form of the Latin *Plus Ultra*) were invented, according to tradition, by the humanist Luigi Marliano, the King's physician, who accompanied him on this voyage[2]; we may assume that the decorations were considered appropriate by the young King's advisers, both Spanish and Burgundian, and that they were intended to impress favorably the leaders of his new subjects in the Peninsula.[3]

The ideals of the House of Burgundy have been convincingly analyzed by Carlos Clavería.[4] They included an attachment to a type of chivalry already somewhat anachronistic, and they kept alive, in the waning Middle Ages, a style of life and a pattern of conduct which Johan Huizinga has called "a renaissance of a fantastic Middle Ages."[5] Yet there was also an awareness of future expansion, of future greatness in a New World unknown to the

Middle Ages. The motto on the sails is *Plus Oultre*—Sail on! And, besides the Pillars of Hercules, St. Christopher—the saint whose task it was to carry travelers across the waters—stands with his feet in the sea.

We shall return in later chapters to the two basic ideas symbolized by the painted sails of the King's flagship: the Spanish Renaissance[6] is an age of expansion, but under Christian banners; the sea is to be crossed by a saint.[7] Before we do so, it will be well to suggest certain dates that may serve us as symbols of the changing attitudes of the Spaniards as they move forward into modern times.

1380 AND 1399

Though in the present work we are studying the Castilian mind in literature, we must again, as in the preceding volumes, give some attention to Catalonia, the northeastern region of Spain which served as a bridge to Renaissance Italy. Ten years before Dante's death, seven years after Petrarch's birth, the Catalans took possession of the Greek Duchy of Athens. This was in 1311; in 1319 they took over also the Duchy of Neopatras, modern Hypate. Their connections with Byzantium and Greece were thus very close. The classical age of Catalan literature begins with Bernat Metge (1350–1410).[8]

In September of 1380, King Pedro of Aragon and Catalonia described the Acropolis of Athens as "the richest jewel in all the world, the like of which no other king of Christendom could match." The jewel was rich, a king's treasure; but it was also beautiful, and Don Pedro gives a strong aesthetic tone to his description. "It is . . . , as Gregorovius and Rubió y Lluch have stated, the first aesthetic recognition of the Acropolis, after almost a thousand years of silence, to appear on the lips of anyone in western Europe."[9] The Catalan Metge is one of the first of modern European writers to utilize the myth of Orpheus in a work composed in the vernacular—his *Lo somni* of 1399. With an aesthetic appreciation not unlike that of King Pedro, he sees in the tale of the Greek musician's descent to Hades not a theme for ethical contemplation or moral edification but a beautiful fable, a symbol of the power of poetry to move beasts and rocks and trees.[10] In this he anticipates the Italian Angelo Poliziano by nearly a hundred years. This sense of the beauty, the elegance and brilliance, and the attraction of the ancient world, and the desire to adapt and assimilate, to equal and even to surpass the life style of the Greeks and Romans, and, at the same time, "to work the pagan marble with Christian hands"—or, as others put it, "to spoil the Egyptians" (Exod. 12:35–36)—was one of the compelling impulses felt by the Spaniards in their suddenly accelerated march toward national self-realization. When Spaniards pass from the apologetic attitude —*Pro adserenda Hispanorum eruditione*[11]—to the proud affirmation that Spain's achievements surpass those of the ancients, as in Tirso de Molina's defense of the national drama, the Renaissance in Spain has reached its end. It will be necessary to revert to this theme in a later chapter.

1456

This is the date of the death of Juan de Mena, pioneer of the Spanish literary renaissance.[12] Mena, like his friend and contemporary the Marqués de Santillana, sought to create for Spain a literature of increased culture, more worthy of learned men.[13] Mena's writing is characterized by "the complex superposition of various classical suggestions and their fusion in the creative imagination of the poet, a quotation from one source, a reminiscence from another, a glancing allusion from a third, transformed into something authentic" (Gillet, *op. cit.*, p. 159). The essential quality of Mena's *Laberinto de Fortuna* is medieval: he appears curiously indifferent to the objective exactness of the traditional data he used. He was strongly influenced by Dante and, like Dante, by the *Aeneid*. His geographic panorama of the world is definitely connected with the medieval *De imagine mundi* ascribed to St. Anselm. Yet, as a contemporary of Henry the Navigator, he looks out upon the world with avid senses. He systematically introduces mythological allusions, not for their exemplary value, but as ornament and pomp. He knows that in his translation of "Homer" (i.e., of the *Ilias Latina*) he has access to merely a pale reflection of a majestic poem which he, not knowing Greek, could not possess directly. He distinguishes clearly between the genuine Homeric tradition and its medieval deformation (Mrs. Malkiel, *op. cit.*, p. 531), and he comes out in defense of the ancient poet, stressing the power that poetic creation possesses to determine forever attributes and characters, and declaring: "The last hours of Priam were no more lamentable than Homer wished them to be, nor was Hector more lamented, nor Paris more enamored, nor Achilles more renowned . . . , nor Ilium more beautiful, nor the harbors more crowded with warships . . . , nor the temples with sacrifices, than the rich pen of Homer, guided by his wise hand, willed that they should be for all posterity."[14]

From the national standpoint, the hope of monarchial unity (soon to be realized) is an essential aspect of Mena's *Laberinto:* a future single monarch will inspire Spain, under the leadership of Castile, to complete the reconquest of all her territory from the Moors. And, though *Plus Ultra* lies some years in the future, there is a prophetic imperial note: the Spanish king will rule not only over Spain, but over the world (*ibid.*, pp. 542–43).

"What Mena wrote and what Mena was," writes Professor Gillet (*op. cit.*, p. 164), "is probably less important than what he achieved in others. His own time certainly found in him an answer to its needs, and . . . his position . . . as patriarch of Spanish letters was hardly ever challenged." Specific indebtedness is shown, in masterly fashion, by Mrs. Malkiel. His commentator Hernán Núñez, known as el Comendador Griego (see below), declared him to be "very eminent and outstanding, particularly in his use of metaphor and simile, so that I proclaim him comparable, not to other Spanish poets, but even to the most excellent Latins." And he consents that Mena be called heroic: "We may call Juan de Mena heroic, since he deals in this poem with many illustrious heroes."[15] This is a fundamental preoccupation of the Spanish Renaissance. In classical theory the epic was the noblest genre, and much of the energy of Renaissance poets, in all of Europe, was devoted to the search for the heroic poem—the poem which seeks to declare all, or at least the essential, truth in any age or generation. Juan de Mena did not write such a poem, nor did any of his countrymen, only the Portuguese Camoëns having been fully successful in his *The Lusiads.*[16] But Mena pointed the way, and won the respect of later generations. He was cited as an authority, a source book; he was the Spanish poet *por antonomasia*, par excellence: throughout the Golden Age it was felt sufficient to refer to him as *El Poeta Español*.[17] Lope de Vega admired him, and Tirso de Molina actually put him on the stage, with full honors (Mrs. Malkiel, pp. 376 ff.). His position as a "primitive classic" is thus somewhat parallel—*longo intervallo*—to that of Dante as a "classic" during the Italian Renaissance.[18]

1458

This year marks the death of the Marqués de Santillana, Don Iñigo López de Mendoza, author of the first-known example of Spanish literary criticism and literary history—the famous *Carta Prohemio* prefacing the copy of his works which he sent as a gift to Don Pedro de Portugal. As a literary historian *avant la lettre*, Santillana "was the first to see the art of the troubadours as a literary tradition in which different nations cooperated."[19] As a literary theoretician, Santillana follows Boccaccio in his definition of poetry: "And what is poetry . . . except an imagining of useful things, covered or veiled with a most lovely covering, composed, set off, and scanned in accordance with a certain syllable count, weight, and measure?" (cited *ibid.*, p. 249). Here he emphasizes the play of fantasy, with its immediate purpose of creating beauty, the essential requisite of metre, and the didactic end of poetry. His definition was not rendered obsolete during the Renaissance, though there were poets, like Góngora (as well as prose writers like Quevedo), who on occasion disclaimed the didactic purpose of literature.[20] Santillana's enthusiasm for poetry and his equating of literary fame with martial fame are definitely Renaissance characteristics.

In Santillana, as in his friend Juan de Mena, we again encounter a deep concern for learned, as against light and circumstantial, poetry. When Santillana cites Livy or Dante, he is not moved by the medieval desire to authenticate every statement, but rather by the urge to show off—with an innocent vanity that is never offensive—what he has recently learned. No Spanish poet of his own or of earlier times could compete with him in the vast sweep of his interests[21]; none had given himself over so avidly to the Latin classics[22] (in compendiums or translations) or to the great writers of Italy.

This intention to create a body of learned poetry for Spain had as a natural consequence the introduction into Spanish of words adapted from Latin and other languages. Another consequence was the cultivation of a rhetorical style, reminiscent of that of the *Grands Rhétoriqueurs* of contemporary France. Cicero's *De Inventione* and *Rhetorica ad Herennium* were available in Spanish translation, and Santillana's use of rhetorical *elegantiae* shows a clear awareness of form; rhetorical devices are successfully, though not always spontaneously, employed. Mythological invocations appear at the beginnings of his longer poems and, internally, in the initial stanzas of the subdivisions. As early as 1436 Santillana had developed a style of his own, brilliant and ostentatious, which surpassed that of his contemporaries. Juan de Mena learned much from him, although Mena, owing to his mastery of Latin, acquired poetic resources that were denied to the Marqués (Lapesa, *op. cit.*, pp. 160 ff.).

Santillana has yet another claim to our attention: inspired by Petrarch, he composed forty-two *Sonetos al itálico modo*, written at intervals during the last twenty years of his life. Some of these are occasional pieces, lamenting the death of a prominent personage or celebrating a royal entry; others have a political intention. One invites the princes of Christendom to restore Byzantium, recently conquered by the Turks. Another gives counsel to the new king, Enrique IV (*ibid.*, pp. 179 ff.). We have to do, therefore, not with a poetic whim, but with a consistent and prolonged effort to introduce the sonnet form—a form deliberately chosen and especially difficult. Yet Santillana's *sonetos* do not show a development, an increasing mastery; the last ones, like those at the beginning of the series, are marked by flashes of genuine poetry, but also by deficiencies characteristic of an experimenter.

The occasional sonnets constitute a minority; most of Santillana's forty-two *sonetos*, like the majority of those in Petrarch's *Canzoniere*, are amatory. They do not reveal, as do those of Petrarch, successive stages in the transformation of the poet's emotional life. Few in number, they show only separate phases of the amorous experience: love at first sight, absence, glances, the appearance of gray hairs, the joy of a renewed relationship. All of them seek to express, in vocabulary, tone, and style, the feeling as well as the form of the Italian *dolce stil nuovo* and of Petrarch's *Canzoniere.*[23] "Into these Petrarchan molds," writes Lapesa, "enters all the subject matter of chivalric love" (p. 187). Santillana's Petrarchism is a new, fair, and prestigious form, a *fermosa cobertura*, such as all true poetry required, according to his own definition (p. 189).

None of Santillana's contemporaries and immediate followers was inspired to follow his example. Some sixty years later a few sporadic efforts were made by Spaniards to use the sonnet form, but the language employed was Italian. It remained for Juan Boscán, and for the infinitely more gifted Garcilaso de la Vega, to naturalize the sonnet in Spain; yet Fernando de Herrera in 1580, in his commentary on Garcilaso, did justice to the forerunner: "The Marqués de Santillana, a great Spanish captain and a brave knight, first made the plunge, with noteworthy boldness, into that unknown sea, and did so with singular success, and returned to his native shores with the spoils of foreign conquest. Testimony of this are some sonnets of his, worthy of veneration because of the nobility of him who wrote them, and because of the light they cast amid the shadows and confusion of that time" (cited in Lapesa, pp. 201–2).

The shadows and confusion of that time . . . Herrera is aware, in 1580, that there has been a sudden development in Spanish literary culture, that his country, between Santillana's day and his own, has seen the beginning of a new cultural span. But we must not get ahead of our story.

1473[24]

This is the year of the return to Spain of Antonio de Nebrija (or Lebrija, d. 1522), father of Spanish philology, after his years of humanistic study in Italy.[25] Nebrija, neither knight nor cleric but a simple lay scholar, represents the linguistic and philological as well as the scriptural preoccupations of the early Renaissance.[26] There is a striking parallel between Nebrija's conviction in these matters and that of Roger Bacon (d. 1294), who wrote that "no Latin[27] will be able to understand the wisdom of the sacred Scripture and of philosophy unless he understands the languages from which they were translated." Nebrija was primarily a Latinist, and his concern was with the correcting of the text of the Vulgate; his position was new in that he proposed to apply all the resources of the new philology of the Italian Renaissance to the understanding of the Scriptures. Italy was the mistress of Spain's Christian humanists.[28]

Ingram Bywater points out[29] that an adaptation of Nebrija's *Vocabularium* was found in the library of Henry VIII, and that as late as 1631 there appeared in England *A Brief Introduction to Syntax . . . Collected for the most Part of Nebrissa his Spanish Copie. . . .* The credit for the working out of a theory of ancient Greek pronunciation is due, says Bywater, not to Aldus Manutius or any other Italian, but to the great Spanish humanist Antonius Nebrissensis, the prophet of the new learning among his countrymen, whose labors gave to Spain a place of her own in the intellectual history of the sixteenth century which, though not so distinguished as that of Italy or France, surpassed anything that was possible in Tudor England.

The seventeenth-century bibliographer, Nicolás Antonio, marshals Nebrija's writings under seven headings: grammar, philology, poetics, history, jurisprudence, medicine, and Biblical studies. To ancient geography Nebrija contributed an edition of Pomponius Mela and a dictionary of ancient place names. As editor or commentator he produced a Virgil, a Persius, a Prudentius, a Sedulius, and also an edition of the Vulgate Psalms. Interested in Hebrew as well as in Greek and Latin, he had some hand in the editing of the Alcalá or Complutensian Polyglot edition of the Bible, of which we shall have more to say below. His position was essentially that of Erasmus: in all matters of interpretation, the first duty of the interpreter is to go back to the original texts. The true text of the venerated Vulgate might need to be determined, he declared, by consulting the ancient manuscripts. So bold were Nebrija's declarations that his post at Salamanca became untenable; but he moved on to the newly created University of Alcalá, where he remained until his death. As royal historiographer he was commissioned to write the official history of the reign of Ferdinand and Isabella.

In the introduction to his *Spanish-Latin Dictionary*, Nebrija tells how he became convinced that, however great the learning of his preceptors in grammar and logic, *en dezir sabían muy poco*—i.e., they were not masters of the Latin language. "And although I had," he continues, "sufficient ability and training to earn a good living and to obtain honors, I was unwilling to tread the common road, but sought out a path, by God's grace revealed to me alone, namely, to go to the source where I might slake my own thirst and that of my countrymen. . . . So it was that at the age of nineteen I went to Italy,[30] not as others do to obtain a benefice or to bring back formulas of civil or canon law, or to return with merchandise: but to restore to the land they had lost[31] the authors of Latin literature, who for many centuries had been exiled from Spain."

1492

This *annus mirabilis* is a year of many beginnings. In January Granada fell to the besieging forces of Ferdinand and Isabella, and Spain's centuries-old thrust to the south not only met with final success but entered a new phase: Spanish domination extending into North Africa. In August, Columbus set sail from Palos, initiating the great policy of expansion to the west and balancing the eastward movement which had begun in the Middle Ages with the conquest of the Balearic Islands and had carried the Aragonese and Catalans to victories in Greece.[32] In a less martial field of endeavor, the year saw the birth of the secular theater in Spain, as Juan del Encina put on the first of his eclogues in the palace of the Duke of Alba. It is, finally, the year which gives us the most eloquent expression of Spain's consciousness of her mission as a carrier of civilization—and the arts of peace—to distant lands and populations as yet unknown.

In 1492, almost certainly after Columbus had set sail but assuredly before his return (March 15, 1493), Nebrija published his *Gramática de la lengua castellana*, the first grammar of a Romance language written with all the rigor of the new philology. This book, says González Llubera in the introduction to his modern edition (cited above), "has a very real and symptomatic importance. An intense and cultured patriotism pervades it. The author is conscious that Spain has begun to accomplish great deeds, that the

Castilian people are on the threshold of an age of conquest. The eloquent pages with which the book opens belong to the noblest utterances inspired by patriotic feeling; and when we reflect that they immediately precede the discoveries of Columbus, we cannot resist the impression that their tone has something of the prophetic."

In his prologue Nebrija addresses Queen Isabella. "When I reflect, most gracious and illustrious Queen, and view in retrospect the antiquity of all the things of which we have written records, I come to one conclusion: that language was always the companion of Empire, so that together they began, increased, and flourished, and together fell into decline." He then sets forth his classical concept of the cyclical movement of history—not too greatly different from that of the modern Spengler—and traces the linguistic and political history of the Hebrews, the Greeks, and the Romans. The Latin language, as those of his generation inherited it from their fathers, "had little more to do with the Latin of the years of Rome's glory than with Arabic."

And what of Castilian? It had its inception in the early centuries of the judges and kings of Castile and León; began to show its strength in the time of Alphonso the Learned (d. 1284); spread to Aragon and Navarre; and finally, in the fifteenth century, was carried to Italy, "following the princes whom we sent to rule [*imperar*] in those Kingdoms" (Naples, Sicily). "So it has grown, up to the moment of unity, peace, and power that we now enjoy, wherein the pieces that formerly composed Spain have been brought together in a union such that many centuries, and the ravages of time, will not be able to break or disunite it."

Thus, with the infidel crushed and expelled, with Christian unity established, all that remains is to foment the arts of peace, among which language occupies first place as the instrument of the human reason. Heretofore the Castilian language has lain in neglect, without learned regulation, and subject to popular forces of change as each generation treated and mistreated it according to whim.[33] In order that whatever shall be written in Castilian in the future may have linguistic permanence and continued validity, the authority of grammar is indispensable. Nebrija would do for Castilian what the grammarians of antiquity did for Greek and Latin. He himself, he continues, has reduced Castilian to rule "in the most opportune time that ever was, since our language is at the height of its development."

And there is another way, he says, in which his new *Grammar* will serve the public weal: when he offered the presentation copy to Her Majesty in the city of Salamanca, and the Queen asked the nature of its usefulness, "the reverend Bishop of Avila answered in my stead, saying that after your Majesty shall have placed under her yoke barbarous nations with strange tongues, and, having conquered them will need to impose on them the laws of the conqueror, and therewith our language; then, by means of this my *Castilian Grammar*, they will come to know that language, just as we now depend on my *Latin Grammar* when we need to learn Latin."

We have already read, in Nebrija's own words, his statement of Renaissance individualism, as he sought out a path revealed to him alone, and of the humanist's desire to return to the sources, to make —as Américo Castro has brilliantly expressed it—"a critical edition of the universe"; we have seen his interest in both profane and sacred antiquity; and we have heard him express his noble concept of an empire devoted to the arts of peace, to the work of civilization. To all this we should add a quotation expressive of his sense of being a reformer, to the greater glory of his nation. He says, in the prologue to his *Latin-Spanish Dictionary:*

> I never ceased to try to hit upon some way whereby I could break through the barbarism that is spread so widely throughout Spain. And I remembered the decision of Saints Peter and Paul, the princes of the apostles, in their determination to banish heathenism. For just as those apostles, in order to lay the foundations of the Church, did not lay siege to obscure and unknown towns, but one of them to Athens, and both to Antioch, cities famed for the study of letters, and thereafter to Rome, queen and mistress of the world, so today, in order to banish ignorance from the men of our nation, I began by attacking no meaner center than the University of Salamanca, which, once taken like a fortress captured by storm, I doubted not that all the other towns and cities of Spain would come to offer their surrender.

So noteworthy was his doctrine, he continues, that even his enemies conceded:

I was the first who set up my campaign tent, proposing to teach Latin and daring to raise a standard of new precepts; I banished from Spain the harshness of the old-style grammarians, so that if any proper sort of Latin is possessed by the men of our nation, all of this must be attributed to me.

In the prologue to the 1495 edition of his *Introductiones Latinae*, Nebrija tells of being busily engaged in the study of the antiquities of Spain and declares that, when once this task is finished, he intends to devote himself exclusively to Biblical studies. This statement leads us to our next symbolic year, or rather span of years.

1502–1517

Between these two dates the edition of the great Complutensian Polyglot or Alcalá Bible, was completed. In it Nebrija saw the partial realization of his ideals of Biblical scholarship: the restoration of the sacred texts by means of a return to their philological sources. The great cardinal Cisneros (Francisco Jiménez de Cisneros, d. 1517) brought together a brilliant group of Hellenists, Latinists, and Hebraists (their names will concern us later), obtained for them the best manuscripts that could be found, and spared no expense in materials or printing. The work was begun in 1502; the printing, begun in 1514, was completed in 1517. Volumes I–IV contained the Old Testament in Greek, Latin, Hebrew, and Chaldean; volume V, the Greek and Latin texts of the New Testament; volume VI, a Hebrew-Chaldean vocabulary, an index of names, and a Hebrew grammar. It was the first polyglot Bible to be printed, and it was the high-water mark of early scriptural science. The Alcalá New Testament in Greek preceded by some two years the Greek New Testament of Erasmus.

Nebrija, who for years had been devoting himself to the study of the texts of the Scriptures, accepted (at a late date) the position of Latin editor on Cisneros' board. He declared: "I came to Alcalá to take part in the emendation of the Latin, which is normally corrupt in all the Latin Bibles, by collating it with the Hebrew, the Chaldean, and the Greek." His proposed emendations aroused the opposition of those who defended the Vulgate text as something untouchable, and Nebrija withdrew from the enterprise.[34] Nebrija's activity in this field of textual criticism had preceded the project of Cisneros. He represents, as Marcel Bataillon says, the autonomous effort of the humanists to restore antiquity in its entirety, Christian as well as pagan, and he deserves a place of his own in the history of Christian humanism. In this field of Biblical studies he is not only a predecessor of Spanish Erasmism but a precursor of Erasmus himself. Bataillon sees in him the heir of the boldness of method of Lorenzo Valla in matters of Biblical philology, perhaps also of Valla's critical attitude in regard to the traditions of the Church.[35]

1508

Ever since becoming primate of Spain, Cardinal Cisneros had devoted large sums from his personal income to the furtherance of learning. His plan to found a university which should be a complete organism for ecclesiastical training[36] strongly based on the humanities, and whose faculty of theology should be open to the novelties of the new scriptural science and the new erudition in the three languages, finally took shape, and he chose Alcalá as the seat of the new university. In 1499 the necessary papal bull was granted; the foundation stone was laid in 1500; instruction began in 1508.

The reason that a new university was felt to be necessary was precisely that in the older University of Salamanca tradition still held sway. Cisneros was determined that, at Alcalá, theology should use as its handmaidens the other sciences and arts—as the statutes of the University (art. XLV) clearly specified. The founding of this university marked not only a triumph of Renaissance humanism, but also a rebirth of Christian antiquity—a fact which differentiates it profoundly from the Collège de France (1530). From the *Distichs* of Cato, beginners in Latin passed to the hymns and prayers of the Church before starting to read Terence; the first half of the next year was devoted to such Christian poets as Sedulius and Juvencus, the pagan Virgil being postponed to make room for them. The Chair of Rhetoric was held by Hernando

Alonso de Herrera, one of the first Spanish Erasmians (in the sense that, like Erasmus of Rotterdam, he called for a reform of institutions and of culture); his successor in this chair was none other than Nebrija. In philosophy, Duns Scotus was placed on an equal footing with Thomas Aquinas. And, after centuries of Scholasticism, there was a direct return to the Church Fathers: Jerome, Augustine, Ambrose, Gregory. The Greek Fathers were read in the original; Cisneros established a university press and had published, at times at his own expense, the necessary Greek textbooks.[37] Greek took root in Alcalá because it was the language of the New Testament, of many Church Fathers, and of the great source of Thomist theology, Aristotle. Had Cisneros not died in 1517, there would have been produced at Alcalá a bilingual edition of Aristotle in Greek and Latin. The work had already begun.

The creation of this university thus reminds us rather strikingly of the motivation that prompted the founding of Harvard, somewhat over a century later. Men of immensely different backgrounds and beliefs, in two completely different environments, sought to provide adequate instruction for the spiritual leaders of their respective societies.

In later chapters of the present volume we shall perceive, as Bataillon's great work has enabled us to see with respect to its special field of study, that the problems which led to the wars of religion in sixteenth-century Europe were present also in Spain; that the Spain of Cisneros contained the germ of all that was to develop in the reign of Charles V (d. 1558), all that the efforts of Philip II (d. 1598) would strive to preserve.[38]

1526–1532

In the first volume of *Spain and the Western Tradition* (Chapter IV), we devoted some attention to another *annus mirabilis*, 1526—the year when a suggestion from the Venetian ambassador to the court of Spain, Andrea Navagiero, convinced the poet Juan Boscán of the desirability of naturalizing in Spain the poetic forms so brilliantly developed in the Italy of the "three modern classics," Dante, Boccaccio, and Petrarch. As a result of Navagiero's persuasiveness and the efforts it inspired on the part of Boscán and—much

more to the purpose – of his supremely talented friend Garcilaso de
la Vega, a world of new symbols and of entirely new artistic possibilities was opened to the Spaniards, affecting the development of
their literature to the present day. Because this was treated at some
length in our earlier volume, it will not be necessary to retrace here
the growth in literary beauty and power as the new poetic symbols
were taken over, together with the new poetic instrument: the
Italian hendecasyllabic line, arranged in new strophe-forms – sonnet,
canzone, terza rima, eclogue, and others.

Lapesa rightly insists on the decisiveness of the Italian
influence.[39] Great as was Garcilaso's debt to Virgil, it was to
Petrarch – primarily – and to Sannazaro, Ariosto, Tansillo, and Bernardo Tasso, that the Spanish poet was indebted for the molds into
which he cast his personal conception of the world of poetic
beauty. Guided by these masters, Garcilaso moves from the
gloomy, despairing, and psychologically-abstract imagery of earlier Spanish *cancionero* poetry to the gentle notes of light and color
which make possible his new treatment of the physical beauty of
his beloved, the hauntingly inaccessible Isabel Freyre – moves so
successfully that he was able to surpass in poetic authenticity the
entirety of the lyric of the Italian *Cinquecento.* From his Italian
models he learned how to write learned poetry, full reminiscences
exquisitely re-elaborated and made new, endowed with a delicate
sense of plasticity and form. By the time Garcilaso achieved the
spiritual peace of his Neapolitan period (from 1532 until his death
four years later), he had reached the fullness of his powers. It is to
this period in Garcilaso's career that I applied, in my earlier volume, C. S. Lewis' designation of *golden.* We may well permit
ourselves to repeat here Lewis' statement of what he means by
golden poetry: "In a Golden Age the right thing to do is obvious:
'good is as visible as green.' " The artist has only "to find the most
beautiful models, pose them in the most graceful attitudes, and get
to work. . . . Men have at last learned how to write; for a few
years nothing more is needed than to play out again and again the
strong, simple music of the uncontorted line and to load one's poem
with all that is naturally delightful – with flowers and swans, with
ladies' hair, hands, lips, breasts, and eyes, with silver and gold,
woods and waters, the stars, the moon and the sun."[40] In Garcilaso

de la Vega all this is achieved; it is the triumph, in the lyric, of the Spanish Renaissance.

Not all genres reach their plenitude at the same time. The drama, fiction, and the essay reach maturity only in the period "when ingenuous taste has been satisfied," when it becomes necessary "to seek for novelty, to set oneself difficult tasks," even "to make beauty out of violence," (*ibid.*) as do Góngora and Quevedo in the baroque. We shall leave discussion of this for Volume IV. In the meantime, there are two additional dates for us to consider.

1580

In 1580 Fernando de Herrera republished the poems of Garcilaso de la Vega, separating them for the first time from the works of Garcilaso's more pedestrian friend Boscán, and providing them with a learned commentary which marks the full tide of the Renaissance in the field of criticism. Some six years earlier, to be sure, the humanist Francisco Sánchez de las Brozas (el Brocense) had made an edition of Garcilaso "with commentary and emendations," but this edition was completely overshadowed by Herrera's. El Brocense's edition is to be recalled only for the principle underlying its avowed purpose: the demonstration of Garcilaso's excellence in terms of his close kinship with the "classical" poets of Italy and Rome. "I say and affirm," wrote el Brocense, "that I do not regard as a good poet him who fails to imitate the excellent poets of antiquity. And if I am asked why, among so many thousands of poets as exist in our Spain, so few can be accounted worthy of this name, I reply that there is no other reason, except that they are not equipped with the knowledge, languages, and doctrine which would enable them to imitate."[41] Herrera had much to say in the same vein; William C. Atkinson suggests that "had he too been merely a university professor the significance of his commentary might likewise have gone no further. Fortunately he was, instead, a poet" (*ibid.*, pp. 208–9). Atkinson points up the positions taken by Herrera in what amounts to a chapter in the "Quarrel of Ancients and Moderns"[42]—positions that attest the maturity of the Spanish Renaissance in the field of criticism applied to the lyric (a genre almost completely disregarded in Aristotle's *Poetics*). Herrera's positions are (1) that the day for Spain's inferiority complex in the matter of culture and civilization is over[43]; (2) that the complaint, so often repeated throughout the century, against the literary neglect and inadequacy of Castilian is no longer valid; (3) that Spaniards have it within their power to write poetry as immortal as any; (4) that poetry is a heightened mode of expression that may address itself to the initiate with words chosen for their sound, their associations, and their symbolism, and that this poetic language is often beyond the grasp of the common man; (5) that languages have their special character, their genius, and that Spanish is incomparably more "grave," is possessed of a greater spirit of magnificence than all the others now called "vulgar"; (6) and that the poet, if he will learn all that the ancients and the Italians have to teach, may hope to set out from that point to achieve his own conquests.[44]

1585

This year marks the triumph of Castilian prose, as 1580 does that of Castilian as a vehicle for poetic expression. Dr. Francisco López de Villalobos, physician to the Catholic Sovereigns and to Charles V, felt that his miscellany entitled *Libro de los problemas*, published in 1543, would suffer from the fact that he had written it in Spanish rather than in Latin; and, although many apologies for, and praises of, the Spanish language appeared during the sixteenth century (we shall study them in a later chapter), "it took the voice of Fray Luis de León to make clear once and for all that Castilian was equal to Latin." After the publication of Book III of Fray Luis' *De los nombres de Cristo*, "all understood . . . that the hour of the vernacular had sounded, announcing and promising for it a brilliant career in the future, and proclaiming that henceforth the fruits of philosophical or religious meditation would be available to all readers," whether they knew Latin or did not.[45]

Fray Luis had published Books I and II of *De los nombres de Cristo* in 1583 and had been censured (in spite of the very successful religious works composed in Castilian by Fray Luis de Granada and others) for venturing to compose them in the vernacular. In 1585 he replied to the censure by reprinting the first two books, with a third book added. In the introduction to the latter, Fray

Luis accuses his detractors of contempt for their own language, since they refuse to read matter composed in it which—were it not for the circumstance of the linguistic vehicle—they would gladly read and regard as good. These detractors, he says, in their ignorance think that to write in the vernacular is necessarily to express oneself as the common man does, carelessly and without giving thought to the sequence and disposition of concepts and words (*desatadamente y sin orden*). Fray Luis explains that, on the contrary, he gives to every word its proper place in the general orchestration (*concierto*). Effective expression requires judgment and special study. Words have their appropriateness, not only as to meaning but as to sound; the master prose writer actually counts syllables and even letters, weighing and composing for clarity, harmony, and sweetness. Readers of good taste, wise and serious readers, refuse to apply themselves to the perusal of what has been badly or carelessly written. Fray Luis' present book is intended for readers of this kind, and its author has naturally given thought to their requirements.

If any should chance to say that this is a novelty, a departure from established ways, Fray Luis willingly admits that it is indeed a new thing to lift ordinary discourse to a higher plane, to give it harmony and rhythm. This is a new path[46] which he has purposely opened, not out of a presumptuous sense of superiority, but rather with the purpose that those having the strength to do so may be encouraged henceforth to treat their native language as the wise and eloquent writers of the past treated theirs, and that by so doing they should make it the equal of the languages which are considered the best—over which Castilian has, in Fray Luis' considered judgment, the advantage of many virtues peculiar to it alone.[47]

SUMMARY AND CONCLUSION

The "symbolic dates" singled out for special attention to represent successive stages of advance, as Spain emerges from the Middle Ages and assumes her place among the cultured nations of Europe, have exemplified various aspects of this cultural coming-of-age: an early awareness of the beauty bequeathed by a more learned past to modern Europeans; the first clearly conscious efforts to give to

Castile a literature worthy of mature and learned men, a literature ennobled by its having come to terms not merely with a part of the ancient heritage but with all of it; a conscious turning toward Italy as to a mistress already in possession of many of the things that the Castilians desired for themselves—the keys to the ancient languages and the philological method that would make possible the restoration, in all their purity, of the sources of the Christian culture which Spain, like her sister nations in Renaissance Europe, had inherited from Palestine, Greece, and Rome. Not that the newly enriched culture sought to become a replica of what had gone before; rather, the new culture, now aware of its powers, was entering into possession of ancient treasures which, through neglect and unawareness, had not yet given their modern fruit. Concretely, we have seen how the Christian humanists of Spain set about the accomplishment of these ends by making available for Christian scholars and theologians the complete body of Holy Writ in its ancient languages, for purposes of determining what, exactly, the Holy Ghost had wished to convey to mankind. We have seen also how the same desire for a renewal of the life of the mind and of the spirit led to the creation of a special university which should cultivate the new learning and to the establishment of a university press which should provide the needed books.

Passing from intellectual and religious to literary history, we have seen how a new poetic instrument, and the approach, by means of it, to Italian models, lent an altogether new dimension of expressiveness and beauty to the Spanish lyric; how the awareness of this achievement found its expression in literary criticism and brought the conviction that the ancients were not giants upon whose shoulders mere moderns stood as pygmies, but rather that the moderns, would they but follow the road marked out by their ancient predecessors, could be as sublime as they and aspire to the same literary immortality. Finally, we have gone one step further and seen how the same spirit manifested itself in Castilian prose, as matters of the highest spiritual significance were set forth in a prose style which consciously aimed to be worthy of the supreme dignity of its subject matter.

With this, the Spanish Renaissance may be regarded as launched. Many of its triumphs still lie ahead; Fray Luis de León could have had no inkling of the vast new literary world soon to be created by Lope de Vega and given expression in the national drama. He could not conceivably have foreseen the rich, human triumph of Cervantes, as he created the modern critical novel and opened to writers of fiction a marvelously new scheme of "incarnation," placing authentic human creatures upon the stage of the imagination, there to work out their destinies to the permanent enrichment of mankind.

Nor was it possible, in 1585, to know that after noonday would come sunset and twilight and dark. Nebrija had considered that his country would develop the arts of peace under a firm governmental organization that could not be broken during any time span he could foresee. By no conceivable stretch of the imagination could Nebrija, before his death in 1522, or even Fray Luis, before committing his spirit into the hands of his Maker in 1591, have known that Quevedo, born in 1585, would one day utter the disconsolate cry:

Life, life, ahoy! Alas, life does not answer![48]

These complications, these shadings from darkness to light and from light to darkness, we shall investigate in later portions of our study.

5 Fingen Los Poetas — *Notes on the* Spanish Attitude toward Pagan Mythology

Boccaccio maintained that the pagan poets were good theologians.[1] Villani said that Dante had reconciled the fictions of the poets with moral and natural philosophy and with Christian literature, and had shown that the ancient poets were divinely inspired to prophesy the Christian mysteries, thus making poetry pleasing not only to the learned, but also to the common and uneducated.[2] "I religiosi stessi," writes Antonio Belloni in his history of *Il poema epico e mitologico*,[3] "quando si diedero a trattar materia sacra, sentirono il bisogno di ricorrere alle divinità pagane." Ernst Walser, in his *Studien zur Weltanschauung der Renaissance*,[4] attacking what was to him the error of earlier students of the Renaissance (Burckhardt, Voigt, Monnier, etc.), namely that the Christian piety of the humanists had been shaken by the revival of antiquity, sets forth as the one fundamentally new element in Renaissance humanism—the one trait that humanism did not share with medieval learning—its new artistic conception of the formal beauty of antique letters and art, and maintained that the content of humanism remained largely medieval, while "the paganism of the Renaissance in all its thousand-fold forms . . . was a purely external, fashionable, formal element."[5]

In seeking an explanation of this phenomenon we must go beyond the fact that the poetry of the ancients was too closely intertwined with contemporary culture to be ignored,[6] in search of a cause closer to the well-springs of human nature. This has been done by C. S. Lewis. "No religion, so long as it is believed," he writes in *The Allegory of Love. A Study in Medieval Tradition*,[7] "can have that kind of beauty which we find in the gods of Titian, of Botticelli, or of our own romantic poets." And he continues:

For poetry to spread its wings fully, there must be, besides the believed religion, a marvellous that knows itself as myth. For this to come about, the old marvellous, which was once taken as fact, must be stored up somewhere, not wholly dead, but in a winter sleep, waiting its time. . . . The decline of the gods, from deity to hypostasis and from hypostasis to decoration, was not, for them nor for us, a history of sheer loss. For decoration may let romance in. The poet is free to invent, beyond the limits of the possible, regions of strangeness and beauty for their own sake.[8]

Arturo Farinelli finds a similar reconciliation in Spain:

L'umanesimo in Ispagna non era in lotta alcuna con Dio e coi Santi; si rappattumava con essi, senza fatica, senz'astio e cruccio. L'Olimpo dei Pagani viveva allegramente e pacificamente accanto al Paradiso dei Cristiani. Il pensiero antico è tratto a reggere ed a fortificare il pensiero moderno.[9]

Mythology and the pagan Parnassus were thus a part, and an increasingly important part, of "la muy fermosa cobertura" which the Marqués de Santillana regarded as the very essence of poetry.[10] Jean Seznec's *La survivance des dieux antiques*[11] is, from beginning to end, a history of this adaptation, whereby the *fingimientos de los poetas* were converted into allegories and symbols—a tendency which had its roots in Greek euphemerism.[12] The adaptation was not, however, perfect: it produced a certain *gène*. In this respect Seznec's book, and the present article, are a corrective to the one-sided statements which I have quoted thus far. Tertullian sought (ineffectually) to eliminate the pagan names of the days of the week; certain *astrothéosophes* sought to transform Cepheus into Adam and Cassiopeia into Eve; and the Priscillianists replaced the signs of the Zodiac by the twelve prophets. Later, Pope Pius V chased the "idols" from the Vatican, and Sixtus Quintus ordered that the fountain of Acqua Felice be adorned by a statue of Moses and not of Neptune.[13] While these efforts are but ripples on a mighty current, they correspond to an essential reality:

Certes, beaucoup de croyants sincères, qui sont en même temps de fervents lettrés, associent naïvement et sans arrière-pensée, leur érudition profane et leur foi; pour eux, l'allégorie n'est qu'un sentier fleuri, qui permet de passer de l'une à l'autre.

Mais, au fond, il faut bien le dire, l'allégorie n'est très souvent qu'une imposture: elle sert à concilier ce qui n'est pas conciliable, comme elle servait, tout à l'heure, à rendre décent ce qui ne l'est point.

A ce double titre, c'est une supercherie dangereuse.[14]

These reasons explain the répugnance with which "les Pères . . . avaient admis . . . la poésie profane dans l'éducation . . . avec la conviction qu'elle était un élément indispensable de la culture," exactly as the Jesuits did after the Council of Trent.[15]

We are now prepared to follow the course of these ideas in Spain. It will be convenient to give attention first to the dissenters. Both Gómez and Jorge Manrique reject the "pagan,"[16] or rather pseudo-pagan[17] invocation. I shall quote from Jorge, who is the more outspoken of the two:

> Dexo las ynuocaçiones
> de los famosos poetas
>   y oradores;
> no curo de sus ficciones,
> que traen yeruas secretas
>   sus sabores;
> Aquél sólo me encomiendo,
> aquél sólo ynuoco yo
>   de verdad,
> que en este mundo biuiendo,
> el mundo no conosció
>   su deydad.[18]

Don Pedro de Portugal is equally outspoken. The yeruas secretas of the Muses of Parnassus are, for him, ponçoña.[19] Juan de Mena, who in the first copla of his Trezientas speaks of God as Júpiter, in the Coplas contra los pecados mortales, turns, not only from the amorous follies of his youth, but also from concern with the sensuous delights of poetic fábulas. Addressing his Christian Muse— "Canta tú, christiana musa"—, he dismisses the Sirens—serenas—

> Que en la mi edad pasada
> tal dulzura emponzoñada
> derramastes por mis venas,

and then, "usando de una comparación de San Basilio el Magno en su célebre homilía sobre la utilidad que se saca de la lectura de los libros de los gentiles," he adds:

Usemos de los poemas
tomando dellos lo bueno,
mas huyan de nuestro seno
los sus fabulosos temas.
Sus ficciones y problemas
desechemos como espinas . . .
. . . .
De la esclava poesía
lo superfluo así tirado,
lo dañoso desechado,
seguiré su compañía,
a la católica vía
reduciéndola por modo,
que valga más que su todo
la parte que fago mía.[20]

This is essentially the position of Juan de Padilla, *el cartuxano*, who in his *Retablo de la vida de Cristo* makes it clear that in his case, as in that of Mena, the turning away from the delights of secular poetry is analogous to the turning away from the delights of courtly love:[21]

Huyan, por ende, las musas dañadas
a las Estigias do reina Plutón,
en nuestro divino muy alto sermón
las tienen los santos por muy reprobadas.
Aquí celebramos las cosas sagradas.[22]
. . . .
Dexa, por ende, las falsas ficciones . . .
sus fábulas falsas y sus opiniones
pintamos[23] en tiempo de la juuentud,
agora mirando la suma virtud
conozco que matan a los corazones.[24]

He proceeds, however, to correct the impression of a general condemnation of "los vanos poemas":

> Los vanos poemas, que pueden dañar,
> dexemos aparte, tomando lo sano;
> como quien quita la paja del grano,
> y más de la cidra su mal amargar.
> Esta sentencia, por muy aprobada,
> tienen los santos decretos y leyes:
> *porque no tengan los pueblos y reyes*
> *la ciencia terrena por menospreciada.*[25]

The prose writers are no less explicit. The stern moralist, Juan Luis Vives, recommends that the reader of the ancient writers "proceda como al andar en parajes señalados como venenosos, esto es, con el antídoto conveniente . . . a fin de tomar de todos ellos lo que es útil, rechazando lo demás."[26] Pedro Mexía, in the prologue to his translation of Isocrates' *Parenesis a Demónico* remarks: "Y también porque Isócrates en algunos lugares habla como gentil, tuve cuidado de traducirlo cristianamente."[27] To Fray Luis de Granada, in the moment of temporary pessimism in which he composed his *Libro de la oración y meditación* (1554), "el estudio de los autores paganos sería, a lo sumo, una calamidad inevitable." Granting that these studies are in part necessary, he yet warns: "todavía los habíamos de tener por una gran plaga de nuestra vida, pues nos roban tanta parte del tiempo," and he insists, "ya que la miserable condición de nuestra vida nos puso en esta necesidad, debríase aguardar tiempo convenible para ella. . . ."[28] Later, in the *Guía de pecadores* (1556), and especially in the *Introducción del Símbolo de la Fe* (1582), Fray Luis becomes very liberal in these matters.[29]

The most curious text of all—to return to the poets—, composed at a time when the educational program of the Jesuits had long since integrated "résolument les lettres païennes dans l'enseignement chrétien,"[30] and when churchmen like Fray Juan de Pineda had proclaimed tolerance toward the *fingimientos de los poetas*,[31] is a *Psalmo*, a sort of *confesión general*, by el Licenciado Agustín Calderón, which appears in the second volume (1611) of the *Flores de poetas ilustres de España*:

> Y, lo que excede a todos mis delitos:
> cual si no fuera hijo de esa sangre,

dioses llamé los ídolos gentiles,
a quien pedia, ¡oh ciego desvario!,
la voz a Citerea,
a Palas el espíritu,
a Apolo plumas y discurso a Clío.
Ya les sacrificaba allí una fiera
mi corazón de cera,
y ya, con alma hereje, *si devota,*
en el templo colgaba
adonde idolatraba,
la túnica mojada o prisión rota.[32]

Agustín Calderón's palinode voices the extreme attitude of that *minority* that saw evil in the *Diana* and rewrote "a lo divino las obras profanas, no sólo los libros de caballerías, mas también autores de espiritualidad tan depurada como Boscán y Garcilaso."[33] This minority felt with Fray Luis de Granada in his *Libro de la oración y meditación:* "Aprende a bien morir." The great majority, like Fray Luis de Granada in the *Introducción del Símbolo de la Fe,* was concerned with the reverse of the medallion: "Aprende a bien vivir."[34] This majority, both inside[35] and outside[36] of Spain had no such scruples. It is time to turn our attention to this majority.

In *El Cancionero de Palacio*[37] there is a poem by Santa Fe, no. 266, entitled *Lohores de la Virgen María,* which begins:

De mi lengua despoblada,
clara estrela Diana,
Cibeles biua fontana,
que'speras ser loada.

In the following stanzas the Virgin is addressed as *Minerva santificada, Juno por nos advocada, Pallas illuminada,* and *crido d'Apolo eterno.* Passing from the end of the *siglo XV* to the very last year of the *siglo XVI,* we find the following text in a *Sermón de San Pedro,* by Fray Alonso de Santa Cruz:

Nunca les ha ido también [*sic:* tan bien] a los que han querido pelear con Dios y ponerse a tú por tú con el Cielo. Miremos la caída de los malos ángeles, *el castigo de los gigantes,* el fin de Faraón y de todo su ejército. . . .[38]

To both poet and preacher, in the fifteenth, sixteenth, and seventeenth centuries, the *merveilleux païen* was but a *fingimiento*. "Assí mesmo *fingen* los poetas Diana auer sido deesa de la castidat . . . ," writes Hernán Núñez, el Comendador Griego, in his commentary on Juan de Mena's *Trezientas*,[39] and the words *fingen los poetas* appear *passim* in his annotations. "Todo esto, Miçilo, cree que es mentira y *ficíon* de fabulosos *poetas*," we read in *El Crotalón*, and a little farther on the author adds: "Avnque quiero que sepas que esto que estos poetas *fingieron* no careçe del todo de misterio algo dello, porque avnque todo fué *fición*, dieron debajo de aquellas fábulas y poesías a entender gran parte de la verdad, grandes y muy admirables secretos y misterios."[40] A similar explanation is given by Hernán Pérez de Oliva in his *Diálogo de la dignidad del hombre*. The heroes of Greece and Rome were real men, he tells us, but their identity has been lost in the course of the centuries, "ya que por sus nombres no conocemos los que fueron, sino otros hombres *fingidos* que han hecho en su lugar con *fábulas*, los *poetas*."[41]

The words *ficciones*, *fición*, and *fingida* are used by Juan del Encina to explain the common use by poets of the pseudo-pagan invocation: *O lúcido loue* (Santillana),[42] *O sumo gran Joue* (Gerónimo de Artés)[43]; *Ioue potente* (Johan de Andújar)[44]; etc. Encina, speaking of the *dinidad de la poesía*, says that its origin was attributed by the ancients to their gods and to the Muses,

> según parece por las inuocaciones de los antiguos poetas: de donde nosotros las tomamos, no porque creamos como ellos ni los tengamos por dioses inuocándolos, que sería grandissimo error y eregia: mas por seguir su gala y orden poética: que es haber de proponer, inuocar y narrar o contar en las ficciones graves y arduas, de tal manera que siendo fición la obra, es mucha razón que no menos sea fingida y no verdadera la inuocación della. Mas quando hazemos alguna obra principal de deuoción o que toque a nuestra fe, inuocamos al que es la mesma Verdad o a su Madre preciosa o a algunos santos que sean intercesores y medianeros para alcanzarnos la gracia.[45]

It is in this spirit that we should interpret Encina's lament on the death of Prince John:

Lleuónoslo Dios, quedamos perdidos,
sin él nuestras glorias quedaron perdidas,
las Parcas *que dizē* que hilan las vidas
sus hilos quebraron no estando torcidos.[46]

Boscán, in his *Octava rima,* shows a similar understanding of the function of the *fingimientos de los poetas:*

Escrito está en las fábulas antiguas,
que infinitas mugeres estimadas
fueron, por ser de Amor siempre enemigas,
en piedras o alimañas transformadas.
No en balde los poetas sus fatigas
pusieron en mentiras tan soñadas;
pues desto que a la letra es vanidad
se saca en su substancia gran verdad.[47]

Fray Luis de León insisted that the poet should "trabajar el mármol pagano con manos cristianas."[48] This precept is carried out by Pedro Espinosa, than whom "ninguno . . . ha utilizado tan resueltamente los mitos antiguos para adorno de los motivos cristianos y ha expresado mejor el sentimiento de renunciamiento del mundo con tan suntuosas figuraciones, colores y efectismos."[49]

Quevedo's *canto épico, Cristo resucitado,* was dedicated to the *cristiana Musa mía.* In his description of Hell, Quevedo places among Satan's legions Alecto, Tisiphone, Megaera, Rhadamanthus, and Discord with her vicious sisters, and introduces the rivers Cocytus and Phlegethon to give a Virgilian coloring to a scene remarkable for its "blending of classical literary tradition and Christian metaphysics."[50] In the mind of Calderón, "la mitología no era más que un resto lejano de la tradición antigua, en la cual habían quedado desfiguradas y oscurecidas . . . altísimas verdades relativas al origen y destino del hombre . . . Hay más: . . . la mitología es considerada por Calderón . . . como una preparación para la ley de gracia."[51]

It is time now to turn again to the theorists. Professor Seznec studies a work published at Madrid in 1585, the *Philosophia secreta, donde debajo de historias fabulosas se contiene mucha doctrina provechosa a todos estudios, con el orijen de los Idolos o Dioses de la gentilidad,* by the mathematician Juan Pérez de Moya:

La description de chaque divinité, et le récit de ses aventures sont le plus souvent suivis d'une triple "Declaración": historique, physique et morale. Ce troisième sens est celui qui le retient davantage: car, comme l'indique son titre, il voit avant tout dans la mythologie "une philosophie cachée"; il consacre tout un livre, le cinquième, à l'étude des fables "qui exhortent les hommes à fuir les vices et à suivre la vertu"; et dans le septième et dernier, il traite de celles qui furent inventées "pour leur inspirer la crainte de Dieu."[52]

Four years later there appeared at Valladolid *Las Transformaciones de Ouidio, traduzidas del verso Latino, en tercetos y octauas rimas, por el Licenciado Viana, en lengua vulgar Castellana, con el Comento y explicación de las fábulas, reduziendolas a philosophia natural y moral y astrologia e historia,* in which there is complete accord between the classic myths and Christian belief. This is shown particularly in Libro Primero, Anotación 26, where Pedro Sánchez de Viana treats of the end of the world, the new Heaven and the new earth. In the Prólogo a los Lectores he declares:

> La vniuersal diuisión de las fábulas de que en este comento tengo de tratar, es que vnas contienen secretos de naturaleza como la de Venus de la spuma del mar, que Phebo matasse a los Cyclopes, y ellos fabriquen a Júpiter sus rayos. Otras declaran la inconstancia de la Fortuna . . . como la de Apolo que vino a ser vaquero de Admeto, otras nos apartan de suzios desseos, como la de Lycaõ, otras se inuentaron para poner terror y espanto a los hombres, y apartarlos de pretensiones feas y deshonestas, como la pena de Ixión en el infierno. Otras nos animan a obrar deligentemente y con esfuerzo los actos virtuosos, como la de los trabajos de Hércules. Otras *se fingen* para quitar la temeridad humana, como la de Phaetón, Belorophonte y Marsias, otras nos atraen a virtud, entereza de vida, fee, equidad y religion, con proponer premios, como la de los campos Elísios. Otras nos auyentan de todo vicio como la de los tres juezes infernales Radamanto, Eaco y Minos. Los quales preceptos disfraçados debaxo de *fictiones,* no sólo son tolerables a la sensibilidad y delicadeza humana: pero suaues y gustosos.

The year 1589 also saw the publication in Salamanca of Fray Juan de Pineda's *Primera Parte de los Treynta y cinco Dialogos*

familiares de la Agricvltvra Christiana, in which "el autor procuró
poner la más varia, prouechosa, curiosa, apazible y mejor prouada
doctrina que supo y pudo." No Jesuit, Pineda was a "Religioso de la
Orden del Seráphico padre Sant Francisco de la obseruancia." On
fol. 20 (and 20 v.) of this book we read:

> *Philale.* Homero entre los Griegos poetas y Ouidio entre los
> Latinos son tenidos por sapientíssimos, luego no son tenidos por
> mentirosos . . . Notad que fingir no es mentir, y se prueua con
> que el Redentor del mundo fingió en el castillo de Emaus, y es
> heregía dezir que mintió: y *los poetas fingieron* . . . aquellas
> sus narraciones para encubrir y escurecer muchas verdades ansí
> naturales como morales (y es estilo en Sacra escritura) por las
> dar a estimar al vulgo que las touiera en poco, si en lenguage
> llano y claro las hallara: y por eso vsaron todas las gentes de
> symbolos y de ceremonias mysticas en el culto divino, por con
> aquello que no es entendido del pueblo, leuantarle más a Dios.[53]

Passing from the sixteenth to the seventeenth century, we find
the *Teatro de los dioses de la Gentilidad* (Salamanca, 1620), of
Fray Baltasar de Vitoria, with an aprobación by Lope de Vega,
from which I quote (in Seznec's translation):

> Il n'est rien, dans cette histoire mythologique, qui répugne à
> notre foi, ni aux bonnes mœurs: au contraire, c'est une science
> fort importante pour l'intelligence de beaucoup de livres. Les
> anciens enveloppèrent la philosophie sous les fables, sous les
> beaux ornements de la poésie, de la peinture et de l'astrologie.
> Tous les théologiens des gentils, depuis Mercure Trismégiste
> jusqu'au divin Platon, cachèrent sous des symboles et des hiéro-
> glyphes l'explication de la nature~comme il est dit dans le *Timée*
> et le *Pimandre* que firent les Egyptiens, pour dissimuler au vul-
> gaire les vérités sacrées.[54]

La philosophie sous les fables. These words are a restatement of
the position of Juan del Encina in regard to ancient mythology.
The seventeenth century is at one with the fifteenth, and to this
extent Olympus "viveva allegramente e pacificamente accanto al
Paradiso dei Cristiani," as Farinelli asserted.[55] But we may not
disregard the dissenting voices which are heard from Juan de Mena
to Agustín Calderón. Such dissent is generally expressed toward

the end of a writer's life, and is analogous to the palinode which many poets wrote renouncing their youthful amatory works.[56] These palinodes represent what Curtius calls "moralisch- dogmatischer Rigorismus."[57] The "rigor" is born of personal attitudes on the part of the writer: Fray Luis de Granada felt it in 1554, before the promulgation of the decrees of the Council of Trent, only to soften his attitude in later years, when those decrees were known to all. The two Calderóns, Agustín and Pedro, represent the two poles; the former, a rigorist, precedes the latter in time. But of greater importance than these minority voices is the fact that the majority felt as Encina did: "siendo *ficíon* la obra, es mucha razón que no menos sea fingida la inuocación della." *Fingen los poetas.* Encina's distinction between the types of poems that allow the pseudo-pagan invocation or exclude it is fundamental. A study of the invocation in Spanish is needed, comparable to that of Curtius on "Die Musen," to show to what extent Encina's practice was followed throughout the *siglo de oro* in *obras principales de deuoción* or that *tocan a nuestra fe*, as Manrique's *Coplas* did.

6 Se Acicalaron Los Auditorios:
An Aspect of the Spanish Literary Baroque

In the year 1581 Don Luis de Góngora, a mere youth of twenty, seems to have perceived, perhaps vaguely, that Spain was entering or was about to enter a Silver Age in which "the magical, the sensory, and the gestural" were to become strong at the expense of "the human and the objectively rational," in which style was to have "a greater sensoriness than would have originally been compatible with *gravitas*."[1] He wrote:

> Ahora, que estoy despacio,
> cantar quiero en mi bandurria
> lo que en *más grave instrumento*
> cantara, mas *no me escuchan.*
> Arrímense ya las veras
> y celébrense las burlas,
> pues da el mundo en niñerías,
> al fin, como quien caduca.[2]

Whether or not this "voluntad de ser raro"[3] was forced upon the young poet as he implies, whether he would have *preferred* the "más grave instrumento" or was actually delighted to devise new ways of commanding attention by inventing *niñerías*, we can only surmise. What we do know is that Góngora was not the first or the only writer to express awareness of the new direction in Spanish taste toward the end of the sixteenth century.

For this statement I propose to offer documentation, but first I would make clear that the search for a *new* elegance, while central for an understanding of late-Renaissance literature is, as the title of the present article suggests, only an *aspect* of that literature: "Au lieu d'un siècle en évolution progressive et monochrone, on verrait se dessiner plusiers XVIIᵉ siècles parallèles, alternés ou entremêlés, au sein desquels on reconnaîtrait au Baroque la valeur d'un ferment actif et d'une composante nécessaire."[4] Literary history has always its *sic* and its *non*.[5] The same Vicente Espinel who wrote in 1587,

> hallo que al mundo seruiran de exemplo
> mis versos, llenos de passion y lloro,
> que todo es vanidad, todo locura,[6]

could declare in 1618, in the Prologue to his *Marcos de Obregón:* "digo que yo he alcanzado la Monarquía de España tan llena y abundante de gallardos espíritus en armas y letras, que no creo que la romana los tuvo mayores, y me arrojo a decir que ni tantos ni tan grandes." Even *desengaño* has its varied meanings and does not always carry the overtones of Quevedo's *¡Ah de la vida! Nadie me responde.* Antonio López de Vega in his *Paradoxas racionales* (1654), over and over again uses *desengañado* in the Stoic sense of *sapiens:* ". . . si no queréis parecer ridículo a los desengañados."[7]

The single *aspect* which I wish to point up here is purely literary: the Spanish public is declared to have ceased to be satisfied with what Ezra Pound defined as the essence of great literature, "simple language charged with meaning to an extreme degree." Readers and auditors were demanding a language which was not simple, a language "sharpened with the new brightness of paradox," as in Chapman's

> The downward-burning flame of her rich hayre.[8]

In Spain as in England writers were no longer concerned solely to communicate an experience; they were concerned—often more concerned—to fabricate a novel, attractive, intricate object, a dainty device. Themes which formerly had been pretexts for formal beauty were becoming pretexts for wit.[9] In 1555, a generation before Góngora's *mas no me escuchan*, Juan Gozález de la Torre, in his *Diálogo llamado Nuncio Legato Mortal*, explained his choice of form and style in these words: "Me movió a escribir en este estilo por ver andar el mundo tan lleno de vanidades, que ya no curan los que son *vulgares*[10] de leer cosa buena en prosa, sino que andan buscando Coplillas, Romances, Disparates y *Farsas*[11] de poco fructo. Pues que ansí es, no sé yo qué mejor *Farsa* ni Romance pueden leer, que esta farsa de la Muerte; pues *se introduzen dos personas;* y hay demandas y respuestas, ejemplos y avisos muy fructuosos."[12]

In 1570 Alfonso García de Matamoros, in his *De methodo concionandi,* criticized the departure from simplicity which he found characteristic of the pulpit oratory of his day: "El arte debe ir tan embebido en la naturaleza que no se eche de ver, como cuando se mezcla con el vino un poco de agua, que parece que todo es vino. El predicador no ha de *respresentar las cosas como en el teatro.* Hay algunos que corren un toro como si estuviesen en la plaza, o fingen que van siguiendo un pajarillo y le echan mano y lo despluman con tal propiedad, con tales muestras primero de ansiedad y luego de regocijo, dando tales saltos y voces, que realmente parecen unos chiquillos."[13]

In 1575 Juan Huarte de San Juan published his famous book on vocational guidance, the *Examen de ingenios para las sciencias,* in which of necessity he dealt with the pulpit orator. "No rechaza de plano el bien decir y hablar en el púlpito," notes Mauricio de Iriarte, S.J., in his study of Huarte's differential psychology, because "hoy, *recibida la fe y de tantos años atrás,*[14] bien se permite predicar con lugares retóricos." But Huarte adds, not without irony: "Esto no es menester encargarlo a los predicadores de nuestro tiempo . . . porque su estudio particular . . . es buscar un buen tema a quien puedan aplicar a propósito muchas sentencias galanas . . . sin perdonar ciencia alguna, hablando copiosamente, con elegancia y dulces palabras; con todo lo cual dilatan y ensanchan el tema una hora y dos si es menester." And he procedes to make sport of the preachers who yield to the popular demand for *farsas* —as Juan González de la Torre had done twenty years earlier: "La acción se ha de moderar haciendo los meneos y gestos que el dicho requiere: alzando la voz y bajándola; enojándose, y tornarse luego a apaciguar; unas veces hablar a priesa, otras a espacio; reñir y halagar; menear el cuerpo a una parte y a otra; coger los brazos y desplegarlos; reír y llorar; y dar una palmada en buena ocasión. Esta gracia es tan importante en los predicadores, que con sola ella, sin tener invención ni disposición, de cosas de poco momento y vulgares hacen un sermón que *espanta* al auditorio."[15]

In 1579 Fray Diego Velades protests against all this in his *Rheto-*

rica christiana: "La verdad recta y sencilla no necesita colores postizos ni luces extrañas; al contrario, eso la hace sospechosa, porque no sabe fingir lo que no es."[16]

In 1580 Francisco de Medina, in his Prologue to Herrera's *Anotaciones,* shared the feeling of González de la Torre against *los que son vulgares*[17]: "Se [pierde] estimación en allanarse a la inteligencia del pueblo." He too spoke of the ornamental style—"de mil colores"—of certain preachers.[18]

In 1588 Fray Pedro Malón de Chaide, in his *Conversión de la Magdalena,* repeated the earlier complaints: "He querido poner aquí este salmo entero . . . porque, como ya he dicho en el prólogo, están los gustos tan estragados con los muchos vicios, que para que puedan comer algo que les sea de provecho, es menester dársele guisado con mil salsillas, y aun plega a Dios que de esta suerte lo detengan y no lo vomiten, como comida indigesta. Y no sé si me engaño, pero pienso que con los versos se desempalagarán, para mejor tragar la prosa."[19]

To the same year of 1588 belongs a complaint from the *De sacra ratione concionandi* of Fray Diego Pérez de Valdivia: "Pero, ¿qué, dirá alguno, no se ha de aderezar un poco la palabra de Dios para que la reciban con más gusto los oyentes? No; porque vendremos a parar a lo de antes: los oyentes, engolosinados con el estilo, se pararán en él y no probarán el alimento sólido del Evangelio. Los Apóstoles lo predicaban con toda sencillez. . . . Y las gentes lo recibían con gusto y con provecho. Ahora, en cambio, lo predicamos con todos los aderezos habidos y por haber, y ya vemos lo que pasa, que muchos no quieren oír la verdad."[20]

In 1589 Juan Bonifacio, S.J., in his *De sapiente fructuoso,* exclaimed: "Es vergonzoso que un predicador ande buscando florecillas y ponga en eso todo su cuidado. La verdadera elocuencia no necesita postizos ni coloretes; le bastan sus colores naturales y la hermosura que le da su propia robustez y la riqueza y pureza de su sangre. . . . No es la voz suave del predicador ni su lenguaje florido lo que cautiva al auditorio, sino la grandeza y hermosura de las cosas que dice."[21]

There is considerable significance, for our problem, in Pedro Simón Abril's analysis of the condition of Spanish eloquence in this same year of 1589. Eloquence, he says, is now restricted to the pulpit, since government in modern times does not depend upon swaying the populace as it did in Athens or in Cicero's Rome. In Spain, even lawsuits are decided *por escrito:* "Por esto convendria, que pues ya ni en los Senados, ni en las Audiencias no hay materia para semejantes oraciones, se traduxessen del Latin, y del Griego las mejores oraciones de Tulio, y de Demostenes, y los Sermones de aquellos grandes Predicadores San Basilio, San Chrisostomo, San Cyrillo, San Leon, por personas que supiessen representar sus virtudes y estilo en la lengua popular, para que estos sirviessen de exemplo y experiencia de como debe usarse y exercitarse la Rhetorica."[22]

In 1601 the "Claustro de doctores y maestros en todas facultades" of the University of Salamanca, considering whether it was wise to permit the use of the vernacular in works of spiritual content, wrote into the record of their meeting that there was "poca devoción el día de oy en oyr los sermones . . . y los que van a oyr, muchos van por curiosidad . . . o por entretenimiento y gusto del lenguaje de las floridas razones, como quien va a oyr un rato de música que suena dulze y suauemente, y no buscan el espíritu y verdad del Evangelio."[23] The professors also stressed the part played in this unfortunate development by the *vulgo:* "los discretos predicadores con mucha razón temen ya el officio de predicar, lo vno porque apenas hallarán cosa que decir que no esté ya escripta en los libros de romançe y lo otro *temen* con mucha razon *la censura del vulgo* que como lo hallan todo escripto en los libros de romançe todos se hazen çensores de lo que el predicador dize."[24]

Sometime around the year 1609 Góngora and Fray Hortensio Félix de Paravicino discovered that, independently and each in his own field, they were endeavoring to do the same thing: "[producir] *sorpresa* y deleite, maravilla y entretenimiento."[25] Pellicer declared Paravicino to be "*assombro* y ornamento de su nación."[26] He, more than any other, gave to Spanish sacred oratory that "sensoriness" which Auerbach found to be characteristic of the Latin writers of the Silver Age.[27] Emilio Alarcos considers him an "ingenio barroco de primera categoría . . . más admirable que imitable" (p. 319). In his own eyes he too was a victim of the *vulgo,* of those who *diserti esse volunt magis quam boni:* "las conversaciones [de Cuaresma] son sermones, todas a costa de los predicadores, con ningún provecho de los oyentes, porque nos venís a juzgar más que a oyr" (p. 173, n. 2). He complains that preaching has become histrionics: "por nuestra desgracia han llegado los sermones tan a la necesidad misma de agrado que las *comedias*" (ibid.).

Another testimony, of the year 1617, when Francisco Terrones del Caño published his *Instrucción de predicadores*, voicing the old lament: "Piensan algunos que se ha de hablar por vocablo y artificio exquisito, con muchas flores de elocución. Si una ciudad estuviese cercada de enemigos y dándole asalto, tirando los enemigos pelotas de artillería, y los de dentro tirasen flores, ¿sería ésta buena defensa? Los vicios acometen, como enemigos, a asaltar las almas; los predicadores, son sus defensores; mejor harían de arrojar pelotas contra los vicios que flores para las orejas del auditorio."[28] In his moments of discouragement he verged on despair: "Y si no hay hombres ni caudal sino para tratar cosas muy vulgares, mejor es dejar el oficio; que *están ya los auditorios tan acicalados* que predicándoles cosas muy comunes, las desprecian."[29]

We shall end our survey in 1629, although the topic extends to Gracián and the end of the century, as Alarcos shows. In his *Aforismos y reglas para mas bien ejercer el alto oficio de la predicacion evangélica segun dotrina de santos y escritores antiguos y modernos*, printed at Antequera in that year, Fray Diego León y Moya insists that "no es oficio de necios el predicar" and concedes that those who practice it should possess "buena gracia y donaire sabroso para dar vida a lo que dijere[n]," although he denounces the tendency to yield to the demands of the *auditorio acicalado*: "Nunca se comience . . . con fábula, hieroglífico o poesía . . . tampoco deben hacerse las entradas con palabras artificiosas que lleven torrente *como loas de comedia*."

The language of the sermon should be "romance casto y limpio," neither *culto* nor *conceptista*: "La elocuencia . . . que se debe seguir . . . no está en hablar con términos nuevos, nunca oídios, esquisitos, frases singulares, locuciones puramente simbólicas, y tan figurativas que ninguno o muy pocos las entiendan; que es multilocuencia y parlería. . . . No se saque el romance de sus quicios, ni se afecte de manera que sea tan dificultoso de entender para el vulgo, como si se hablara latín."

He rejects all histrionics: "Si dijese que uno se rascaba, no se ha de rascar el predicador." "No ha de haber en el púlpito . . . lo que en los *tablados*. 'La yerba verde y aljofarada matizada con la roja sangre, que la cruda mano de la sobrehumana ninfa derramó—el pajarillo con su harpada lengua,' etc., que esto es mejor para *farsa*, y propio lenguaje de *cómicos*."

Of special interest is a protest not heard before—that there be no exploitation of the picaresque style in the pulpit: "téngase recato que no se usen jamás vocablos *apicarados*. Uno dijo que 'Acabando que acabó Noé de beber el vino . . . quedó hecho équis uñas arriba . . . ' Otros por decir 'golpe o cuchillada' dicen 'decendimiento de manos' y 'No lo conocerá Galván,' 'a lo de Vive Cristo': cosas todas más de la *seguida* [i.e., de la vida airada] que del lenguaje del cristiano, cuanto y más del púlpito."

And he is no less severe against an earlier abuse—the insertion into the sermon of the preacher's professional jargon: "No se digan en ninguna manera términos ni vocablos escolásticos."[30]

It will have been observed that in these protests there are two *leitmotifs:* the auditors, often referred to as the *vulgo*, are, like Lope's *mosqueteros*, the ones who have called the tune and they therefore share with the preachers responsibility for a state of affairs which is religious and moral, to be sure, but also *literary*. According to the testimony, it was the auditors who in large part determined the development away from simplicity to an ever increasing *afán de novedad*. And these same auditors, blood brothers of the *mosqueteros*, demanded *dramatic* action in the pulpit: "han llegado los sermones tan a la necesidad misma de agrado que las comedias."

In an earlier study I have shown that there was a creativeness in the action of the *vulgo* on the development of the Spanish *comedia*, and that this creativeness was at times recognized by critics, notably by Jusepe Antonio González de Salas.[31] If we look forward to Fray Gerundio, we must regard as deleterious the influence of the *vulgo* on the development of prose style; but if we stop with Paravicino, Góngora's contemporary and friend, the judgment will be more favorable. His *afán de novedad*, his *sutileza y ornamentación* in prose are the counterpart of Góngora's revolution in verse and make of him the "ingenio barroco de primera categoría" that

he unquestionably was.[32] It was because he found a ready acceptance of the newness he had to offer, because audiences were *ya
acicalados*, that he became the most influential preacher of his age,
the master of "the magical, the sensory, and the gestural."[33] It is
thus seen that the *comedia* was not the only genre that was—almost
—a communal enterprise. In pulpit oratory also, and in prose generally, the nation as a whole determined the character of its culture:
se acicalaron los ingenios, even among the *vulgo*.

There is an interesting sequel. In an article entitled "La oratoria
sagrada en el seiscientos"[34] Luis López Santos published the record
of a polemic between two Jesuits, Padre Valentín Céspedes and
Padre Joseph de Ormaza, in the year 1648. Each defends tenaciously his own choice between the two prevailing schools of
pulpit oratory—the *antiguos* and the *modernos*, Céspedes speaking
for the old school and Ormaza for the new—and each accuses the
rival school of "delitos y vicios." The *antiguos* are accused of
lumbering up their sermons with quotations from the Bible and the
Fathers: "todo son pegotes." What is worse, these quotations do
not bolster doctrine; they are mostly "narraciones e historias." But
contrary to what might be expected, this extraneous erudition, far
from boring the audiences, delights them with profane enticements
because the *antiguos* actually *act out* the stories. They are, in short,
farsantes[35]: "cruje la honda, truena el estallido y ondean las mangas
del orador," as Goliath falls. Such procedure is stoutly defended by
Céspedes: "el predicador es *un representante a lo divino*, y sólo se
distingue del farsante en las materias que trata." He insists: "La
representación . . . perfecta con las partes que he dicho deleita y
suspende." Giving actual examples of such dramatizing, he declares
that those of his school "lo [hacen] con tal propiedad, viveza y
gracia que [prorrumpen] los oyentes en aplausos gritados, siendo
necesario parar hasta que [cese] el tumulto."[36] And he explains the
theory which lies back of his approval: the preacher should rely
for his *idea*s on authority, as do lawyers, physicians, and "los
escolásticos." Only the *manner* of presentation should be original.
Indeed, the elimination of "authorities"—"el afán de rechazar los
textos e historias bíblicas"—continues to be, he asserts, "uno de los
más perjudiciales huevos que empolló Erasmo para que Lutero
sacase a luz."

The school of the *modernos* condemns both this theory and this procedure, believing—with Huarte de San Juan—that where religious assent is universal ideas are not important, *there being nothing to prove.* The preacher, says Ormaza, should use his originality to invent *conceptos* for the purpose of *moving the will.* Doctrine should be introduced only by indirection, "de rebozo." Style is not merely "la parte principal, sino *el todo* de la oración." His opponent Céspedes describes "modern" preaching in terms which, except for the use of pejorative suffixes and adjectives, might well be those of Ormaza himself: "es [una predicación] con punticos de mucho garbo, adornados de unos concepticos picados y picantes . . . atendiendo a la dulce cadencia del estilo." The "moderns," says Céspedes, have only one purpose: "la vana ostentación de la agudeza . . . el agrado y el aplauso de los cultos."[37]

De los cultos. But certainly not only the *cultos* listened to sermons. Here, as in the case of the *comedia,* we have the intermingling and the interaction of *cortesano* and *oficial.* Here again we have proof that Cervantes was right when—in the *Viaje del Parnaso*—he declared the *vulgo* of Madrid to be *discreto.*[38] The public that would hiss a *comedia* from the boards if its scansion were faulty could—and did—demand of its preachers a language worthy of an *auditorio acicalado*—a demand which appears to have had more than a small part in the development of the baroque in Spain.

7 *Boscán and* Il Cortegiano: *The* Historia de Leandro y Hero

It is well known that in this expansion of the 341 hexameters of Musaeus' καθ' 'Ηρὼ καὶ Λέανδρον into the 2793 hendecasyllables of his own *Historia de Leandro y Hero*, Boscán made use not only of the Greek text or its Latin translation,[1] but also of Ovid's epistles *Leander Heroni* and *Hero Leandro*,[2] from which he took certain details; of Bernardo Tasso's *Favola di Leandro ed Hero*[3]; and of Virgil's *Georgics*, from which he took the long episode of Aristaeus.[4]

Menéndez y Pelayo attributes to the influence of the *Heroides*, the fact that Boscán chose to make of his *Historia* "no una viva y eficaz representación de los afectos . . . sino un comentario perpetuo y prolijo de los pensamientos y acciones de sus personajes, como anuncia desde los primeros versos:

> El mirar, el hablar, el entenderse,
> el ir del uno, el esperar del otro,
> El desear y el acudir *conforme*,"

and insists that

> Con esto alteró torpemente la índole del poema griego, desconoció su bellísima sobriedad, enervó su estilo con insípidas menudencias y . . . se perdió en un mar de palabrería insubstancial. . . .[5]

The word *conforme* in the lines just quoted is one of many Platonic echoes in Boscán's poem. Indeed, what Boscán endeavored to do was to convert Musaeus' priestess of Aphrodite into a Renaissance *dama*, and to bring the passion of both lovers into conformity with the code of Platonic love as set forth in Castiglione's *Il Cortegiano*, of which Boscán was the brilliant translator.[6]

After the Invocation, Boscán expands Musaeus' lines 16–23 into 23 *versos sueltos*. One word—*saber*—looks forward to the development which is to follow. Musaeus' "similes inter se"[7] becomes "Iguales en linaje y en hacienda, / En valer, en *saber* y en hermosura."[8] It is the first indication of the Castiglione-Boscán ideal of aristocratic womanhood:

> . . . es necesario que la Dama . . . tenga noticia de muchas cosas, porque, tratando agora de las unas y agora de las otras, haga su conversación larga, agradable y sustancial.[9]
> . . . quiero que esta Dama tenga noticia de letras, de música, de pinturas.[10]

The next 19 hexameters become, by a similar process of expansion, 53 *endecasílabos* in which Boscán presents the *dama* as he conceives her:

> . . . repartiendo
> Sus horas en honestos exercicios,
> Para vivir sabrosa y *cuerdamente*.
> Este lugar sus padres se le dieron;
> Pero no se le dieron por guardalla
> Con guardas, ni con premias, ni estrechezas;
> *Su misma voluntad era su guarda*.
> Su vivir era *libre*, mas no suelto;
> Haciendo sin querer quanto quería,
> No hacía sino *lo razonable*
> Y en esta discordancia concordaba.[11]

She is thus a perfect type of Renaissance *temperancia*, of Stoic *virtus*, and of Platonic harmony:

> la temperancia *libre* de toda turbación y movimiento es semejante al . . . capitán, que sin pelea y sin contradición vence y reina, y habiendo en el alma donde se halla, no solamente remediado en parte, mas del todo muerto el fuego de los deseos, como buen príncipe, cuando un pueblo echa a dos partes y pelean entre sí unos con otros, destruye los alborotadores enemigos familiares y *da el mando y señorío entero a la razón*, y *no forzando a nuestro sentido*, sino infundiéndonos sabrosamente una fuerte y firme *persuasión* que nos inclina al bien, hácenos estar *sosegados*

y llenos de reposo, iguales en todo y bien medidos, y por donde quiera compuestos de una cierta *concordia con nosotros mismos,* que nos mejora y nos da lustre con una bonanza tan clara, que jamás nos añublamos ni nos turbamos, sino que somos hechos en todo *conformes con la razón,* y prestos y aparejados a enderezar hacia ella todos nuestros movimientos.[12]

Musaeus' lines 55–85 describe Hero's beauty, and its effect on the young men of Sestos. Boscán, in his expansion (p. 294), gives to this beauty a new quality:

> En su cuerpo su alma se mostraba,
> Y víase también claro en su alma,
> Que a tal alma tal cuerpo se debía.[13]

Hero exemplifies the courtly virtue par excellence: *huir de la afectación:*

> Levantaba los ojos a su tiempo,
> Sin parecer que se acordaba dello,
> Dando con un descuido mil cuidados.[14]

And she has the supreme gift of "tener gracia natural en todas las cosas"[15]:

> El andar, el mirar, *el estar queda,*
> Andaban en tal son, que descubrían
> *Un cierto no sé qué,* tan admirable,
> Tan tendido por todo y por sus partes,
> Con tal orden y fuerza recogido,
> Que era imposible dalle lugar cierto.[16]

There is a very clear reference to Platonic contemplation:

> Decía más: Mis ojos son vencidos
> De tanta luz, de *contemplar* tan alto;
> Mas *la parte inmortal* nunca se vence
> Del *manjar natural* de que ella vive.[17]

Among Hero's admirers is Leander, a non-Platonic lover in Musaeus,[18] in Boscán an exemplar of "el verdadero amor" which

ha de ser bueno y siempre ha de producir efetos buenos en las
almas de aquellos que con el freno de la razón corrigen la malicia
del sentido.[19]

It is through the avenue of the eyes that the heart is smitten:

> Y empezó a recebir aquella vista,
> De aquel sol que aserenaba el mundo.
> Dexó estender sus rayos por su alma
> Echando su calor y luz por ella;
> Y así le esclareció y él levantóse,
> Con nuevos alborozos levantados,
> Y empezó con Amor a entrar en cuenta,
> Acordando de no dexar morirse.[20]

As the moments pass, Leandro

> . . . empezó de dar indicios
> De temor y de amor y de deseo,[21]

of that *deseo* which by definition is identical with love:

> Digo, pues, que según la definición de los antiguos sabios,
> amor no es otra cosa sino un deseo de gozar lo que es hermoso.[22]

Hero is at first gently flattered by his attentions

> Que la hacían pensar su hermosura,
> Teniéndola contenta de sus gracias (p. 299).

There is progression, however:

> Aquésta fué la principal entrada,
> La primera a lo menos por donde ella
> Al deleite empezó de abrir la puerta.
> Comenzó a querer bien sanamente,
> Sanamente según ella entendía,
> Mas este su entender era engañoso.
> Debaxo de esta sanidad andaba
> La pestilencia, entrando por las venas,
> Esperando matar súpitamente.
> Y la razón estaba descuidada. . . (p. 300).

This also is in accord with the *Cortesano*'s code: the force of passion is recognized as existing, with some degree of inevitability, especially in the young:

> . . . y puesto que la razón, procediendo por sus argumentos adelante, llegue a escoger el bien, y conozca la hermosura no nacer del cuerpo, y por el mismo caso tenga la rienda corta a los deseos no buenos, todavía contemplándola siempre el entendimiento en aquel cuerpo de la persona amada, *se le turba y trastorna hartas veces el verdadero juicio*.[23]

And Hero

> Abaxó los sus ojos *blandamente*
> Con una pura virginal vergüenza. . .
> Luego después los levantó a su tiempo,
> Volviéndose a Leandro mansamente.
> Mas esto fué con ademán tan *cuerdo*,
> Que el *seso* se mostró muy descubierto,
> Y de amor pareció solo una sombra (pp. 300–301).[24]

Her love is "un puro amor" (p. 301), in accordance with the code, as is that of Leandro: "Mostró con puro amor puro deseo" (p. 303).[25]

But love is, by definition, desire:

> El deseo empezó a tomar la mano,
> Siguiendo el esperanza por sus pasos (p. 302),

and Leandro:

> . . . sin ver lo que hacía,
> Perdido el miedo que el amor le daba,
> Perdido el conocer del desacato,
> Perdido el contemplar del valer della,
> Perdido el contentarse con miralla, . . .
> Perdida, en fin, la fuerza de su alma,
> Atrevióse a tomar *la mano* de Hero,
> De Hero la mano se atrevió a tomalla;
> Mas esto fue con un ardor tamaño,
> De una congoxa tal, tan entrañable,

> Con un gemir tan baxo y tan profundo,
> De su necesidad tan gran testigo,
> Que desculpó la culpa del *pecado* (p. 305).[26]

Hero's reaction would have pleased Castiglione's Bembo:

> Ella al punto que vió tan nuevo hecho,
> Y se sintió tan presto salteada,
> No supo qué hacer de sí, ni supo
> Sino quedar tan atajada desto,
> Que *ni pudo estar brava ni enojarse,*
> Ni pudo atrás tirar su blanca mano,
> Por *no dar a entender lo que entendía,*
> Y por *disimular* consigo misma
> Lo que después disimular no pudo.
> Así que estando honesta estuvo queda (p. 306).[27]

Leandro's advances having been excessively rapid, the priestess of Venus, like Bembo's *dama,* reacts with *esquivez:*

> —O hombre, que veniste por mal tuyo
> A este templo a deslustrar mi honra,
> Sin entender quán gran locura emprendes,
> No sabes tú que soy sierva de Venus,
> Y virgen, y por virgen que la sirvo? . . .
> Vete y jamás parezcas do estuviere (p. 307).[28]

Greatly expanding Musaeus' lines 132–237, Boscán traces the course of true love in accordance with Renaissance concepts (pp. 307–323). Leandro's love is as far removed from the body as nature and youth permit:

> Constreñido por él [el amor] a tus pies me echo,
> Ofreciéndote el alma por don grande
> Para Dios, quanto más para los hombres!
> El cuerpo ha de ir tras ella en compañía,
> Súfrele, pues es cuerpo de tu alma,
> Que la mía es ya tuya puramente,
> Por ley de amor escrita en nuestras almas (p. 308).[29]

Yet the tradition of these lovers required that their love should consist of more than sight:

Las vírgenes irán tras su Diana. . .
Tú y las que estáis a Venus consagradas,
En lecho conyugal habéis de veros. . .
Si quieres tanto honrarme que me quieras
Por marido y por siervo, yo soy tuyo (pp. 309–310).[30]

This declaration is followed by "sollozos,"

De lágrimas cuajada su garganta (p. 311).[31]

The *ley de amor* asserts itself with unwonted speed:

Quererte por señor y por marido
Juzga tú mismo aquí si he de querello.
Pero cómo será? que abiertamente
No podrá ser, que no querrán mis padres (p. 314).

There follows the "marriage," without ceremonies or witnesses
—a procedure which had ample classical precedent[32] and which was
to assume great importance in Spanish literature[33]:

Desta arte platicaban sus conciertos,
Y en palabras y en obras pretendían
Entre ellos concluído casamiento.
Mas al cabo lo más que refirmaron,
Fue venir él a nado como dixo (p. 319).

As he prepares to leave Sestos, Leander passes by Hero's tower
in order to note well its situation against his return,

Y acudiéronle mil cosas tan juntas
Que un rato le turbaron el juicio (p. 320).[34]

Turning from Musaeus to Ovid's epistle *Leander Heroni*, Boscán inserts an interval of ten days[35] between the lovers' first encounter and the first showing of the light, and includes, by way of
explanation, the tale of Aristaeus as given in the *Georgics*, IV,
317 ff. His possible reasons for doing this, and the inartistic result,
should not concern us here, and we skip 794 *versos sueltos*, after
which we are told of the first crossing, and how Leandro

A todo satisfizo de tal arte
Que el amor de los dos quedó en un punto

Correspondiente el uno con el otro. . .
Y quedaron entrambos desde entonces
Atados a la ley del matrimonio (p. 359).

With this, love ceases to be Platonic, and Castiglione is no longer guide. The transition is bold, but effective:

Vuélvete a mí, y en mí toma venganza
Del viento y de la mar y de la noche;
Entrégate de quanto has trabajado,
Entrégate de quanto has padecido,
Y entrégate de mí, que estó entregada (p. 359).

There follows the long separation during the winter's storms, the fatal crossing, and the final despair and suicidal plunge of Hero:

Tras esto, así sin más pensar su muerte,
Dexándose caer de la ventana,
Dió sobre el cuerpo muerto de Leandro,
Que aun entonces se le acababa el mundo.
Así fueron juntas las dos almas
A los campos Elíseos para siempre (p. 376).[36]

Neither this act of suicide, nor Boscán's concern with Platonic and Stoic concepts, can be regarded as pointing toward non-christian tendencies in Boscán's thinking or feeling, as a complete study of Boscán will show. Greek and Roman ethics and moral wisdom were regarded, both by Boscán and by Castiglione, as aids and handmaidens of Christian morality:

. . . acordaríale más. . . , que fuese verdaderamente buen cristiano . . . porque desta manera juntando *con la humana prudencia* el temor de Dios y la verdad de nuestra religión cristiana, terná de su mano la buena fortuna, y a Dios por protector, el cual siempre le hará próspero en la paz y en la guerra.[37]

8 Desengaño

It is doubtful whether any institution can survive very long when it directs desire towards ends without, at the same time, supplying the adequate means for achieving those ends.[1]

Rancor is the antithesis of the Christian spirit. The Christian knows that the Creation is nothing in comparison to God; but he mitigates this nihilism with his respect for the work of God's hands.[2]

Independent of and quite separate from the awareness of national decline . . . ; independent, also, of the widespread idea of a cyclical movement of history and a growing-old both of the world and of the human race; independent of—or at least not caused by— Counter-Reformational pressures imposed from above to cause a return to a hell-fire conception of humanity; and finally no less independent of causative effects produced by the racism that darkened many aspects of the life of Spain, there grew up in our period a literature of considerable bulk on the subject of disillusionment.

This was no new phenomenon, but a differentiating tone of intensity was perceived even by contemporaries. Fray Francisco Palanco, in his approbation of Quevedo's treatise *On the Constancy and Patience of Saintly Job* (1641), declared that those meditations have a greater Christian utility

> than other works of the author; for although he always has appeared as *desengañado* [that is to say, undeceived by the beguilements of life] even when his writings were festive and jocose in nature, in his earlier poems and essays the disillusionment was a sort of play-acting, a holiday jousting in which the lances were

thrown for pleasure, not in anger. Here, on the contrary, there is no play, no jesting. The lances are thrown in all seriousness, and their steel points are so sharp that they penetrate to the inmost recesses of any thoughtful heart. The author does not flatter; he strikes.[3]

This *desengaño* is related to the sort of awakening to the nature of reality that the Prodigal Son must have experienced: "I will arise and go to my father." This waking to true awareness is called *caer en la cuenta:* to have the scales fall from one's eyes, to see things as they are. Such a state of mind is desirable. Disillusionment comes to be viewed, even to be venerated, as a sort of wisdom—the wisdom of the Stoic *sapiens*, or wise man of antiquity, who was fully aware of what constituted the *summum bonum*, the supreme good, and was utterly unenticed by everything else; a wisdom perhaps not unlike what the French mean today by their phrase *n'être pas dupe*, to be nobody's fool. Antonio López de Vega in his *Paradoxas racionales* (1635) uses the word *desengaño* (or *desengañado* or even *cuerdo*, "sane") in this sense over and over again: "but I warn you that if you do not wish to appear ridiculous in the eyes of the undeceived . . ."[4]; "and so we who are undeceived laugh heartily and justly at their silly choice and misguided complacency" (*ed. cit.*, p. 73); "Eternal Providence even makes use of the stupidity of mankind for the good government of the universe; and though the deceived ones are so numerous, we who are wise may rejoice in the better portion that is ours" (p. 74).

Covarrubias, in his *Tesoro de la lengua castellana*, recognizes the positive values that the word *desengaño* may connote. Under the key word *Desengañar* he defines the noun *desengaño* as "the clear and straightforward manner whereby we undeceive another; or the truth itself which undeceives us."[5] In harmony with the second of these meanings, Fray Luis de León, in the dedication of his edition of the works of Santa Teresa, tells how the human soul becomes *desengañada de lo que la falsa imaginación le ofrecía*—freed from the enticements of the false images of things, conjured up by the imagination—and Quevedo in his treatise *The Cradle and the Grave* (1633) applies the same figure of speech to the last breath of every person: *desengaña al hombre de sí mismo*—it corrects all false ideas of the self.[6]

Much earlier use of this acceptation of both verb and noun is found in the *Segunda comedia de Celestina* (1534) of Feliciano de Silva: *desengáñate dese engaño el desengaño que en todas las cosas desta vida hay*—"open your eyes to the deceitfulness of the deception of the things of the world."[7] On the whole, however, I find that the state of mind—or the transformation of mental and emotional attitudes—here studied is normally expressed in the earlier period by words other than *desengaño*[8]—a fact which may account for the contention of so many observers that *desengaño* was born around 1550 and extended onward through the seventeenth century, becoming the key word for the interpretation of the years of Spain's waning fortunes.[9] The word is not used, for example, where it might reasonably be expected to be employed with telling effect in an early poem of "consolation": Don Francisco de Castilla's *Dialogue between Human Misery and Consolation*, first printed in the 1518 edition of the *Cancionero general* of Hernando del Castillo,[10] and reprinted (in shorter form) in the *Cancionero* printed at Sevilla in 1527 and (in full) in Don Francisco's *Theórica de virtudes* (1564). Yet the word was known and used in the acceptation that concerns us in a manuscript listed by Gallardo, composed many years before 1550: *El consejero del desengaño, delineado en la vida de Felipe el Hermoso*—"Disillusionment the Best Counselor, as Seen in the Life of Philip the Fair." This is not Philip the Fair of France but Philip of Burgundy (Philip I of Spain, consort of Queen Joanna the Mad), who died in the year 1506.

As an element in the titles of printed books, the word *desengaño* belongs almost entirely to the seventeenth century, if one may judge by the portion of the index of Nicolás Antonio's *Bibliotheca Hispana Nova* entitled "Moralia, Documenta, Politico-Moralia, Philosophico-Moralia," which lists the following: *El desengaño del mundo* (ca. 1602); *Desengaños del mundo* (1611); *Engaños y desengaños del mundo* (1656); *Desengaño del eclesiástico en el amor de los parientes* (1670).[11]

The attitude of mental and emotional superiority—"to see life steadily and see it whole"—which the word *desengaño* and its derivatives so constantly imply is characteristic of a manuscript written in the decidedly early year of 1576 by Dr. Francisco de Abila: *Dialogues in Which an Effort Is Made to Remove the Presumption and Pride of the Man Whom the Favor and Prosperity of the World Have Rendered Proud and Vainglorious; and to*

*Instill Courage and Spirit into the Man Who Is Weary and Bowed
Down by Hardship and Adversity.* This book, obviously a reincar-
nation of old works of Stoic consolation such as Petrarch's *Reme-
dies for Good and Evil Fortune,* is described by Gallardo in his
bibliographical *Ensayo.*[12] It is unavailable to me, but Gallardo's
account of its "Argument" is highly suggestive. The author explains that there is one reappearing personage in every one of his
dialogues—the allegorical figure of *Desengaño*—according to the
following plan: in the "Dialogue of the King's Favorite," we have
the Favorite plus *Desengaño;* in the "Dialogue of the Man with No
Friend at Court (*desfavorecido*), we have the Unfavored One plus
Desengaño; and so on for each of the twenty-six divisions of the
volume.

All of this is instructive. *Desengaño* is here the voice of wisdom,
presumably of Stoic wisdom. One is to be neither elated when he
becomes the king's favorite (*Desengaño* will undeceive him) nor
downcast when he has no friend at court (*Desengaño* will show
him the blessedness of more humble callings than that of royal
favorite).

Taking a long leap forward into time (and into changed circumstances),[13] we encounter another manuscript, also described by
Gallardo (II, cols. 930–31), which, though unseen and unread,
may teach us much: Francisco de Eraso y Arteaga's *El desengaño
discreto y retiro entretenido,* composed some time after 1636. We
should first note the adjective *discreto*—discreet in the sense of
intellectually distinguished[14]—applied to the noun *desengaño;* the
noun *retiro* (a pleasure ground laid out with trees, shrubbery,
pleasant walks, etc.); and finally the adjective *entretenido,* suggestive of enjoyable entertainment, as in Agustín de Rojas' *El viaje
entretenido* (1603). There is not the slightest suggestion of asceticism, not to mention hatred of the world or contempt for human
existence.

The first chapter of the manuscript contains an introductory
explanation, copied by Gallardo: A melancholy frame of mind of
long standing which disturbed the spirit of the ever great lord Don
Manuel Alonso Pérez de Guzmán el Bueno, eighth duke of Medina
Sidonia, caused him to construct in a brief space of time an elaborate palace and pleasure garden in the best of conceivable retreats, a

pleasance which was recognized as truly great. To it he gave the name of *Desengaño*, a title well suited to the disillusionment which the duke felt in the midst of his greatness. Its site was in the most elevated and pleasing portion of a wide valley, so brightly abundant in flowers and fruits that it seemed to be the habitation of all the springs that ever were. This flower-dotted slope was watered by a brook, not of ordinary snow, but of silver and pearls flowing over white slate and clean stones on its way to the sea. Beyond there were numerous gardens and groves.

Many of the rooms had as their chief adornment fine tapestries and wise and learned books, wherein the sciences appeared to best advantage and gave best proof of their valuable contributions to mankind. After its illustrious owner passed on to a better life, in 1636, the glory of this marvelous place lasted but a few years. Although the ninth duke of Medina Sidonia maintained and rebuilt certain parts of this monument to his father, he at length desisted, giving his attention "to matters of greater importance"—for which cause that which could not have been greater fell to a diminished state.

Mention has been made of the adjective *discreto* ("intelligent") in the title of the book and of the presence of an excellent library in the duke's palace. We are given further information on this aspect of the remarkable "pleasure dome." It was the seat of a sort of private academy, composed of seven men of talent (*ingenios*), which held its meetings on the seven days of the week. Gallardo tells us the subjects of seven of the weekly discourses. We shall note five of them, delivered by the academicians under assumed poetic names: "On the Excellence of Solitude"; "On Self-Knowledge"; "Explanation of Love and Its Effects"; "On the Source and the Effects of Jealousy"; "Whether Knowledge or Experience Is More Important for the Preservation of Mankind." On the seventh day a comedy was performed, "Where There's Love There's No Offense."

GRACIÁN AND EL CRITICÓN

Caer en la cuenta—to come to oneself—was the phrase most used in connection with the type of *desengaño* we are considering here. It signified a passing from ignorance to knowledge, an awakening from the falsity of one's dream. Baltasar Gracián—no pessimist—in the allegory of this awakening which he entitled *El Criticón*, places the blame for life's confusion where it belongs: on man, not on the Creator. "Numerous and great are the monstrosities which appear each day in the dangerous pilgrimage which is our life," he causes Critilo to lament at the beginning of *Crisi* V of Part III, and continues:

> The most monstrous of all is the placing of Deceit at the world's front gate and Disillusionment at the exit—a disastrous handicap sufficient to ruin our life entirely, since . . . to make a misstep at the beginning of life causes one to lurch headlong with greater speed each day and end up in utter perdition. Who made such an arrangement, who ordained it? Now I am more convinced than ever that all is upside down in this world. Disillusionment should stand at the world's entrance and should place himself immediately at the shoulder of the neophyte, to free him from the dangers that lie in wait for him. But since the new-comer—by an opposite and contrary arrangement—makes his first encounter with Deceit (who at the beginning presents everything to him in perverted and reversed order), he heads for the left-hand road, and strides on to destruction.[15]

Critilo looks about in vain for his Decipherer, but the latter has disappeared in the universal confusion of smoke and ignorance. By rare good fortune, however, a bystander who has overheard the lament comes forward and says: "You have every reason to complain of the senselessness of the world, but you should not ask who ordained it, but who has upset it; not who disposed it as it is, but who has put everything into reverse. For you must know that the Supreme Artificer planned things very differently at the beginning, since He stationed Disillusionment on the threshold of the world, and cast Deceit into outer darkness" (*ibid.*, p. 150).

To Critilo's repeated question, who did bring this about?, the stranger replies: "Who? Men themselves."

The allegory has its key. The author refers, under the name of *Disillusionment*, to the Tree of the Knowledge of Good and Evil; under the name of *Deceit*, to Lucifer, the leader of the rebellious angels and universal adversary of mankind (see Gen. 2:17; 3:3 and 7). The stranger explains to Critilo that, had it not been for man's initial willful sin, every new entrant into the world would have been warned by the Tree of the Knowledge of Good and Evil: "Remember that you were not born for the world but for heaven; the enticements of the worldly vices will bring you only death, as the rigors of virtue will give you life; trust not in your youth: its substance is mere glass" (p. 150).

In *Crisi* VIII (*ed. cit.*, III, 244–74) of Part III, Critilo and Andrenio arrive at the Cave of Nothingness. On learning its name, Andrenio asks, "What do you mean, Cave of Nothingness, when into it plunge the great current of the century, the torrent of the world, populous cities, great courts, entire kingdoms?" The Honest One replies that, in spite of appearances, there is absolutely nothing in that cave. "But what do they do who plunge into it?" Andrenio asks, and is told: "What they alway did." "What do they end up as?" he asks again, and is answered: "They become their own achievement: they were nothing, they did nothing, they end up as nothing." At that moment someone rushes forward and, explaining that he has found no profession so attractive as doing nothing, slips inside the cave. Another man, a gentleman followed by a retinue of servitors, comes with the same purpose and, disregarding the pleas of the Honest One, follows his predecessor into Nothingness, never to be heard from again. Men of valor disappear to become men of no value; flowering geniuses, to wither and decay.

In *Crisi* VII of Part II Andrenio asks the Hermit: "What is the purpose of all the statues that you have here?" "Oh," replies the Hermit, "they are idols of the imagination, phantoms of appearance; they are all empty, but we make believe they are full of substance and solidity. A man crawls into the statue of a wise man, imitates his voice and words, and all obey him" (*ed. cit.*, II, 238).

But not everything is farce in this world of farces. In *Crisi* X the pilgrims ask the Queen of Equity how they may arrive at the dwelling of her ladyship Happiness. By way of answer the Queen calls four of her handmaidens (the cardinal virtues), points to the first of them, and says: "This one, who is Justice, will tell you where and how to look; this second one, Prudence, will reveal her to you; with the third, who is Fortitude, you shall reach her; and with the fourth, whose name is Temperance, you will make her yours." At this point there is a harmonious blast of trumpets as a fragrant zephyr begins to stir. The pull of the stars becomes actually perceptible, and the wind, growing stronger, lifts them toward heaven. "He who wishes to know where they stopped must seek them farther on" (*ibid.*, pp. 317–18).

"He . . . must seek them farther on"—here is another indication, among so many that seem to have been overlooked in the writings of Gracián, that his "essays"—in the sense of *experiments* in the manner of Montaigne—have to do with this world only, though the beyond is ever present in the author's mind as the haven where life's little bark comes to rest, where—to revert to abstract language—confusion gives way to meaning.[16]

Caer en la cuenta—to awaken to awareness—is really an extension of the task laid upon the individual not only by Socrates but by the whole tradition of Christian theology. Gracián's innocent savage Andrenio—Everyman—starts his journey toward comprehension from exactly this point of departure: "the first time that I recognized myself and was able to form a conception of my person."[17] On this basis he forms his ideas of the world and of his fellow men. *Thou* is but an extension of *I*: "in you I perceive myself portrayed more vividly than in the silent crystal of a fountain" (*ibid.*). Thus for Gracián—more Augustinian than Cartesian—*existence* is the primary datum: I live, therefore I am. "In a confused and disoriented way," writes José Antonio Maravall, "Gracián is the first writer to consider life as a radical and inexorable reality upon which other realities depend."[18]

The awakening to awareness of Gracián's Andrenio, his *caer en la cuenta*, is portrayed in a vivid allegory in *Crisi* VIII of Part I. In the "Court of Confusion" Andrenio (*ed. cit.*, I, 243) had suffered a general obfuscation of the senses and of the mind, had become separated from his mentor Critilo, and was lost. The latter, searching for him, appealed to Artemia, later (p. 262) revealed as none other than Wisdom or Knowledge, a worker of marvels and prodigies who was by many considered a sorceress; unlike Circe, however, she did not convert men into beasts but used her magic to transform bestial men into men of reason (p. 244). Critilo tells her that his alter ego (*otro yo*, p. 249) must surely be at the court of the King Who Is Famous Without Being Named. Artemia comprehends at once: surely Andrenio is at the Babylonlike court of her great enemy, King Falseworld. She calls one of her chief ministers, the Prudent One, and entrusts the quest to him. It is a wise choice. El Prudente has difficulties. All he has to go by is a description, and Andrenio, after residing in the city of King Falimundo, is so changed that not even his mentor Critilo would recognize him (p. 255). His eyes are dull, half closed, and almost blind, since the ministers of Falimundo take great care to obfuscate every man's vision; he could not even hear well in that court and Center of Lies. Even so, the Prudent One finds him one day, "losing many days in seeing how other men lost their property and even their conscience." It happens that there is a great ball game going on, and the huge balls have a strange appearance. "They seem to be human heads," Andrenio remarks to the man who has come to seek him (p. 257). The fact is, they are indeed human heads—heads more full of wind than of understanding, full of tow or cotton stuffing, full of trickery and of lies. One party of players throws them upward toward their felicity, the other band casts them down amid suffering and calamities; and this goes on until the ball bursts and lands in the stinking mud of a grave.

"Who are you, who see so much?" asks the neophyte. "Who are you who are so blind?" asks the Prudent One. The conversation thus begun, Andrenio is assured that he will never have access to King Falseworld, whose very existence depends on his not being recognized (p. 257). That is the reason that visitors to his court are all but blinded. Since the king cannot be seen face to face and in direct light, Andrenio is led up onto a high hill. "It seems to me that I see much better than before," says the younger man, and the older one rejoices, since in seeing and in knowing lies the young man's salvation. Straining his eyes "to see if he could perceive any reality," Andrenio is thwarted by the window blinds of the palace. He is told to turn his back, since the things of this world must be seen in reverse in order to be seen straight. Then the Prudent One brings out a mirror: "Look well, and try to satisfy your desire." Andrenio looks, trembles, utters a cry. "What is the matter? What do you see?" "What do you expect me to see? A monster, the most horrible sight of my life! Get him out of my sight!"

"Keep your promise," the Prudent Ones replies. "Note well that face of a fox, that torso of a serpent, that camel's spine, those lower parts of a siren, those leper's hands . . . He even speaks in falsetto." To Andrenio's cries of horror the old man replies: "Enough; this is what I desired" (p. 259). The cause of so much horror is the famous king, unknown to all, who holds the world in his grasp because he lacks one thing only—the truth. This is the great hunter who with a universal net ensnares mankind, the judge to whom all appeal in order to condemn themselves. This is none other than King Deceit.

Andrenio would fain seek the safety of distance, but the old man is still not satisfied: Andrenio must know those surrounding the king. A sea monster more frightful than Ariosto's woman-devouring Orc and more false than Rojas' Celestina is the king's mother. Her name is Falsehood (*Mentira*), and her attendants are Yes and No; others in her train are Ignorance, Malice, Human Folly, Perdition, Confusion, Scorn, Intrigue.

As they leave that Babel the old man asks: "Are you content, Andrenio?" "No, not content," is the reply, "but enlightened" (*desengañado*). They move out into the daylight, and Andrenio seems actually half happy (full happiness being impossible). Asked what is lacking, he tells the old man of his lost companion and mentor, Critilo, who had departed for Queen Artemia's court. "Be comforted," says el Prudente, "for we too shall go there. He who freed you from Deceit, where else could he take you but to the presence of Knowledge, by which I mean to the court of the discreet Queen you mention" (p. 262).

In all of this we have the exposition of an optimistic doctrine. Andrenio goes forth from his encounter with Falimundo not only *desengañado* but also relatively content, which is all any man can aspire to. He is on his way to the court of Queen Artemia, who is none other than Knowledge. His guides to happiness are the four cardinal virtues. Andrenio is, thus, a sort of primeval Adam on the human level. (There is no Fall in Gracián's anthropology, purposely limited to the secular sphere.) From within his imperfection (ever with him), Andrenio exercises the power of relative self-perfection; achievement of his self-realization is what Critilo, his mentor, represents. Critilo, or Human Reason, is not perfection;

but in Gracián's thought he is the possibility of—the gift of striving toward—perfection. When Andrenio has his relapses, Critilo needs the help of a transcendent ethic, of someone outside himself who will help him "ransom his 'other I,' who has fallen captive, one knows not how, nor into whose power." The world for Andrenio is thus a balcony from which to see, a platform on which to live. From it he contemplates reality, receiving the testimony not only of things but of their Creator, of men, and of himself.[19]

A similar optimism lies at the heart of Gracián's other great concept, that of the Superior Man. In this sense he is a precursor of Carlyle's *Heroes and Hero Worship*. The very existence of these culture heroes implies an anthropological optimism. Man, says Gracián, "is not born ready-made." His self-realization incorporates new elements into his own being. Critilo is the symbol of the myth of Prometheus, complementary to the myth of Adam. Gracián in all these matters moves within the inherited orbit of Aristotelianism; to him, "becoming a person" consists in achieving full rational development. This every man does by making choices: "where there is no choice there is no perfection." The human personality is, therefore, an artistic artifact.

The process of maturation can occur only in society: the great individual rises above the common and general human condition. Precisely because this condition is general, Gracián pays scant attention to lineage, to nobility: all anyone needs is to be a man. Self-transformation from an ordinary into an extraordinary creature is a general human trait. Gracián's individuals are merely that —individuals—and yet the life adventure of each is similar to that of every other. What one individual can offer, in opposition to other individuals, is eminence—the exaltation of this quality or that.[20] Gracián's *Discreto*, his Intelligent Man or *Sapiens*, obtains a universal knowledge, so that moral philosophy makes him prudent; natural philosophy makes him wise; history makes him well-informed; poetry awakens his creative powers; rhetoric renders him eloquent; classical studies give him discretion; cosmography imparts to him an acquaintance with the world; and the reading of the Holy Scripture makes him devout. Thus in every branch of learning— human and divine—he achieves perfection.[21]

Engaño (the only escape from which is blessed *desengaño*) is a strictly human deceit. At the beginning of *Crisi* IV of Part III of *El Criticón*, a pilgrim surveys the starry heavens and declares that the best book in the world is the world itself—an extended parchment, with stars for letters. "The words of that heavenly scroll are easy to understand, even though the astrologers call them enigmas. The difficulty—the real difficulty—is in learning to read what lies below, from the rooftops downward, because, since all is in cipher and human hearts are sealed and inscrutable, the best of readers is constantly at fault. And if you have not studied well and memorized the code to the cipher, you will be simply lost, unable to read a word or recognize a letter, not even a pen-stroke or a tilde."[22] God, in other words, does not deceive; the universe was created in holy wisdom and love. It is human hearts that are "sealed."

QUEVEDO

It is necessary to distinguish Quevedo the satirist from Quevedo the preacher of *desengaño*. We shall therefore pass rapidly over his laments—some of them noteworthy for the poetic shock of their conceptistic language.

> Perdieron su esfuerzo pechos españoles
> porque se sustentan de tronchos de coles[23]

produces an effect in Spanish which the transfer to another language all but destroys:

> The hearts of Spanish men have lost their mettle
> Because their bodies feed on cabbage stalks.

> You will answer in my stead,
> Saying that I fear you not:
> My strength's identical with Spain's
> For both she and I are starving.[24]

Or again:

> My cheeks are hollow and my sunken eyes
> Pour forth their sadness from two weeping urns
> On the sepulchral slab of both Castiles.[25]

Except for the force of the poetry—the product of a literature now fully mature—these sentiments could be duplicated, or at least striking analogues of them could be found, in the works of the fifteenth-century satirists. I do not consider this to be *desengaño*. Nor would I regard as expressive of a true "coming to oneself" Quevedo's poems of amatory disillusionment—notably the sonnet, an echo of the book of Job, which begins *Cargado voy de mí; veo delante*—rendered in our Volume I (p. 252) as: "I have become a burden to myself." A ballad, *Son las torres de Joray*, addressed to a faithless Floris, is closer to our theme: it describes the ruined fortress to which Quevedo has been sent as a prisoner, a fortress

> Which had a chatelain, and now has owls.

Here the poet listens to *Desengaño* as he writes, repeating his refrain at the end of each of three separate stanzas:

> The glories of this world
> Entice with light, only to blind with smoke.[26]

Not infrequently Quevedo's complaints are given an economic cast: the evil men do for gain.[27] They are constantly political, as in the *Sonnet on the Bad Government* of Philip IV (*ibid.*, p. 138a). Social satire, however, is not *desengaño* as I here interpret it.

Quevedo's drama lay elsewhere; it was personal. As Pedro Laín Entralgo has shown so well, Quevedo was too attached to this life, too eager to convert the Christian idea of immortality—which he wholeheartedly adhered to as a Catholic—into "a better this-world to come." Everything tells us—and here I follow Laín Entralgo—that Francisco de Quevedo lived historically in insecurity and was beset by despair, not because his country did not retain its power, but because he, having aspired to do and to possess all things, saw—amid ruin and defeat—that everything he still possessed was a mere mockery. Hence the unsurpassable bitterness of some of his lines:

> King Philip, you are great—just like a hole.

Quevedo's earthly hope, therefore, is a mixture of avidity and despair. His ultimate hope—eschatological in character and rising above despair—may at any time be weak or robust, ascetic or worldly, resigned or exultant, but it never yields to metaphysical pessimism: it rests, always, on his conviction that the creation and its mutations are somehow the result of an act of love.[28] This aspect of his thought will concern us in our chapter on death.

CALDERÓN

Pedro Calderón de la Barca is repeatedly cited—with Quevedo and Gracián—as one of the three great exponents of *desengaño*.[29] That Calderón, the dramatist of Scholasticism[30]—with Platonic and Augustinian overtones (see our Volume I, p. 259)—should proclaim the unsubstantiality of this world below,[31] in which the Christian is but a pilgrim, and should insist on the unreliability of all that is of the earth (I Cor. 15:47), is in every way normal. Yet, a distinction must be made between the preacher and his preaching. Calderón is not attached so emotionally to the ephemeral values of this world as is Quevedo: Calderón knows the score from the beginning. Therefore, there is much more lyrical beauty than rending passion in his famous sonnet on mutability:

> These that this morning opened to the light,
> Awakened by the rosy tints of dawn,
> When evening comes will be a heap of petals
> Clasped in the arms of cold, encircling night.
> This tint that vies with heaven's brightest hue,
> A spectrum streaked with gold and white and crimson,
> Is but a symbol of our human error
> That undertakes too much in life's brief day.
> The roses opened with the morning's light,
> Born to grow old, in so few hours to find
> Their grave and cradle in a single bud.
> Such is the life of man, a fleeting day
> In which we enter life and then depart it:
> A century, once past, is but an hour.[32]

The thought of the sonnet is sobering, yet in its contemplation of mutability it is as serene as the Protestant hymn:

> Our lives are like the shadows
> On sunny hills that lie. . . .

To his dramatic personages, however, Calderón can impart passion. His Segismundo, in *Life is a Dream,* undergoes a metamorphosis similar—though infinitely more violent—to the transformation of Gracián's Andrenio: from initial ignorance in his tower prison, to the heights of royal command, and thence to humble acceptance of the natural and the supernatural destiny assigned to him and reserved for him by Providence. In the throes of his worldly experience he gradually sees through the painful deceptiveness of the world of phenomena and "becomes a person." He learns

> That every joy of mankind
> Must fade into the night as does a dream.[33]

When enlightenment comes, he asks:

> Who for human vainglory
> Would lose the glory of heaven?[34]

and decides:

> Let us turn to things eternal.[35]

In the realm of the eternal, transitory things are left behind:

> There happiness never sleeps,
> Nor does greatness fade away.[36]

CERVANTES AND DON QUIJOTE

The clearest example of *desengaño*—of becoming undeceived and coming to oneself—that can be found in all of Spanish literature is the gradual return of Don Quijote from the world of phantoms, born in the minds of the authors of the romances of chivalry that he read with such absorbing avidity, to the changeless eternal world of God's truth that from the beginning was destined (by the artistic will of Cervantes) to be the Knight's ultimate center of respose. I have treated this subject at length in an article, and a summary of this article will bring our study of Spanish *desengaño* to a fitting close.[37]

Paul Hazard was correct in asserting that Cervantes' attack on the romances of chivalry is a mere point of departure, a convenient mold into which he pours the content of his powerful spirit,[38] just as he avails himself of another device—that of a fictitious author whose manuscript he, Cervantes, is merely translating—to give his novel the fundamental element of *artistic distance*, as a frame sets off a picture on a wall.[39] The introduction of the Arabic chronicler is a joke—"and such a successful one that the significance of its absurdity is almost invariably passed over" (*ibid*). In similar fashion, Cervantes makes very conscious use of the romances of chivalry to achieve a purely literary purpose.[40]

Cervantes did not smile Spain's chivalry away, as Byron regretfully asserted. Nor did he laugh out of court the romances of chivalry, which had already lost their vogue as the new picaresque tales and Lope de Vega's new *comedia* supplanted them in popular favor.[41] *Don Quijote* is much more than a parodic satire. It is, rather, an original exploration of reality,[42] which is exemplified by the life of an intermittently deranged literary hero and is achieved by means of two brilliantly conceived techniques: the utilization of the romances of chivalry as a framework for a critical presentation of reality, and the utilization of Juan Huarte de San Juan's differential and typological psychology as a rational and (for that age) scientific pattern for the hero's metamorphosis.[43]

The details of the phases of the metamorphosis are exquisitely planned and brought to their conclusion. There are three of them: an initial psychosomatic disturbance (excessive heat in the brain) that causes the Knight's three sallies; a resolving crisis (involving defeat, discouragement, and loss of cerebral temperature) that three times brings Don Quijote back to his village and to his bed; and a long sleep which, with other physical agencies, brings about a general cooling with consequent restoration (partial or complete) of the mental faculties. Twice the therapy of sleep returns the Knight to a merely relative sanity (till a new crisis sets him off again). After the third and last return, complete lucidity is achieved as the adust humor yields to its opposite, the ultimate cold of death—a death preceded, however, not only by a fully rational perception of reality, but also by a glimpse and a foretaste of the Reality that, as in Gracián's *Criticón* (see above), lies beyond the world of phenomena.

We must therefore reject the idea that Don Quijote "is absolute in valor, in chastity, in justice."[44] These attributes he possesses only in relative measure, as do all other men. Nor is Don Quijote "defeated only when his ideals have snapped, and he . . . returns, full of hard realism, to die" (*ibid.*). His death is, on the contrary, his noblest achievement. Professor Entwistle, whose analysis of Don Quijote as a human being I am here following, is correct, however, in what follows: The Knight "imposes his will on all he meets, and they revolve around him. He addresses wantons as ladies, and they act as ladies for the nonce; an innkeeper, a barber, a priest, a peasant are forced into chivalrous roles by the power of his enthusiasm. He compels country gentlemen, nobles, clergymen to reflect seriously upon great themes: public service, the function of culture, the principles of the arts, the duties of government" (*ibid.*). But it is not now possible to hold, as Professor Entwistle did in 1940, that in Cervantes' masterpiece "life puts its own construction on the universe, and dies only through loss of faith" (*ibid.*). In the remainder of the chapter I offer a demonstration that faith is the essence of the deathbed scene in the final pages—a scene which so many critics, and so many lovers of Cervantes, have found disturbing.

Will[45]

Some critic has said of the modern philosopher Miguel de Unamuno that he desired the immortality of his own person so ardently that, by the mere act of wishing it, he made it true. This mental and emotional attitude was congenial to Cervantes. In one of his *Exemplary Tales* (*La fuerza de la sangre*), a father addresses his daughter, a victim of brutal assault: "Since you neither in word nor thought have offended [God], consider yourself to be as honorable as before; I shall always so consider you."[46]

In the first chapter of Part I of *Don Quijote* we have telling examples of the psychological miracle of making a thing true simply because it is desired. Don Quijote, in order to sally forth as a knight-errant, must have a suit of armor. The arms inherited from his grandfather are in a sorry state and require a general refurbishing. But more than refurbishing is necessary when it comes to the sallet, or rounded helmet: it is simply lacking. Don Quijote manu-factures one out of cardboard and puts it to the test with a sword blow, demolishing it with one stroke. He then proceeds to make a second one, after which he "commissioned and accepted it as a complete and perfect helmet"—without testing it.

Much later, in chapter 25, Don Quijote declares that his lady Dulcinea is the creation of his own will: "I picture her in my imagination as I desire her . . . it suffices me to think and believe that she is beautiful and chaste." Still later, in chapter 49, Don Quijote is riding on an ox cart, enclosed in a wooden cage, and is convinced (by his captors) that his plight (intended to get him home again) is the work of enchanters. Sancho doubts this, and points out the indubitable fact that his master, unlike enchanted heroes, still has to perform the inconvenient physical necessities of a fully activated human body. The Knight will not be convinced: "I know and firmly believe that I am enchanted, and that is suffi-cient for me."

Doubt

In the episodes described above Don Quijote rejects doubt by an act of will, remaining relatively satisfied. Yet he is not always able to do this. His insistent inquiries as to whether his experience in the Cave of Montesinos had actually occurred or whether it was only a dream receive an ambiguous answer: what the Knight saw and experienced there was both reality and dream. The fact that he is haunted by this perplexity is proof to Don Quijote that his exis-tence as a knight-errant is a tissue of both truth and falsehood. Faced with this perplexity, the Knight simply prefers to tip the balance in favor of believing that this existence is real, while San-cho insists on the opposite.

In chapter 31 of Part II there is a revealing text which tells us that Don Quijote had never (in his lucid moments, that is) been fully convinced of the authenticity of his knight-errantry. Treated as a knight by the Duke and Duchess, the hero for the first time "knew and believed that he was a true knight-errant." Prior to that moment, the thought that his adventures were fantastic had not been fully overcome; and in chapter 34 the doubts are renewed as

Don Quijote again seeks certainty regarding what happened in the cave.

In chapter 55 of Part II he writes to Sancho, now separated from him because (owing to the Duke's role as *deus ex machina*) the squire has at length become governor of his "island." In the letter Don Quijote expresses a doubt newly added to those that have long tormented him: "Let me have your report as to whether your major-domo is the same man who intervened in the hoax of La Trifaldi, *as you suspected.*" The words underlined show that the questioner shares the suspicion. And again, in chapter 64, one of the old questions is repeated, addressed this time to the "enchanted head" in Barcelona: "What I report as having happened to me in the Cave, was it fact or fancy?"

These probings of reality become more insistent in proportion as Don Quijote's choler (yellow bile, the excess of which is the cause of his fluctuating derangements) wears off; but it must not be forgotten that the doubts appear in the very first chapter of the first part and are repeated throughout the work. In other words: Don Quijote lacks certainty and seeks conviction—in his lucid moments. At other times, at the moments of violent action caused by his adust humor, he rides forth to meet his enemy—windmills, sheep, an armed Biscayan—without the slightest vacillation.

Sancho too has his doubts, though their source is different. Sancho believes in the veracity of the books of chivalry because men of his class simply did. On the basis of such a misconception of reality, Sancho leaves farm and family to go forth with a monomaniac in search of an island that he may govern. Why should not he, Sancho Panza, be favored by Fortune as was Gandalín, the squire of Amadís? As early as chapter 32 of Part I, however, Sancho is shaken on hearing the innkeeper say that "that business of famous knights belongs to the times of long ago." Indeed, he is so upset that he even conceives the idea of leaving his master. At the same time, Sancho himself becomes a deceiver: first when he merely feigns delivery of his master's message to Dulcinea; later when he "enchants" that fair lady, "converting" her into a rude peasant woman. There comes a time (II, 23) when he says: "Pardon me, worshipful sir, if I say that of all you have just told me, I believe nary a word, so help me God!"

Falsification of the Truth

Alexander A. Parker has written a luminous article on "The Concept of Reality in Don Quijote,"[47] which I shall summarize for the purpose of using it as my springboard for further exposition and a somewhat more far-reaching conclusion. Why do the personages in Cervantes' book deform the truth? They do so because each feels the need to distort it in order that he may be as he wishes to be, or for still baser motives: the desire for amusement, or personal interest in the fruits of falsification. In Don Quijote, the need for falsification is produced by his adust humor, his choler, which makes him a monomaniac. "All the action of the novel," says Parker, "is based on the interplay of Don Quijote's madness (which causes him to deceive himself) and the tricks by means of which others deceive him" (p. 292). Sancho stands in the middle, now deceived, now deceiving. In every case the falsity, the distortion, is the work of men: only men know how to lie. It is all a matter of deceit; reality itself is never presented as unreliable.

Don Quijote's motives. Why does the Knight falsify the truth? In the first place (and here I inject a thought of my own, not of Parker), Don Quijote does this because he needs to realize himself as a superior man. In his initial act of distortion (the repaired helmet), he must do the thing he does in order to be Don Quijote. And he needs light on the problem of the cave because the greater problem of reality in general is a constant preoccupation to him. He even grants to Sancho the self-assumed right to distort things according to his fancy, offering to believe Sancho's account of things seen in the heavens (as he rides, supposedly blindfolded, on the hobbyhorse Clavileño), on the condition that Sancho accept as authentic Don Quijote's visions and adventures below ground (II, 41).

But the virtue of desiring to be authentically what one wishes oneself to be has its corresponding vice: the Knight wants to be a hero. And this is true at certain times when the force of his madness is mitigated. He then does things with wise deliberation because he desires fame. The acts carried out under this impulse should, theoretically, redound to the welfare of mankind; in practice they injure innocent parties. In Parker's words, Don Quijote had come to be filled "with an enormous vanity." Almost all the falsifications are born of this megalomania. The texts marshaled by Parker are convincing (pp. 296–99).

Three calls to sanity. Three persons recommend to the Knight that he depart from his extravagant adventures and return to a normal life. These are: the Canon of Toledo, who does so in all friendliness; the chaplain in the Duke's palace, who gives his advice with revolting crudeness; and the man in the streets of Barcelona, who speaks with the folly of a madman. Nothing here raises epistemological questions. It is rather a matter of ethics: all the difficulty stems from arrogance, egotism, frivolity—the innate or the accidental folly of men. The world is ever a reasonable creation; men are the falsifiers. But there is more than this: there is always one Reality, the last and ultimate one, which no man can distort.

The hero's vainglory. At this point I depart from Parker and offer my own interpretation. Roy W. Battenhouse, in an article entitled "Shakespearean Tragedy: A Christian Interpretation,"[48] notes that "in each tragedy the hero . . . inclines toward some form of inordinate self-interest; and accordingly spends himself in destructive passion which ends in his own spiritual death, often concurrent with physical death." But in Shakespeare's Lear, as in Don Quijote, something quite different is the result: "Then to this wasteland of the self comes a vision as by miracle, and Lear can depart in peace. The experience marks tragedy's utmost limit, at the very gates of comedy." Neither of these masterpieces ends on a note of despair. Don Quijote has his miraculous vision; like Lear, he can depart in peace. His tragedy—that of a wasted life—is converted into a song of life and hope.[49]

Glimpses of the truth. In chapter 8 of Part II, we have the first inkling of the change which the author plans to carry out in the chapters having to do with Don Quijote's final return from the world of illusion and falsehood. He and Sancho are on the way to El Toboso in search of her ladyship, the fair Dulcinea. It is natural that under these circumstances the hero's thoughts should move on a lofty plane. Here there is discussion of two kinds of fame—one infamous, the other saintly. There are sainted knights in Heaven, and knights here below should seek out occasions for battle that will render them not only famous men-at-arms, but also good

Christians. This is a first anticipation of what is to come fifty chapters later (II, 58), when Don Quijote will find himself facing the Holy Images and, in that awe-inspiring presence, will feel humble and desirous of directing his steps over a better road than the one he has traveled up to that point, a road which will lead him —very soon—to the gates that open upon the fairer world of the Beyond.[50] In the remaining chapters, Cervantes will cause his hero to suffer all manner of indignities and humiliations: not because of cruelty to the dearly-loved creature of his artist's imagination, nor yet because he is disillusioned with life and with men, but because this is necessary for Don Quijote's transformation in two respects. First, he must be made to lose his choler (the adust humor which is the cause of all his aberrations), and this can be accomplished only by producing in him a predominance of the opposite humor, which is melancholy (black bile). Second, he must also cast off his burden of pride, of vainglory, and embrace the Christian virtue of humility. In short: it is not the author's intention to let him die in his error.

The hero's backsliding. Don Quijote could not possibly maintain himself through fifty chapters on the lofty plane of II, 8. In chapter 14 he has the good fortune to defeat the Knight of the Mirrors, becoming, as the author tells us, "extremely vainglorious" as a result. In chapter 17 occurs the adventure of the lions, an adventure purposely sought in all foolhardiness with no other end in view than the conquest of renown. Don Quijote asks: "Surely you regard me—who could think otherwise—as a madman?" Later, in chapter 58, Don Quijote sadly reviews his past life: "up to this point I know not what I have achieved by so much suffering and effort; but if my Dulcinea might be disenchanted, and if I might be granted better fortune, and the restoration of my judgment, it could happen that I would find a better path than the one I tread." The discouragement does not last long. In the very same chapter the hero, coming upon some hunter's nets, threatens to break them by mere strength, though they were strong and resistant as diamond. In chapter 64 he still thinks himself capable of defeating all the Moors of Africa. Even after his defeat at the hands of the

Knight of the White Moon on the strand of Barcelona, he can dream of achieving another type of fame, though deeds of derring-do be forbidden to him. He and Sancho will become amorous shepherds: "Apollo will give us sweet verses: Cupid, elgeant conceits whereby we can eternalize our fame" (ch. 67).

The road to perfection. In order to bring about the necessary psychological and physical changes in Don Quijote and to bring him home from the *outward and centrifugal* journey on which his overheated brain launched him in Part I and the early chapters of Part II; in order, that is, to initiate and complete the *centripetal return* to sanity and recognition of the error that the worldly virtues of a knight inevitably involved (see Chapter I of our Volume I), Cervantes subjects him to a series of cruel disillusionments and humiliations that bring about his ultimate *desengaño*, dissipating his choler and increasing his melancholy (caused by black bile, the enemy of choler). The sequence of disasters seems interminable: the "enchanting" of Dulcinea; Sancho's unwillingness to do his part to end her enchantment; the shameful exposure, by the challenged lion, of his buttocks to our hero (who had hoped to meet claw and fang); the "error" (recognized by Don Quijote) in having decapitated the marionettes of Maese Pedro; the scarcely heroic flight of Don Quijote after the adventure of the ass-calling contest (as the unfortunate upholder of the right fearfully expects to receive a bullet from behind); Sancho's lack of respectfulness in the palace of the Duke and Duchess—so conspicuous as to cause Don Quijote to "be consumed with inner rage"; the unspeakable discourtesy of the chaplain in that palace; the doubts about the cave; the sadness caused by separation from Sancho when the latter goes to rule his "island"; and another, an unexplained melancholy ("That is not the principal cause that makes me appear to be sad" [ch. 44]); the attacks against his person by cats, bulls, and swine; the finding of himself suspended by the wrist from an upper window because of the mischievousness of a shameless girl; the pinching by demons or goblins that "pulled back the sheet" to get at him; the inability to eat out of sheer depression ("Eat, friend Sancho . . . and let me die at the hands of my sad thoughts" [ch. 59]—the gravest of sins, this, the sin of despair); the pummeling (horror of horrors!) by the fists of his own squire (ch. 60); the sadness caused by his own lack of care, so that certain soldiers found him with unbridled horse (Don Quijote, whose profession required that he be ever alert!); the boys' running after him through the streets of Barcelona with insulting remarks (ch. 61); the reviling by adults in the streets of that same city (ch. 62); the feeling himself sick to the heart because the dancing girls made sport of him (*ibid.*); his final defeat in battle, which made him take to his bed for six days, "sad, pensive, and unable to pull himself together" (ch. 65); the necessity of confessing that "sad thoughts and events cause me to appear discourteous" (ch. 66); the melancholy described at the beginning of chapter 67; the finding of himself a prisoner in the power of men armed with lances and shields (ch. 68); the hearing of himself called Sir Codfish by the evil-minded Altisidora—all of this tended to make Don Quijote "more judicious since he was defeated, with better judgment in all the matters he discoursed upon" (ch. 71). We now know why Cervantes included in one of his latest chapters the words just transcribed: they reveal to us that Don Quijote is returning to sanity. He is returning to his original soundness of mind because melancholy is cooling, or has already cooled, the choler which was the cause, the perturbing source of all his acts of madness and of all his deceits—his distortions of reality in order to assuage a thirst for renown.

The denouement. The untying of the knot begins with certain omens. Cervantes knows that these must not be believed, but he uses them for ends which are artistic.[51] As Don Quijote approaches his village, it happens that two boys are engaged in a quarrel. One of them shouts: "You shall never see it as long as you live." The word "it," being grammatically feminine in this case, seems to Don Quijote to refer to the "her" who is uppermost in his thoughts, his enchanted Dulcinea. A pursued hare runs up and takes refuge between the feet of Sancho's donkey. "*Malum signum*, a bad omen!" cries Don Quijote, yielding to popular superstition: "Dulcinea will not reappear."

All of this is burdened with significance—a significance that is all but lost on the reader unless he is familiar with the set of psychological beliefs which Cervantes manipulates to achieve his effects.

In spite of the brief flickering up of hope when the thought of becoming amorous shepherds is briefly entertained, and in spite of the common sense of the housekeeper, who advises her employer to attend to his affairs, to go frequently to confession, and to succor the needy, the ex-knight becomes aware that none of these things can be: "Silence, my daughters," he says to housekeeper and niece, "for I know what I need to do. Take me to my bed, for it seems to me that I am not well" (ch. 73). "Take me to my bed"—it is the now familiar remedy that Cervantes applies after each one of his hero's three sallies: the great balm of sleep! Sleep, aided by melancholy, will now repair—definitively—Don Quijote's injured brain, and when he wakens he will see the doors of the other world beckoning to him. Recognizing the falseness of all enchantments and of all worldly knighthood, Don Quijote embraces holy humility, abandoning that portion of the values of his culture that are limited to this side of the grave. "There are no birds in last year's nest."

Eternal reality. "Praised be God, who has granted me such a blessing! In short, his mercies know no end, nor are they diminished by the sinfulness of men." In the deathbed scene there is an air of eternity which makes us think that the ex-knight experiences more than he tells. So great were God's mercies that the dying man "cried out with a great shout." He does what he must: he renounces his past errors, dictates his last will and testament, thinks of the fame as a good man (not as a famous knight) that he wishes to leave behind him, and is shriven in secret by the priest.

And perhaps there is more than this. There is a passage in the *Persiles* that strongly recalls the death scene in *Don Quijote*. Auristela, having been converted into a loathsome creature by an evil spell and, as she begins to recover her health, "giving thanks to heaven for the mercy and the joy vouchsafed her," calls Periandro and says to him: "I could wish that my present happiness might last forever. . . . Our souls, as you know and as I have been taught here, are ever in ceaseless movement, unable to rest until they rest in God, as in their center. In this life our desires are infinite, and interlocking they at times form a chain that reaches to heaven" (*Obras, ed. cit.*, p. 1706b). This, as I have pointed out in Volume III (p. 291), is one of eight expressions by Cervantes of his preoccupation with an eloquent phrase from the first chapter of St. Augustine's *Confessions*: "Thou has made us for Thyself, and our hearts are restless till they rest in Thee." We may confidently believe that the mercies received by Don Quijote on his deathbed are akin to the mercies and the joy, the happiness that Auristela experienced on her return from the antechamber of death. In the light that streams from the Eternal, something human—including the plots of Cervantes' novels—ceases in its movement as it finds its center.

Grace

We have now seen how in Cervantes' works the object of desire is converted into reality when the characters give themselves over to the dominion, not only of the ought-to-be but of the I-will-have-it-to-be-so. It is an ancient doctrine, central to medieval Christian psychology. The will is the appetitive faculty of the soul, and so powerful that it can overcome reason, because will (*voluntad* or *gusto*) is a child of the free will granted to every person. A character in Cervantes' tale, *El coloquio de los perros*, says of herself: "as it is a sin of the flesh it inevitably dulls all the senses . . . not permitting them to function as they should; and thus the soul, defenseless and useless, cannot raise its spirit to entertain a single good thought; but rather, sunk in an abyss of misery, it refuses to lift its hand to God, who is extending His own hand downward toward the sinner, moved only by His Grace" (*Obras*, p. 1017ab).

This is the situation of Don Quijote in chapters 8 and 58 of the second part. The Knight would wish to depart from his error, to follow a "better path." He feels above him the presence of the Divine Hand, but he does not see clearly nor can he yet renounce the will-o'-the wisp toward which he struggles: if only Dulcinea might be disenchanted! And the reason for this sad state is that the choler which causes his infirmity has not yet been dissipated. We must wait.

Let us fix our attention on the final words of the text last cited: "moved only by His Grace." The human soul is helpless without contact with the downward-reaching Hand, which is the gift, the help, of grace, of mercy—a gift not deserved but granted to man by his Maker, who is all love.

From the beginning to the penultimate scene of his long history, Don Quijote is ruled by his desire, by his will: "I imagine that everything I say is as I say it is, and I picture her in my imagination as I desire her" (I, 25). But that will gradually weakens; it is diminished by imperceptible degrees as we advance through the marvelous architectural structure that is *Don Quijote*. Already in chapter 58 of Part II Don Quijote is in what we might call the antechamber of the state of grace: what he now desires is not to see his fame extended throughout the world, but to see his lady disenchanted, and himself with feet firmly planted "on a better path than the one I follow." This inclination of desire toward the good is simply the step that every man must take before receiving the gift of grace. And that desire—in Don Quijote—will be fulfilled. The hour of liberation from "the power of the enchanters" is, in this chapter, still distant; but that hour will come. It will come when, the mists that becloud his judgment having been removed by natural causes (the cooling agents of sleep and melancholy emotions), the hero shall receive the supreme gift of grace, the final mercy, which both he and Auristela of the *Persiles* recognize and accept—he by direct contact with, she by a foretaste of, the releasing power of death.

Such a seeing into the heart of things, such a direct knowing of reality, is the very essence of *desengaño*. Because this is so, *desengaño*, in the deepest sense, is a sort of wisdom. It is a liberation from error. As the Portuguese poet André Froes wrote, in a collection of verse entitled *Amores divinos* (1631), in one of a sequence of sonnets intended to "move the reader to the love of God":

> I saw my folly, knew my disillusion,
> Became a turncoat as my fortune turned
> And reaped by that one act a marvelous harvest:
>   Amid the deceit that mocked each fair illusion,
> Amid those miseries, bordering those abysses,
> I was myself converted, born anew[52];

or, as Petrarch expressed it almost three centuries earlier: *Che quanto piace al mondo è breve sogno*—"all that the world esteems is but a dream."

DESENGAÑO IN THE REST OF EUROPE

Desengaño is a Spanish word, and disillusionment is often thought of as a peculiarly Spanish phenomenon, caused (as some critics hold) by an un-European incapacity inherent in the Spanish culture and dating from that culture's birth in the centuries-long struggle against a hostile culture—the Mohammedan. Such a view is excessively narrow. *Desengaño*—as well as optimism—characterizes all of Europe during our period. Herschel Baker, in *The Wars of Truth: Studies in the Decay of Christian Humanism in the Earlier Seventeenth Century*,[53] devotes a section of chapter ii to "The Literature of Disenchantment" and another to "The Great Threnodists." Here, as always, we encounter our *Sic et Non*. Not all was joy during the "joyous" age of the "discovery of the world and man." The miseries of the human situation, so frequently emphasized in medieval literature, were never forgotten by the writers of the Renaissance.[54] There were concrete miseries also: Juan Luis Vives, writing to Cranevelt in 1526 on the sad state of affairs—everyone accusing everyone else of heresy—is not thinking specifically of Spain; he has in mind Lefèvre d'Etaples and Briçonnet, Noël Beda and Ulrich von Hutten. And what is more, Vives, although writing in Flanders, feels it expedient to express himself with as great caution, with as delicate an ambiguity, as Cervantes ever did.[55]

Joachim du Bellay's *Regrets*, which was inspired by the poet's journey to Rome in 1553 and published after his return to France in 1558, symbolizes, according to R. Jasinski, the entire epoch:

> The bewildered dreams of the Pléiade, the more general aspirations of the humanists, were destined to be cut short by disappointing realities. One has only to think of the disillusion of Ronsard, or to recall the disenchantment of Rabelais after the *affaire des placards* and the reaction that followed it; the somewhat saddened wisdom of his *Tiers Livre*, following so soon after the radiant visions of Thélème. These crises resemble to some degree those of the Romantics after the ebb tide of the great dreams of 1830. The sixteenth century, no less than the nineteenth, had its *mal du siècle*.[56]

"In every period," writes Lucien Febvre, "there existed . . . heroes . . . , burning minds that the sixteenth century willingly converted into burned bodies. That perspective did not frighten them—the number of the martyrs is proof: martyrs who faced torture without fear, martyrs of the Reformation or of the Counter Reformation, martyrs of Anabaptism or of anti-Trinitarianism, martyrs of all sectarian doctrines, martyrs even of what people then referred to as atheism."[57] In spite of these miseries, however, "John Donne [d. 1631] and his fellows inherited a unified worldview which related everything in the universe, concrete or abstract, to everything else and to God."[58] It is significant, Theodore Spencer insists (*op. cit.*, p. 203), that the three chief satirists of the 1590's in England—Donne, Hull, Marston, men who used literature to expose the evil in human nature—all ended in the Anglican Church.

In two respects—important ones—the Spaniards maintained themselves in a world apart: clinging tenaciously to the Aristotelian-Thomistic world view, they did not suffer appreciably from the upsetting astronomical discoveries of the time; nor did they find a comfortable new world view that embraced the resulting changes in cosmological theory. Robert Boyle (d. 1691) "was appalled by Descartes' implicitly mechanistic view of God, because to relegate Him to the role of a removed spectator, or to deprive man and nature of His constant surveillance and intervention, was in his view impious."[59] For Molière (d. 1673), on the other hand, "the conflict between Nature and Grace vanishes; there remains only Nature. . . . Not that he rejects religion. . . . But religion is now but an adornment."[60] And as the seventeenth century wore on, "men who thought they understood Galileo and Newton could identify providence with mechanism—even after God was well on his way to becoming an unnecessary hypothesis" (Baker, *op. cit.*, p. 13).

To say that Raleigh, the last Elizabethan; Dr. Browne, the amateur of Baconian science; Donne, the sporadic skeptic; and Taylor, the exponent of the Anglican *via media*, "could draw at will on the venerable tradition of pessimism is not to charge them with insincerity; it is to suggest that in the early seventeenth century men were still close to their medieval heritage, and that the inherited patterns of thought and emotion were still powerful" (*ibid.*, p. 57). Sir Walter Raleigh—like Francisco de Quevedo—could write that glory is the only vanity, a vanity that leads inexorably to the point where men "by workmanship of death, finish the sorrowful business of a wretched life; towards which we travel both sleeping and waking" (*ibid.*). When Sir Thomas Browne meditated on eternity, "he did so in terms most readily available, and his thought was patterned by those ancient dogmas dramatizing man's impotence before the facts of death and judgment: ' 'Tis that unruly regimen within me, that will destroy me; 'tis I that do infect myself; the man without a Navel yet lives in me; I feel that original canker corrode and devour me' " (*ibid.*, p. 59).

All of this was on the point of vanishing "towards the end of the seventeenth century, with the general acceptance of Copernicanism, the dominance of Descartes, and (in England) the foundation of the Royal Society." Later, "when Watt makes his engine, when Darwin starts monkeying with the ancestry of Man, and Freud with his soul, and the economists with all that is his, then indeed the lion will have got out of his cage. Its liberated presence in our midst will become one of the most important factors in everyone's daily life. But not yet; not in the seventeenth century."[61]

Most certainly not in Spain, where the greatest exponents of the Castilian mind as expressed in literature cling steadfastly to the patristic and Thomistic world view which, for them, showed no signs of vanishing. In their *desengaño*, their disenchantment, there is no evidence of a weakening of this preferred *Weltanschauung*. "As for man, his days are as grass," the Psalmist had written some two millenniums earlier. To remember his words, and to hold with Sir Walter Raleigh that glory is vanity, and with Sir Thomas Browne that man is impotent before the facts of death and judgment, was the ultimate wisdom.[62]

9 El Ingenioso Hidalgo

That Cervantes had a very special reason for calling his hero *ingenioso* is a fact unnoticed by the commentators, although it seems natural for any reader to ask why that particular adjective was chosen. It is evident that *ingenioso* has been a source of difficulty or at least of uncertainty to translators. In French, Italian, or Portuguese it was possible to use a cognate, and this became common practice: *ingénieux, ingegnoso, engenhoso*. Jarvis and other English translators have likewise been content with merely transferring Cervantes' word: *the ingenious gentleman*. Shelton used *valorous and witty*, revised by Captain John Stevens to *ingenious and renowned*, apparently in view of the fact that the Caballero de la Triste Figura may not properly be called a man of wit. Most other translators disregarded *ingenioso* and provided an adjective of their own: *most renowned, much esteemed*. The French sometimes preferred *valereux* or *admirable*. In German we find *berühmt, weise, scharfsinnig, sinnreich*. It is not until 1910, when Robinson Smith first published his translation, that we are given a reasonable approximation of *ingenioso: the imaginative gentleman*, which Smith replaced in his third edition (1932) by *visionary*. That there are special overtones in the word *ingenioso* every perceptive reader is aware. That the translators generally failed to render them and often merely cut the Gordian knot is equally clear. Only Robinson Smith is correct and even he gives no explanation, no reference to an all-but-forgotten study which may have put him on the right track: Rafael Salillas' *Un gran inspirador de Cervantes. El doctor Huarte de San Juan y su Examen de Ingenios*, Madrid, 1905. Smith could not have known a later illuminating investigation of the problem by Mauricio de Iriarte, S.J.[1]

It is the purpose of the present article to call attention to Father Iriarte's findings and to show, in addition, that well-read contemporaries of Cervantes, even if they did not know Huarte's extremely popular book (1575), would have followed with clear understanding the course of Alonso Quijano's transition from a country gentleman of *choleric temper* to an *imaginative* and *visionary* monomaniac, and would have interpreted this transformation, as Cervantes had conceived it, in the light of their knowledge of Greek-Arabic physiological and psychological theories regarding the balance and imbalance of the bodily humors.[2] More specifically it will be shown that Alonso Quijano is a man primarily *colérico;* that his natural condition is exacerbated by a *passion* and by *lack of sleep*, which produce a hypertrophy of his *imaginative faculty;* that his madness follows a natural trajectory away from, and back to, normality; that his moments of temporary improvement after his first two *vueltas*, and his final return to sanity, correspond to relaxations in, or the removal of, the causes of his aberration. In short, it will be shown—if my arguments carry conviction—that Don Quijote's adventures could have happened only to a *colérico*, a man by nature *caliente y seco*, and that such a man was, according to Renaissance psychology, of necessity *ingenioso*.

It will be well to make clear at once the mechanics of this transformation. Alonso Quijano is described as a man of the type in which *choler* (yellow bile) prevails over blood, melancholy (black bile), and phlegm. He is thus a person more akin to the element *fire* than to the other three: air, water, earth. Such an imbalance would normally have been bearable, would naturally have made of Alonso Quijano what he was: a man of great enthusiasm, quick to anger, a lover of justice more fit to execute it than to administer it wisely.[3] His natural enthusiasm caused him to develop a *passion*[4]—the reading of novels of chivalry—and this passion deprived him of *sleep*, the great restorative, the means whereby the brain rehumidifies itself and keeps in check the *fiery* element in an individual's make-up. Lacking this restoration of its humidity, the hidalgo's brain *se le secó* and *for this reason* gave free rein to the *imaginative* and *visionary*, as against the ponderative faculties. His illness was the opposite of that of Democritus of Abdera, who suffered a hypertrophy of the *entendimiento*.[5] His physical make-up was identical with that of Saul of Tarsus, struck down by a *vision* on the road to Damascus.[6] It was the opposite of that of Sancho Panza, a man "de boto ingenio" and much given to *sleep*.[7]

These physiological and psychological ideas were current during the Middle Ages and the Renaissance. They derived from Aristotle and Galen and the medieval physicians, both in the Muslim and in the Western World.[8] Renaissance audiences and reading public "had a general acquaintance with this framework, comparable, we may believe, to our own vague familiarity with the terminology and the doctrines of modern psychiatry, which we bring with us to a performance of *Mourning becomes Electra* or *The Cocktail Party*."[9] The source books were numerous. The Archpriest of Talavera, in his very ample fifteenth-century treatment of these matters, cites "el libro *De Secretis* que fizo Aristotyles a Alixandre."[10] Alejo Venegas del Busto in the sixteenth century refers to Michael Scott and Joannes ab Indagine.[11] Later works were Levinus Lemnius' *De habitu et constitutione corporis* or *Touchstone of Constitutions* and Jean Fernel's *Physiologia* and *De abditis rerum causis* where "des milliers d'hommes . . . ont puisé pendant un siècle et demi au moins leurs idées et leurs doctrines."[12]

The fundamental principle is that of the four humors. Each of these has two primary qualities: *blood, hot and moist; choler, hot and dry; melancholy, cold and dry; phlegm, cold and moist*. These correspond to the four elements: *air is hot and moist; fire hot and dry; earth cold and dry; water cold and moist*. Each humor has its bodily function: blood warms and moistens the body; choler nourishes those parts regarded as hot and dry; melancholy nourishes the bones and sinews; phlegm—at the opposite pole from choler—nourishes the *cold and moist* parts such as the *brain* and kidneys.[13] Alonso Quijano's excess of *heat and dryness*—as a *colérico* he inevitably had these in excess, as we shall see—went hand in hand with a corresponding *deficiency of phlegm*, and, when through lack of sleep this excess became acute, his brain suffered from lack of moisture: *se le secó el cerebro*.

Such pathological conditions Renaissance medical theorists traced to humoral abnormalities, explaining every disease thereby. Their cause was either the *burning* of a natural humor by *unnatural heat*—and this is Alonso Quijano's case—, the putrefaction of a natural humor, or the improper mixture of natural humors.[14] Cure depended on restoration of the normal by blood-letting or by purgation: hellebore for melancholy, rhubarb for choler. Diet was also used. A patient suffering from a hot and dry disease was given cooling food such as lettuce and cress. When Don Quijote was struck down by his last illness, the Priest ordered "que tuviesen cuenta con regalarle, dándole a comer cosas confortativas y apropiadas para el corazón[15] y el cerebro." But the complete remedy, in Don Quijote's case, was triple: an attack of melancholy,[16] and acute fever,[17] and a prolonged sleep.[18]

With this *mise en matière* we may regard the problem as set. Before turning to Father Iriarte's analysis of Don Quijote as a *colérico* who could easily become—like the Licenciado Vidriera—a *loco ingenioso*, we shall find it useful to consider a Spanish medieval antecedent: the description of the *colérico* as set forth by the Archpriest of Talavera in the *Corbacho*[19]: "Estos son *calientes e secos*," we are told, "por quanto el elemento del *fuego* es su correspondiente." They are "*yrados muy de recio*"; they are "muy *soberbios*, fuertes, e de mala conplisyon arrebatada, pero dura breve tienpo, pero el tienpo que dura son muy perigrosos." They are "muy *sueltos en fablar, osados en toda plaça*, animosos de corazón, ligeros por sus cuerpos, *mucho sabyos, sobtiles e engeniosos*." They are competent: "onbres para mucho." They are lovers of justice: "*aman justicia* e non todavía [siempre] son buenos para la mandar, mejores para la exsecutar . . . vindicativos al tienpo de su *cólera* . . . ardientes como *fuego*." Such men are born under the planet *Mars*.[20]

One is struck by the parallels. Born under the planet Mars: "Yo . . . nací, según me inclino a las armas, debajo de la influencia del planeta Marte" (II, 6). *Yrados muy de recio:* "Oh, válame Dios y cuán grande fué el enojo que recibió don Quijote oyendo las descompuestas palabras de su escudero!" (II, 46). "Sois un grandísimo bellaco, y vos sois el vacío y el menguado," he cries in II, 56, accompanying the words with the *furia* of his action. *Soberbios:* Don Quijote's besetting sin is *hubris*, and it is only in the final chapters of the book that he achieves Christian humility, starting in II, 58.[21] *Muy sueltos en fablar . . . osados en toda plaça.* We recall the eloquence displayed at the goatherds' campfire (I, 11), the *discurso de las armas y las letras* (I, 38), and the overwhelming *osadía* of his reply to the meddling ecclesiastic (II, 32). *Aman justicia . . . mejores para la exsecutar:* We think of the *galeotes*, freed out of love of justice, freed by an *executive* act, yet *unwisely* freed (I, 22). Finally we come to the key words: *mucho sabyos, sobtiles e engeniosos.* Don Quijote is *ingenioso.* Even Sancho exclaims: "Digo de verdad que es vuestra merced el mesmo diablo y que no ay cosa que no sepa" (I, 25).

This fórmula *colérico-sutil-ingenioso* reappears in 1562, 1572 and 1586 in a book which Cervantes may well have read,[22] Francisco Núñez de Oria's *Régimen y aviso de sanidad.* According to this author, "el colérico es osado, súbito, agudo, delicado, *ingenioso*, se enfurece y tranquiliza fácilmente."[23] But Cervantes' guide and direct inspiration was the *Examen de ingenios* of Juan Huarte de San Juan and we shall have to turn for guidance to the study of Father Iriarte on Huarte's differential psychology.

That Cervantes had read Huarte's book may be regarded as certain.[24] Its full title is *Examen de ingenios para las sciencias* and it was first published in 1575. Before we examine its influence on the psychology of Don Quijote it will be well to establish the meaning of the word *ingenio.* To Vives it was the *universa vis mentis nostrae.*[25] To Huarte it was "lo mismo que fecundidad de la inteligencia . . . , capacidad de engendrar *conceptos* o figuras representativas de la naturaleza de las cosas, con carácter científico." The types or forms of *ingenio* depended on the forms, combinations or predominance of the *temperamento*, or mixture of bodily humors.[26] Herrera in 1580 defined *ingenio* as "aquella fuerza y potencia natural y aprehensión fácil y nativa en nosotros, por la cual somos dispuestos a las operaciones *peregrinas* y la noticia *sutil* de las cosas *altas.*"[27] Covarrubias in 1611 derives the word from Latin *gigno*, to beget, bring forth, produce: *proprie natura dicitur cuique ingenita indoles.* "Vulgarmente llamamos *ingenio*," the definition continues, "una fuerza natural de entendimiento, investigadora de lo que por razón y discurso se puede alcançar en todo género de ciencias, disciplinas, artes liberales y mecánicas, *sutilezas, invenciones* y engaños. . . . Ingenioso, el que tiene sutil y delgado ingenio. . . ."[28] Cervantes grants some degree of *ingenio* to virtually all men, and rightly so, for both Huarte and Covarrubias attribute it to the masters of the mechanical arts. Sancho Panza is "de boto ingenio" (I, 25). Cejador lists a number of passages in the *Quijote* where the word is used. Particularly interesting are these lines from *La elec-*

ción de los alcaldes de Daganzo, reproduced by Iriarte, in which Cervantes echoes the *Proemio* of Huarte's *Examen de ingenios:*

> Digo
> que, pues se hace examen de barberos,
> de herradores, de sastres, y se hace
> de cirujanos y otras zarandajas,
> también se examinasen para alcaldes.
> . . . .
> Llamen a Berrocal, entre, y veamos
> dónde llega la raya de su ingenio.²⁹

All intelligent men have *ingenio,* whether *boto* or *sutil,* but the *ingenioso* is "el que tiene *sutil* y *delgado* ingenio" (Covarrubias). Such a man is *colérico,* partakes of the element of *fire* in greater proportion than of the others, and is born under the planet Mars. He symbolizes *iuventus, aestas,* and the wind *Favonius.*³⁰ The *ingenioso* possesses "una índole de ánimo vivaz inclinada a singulares y raras (Cervantes diría descomunales) ocurrencias."³¹ Furthermore, his psychological balance is precarious. Huarte says: "por maravilla se halla un hombre de *muy subido ingenio* que no pique algo en *manía,*³² que es una destemplanza *caliente* y *seca* del cerebro."³³ According to this, Alonso Quijano was properly called *ingenioso* "porque era *caliente* y *seco* de temperamento . . . y de *subido ingenio,* con su tanto de *manía,* primero por la caza, y después por la lectura; hasta que *recalentándose* y *desecándosele* el cerebro, vino a dar en la monomanía delirante."³⁴ That is to say, Cervantes thought *ingenioso* a fitting adjective to describe his hero's original pre-psychotic inclination and his subsequent psychotic excess.

Both the original inclination and the subsequent excess are described in accordance with Cervantes' belief in the correspondence of mental-moral and physical characteristics, a belief born of his reading of Huarte. Don Quijote himself shares this belief. In the first chapter of the Second Part he *describes* Amadís and claims he could have derived a *similar description* of any and all of the heroes of his dream-world on the basis of their *characters* as revealed in their printed histories: "por las hazañas que hicieron y condiciones que tuvieron se puede sacar *por buena filosofía* sus colores y estaturas."[35]

Iriarte has brought together the passages wherein Don Quijote's physique and personal appearance are described. The result is the image of a man "alto de talla, largo de miembros, flaco pero recio, *seco* de carnes, huesudo y musculoso, rostro estirado y *enjuto*, el color moreno y amarillo, la nariz aguileña, lacio el cabello que antes fué negro y ahora entrecano, abundante vellosidad, venas abultadas, voz ronca; y en conjunto feo y mal tallado."[36] These are the traits of Huarte's *hombre caliente y seco*, that is to say, of the *hombre colérico*. Huarte writes: "el hombre que as caliente y seco . . . tiene muy pocas carnes, duras y ásperas, hechas de nervios y murecillos [músculos], y las venas muy anchas . . . el color . . . moreno, tostado, verdinegro y cenizoso . . . la voz . . . abultada y un poco áspera. . . . Los hombres calientes y secos por maravilla aciertan a salir hermosos, antes feos y mal tallados."[37] Readers of the *Quijote* will recall "seco de carnes, enjuto de rostro" (I, 1). They may also recall that in the Prologue to Part I Cervantes calls his brain-child "un hijo seco." Other parallels may well be repeated here: "las piernas . . . muy largas y flacas, llenas de vello"; "su rostro . . . seco y amarillo"; "avellanado de miembros"; "con una voz ronquilla, aunque entonada"; "no teniendo vuestra merced ninguna [hermosura], no sé de qué cosa se enamoró la pobre." Most noteworthy, it seems to me, is the passage in which Don Quijote describes his hand: "Tomad, señora, esa mano. . . . No os la doy para que la beséis, sino para que miréis la contextura de sus nervios, la trabazón de sus músculos, la anchura y espaciosidad de sus venas, de donde sacaréis qué tal debe de ser la fuerza del brazo que tal mano sostiene."[38]

Don Quijote is thus clearly a *colérico*. As a man of *subido ingenio*, he was, according to Iriarte, "constitucionalmente prepsicótico."[39] In the "síndrome sintomatológico" of his psychosis there are two telling details which belong "de pleno a pleno" to the psychopathology of Huarte. They are: *el resecamiento del cerebro* and *la lesión imaginativa*. It was Huarte who taught Cervantes that "la vigilia de todo el día *deseca* y endurece el cerebro, y *el sueño lo humedece* y fortifica."[40] If the brain's moisture is not restored in the repose of sleep there develops a "trastorno . . . que ha de repercutir en las facultades psíquicas, y primero en . . . *la imaginación*."[41] When Don Quijote had suffered this upset, "llenósele la fantasía de todo aquello que leía en sus libros . . . y asentósele de tal modo en *la imaginación* que era verdad toda aquella máquina de invenciones que leía" (I, 1). Don Quijote the *colérico*, "sobtil e engenioso" (Talavera), by virtue of his "sutil y delgado ingenio" (Covarrubias) was liable to "picar algo en manía, que es una destemplanza *caliente* y *seca* de cerebro" (Huarte). This became acute: "se le secó el cerebro, de manera, que vino a perder el juicio" (I, 1). The precipitating cause was a lack of *moisture* brought about by loss of sleep: "las noches de claro en claro."[42]

In each of the three *vueltas* of Don Quijote, *sleep* was a factor in bringing about partial and temporary, or complete and final recovery. After his first encounter and his return, "mal ferido por culpa de mi caballo" (I, 5), the Knight "a ninguna [pregunta] quiso responder otra cosa sino que le diesen de *comer*[43] y le dejasen *dormir*, que era lo que más le importaba. Hízose así. . . ." After the passage of some time he awoke shouting, and "cuando llegaron a don Quijote, ya estaba él levantado de la cama" but still a victim of his *desatinos* (I, 7). He *again* called for food "y quedóse *otra vez* dormido, y ellos admirados de su locura." Two days later he arose from his bed sufficiently well to go in search of his library, still deranged, however. Over the disappearance of his library there was some discussion between the Knight and his Niece and Housekeeper, the Niece even permitting herself to suggest that he should not go through the world "a buscar pan de trastrigo." He answered testily and "no quisieron las dos replicarle más, porque vieron que se le encendía la *cólera*." Anger is a dry passion which causes the gall to pour forth choler.[44] In this same chapter Don Quijote sets out again, now accompanied by Sancho, a man fully contaminated by the *imaginativa* of his master, "con mucho deseo de verse ya gobernador."

After a long series of adventures in the First Part, Don Quijote returns "enchanted" to his village, having received a tremendous blow from one of the *diciplinantes* (I, 52). On this occasion the curative factors are much less obvious, and would pass unnoticed except for the fact that we now share Cervantes' secret. The Housekeeper and Niece "le recibieron, y le desnudaron, y le tendieron en su antiguo *lecho*." Here ends the Primera Parte; but at the beginning of the sequel we learn that during almost a month the Priest and the Barber refrained from visiting their unfortunate friend, without, however, ceasing to supervise the care he received: "[que] tuviesen cuenta con regalarle, dándole a comer cosas confortativas y apropiadas para el corazón[45] y el cerebro." The patient seemed to respond: "iba dando muestras de estar en su entero juicio." But the diet, and the sleep implied by the word *lecho* were of no avail. "Visitáronle, en fin, y halláronle sentado en la cama . . . ; y estaba tan *seco* y amojamado, que no parecía sino hecho de carne de momia." A mention of the Turks brings back hot and dry passions—boldness and aggressiveness—and the Niece perceives clearly "que quiere mi señor volver a ser caballero andante." Indeed, she herself causes a new outpouring of choler: "Por el Dios que me sustenta, que si no fueras mi sobrina derechamente, como hija de mi hermana, que había de hacer un tal castigo en ti, por la blasfemia que has dicho, que sonara por todo el mundo" (II, 6). At the end of the very next chapter Don Quijote and Sancho head for "la gran ciudad del Toboso."

The decline of Don Quijote's *bríos* toward the end of the Second Part needs no recording here. There are recurring fits of melancholy,[46] beginning with the encounter with the Holy Images: "y yo hasta agora no sé lo que conquisto a fuerza de mis trabajos" (II, 68).[47] On the sands of Barcelona he is defeated by the Knight of the White Moon. Entering his village he sees a hare crossing his path: "*Malum signum!*" Thereafter an acute attack of melancholy, a physical crisis in the form of a fever, and a long sleep effect the final cure of his mind and bring on his death.

Don Quijote is beset by melancholy[48]: "Fué el parecer del médico que melancolía y desabrimiento le acababa."[49] Sancho confirms the diagnosis: "la mayor locura que puede hacer un hombre es dejarse morir, sin más ni más, sin que nadie le mate, ni otras manos le acaben que las de su melancolía." In Renaissance theory unnatural melancholy born of passion produces a "strange and foreign heat" that burns the natural humors "into ashes," and the product of this combustion is "far worse and more pernicious" than natural melancholy, according to the doctrine of Levinus Lemnius.[50] Any infinite sadness tends to produce death.[51]

Don Quijote suffers a fever "que le tuvo en la cama seis días." Huarte, it will be remembered,[52] declares that a rise in the brain's temperature through illness causes a change in the patient from wisdom to foolishness or vice versa. He gives an example which clearly is an antecedent of the death-scene that Cervantes is preparing: "En confirmación de lo cual no puedo dejar de referir lo que pasó en Córdoba el año 1570, estando la corte en esta ciudad, en la muerte de un loco cortesano que se llamaba Luis López." This man, when sane, "tenía perdidas las obras del entendimiento, y de lo que tocaba a la *imaginativa* decía . . . donaires de mucho contento." He was smitten by "una calentura maligna de tabardillo" and "*vino de repente a tanto juicio . . .* que espantó toda la corte." For this reason "le administraron los santos sacramentos, y *testó* con toda la *cordura* del mundo, y así *murió* . . . pidiendo perdón de sus pecados."[53]

A third factor was sleep. "Rogó don Quijote que le dejasen solo, porque quería dormir un poco. Hiciéronlo así, y durmió de un tirón . . . más de seis horas, y tanto que pensaron el Ama y la Sobrina que se había de quedar en el sueño." At the end of that time he awoke, "dando una gran voz," praising God for the restoration of his faculties, and declaring: "Yo me siento, Sobrina, a punto de muerte." All were inclined to believe him, and one of the reasons was "el haber vuelto con tanta facilidad de loco a cuerdo," like Huarte's *cortesano* in the year 1570. Like that *cortesano*, Don Quijote makes his will. His sands run out rapidly. Sansón Carrasco prepares en epitaph and Cide Hamete Benengeli places his pen in the rack, his long chronicle at last completed.

All has come full cycle. Don Quijote has lived out his destiny as a *colérico ingenioso* to the enrichment of all thoughtful men who know or have known his story. To achieve this end Cervantes made use of two vehicles whose possibilities his own *ingenio*, his own great power of *invención*, enabled him to perceive: the novels of chivalry as a framework for a newly conceived reality and Juan Huarte de San Juan's typological psychology as a pattern for the metamorphosis of his hero. The phases of the metamorphosis are exquisitely planned and brought to their conclusion.[54] There are three of them. An exciting cause, a resolving crisis, a diminution of cerebral heat, three times repeated and all eventually joined together in a greater unity as the initial adust humor yields to its enemy, the ultimate cold of death.

ADDENDUM

The present article had been completed when I received from Germany Harald Weinrich's *Das Ingenium Don Quijotes. Ein Beitrag zur literarischen Charakterkunde* (*Forschungen zur romanischen Philologie*, herausg. v. Heinrich Lausberg, Heft 1), Münster, 1956. I began to read it expecting that it would render superfluous the publication of my study. Such has not been the case. Although a complete review of Herr Weinrich's monograph belongs properly to another place, it is necessary to give here some account of his findings and their relation to my own. Weinrich knows the studies of Salillas and Iriarte, but fails to see the importance—and frequently the presence—of the medical aspects of Cervantes' conception of his hero. "Cervantes versteht also den Vorgang der Geistesverwirrung im Rahmen der Temperamentenlehre; die *cagione intrinsica* ist eine medizinische Begründung. Cervantes war zweifellos medizinisch interessiert" (p. 30). Yet Salillas "begeht . . . den Fehler, dass er das Ingenium als pathologisches Vermögen begreifen will (*comprender lo ingenioso en lo patológico*), während umgekehrt die Absonderlichkeiten vom Ingenium her verstanden sein wollen" (p. 36). Although Weinrich sees a connection between *se le secó el cerebro* and Don Quijote's derangement, he does not connect it with lack of sleep: Dass die unmässige geistige Anstrengung das Gehirn austrocknet, ist eine der zeitgenössischen Psychologie sehr geläufige Vorstellung" (p. 29). As a consequence of this disregarding of the *Temperamentenlehre*, he fails to understand the interplay of Don Quijote's moments of excitement—with their outpouring of gall and the resulting exaltation of the imagination—and his moments of relative quiet (as at the goatherds' campfire) which make possible his intervals of lucidity.

Because of this incompleteness of his comprehension, Weinrich

conceives a thesis which he cannot prove: that it is "kaum zweifel-
haft, dass Cervantes erst im Laufe der Komposition über das Ingenium Don Quijotes klar geworden ist, und zwar etwa zu dem
Zeitpunkt, da die beiden erwähnten neuen Elemente (loss of interest in parody, desire to write a *good* novel of chivalry) in den
Roman eintreten" (p. 12). This "point" is "etwa von der Mitte des
ersten Teils ab," when the book takes on "einen völlig anderen
Charakter" (p. 11). We are told that, as Don Quijote sallies forth
for the first time, he is a mere *quidam*, because of the "Sparsamkeit
der Charakterisierung"; that "über sein Ingenium erfahren wir
nichts"; that there is no correspondence between *ingenio* and the
contents of the first chapters (p. 10); that only about the middle of
Part I "mag [Cervantes] auch den endgültigen Titel seines Werkes
formuliert haben, oder auch erst nach Abschluss des ersten Teils, so
wie die Prologe bei Cervantes Epiloge zu sein pflegen" (pp. 12–13).

To all of this I would answer that Cervantes had his title and its
meaning clearly in mind from the first. As we have seen, the
physical description of Don Quijote makes this evident, as do the
references to sleep, to the desiccation of his brain (I, i), and to the
restoration of his sanity and *sosiego* after drinking quantities of
cold water (I, v). I would also point out—and this I treat here for
the first time—that Cervantes knew, as early as I, vi, that his
purpose was to write a *good* romance of chivalry.

Certainly we can only surmise what may have been in Cervantes'
mind as he began to write, and what caused him later to play down
the parody of the old romances and concern himself, progressively,
with the problem of presenting an analysis of reality within the
framework of a book of entertainment. It seems to me that we
cannot now be so sure as formerly that he was at first *unaware* of
what he wanted to do. It could well have been that the very nature
of Don Quijote's illness required the *first* stages of his madness to
be the most violent; that only with the *subsidence* of the flow of
gall could the "lucid intervals" become frequent, and that this
subsidence occurred gradually. I believe it is possible to see in the
escrutinio, and specifically in the comments on *Tirant lo Blanch*, an
early inkling of Cervantes' deeper intention. In *Olivante de Laura*
Cervantes apparently saw *some* elements of verisimilitude—the essence of a *good* romance—, else the Priest would not have said
(comparing this book to its author's *Jardín de flores*), "no sé cuál

de los dos es *más verdadero, o . . . menos mentiroso.*" It would seem that its condemnation to the flames *por disparatado* corresponds to a failure on the part of its author to utilize its elements of truth to create a real work of art. *Florismarte de Hircania* is condemned "*a pesar de* su extraño nacimiento y soñadas aventuras." Cervantes is pleased with the "extraño nacimiento." And do the "soñadas aventuras" have anything to do with the use of *cosas soñadas* in the Cueva de Montesinos? Next comes the *Espejo de caballerías,* "con el *verdadero historiador* Turpín." Surely the concept of poetry-history must *already* have been in Cervantes' mind. For this reason the *Espejo* is condemned merely to banishment, not to the bonfire. There follow the romances of the Palmerin cycle. *Palmerín de Inglaterra* is saved, supposedly because some of the adventures are "bonísimas y de grande artificio" (*poetry* as against history), and also because it observes the rational principle of decorum (cf. Weinrich's final chapter on decorum). *Don Belianís* is put in confinement, since this book requires emendation of the "impertinencias de más importancia." And last of all comes the *Historia del famoso caballero Tirante el Blanco,* a "tesoro de contento" and a "mina de pasatiempos." These are the very merits for which Cervantes praises his own work in the *Viaje del Parnaso:* "Yo he dado en el Quijote pasatiempo/al pecho melancólico y mohino." The "pasaje más obscuro del Quijote" is no longer obscure.[55] Indeed, it throws much light on Cervantes' purpose, and as early as I, vi. In spite of *Tirante el Blanco's* realistic "verisimilitude" (*con todo esto*), its author is to be sent permanently to the galleys "porque *no* hizo tantas necedades *de industria*"—that is to say, purposely and purposefully, with full knowledge that they *were* absurdities, with the superiority of the knowing artist who uses the unreal to interpret the real, who mixes experiential and fantastic elements for the sake of higher purpose. For this failure to seize a wonderful opportunity, for this "missing of the boat" when the slightest additional leap would have enabled him to catch it, for this supreme *necedad,* Martorell should be punished—but his book shall not be burned. It is to be read carefully by the Barber for confirmation of the judgment just rendered. I conclude that even in I, vi, Cervantes knew what he was doing.

The conclusion just given rests, admittedly, on hypothesis; the interpretation can be accepted or rejected. Not so with my next

argument. Don Quijote's "lucid intervals" ("Don Quijotes Ingenium zeigt sich vor allem in den lichten Augenblicken" [p. 66])
make their appearance long before "the middle of Part I." As Don
Quijote's *cólera*–the hyperactivity of his *imaginativa* produced by
dryness (lack of sleep) and heat (passion, enthusiasm, *manía*) –
wears off in moments of relaxation, he displays that *other* type of
ingenio, the *universa vis mentis nostrae* of Vives, and he does so
early in the novel. Already in I, xii, there appear cracks in the
curtain of obsession. Don Quijote corrects the goatherds' speech,
insisting on *eclipse* instead of *cris*, *estéril* in place of *estil*, *Sarra* as a
correction of *sarna*. And he says, with all the *gravitas* of his later
self: "Esa ciencia se llama Astrología." He shows literary judgment: "el cuento es muy bueno, y vos, buen Pedro, le contáis con
buena gracia." In I, xiii, he recognizes and proposes to defend the
"claras y suficientes razones" of Marcela. All of this is a product of
"das gute Ingenium" as understood–all but exclusively–by Weinrich: "die Vollkommenheit im *officium* als Vereinigung universaler
Bildung und Tugend mit der speziellen Fähigkeit für einen besti-
mmten Beruf." This is none other than the perfection of Cicero's
orator: "Zum vollkommenen Redner gehört nicht nur die Bered-
samkeit, sondern alle Wissenschaften, da der Redner in der Lage
sein muss, über alle Themen zu sprechen. Voraussetzung solcher
Vollkommenheit ist ein *summun ingenium*" (p. 72). "Don Quijote
kann in seinen Reden und Gesprächen den ganzen Kreis der Bildung abschreiten, weil er *ingenioso* ist" (p. 70).

These statements are indeed true. But it is no less true that Don
Quijote is *ingenioso* because he is *colérico*, that the flow and ebb of
cólera determine the alternation of his spates of *disparates* with
those "lucid intervals" in which the Knight recognizes a science for
what it is, or discourses on the problems of the State. When *both*
"das gute Ingenium" and its pathological hypertrophy are taken
into account, *Don Quijote*, as a work of art, acquires a unity which
it has perhaps never before been possible to appreciate so fully. We
read in López Pinciano's *Filosofía antigua poética* (Madrid, 1953,
I, 48–49): "No atiende la *imaginación* a las verdaderas especies,
mas *finge* otras nueuas, y acerca dellas obra de mil maneras. . . . El
instrumento desta facultad pide *calor* con *sequedad*, compañeros
del *furor*."

IO El Licenciado Vidriera: *Its Relation to the* Viaje del Parnaso *and the* Examen de Ingenios *of* Huarte

In Cervantes studies today it is no longer possible to attribute things we do not understand to a supposed haphazardness on the part of Cervantes. If a work appears to be haphazard, the reason is almost certainly to be found in the faulty vision of the critic, not in an unawareness in Cervantes of the requirements of form. When, therefore, a critic affirms that neither of the two aspects of the madness of Tomás Rodaja (its cause and its nature) "is connected with the framework of the last two thirds of the story" (a madman uttering sage observations on society), and further asserts that "the framework of the story bears no relation to its contents"[1] and makes bold to say that "such slipshod planning in a man at the height of his powers, seems hard to believe"[2]—when such statements as these are made by a critic who in other respects is fully responsible, we are challenged to look deeper. If we do,[3] we shall find that the structure of this tale is admirably suited to express the thoughts and emotions Cervantes was seeking—quite apparently—to convey to his readers.

El Licenciado Vidriera sets forth one of the grave problems of human life. The problem—unresolved—is that of the individual whose happiness is destroyed by a society that will not allow him the right of self-realization, a society that will not permit him to live in peace in accordance with his desires. It is the same problem that Unamuno treats, in an entirely different way, in *La locura del Doctor Montarco*, a *cuento* in which a physician is driven to madness because society is unwilling to concede that a *good* physician could devote his leisure to purely literary composition. In *El Licenciado Vidriera*, a *licenciado en leyes* is prevented from practicing his profession and compelled to *poner una pica en Flandes* because society, which had enjoyed his *ingeniosidades* during his temporary derangement, insists that he *continue* to provide similar free entertainment, and by its insistence drives him to desperation — compels him to accept a way of life foreign to his natural bent. Tomás Rodaja, a young man of great *ingenio* (like Don Quijote) whose desire in life (like that of Don Quijote) is to win *fame* (in this case, in the world of the intellect), is forced to embrace *armas*, not *letras:* "murió . . . dejando fama . . . de . . . valentísimo soldado."

Rodaja is thus presented to us as a sort of Don Quijote in reverse: "mis *estudios*, siendo *famoso* por ellos." But Cervantes, we may believe, is really thinking of himself, embittered by the fact that Lope (intellectually unqualified to unlace the latchet of his shoe) was the darling of the public while he, the *raro inventor*, had been forced, first to become a *valentísimo soldado*, and later (having failed to receive an administrative post in the Indies) to tread the roads of Spain as a collector of wine and oil and grain for the Navy; and—always—to struggle with poverty, to which he never gave the name of "our lady." In this tale, however, it is *glory*, not gold that is principally in his mind, as we shall see.

All of this was a source of pain and resentment to Cervantes, a pain and a resentment from which he sought release through the medium of art.[4] Art is *form*,[5] and the artist's first problem is one of structure. This particular formal problem—to find a vehicle for the artistic exteriorization of personal frustration—was solved by Cervantes twice: in *El Licenciado Vidriera* and in the *Viaje del Parnaso*. Let us examine the latter first.

In Capítulo IV of the *Viaje* Cervantes declares:

> Jamás me contenté ni satisfice
> de hipócritas melindres. Llanamente
> *quise alabanzas de lo que bien hice.*[6]

That he feels *cheated* in the exchange of recognition for achievement is abundantly clear in his complaints at the end of Capítulo III, where he describes the arrival of the poets before Apollo and the assignment of seats of honor to each of them, beneath the laurels. When all are seated except Cervantes he protests—*con turbada lengua*–and continues to voice his indignation in the following Capítulo (p. 80):

> No se estima,
> señor, *del vulgo vano*, el que te sigue
> y al árbol sacro del laurel se arrima.

He then presents his *hoja de servicios:* it is he who designed and cut the dress "con que al mundo la hermosa *Galatea*/ salió para librarse del olvido"; it is he "por quien la *Confusa*, nada fea/ pareció en los teatros admirable"; he who "con estilo en parte razonable" composed *comedias* that, in their time, "tuvieron de lo grave y de lo afable'"; and:

> Yo he dado en *Don Quijote* pasatiempo
> al pecho melancólico y mohino.

It is he who

> he abierto en mis *Novelas* un camino
> por do la lengua castellana puede
> mostrar con *propiedad* un *desatino* –

which is the summing up of his personal and original formula for the writing of fiction: the presentation of the flights of the imagination *well anchored* to the bedrock of reality. Furthermore:

> Yo soy aquel que en la *invención* excede
> a muchos, y al que falta en esta parte,
> es fuerza que su *fama* falta quede –

that is to say that he, Cervantes, who is the greatest *inventor* of all, *should* have the greatest *acclaim*. He has composed–he says–an infinite number of *romances*, the best being the one on *Celos;* and he is about to give to the press his *Persiles*

> con que mi *nombre* y obras *multiplique.*

Because of these *rights* to *recognition,*

> me *congojo* y me *lastimo*
> de verme solo en pie. . . .

It is time for Apollo to make reply, and the god does so in words that Don Quijote had applied to himself:

> Tú mismo te has forjado tu ventura,
> y yo te he visto alguna vez con ella,
> pero en el imprudente poco dura.

The only consolation offered is meager enough:

> *dobla la capa y siéntate sobre ella,*

for an honored place may

> honrar más *merecido* que alcanzado.

There is a difficulty, however, and Cervantes does not hesitate to point it out:

> "Bien parece, señor, que no se advierte
> —le respondí—que *yo no tengo capa.*"
> El dijo: "Aunque sea así, gusto de verte."

Gusto de verte! Coming from Apollo, these words may be the equivalent of a *succès d'estime*, but they do not give consolation. Cervantes can only bow his head and remain standing,

> que no hay asiento bueno
> si el *favor* no le labra o la *riqueza.*

Thus approximately one year before his death Cervantes expresses a dissatisfaction with society which could hardly be more deep-seated. He is grateful for the *favor* of the Conde de Lemos, as he will make clear on his deathbed, but it has come late and has not been sufficient. As for *riqueza*, the tremendous *succès de librairie* of *Don Quijote* relieved his poverty not at all. As for public recognition, *no hay asiento bueno* when the requisites specified are lacking.

Let us turn now to the second work in which Cervantes gives expression—*feeling and form*—to this same resentment. *El Licenciado Vidriera* no longer puzzles us, and is seen to have complete artistic adequacy, when we consider it as an allegory composed on the same theme that we have been analyzing, written in the same key. Let us recapitulate: Tomás Rodaja, born to cultivate the life of the mind, is compelled–by the threat of starvation–to take up an employment that never should have been his: *las armas*. Cervantes, born for poetry and literary glory, had to devote his efforts –in order not to starve–to a task altogether foreign to his temperament: *comisario de la armada*. Cervantes, born to enjoy the company of the Muses, had to seek "la última esperanza de los desesperados": the Indies. Cervantes, like Don Quijote, had been *artífice de su ventura*, but his *ventura* had amounted to little: Lope de Vega was the darling of the nation.

If we read with care the *respuestas* which the Licenciado makes to the *preguntas*[8] addressed to him by the curious idlers responsible for his fate, we shall find parallels with the complaints of Cervantes, the neglected author. Singer, in his second article on the *Licenciado Vidriera*,[9] shows that "again and again, the personal philosophy and experiences of Miguel de Cervantes are echoed in the satire and wit of the mad Licenciate's replies. If the term apothegm applies to over half of them in number, it applies far less in bulk, and withal counts for little in whatever charm and interest the author of *Don Quijote* has given his *novela*" (p. 30). This is indeed true–the apothegms are far less interesting than Cervantes' own observations on the nature of the world and man–and in pointing it out Singer has rendered a genuine service. But all concern over the statistical balance of apothegms and *nonapothegmatical replies* disappears in the light of Gillet's study of the ancient game of *preguntas y respuestas*.

The latter part of *El Licenciado Vidriera* is not a series of apothegms at all; in it Cervantes merely avails himself–for his *artistic* purpose–of the tradition, centuries old in the folklore of many nations, of *preguntas y respuestas*.[10] Furthermore, it is possible to see in Tomás Rodaja's *respuestas* much more than Singer has seen; to see in them, indeed, the central unifying nucleus about which the other parts of *El Licenciado Vidriera* move and from which they derive their significance.

We should remember, first, that *El Licenciado Vidriera* has a frame-story similar to that of *Don Quijote*, but with this difference: in *Don Quijote* the problematical element–that which has to do with the individual's struggle for self-realization—arises from *within*. Don Quijote's madness is born of an act of his own free will: he deprives himself of *sleep*, until "se le secó el cerebro." It was that *sequedad* which caused all his aberrations.[11] The Licenciado, on the other hand, suffers madness through the action upon him of an evil member of *society*, and his self-realization is impeded by outside forces: the *dama de todo rumbo*, the *muchachos*, in short *todos*.

We should also bear in mind that in the *novela ejemplar*—as against *Don Quijote*—the protagonist embraces the career of arms, not because the soldier's career is glorious and leads to fame, but as a *pis aller*, because he can do nothing else. He has no other means, not merely of living free from his tormentors, but of living at all. In *Don Quijote*, quite the other way around, *las armas* remain glorious to the end, when all earthly glory fades in the light of Heaven.

There is another thing we should realize, a thing strangely forgotten, though it was pointed out by Rafael Salillas in 1905, and in 1939 and 1948 by Mauricio Iriarte, S.J., and this is that both Don Quijote and Tomás Rodaja are conceived in accordance with the medical and psychological doctrines of Juan Huarte de San Juan's *Examen de ingenios para las sciencias*.[12] Don Quijote is an *ingenioso*, which is to say that he is *de temperamento caliente y seco*, born under the sign of Mars. Rodaja is less *caliente* (though *seco*), inclining more toward *melancolía* (black bile), since intellectuals are by nature *melancólicos*, that is to say *de temperamento frío y seco*. Rodaja, though possessed of sufficient *cólera* (yellow bile) to enable him to be a valiant soldier, shows by his typically melancholy illness and his fear of breakage that *melancolía* is his dominant humor. Lawrence Babb, in *The Elizabethan Malady*,[13] gives this description of the melancholy man: "Melancholy men . . . are peculiarly subject to hallucinations and fixed ideas. . . . [They] have absurd anxieties regarding their own persons. Some think that they are earthen pots and are continually afraid of being broken. . . . One . . . is afraid to sit down because he thinks that his buttocks are made of glass. . . ."

Whereas Don Quijote, being *caliente y seco* dreams wild dreams, Rodaja, who is *seco y frío*, is more cerebrative than imaginative and is never aggressive (as Don Quijote is countless times). Like the typical melancholy man, Rodaja has the potentiality of becoming, according to Burton's *Anatomy of Melancholy*, an excellent philosopher, poet, or prophet (Babb, p. 55). Only when melancholy exists in excess in the body is it harmful. Ficino believed all men of letters to be melancholy; Vives, that melancholy greatly enhances the mental powers (Babb, p. 61). The *harm* in Rodaja's case arises from the fact that his natural tendency to melancholy is rendered acute and pathological by the administering of a poison.

In Renaissance literature the typical melancholy man, regarding himself as a case of *neglected superiority*, tends to snarl at the world in his frustration (Babb, 76 ff., 96 ff.). Rodaja does not snarl, for the simple reason that Cervantes himself, a man of even and festive temperament, was no snarler. Yet Cervantes was not without his *melancolías*, caused, as we have seen very clearly, by poverty, *neglect by society*, failure to achieve adequate fame. Being Cervantes, he could not snarl at the world, but he could protest and he did so—eloquently—in the *Viaje del Parnaso* and in *El Licenciado Vidriera:*

> *Quise alabanza de lo que bien hice.*

Each of these two works of his old age—the *Viaje del Parnaso* and *El Licenciado*—is a perfect expression of Cervantes' grievance. As he planned *El Licenciado Vidriera*, Cervantes, casting about in his mind in search of a vehicle, a *form*, for the exteriorization of his *discontent*, hit upon various things that he could fuse into a unified artistic whole: 1) the glass-delusion, no invention of his, but common medical and psychiatric knowledge; 2) Huarte's familiar theory of the effects on the personality of an extreme imbalance of the bodily humors; 3) the same author's account of the *paje* whose cure caused public dismay over the loss of so delightful an entertainer; 4) the personal experiences of Cervantes' own *Wanderjahre;* 5) the stock-in-trade device of the love-philter; 6) the folkloric game of *preguntas y respuestas;* 7) the case of the intellectual forced into military service because society offers him no other livelihood. Each of these elements has its task to perform; each is subordinated to the semi-tragic ending.

Singer, in his second article, has rightly pointed out the autobiographical character of Rodaja's denunciation of the knaveries of publishers and the injustice and severity of judges; of his exultant assertion of the right to freedom of body and will; of his praise of poetry and poets and of actors and their profession; of his hatred of money-lenders; of his sympathy for public functionaries. Thus positive as well as negative aspects of Cervantes' personal philosophy and experiences are echoed in the satire and wit of the mad Licenciado's replies—a satire and a wit full of that Cervantine humanity that makes unforgettable the first reading of *El coloquio de los perros*. And the experiences and attitudes are not merely echoed. They are *fused* into a work that leads the reader as *naturally* to its last phrase: "dejando fama de valentísimo soldado," as the entirety of *Don Quijote*—1605, 1615—leads to the death-scene of Alonso Quijano el Bueno.[14] The stages are clearly marked: the early years of study; the *Wanderjahre;* the return to Salamanca in the hope of success in the legal profession, the illness and persecution, the cure and renewal of persecution, the lament and the departure for Flanders; the report of valiant fighting and a soldier's death. The final words, *dejando fama de valentísimo soldado*, should recall to the reader the early expression of Tomás Rodaja's ideal in life: *mis estudios, siendo famoso por ellos*. It was not to be. Tomás is a *figura* of Miguel de Cervantes, for whom there was no *asiento bueno* on Parnassus, insufficient *favor*, no *riqueza*. In 1615 Noel Brûlart de Sillery and the members of his mission from the French Court sought to find out what they could about Cervantes. They learned that he was "old, a soldier, a gentleman, and poor."[15]

II *Don Quijote and the* Alcahuete

In the dramatic character study *Doña Clarines*, by Serafín and Joaquín Álvarez Quintero, there is a scene in which Doña Clarines accuses her niece of telling falsehoods to explain her constant visits to the house across the street: "la niña de la casa es amiga tuya a partir de una larga temporada que estuvo en Madrid." Such is not the case, insists Doña Clarines. The "niña" in question has no attractions whatsoever, "pero tiene una tía, hermana de su madre, que siempre se distinguió grandemente en un oficio que elogiaba mucho Don Quijote." The *oficio* is that of *tercera* in love affairs. S. Griswold Morley, in his edition of the Quintero play, provides this note: "It is in the Adventure of the Galley-slaves (Part I, chapter 22) that Don Quijote delivers a eulogy of one who acts as intermediary between lovers. It has been called the only passage in which the words of the gentle-hearted knight sound out of character."[1] Rodríguez Marín, in his critical edition of 1947 (vol. II, p. 173, n. 7) regards Don Quijote's opinion of *alcahuetes* as "festiva" and offers a parallel text from a MS in the Biblioteca Nacional by Juan Antonio de Vera y Figueroa,[2] as well as references to Act I of Lope's *El amigo hasta la muerte* and to Rodríguez Lobo's *Corte na aldea* (Lisbon, 1630). All three of these collateral texts appear to be derived from *Don Quijote* (Lope's play was composed probably between 1610 and 1612, according to Morley-Bruerton, *Chronology*, p. 167), inasmuch as the influence of Huarte de San Juan's *Examen de ingenios para las ciencias*, a book to which Cervantes owed so much, is apparent in all four texts (see below). The three collateral texts give us no help, however, as we face the heretofore baffling question of *why* Cervantes made this supposedly "festive" outburst.

F. Sánchez y Escribano has endeavored to show a connection with the traditional exercises of wit in praise of fleas, flies, and other harmful, loathesome, unworthy or simply annoying things, and in particular has sought to show a genetic relationship with Erasmus' *Praise of Folly*. But the difficulty here is that there is no verbal connection between the *Encomium Moriae* and *Don Quijote*.[3]

It is now possible to see more deeply into the working of Cervantes' mind as he placed this disquieting speech on the lips of his Knight. Our first step is to analyze the passage in the setting of the Adventure of the Galley-slaves.

I

Before proceeding to the physical liberation of the chain-gang, Don Quijote explains to the officers in charge that he would like to know "the cause of the misfortune" of each of the prisoners. He is told to address his question to each individual man. The questions and the replies are—with the one exception of our perplexing text—chosen by Cervantes to provide an opportunity for the interplay of wit and naiveté.

The first man replies that he is going to the *gurapas* (to the galleys, a word unknown to Don Quijote) "por enamorado." "¿Por eso no más?" asks the Knight. That being so, he himself might well be chained to an oar. But it turns out that it was a different kind of "amor," that had led to an act of larceny.

The second prisoner refuses to answer Don Quijote's question, but a companion does so for him: "va por canario." Again the Knight's innocence is such that he has to be told the meaning: the culprit "sang" under torture, admitting his guilt, and is therefore the object of general contempt.

The naiveté continues. The third man replies: "Voy . . . por faltarme diez ducados." Don Quijote expresses a willingness to pay twenty ducats "por libraros desa pesadumbre." But it so happens that the condemnation (for something far different) was pronounced because there were no ducats available at the trial to pervert justice: "hubiera untado la péndola del escribano y avivado el ingenio del procurador."

The fourth man is our *alcahuete*, an emotional and physical wreck. When addressed by the Knight he bursts into tears, and the fifth man replies for him. There is still a certain degree of naiveté:

Sancho helps his master to understand the language of the *pícaros*, and the spokesman of the *galeotes* makes matters amply clear: "va por alcahuete, y por tener asímesmo sus puntas y collar de hechicero."

Don Quijote's tone changes immediately, and his naiveté drops from him. If it were simply a matter of pimping, i. e., if there were no complicating sorcery, the prisoner should not row in the galleys, but should have charge of them as their *general*. Because pimping is "oficio de discretos, y necesarísimo en la república bien ordenada." Only honorable persons should exercise the profession, and there should be an examining board to determine who the practitioners are to be. "Desta manera se excusarían muchos males" that arise from the fact that it is an occupation manned by contemptible persons—"pajecillos y truhanes de pocos años y de poca experiencia." The Knight would gladly "pasar adelante," he remarks, "y dar las razones porque convenía hacer *elección* de los que en la república habían de tener tan necesario oficio." This is not the time or the place to amplify his thought, he says; some day he will express his ideas to persons in authority, who will be able to do something to remedy this social evil.

Cervantes is speaking through his hero, and in all seriousness.[4] He is thinking in terms, not of witticisms,[5] but of the good of the state.[6] One is reminded of a passage in Cervantes' *entremés*, *La elección de los alcaldes de Daganzo:*

> Digo
> que, pues se hace examen de barberos,
> de herradores, de sastres, y se hace
> de cirujanos y otras zarandajas,
> también se examinasen para alcaldes.
>
> . . . .
>
> Llamen a Berrocal, entre, y veamos
> dónde llega la raya de su ingenio.[7]

II

This leads us to the consideration of an extremely important point involving Cervantes' conception of the new type of novel he was creating[8] as a vehicle for all sorts of ideas, a "Barojian" concept of the novel "en que cabe todo." It is a question of the much debated problem of "digressions," or "episodes."[9] In *Don Quijote* Cervantes' expressed ideas on the unity of the novel "are based on current ideas of epic poetry. In execution, more especially in Part II, he goes deeper than the mere formal observance of these, achieving a unity that is neither skin-deep nor buried beneath layers of symbol and abstraction, one that is neither superficial nor occult, but vital."[10] In the Adventure of the Galley-slaves, Cervantes makes a literary judgment: to develop at this point (as he would like to) his ideas on public control of prostitution, and (more deeply) on the inevitability of evil in a world considered to be part of a moral universe, would detract from the vital unity of his book. He therefore restrains Don Quijote's philosophizing and gets on with the interrogation of prisoners in the chain-gang.

Necessary as this literary restraint is judged to be, it goes against the grain. In the Second Part (Ch. 44) Cervantes explains that it is almost unendurable for him ("trabajo incomportable") to avoid "estenderse a otras digresiones y episodios más graves" (such as the disquisition suppressed in I, 22) "y más entretenidos" (for example, the tales of the *Cautivo* and of the *Curioso impertinente*, in Part I). In his Second Part, Cervantes explains, he has decided to maintain greater unity—a decision for which he requests the reward of praise: "y pues se contiene y cierra en los estrechos límites de la narración, teniendo habilidad, suficiencia y entretenimiento *para tratar del universo todo*, pide . . . se le den alabanzas, no por lo que escribe, sino por lo que ha dejado de escribir."

III

As the result of a chance discovery of a text in St. Augustine's *De Ordine*, it is possible to form a fairly concrete idea of what Don Quijote might have said in the disquisition on *alcahuetes* which he promises for another occasion (I, 22). In the Second Book of his treatise, St. Augustine uses the following question with its answer to serve as heading for Chapter 4: *Are man's sinful acts performed in accordance with God's plan?-[Yes]; evil, when brought into line with, and considered within the framework of the Divine Order, redounds to the splendor of the universe.*[11] In paragraph 12 of this Chapter 4, vile things are considered in the light of the over-arching goodness and beauty of the world, including whores and pimps, as well as the torn and bloodied body of the victim of a cock-fight:

> For you say things which—unless one has seen them—appear to me unsayable; nor do I [Zenobius is speaking] understand how you perceive them; so true and sublime do they appear to me. You, moreover, in your allegation, sought perhaps only *one* example, whereas to me innumerable things occur which incline me to agree. For what is more loathsome than an executioner, more truculent in spirit, more horrible? Yet, in the scheme of things you mention, he has a necessary place in the order of a well governed city. By reason of his own condition he is an evildoer; but as a functioning part of an order that is not his, he injures only those who have done harm. *What could be dirtier, more bereft of decorum and more shameful than whores and pimps and other pests of this sort?* Remove whores from human society, and you would turn everything over to the lecherous. Set them on the same plane as chaste matrons, and you would stain everything with disgusting blemishes. It thus becomes obvious that this type of human beings is utterly impure with respect to life and conduct, and altogether vile when judged by the laws of order. In the bodies of living creatures, are there not certain members, which if you contemplate them only as they appear, are impossible to look at? Nevertheless the order of Nature does not wish them to be absent (for they are necessary) and likewise does not permit them to stand out too conspicuously (for they are indecorous). Nevertheless, these horrid things, if restricted to their proper place, make possible a *better* place for things that are better than they are. What was more pleasant, more in keeping with the rustic life of the fields, than that fight between game cocks which we mentioned in the preceding Book (Chap. VIII, section 25)? What could be more abject than the ugliness of the victim? *And yet by that very ugliness the more perfect beauty of the fight was made manifest.*[12]

I do not argue that Cervantes knew this passage; merely that he had in mind the centuries-old idea of an Order in which the positives and negatives agree, and of a State whose organization should permit men to adjust their lives—their necessities and their passions—to the rational harmony of that Order.[13] I believe that Don Quijote is concerned here more with civics than with theology (although in his day the two could scarcely be separated). He applies to the occupation of the pander the same words that St. Augustine applies to the contemptible occupation of the executioner, and (by implication) to that of whores and pimps as well: "necesarísimo en la república bien ordenada" ("inter ipsas leges locum necessarium tenet, et in bene moderatae civitatis ordinem inseritur"). The remainder of the Knight's speech dwells entirely on the civic aspect of the problem of prostitution (or of illicit cohabitation arranged by an intermediary). Yet there is more than just plain civics: both Don Quijote and his squire are deeply moved and bestow their pity on a vile wretch—Sancho (the money-minded and often greedy Sancho) to the point of giving him an alms.

This civic aspect of Cervantes' thought is better understood when one has read a *Discurso*, composed by Bartolomé Leonardo de Argensola at the request of the ministers of Philip III and entitled *De cómo se remediarán los vicios de la Corte y que no acuda a ella tanta gente inútil*.[14] This *Discurso* makes reasonable the hypothesis that Cervantes was thinking of the social organization of Venice, concerning which he could have become informed during his Italian years, or merely through his own voracious reading. Argensola is advocating what Don Quijote had in mind: the authoritarian control by government of individual conduct through the action of well-chosen and responsible officers.

Argensola would entrust this delicate task to a magistrate possessing the broadest imaginable powers, an official who would know about, investigate, and control all aspects of urban life. Such magistrates had existed in antiquity, of course; but along with the classical references Argensola cites Gasparo Cardinal Contarini's *De magistratibus et Republica Venetorum libri quinque*,[15] together with Guerino Piso Soacius' *De Romanorum et Venetorum magistratum inter se comparatione libellus* (Patavii, 1563), especially the exposition in the latter book "De officio ejus cui mandata est jurisdictio."

In Rome, Argensola notes, the Pope is informed of everything

that happens in the city each day (and night). Even in Madrid, in
the parish of San Martín, the Junta de la Hermandad knows how
each person lives—information supplied by an Administrator who
works with two deputies who are constantly rotated. The munici-
pal organization of Palermo is also cited. Argensola would have all
Madrid imitate these examples: his ideal magistrate would have the
power and the freedom of action of a censor-dictator.

We may conclude with a quotation from the article on prostitution in the Espasa *Enciclopedia universal ilustrada* (vol. XLVII,
italics mine), which seems to apply directly to our problem:

"La cuestión se reduce, pues, a preguntar si dado caso que en
determinadas circumstancias sean un mal menor [las 'casas públi-
cas'], podrán permitirse para evitarlos mayores. Las autoridades
comúnmente se inclinan a la parte afirmative, *siguiendo a San
Agustín y a Santo Tomás y apoyándose en la misma razón que
aducen estos santos doctores* . . . El mayor mal que se trata de
evitar es la sodomía, el adulterio y la seducción de las mujeres
honestas, y otros, los cuales cundirían en la sociedad si los hombres
voluptuosos no tuviesen donde saciar su desordenado apetito."

This judgment of the *santos doctores* had long since been put
into practice by Alfonso el Sabio, under whom "la prostitución
adquiere un sello moderno, es reconocida como oficio, se la encierra
aparte y, por razón de su mismo oficio, se la considera dueña de su
salario."[16]

If we now ask *Quid demonstratum est?* the reply should be
clear. It has been shown that Don Quijote's opinion of the occupation represented by the unfortunate *galeote* is not "festiva," but is
born of convictions so strong that they move even Sancho to a
most unaccustomed act of generosity. These convictions have their
theoretical basis in the teaching of St. Augustine and the Church
Fathers. It has been shown also that there is little reason to see a
genetic relationship between this Cervantine text and Erasmus'
Praise of Folly. Nor should we be content with relating Cervantes'
apparently paradoxical statements to the long tradition of display-
ing rhetorical wit by praising things unpraisable. On the contrary,
it is apparent that Cervantes is guided, as he pens the speech which
Don Quijote addresses to the *galeote*, by his theory of the novel
(the forward movement of a tale should not be unduly held up by

digressions) and by his recollection of Huarte's *Examen de ingenios para las ciencias* (pimping should not be the work of *mujerzuelas*, of *mozos de caballos*, and *rufianes* but should be converted into a socially controlled activity officially permitted in order to avoid greater evils, and placed in the hands of rigorously selected social workers). He may have been guided, also, by his awareness of the existence of various measures of social control in Rome, Palermo, the parish of San Martín in Madrid, and, especially, in the Republic of Venice.[17]

12 *Lope and Cervantes:*
Peripeteia and Resolution[1]

Deleitar aprovechando (instructional delight) is the title of an edifying miscellany published by the Mercedarian Friar Tirso de Molina in 1635. It sets forth the pious conversation of three Madrid families during three days of Carnival, on the banks of the Manzanares river, in the gardens of Juan Fernández and del Duque. Its title is highly significant, and might be applied, in theory to nearly all, in practice to a very large portion, of Spanish belles-lettres not only during the Renaissance but also before and after that period.

The distinguished fourteenth-century prose writer, Don Juan Manuel, Prince of Castile, in his *Treatise on the Three Estates* of medieval Spanish society, expressed the literary ideal of that early time in these words:

> And when he shall have eaten and drunk at table fittingly and with temperance, he should (if he so wishes) hear minstrels sing and play their instruments, repeating good songs and good reports of chivalrous deeds capable of stirring the hearts of those who hear them to act nobly.[2]

Here the minstrels are expected to sing heroic poetry, very much as Homer did, in the presence of a Lord who has dined and wined wisely and well: the social justification of their art resides in its power to inspire noble listeners to acquit themselves fittingly, as a Spanish knight of the fourteenth century understood this duty.

A man of humbler origin, now in the fifteenth century, expressed the same general thought in a more pious frame of reference:

> That poetry is a divine art is proved by many passages in many books; Solomon uses it in his *Song of Songs*, and the holy Doctor

Friar Thomas Aquinas, in that great hymn that the Church sets such store by; therefore if I myself take pleasure in this art, I do so with full justification.

This is the voice of a lay moralist, Fernán Pérez de Guzmán, a pre-humanistic translator of Seneca and compiler of Senecan *sententiae;* the first Spaniard, indeed, to write a collection of modern biographies after the manner of Plutarch. There is nothing in his early humanistic conception of poetry—its uplifting power, its divine origin—to set off this fifteenth-century moralist from the sixteenth-century writer whom we next shall quote, the eminent poet and scholar Fray Luis de León who stands at the height of the humanistic period in Spain. Fray Luis' idea of poetry as God-inspired is not "medieval" in any distinctive or privative sense; it still found acceptance by Robert Lowth in the English eighteenth century.[3] But let us consider Fray Luis' own words:

> The idea of poetry in the minds of men is surely God-inspired, to the end that by its movement and spirit we might be directed toward Heaven, whence poetry came; for poetry is nothing if not a sharing in the celestial, the divine breath.

The late Miguel de Unamuno complained of the homiletic character of his nation's literature, calling it a *literatura de dómines,* of school masters. But the Spaniards were not the only ones to hold these ideas, inherited from the classical world and reinforced by the presence of poetry in the Bible. I invite your attention to the indices of two important books, under the key-words *delight, instruction, profit, utility, instrumental end.* The first book is Allan Gilbert's *Literary Criticism from Plato to Dryden* (New York, 1940); the other, *A History of Literary Criticism in the Italian Renaissance,* by Bernard Weinberg (Chicago, 1961). Ample space is given in each to the concept of literature as delightful instruction.

This idea of the moral responsibility of the man of letters was scarcely ever questioned, however frequently the "authorities," the *preceptistas,* might be locked up in the closet when the dramatist or the novelist sat down to write. So it is that when Garci Rodríguez de Montalvo, in the preface of his own version of the old tale of

Amadis of Gaul (1508), insists that a work of fiction of this sort—a romance of chivalry—can have virtue only by reason of the moralizing matter which the author interpolates into the story, he is echoing a commonplace of medieval aesthetics. And when, later in the same century, Sir Philip Sidney defines the first purpose of poetry as teaching, he is advocating the commonly accepted formula of Renaissance criticism: the Horatio-Aristotelian admixture of instruction and pleasure. Both Lope and Cervantes were convinced that the literary artist had this double responsibility.

Thus poetry was considered, by all the theorizers and by almost all the practitioners, as "an inferior form of philosophy, as philosophy for children or for a childlike public, or for those who were deficient and immature in philosophy proper," as the philosopher-critic Benedetto Croce so clearly stated.[4]

On the other hand, many of the countless novels and plays composed and performed in the Spanish Golden Age could scarcely claim to be more than show business or mere entertainment; the motive of the writers and producers was worldly—to obtain public acclaim and financial gain. Yet nobler motives existed. Impelled by them, Spanish dramatists and novelists of the seventeenth century produced, in surprising number, dramatic and narrative artifacts of value.

We are fortunate in having a new book on the dramatic aspect of this general subject—Charles V. Aubrun's *La comédie espagnole* (*1600–1680*) (Paris, 1967). The book is excessively condensed, so that many statements are offered without textual evidence. These, of course, will need to be tested. But in the 150 pages of text that are now before us, Aubrun has made clearer than it was before, that the Spanish *comedia* is not a copy of lived reality, though Lope de Vega loved to call it (following Cicero) a "mirror of our customs." Nor is it an image of the City of God on earth. The dramatist's purpose, rather, was to project upon the stage an idealized reality, a political and social and ethical ideology interpreted, for the benefit of the community, by the Spanish *intelligenzia*—by the guild of writers, if one may use the term—as a means of satisfying deep-seated needs of the individual and of the nation.

The dramatic projection of this idealized reality presents superbly—to use Aubrun's adverb—the Spanish nation's wish to be egalitarian, from the king on down: a man's honor is a patrimony received from Heaven, to be rendered back only to God. In their striving to maintain this ideal, king and commoner follow different paths: of heroism, of asceticism, of purity of heart. Though its goal is often illusory (Lope did not act like a stage-father when his daughter's reputation became clouded), this theater is exemplary: it shows how an individual and natural force might become socially useful.

Once the Siglo de Oro dramatist has chosen his specific and limited theme, he must manage to produce a change in the consciousness of the spectator, whose confused and confusing life must be made to appear reducible to the simplification that the set scheme of the *comedia* offers, and this must occur on the spectator's level, that of a *caballero*, not that of a hero or a saint, types that must have been rare indeed in the *corrales de comedias* that Lope knew.

When the change has been accomplished, human life no longer appears unsatisfactory and absurd, but rather as something explorable and usable. The inner wasteland becomes a fallow field, the *terra incognita* becomes a garden, as the perplexed man, guided by the dramatist, interprets the forces of Good and Evil. The life thus renewed becomes subject to poetic, i.e., divine justice.

The distinguishing—and limiting—fact about such plays is that they represent a reality that is changeless; their efficacy is magical and sociological. The justification of this theater is its revelatory quality. These dramatic characters do not *grow;* they are *revealed,* to themselves and to the audience. Society does not change; its members—those involved—return, after the peripeteias of the action, to an awareness of the immutable truth that lies behind all appearances. Spanish society had become a closed society.

This interpretation is not new. As early as 1919 Américo Castro wrote: "In the drama of the seventeenth century one must not expect to find the author leading his audience to points of view to which it is not accustomed, or writing in opposition to what the public already sanctioned."[5] What *is* new is the systematic exposition by M. Aubrun of this interpretation. It is this sense of immutability that distinguishes the older Spanish theater (and, in general, the culture of the Spanish baroque period): the world is *un édifice déjà construit*.[6]

The dramatist thus reveals the essence of the exterior world as he and his spectators conceive it, and places its resources at the disposal of the ordinary man, offering him a mirror wherein all things are clarified; the playwright becomes the revealer and the instrument of the public's consciousness, of its conscience.

II

Lope's dramatic personages, as has been said, do not change. In this they are the exact opposite of Don Quixote and his companions, whom their creator launches into the world of fiction, offers them incitements of every sort, and compels them to work out their own salvation—a concept which is the great gift of Américo Castro to Cervantes criticism.[7]

What I would add here as the outgrowth of my own studies is that there is a perhaps unexpected point of similarity—of fundamental similarity—between the personages of Cervantes and those of Lope de Vega in spite of the flexibility of the former and the rigidity of the latter. It is this: just as Lope's characters are brought back, at the end of the third *jornada* or act, to the state of calm from which the first disturbing *peripeteia* started them on their tangential course (as each personage finds that marriage, or death, or entrance into a convent, has stilled his life's angry waters by restoring the divinely willed tranquility to his little world), so Cervantes' Don Quixote, and other main characters such as the Jealous Extremanduran, are brought back to a final perception of unchanging truth, of perfectly *reliable* reality. After Don Quixote's choler-heated brain has sent him outward on his long centrifugal journey (with a temporary return at the end of Part I), there follows in Part II a new set of disturbing circumstances that again raise the temperature (and hence the disquieting force) of the Knight's troubled brain, and place Rocinante's hooves on the road again; but these stimuli are now (in Part II) a mental heat and a mental disturbance from which the author causes his hero slowly to recover, by inflicting upon him an endless series of depressing and humiliating (i.e. brain-cooling) misadventures that lead him, from Chapter VIII to the book's very end, *back* to his original state of sanity and to the serenity of his death—a death accompanied by a vision of his heavenly home so ravishing that it causes him to cry out in gratitude for God's pardoning mercies: across the shining river wait the saints. Don Quixote's errors, his confusions, his sin of overweening pride and vainglory, all fall from him as he *returns*, in the Augustinian sense, to God as to his soul's center and home: restlessness and disquietude give way to eternal rest.[8]

III

Although the characters in Spain's best classic plays are mere chessmen compared to the dynamic Don Quixote, Spain's drama of the Renaissance is comparable to *Don Quixote* in the sense already suggested: the *comedia* always presents a *return* to the social order that had been disturbed by some dramatic *peripeteia*. It is this disturbance and this return to serenity that constitute the *theme* of the Spanish *comedia*—the theme of poetic justice in a moral universe.[9] The social order of the *comedia* is not presented as undergoing alteration: at the end of the play, as at the end of *Don Quixote*, events revert to their former calm as the protagonists obtain a clear vision of their place in the Great Chain of Being.

Charles Aubrun has shown how the themes treated in the *comedia* are still operative among us, and how the Spanish way of treating them can still have meaning if we approach the *comedia* seeking only what it has to give: *not* a logical division and sub-division and ordering of reality, but rather an essentially emotional insight into a conception of reality which is, at bottom, primitive and magical—as magical as the sacrifice of the mass. As M. Aubrun has clearly put it:

> The Spanish public of the seventeenth century would have been blinded and plunged into the darkness of despair if it had looked directly at the nation's sinking sun. Through the screen of its doctrinal theater, it was merely dazzled by the vision. (p. 36)

The fact that the Spanish *comedia* is so static explains, in my opinion, its failure to affect the evolution of European drama more powerfully than it did. The fact that Cervantes' literary technique *is* dynamic explains, if I am not mistaken, why European fiction could not escape the Spanish influence that has been traced from the eighteenth century to our own day.

It may be asked, what has happened, in this drama of souls in search of firm footing, to the greatly vaunted Spanish "realism"? The answer is simply that Spanish playwrights employ what we call realism when it suits their literary purposes to do so, while over all there reigns a higher, a universal decorum. Alonso López, the great Aristotelian theoretician, confesses in 1596 in his *Philosophía antigua poética*, that when in a dramatic representation he hears slaves or shepherds or other folk of lowly station delivering themselves of lofty and well reasoned speeches (in violation of the accepted principle of decorum), he takes delight therein, *provided the medium* be verse, not prose. This last requirement has to do with art as illusion: the verse is like the frame that sets off a painting from the wall space which it adorns: it provides evidence that the world of the authentically poetic imagination obeys laws unknown to the every-day genre painting that captures the repetitions and weary comings and goings of our quite ordinary mundane existence, whose language is unmeasured and uncadenced prose.[10]

And one must point out also that Cervantes' realism is only ideally "real"—it is realism of the spirit only. For all his earthy reality, Sancho Panza leaves wife and children and farm to follow a monomaniac in search of fame and greatness, and in spite of various hesitations he stays with him to the end, suggesting in the final chapters that his master—defeated in combat and forbidden to pursue chivalrous adventures—become an Arcadian shepherd—and take Sancho along as an Arcadian squire. And among the women characters, the scullery maid Maritornes is as ideally ugly as Dulcinea and Marcela are ideally beautiful. No; Spanish realism is not "realistic": it holds up a revealing mirror not to the world, but to the heart.

The ideology of Cervantes is not rigorous, except for his firmly held belief in an ultimate over-arching harmony wherein the positives and the negatives agree. Because of this infinite flexibility, *Don Quixote* belongs to the literature of all times and all nations,[11] whereas Lope—Cervantes' great rival in his struggle for popular acclaim—takes his seat on the European Parnassus only by special invitation, well sponsored by the erudition of the *Lopistas.*

Every great literature, says M. Aubrun in his Conclusion, is ambiguous, in that it endeavors to reduce multiplicity to unity, to overcome dialectically all contradictions, to relate all parts to the whole. This is exactly the intention of the *Spanish* comedia. What differentiates this dramatic form from other forms of theater is its propensity to bring the extremes together—on the one hand the naturalistic welling up of irresistible life; on the other, the rigor of an ideology as unyielding as a strait-jacket. The artistic value of the *comedia* is not determined by either of the elements just mentioned —ideology or upsurging life—but, rather, by the *internal coherence* and the *unstable equilibrium* of its component parts. This instability is not baroque in any distinctive sense: it has been the object of human concern and striving since the time when man's dwellings were caverns. Without this striving man, either in his Spanish or his universal varieties, would not have been able to confront the savage nudity of his own person (p. 141).

Notes

CHAPTER ONE

[1] E. Harris Harbison, *The Christian Scholar in the Age of the Reformation* (Princeton, 1956), pp. 28–29.

[2] Heraclitus, Frag. 26: "It should be understood . . . that all things come to pass through the compulsion of strife" (quoted in Philip Wheelwright, *Heraclitus* [Princeton, 1959], p. 29). Bywater calls this fragment no. 62; Diels, no. 80.

[3] E. H. Kantorowicz, reviewing C. T. Davis, *Dante and the Idea of Rome* in *Speculum*, XXXIV (1959), 104.

[4] Norman Kohn, *The Pursuit of the Millenium* (Fairlawn, New Jersey, 1957) pp. 36, 64–66, 92–93, 123, 150, *et. alibi.*

[5] Edgar de Bruyne, *Estudios de estética medieval*, trans. Fr. A. Suárez (Madrid, 1958–59), I, 119, 126, 131, and the whole section entitled "Aticismo y Asianismo" at the beginning of Vol. I, Ch. 4.

[6] F. Chabod, *Machiavelli and the Renaissance* (Cambridge, Massachusetts, 1958), p. 170. The Augustinian temper persisted from Hippo to about 1350. See S. Harrison Thomson, reviewing Gordon Leff, *Medieval Thought from Saint Augustine to Ockham* (London, 1958), *Speculum*, XXXV (1960), 470.

[7] I am well aware that "Neoplatonism" is a dangerous word. Sergio Rabade Romeo in an article entitled "¿Neoplatonismos medievales?" (*Estudios filosóficos*, VIII [1959], 407–17), argues that the term Neoplatonism embraces concepts so diverse that they cannot properly be included under this designation. He distinguishes five different philosophical currents: (1) that of Augustine and Plotinus; (2) that of the pseudo-Dionysius and Scotus Erigena; (3) that derived directly from Plato as translated by Chalcidius; (4) the Judaeo-Arabic current of Avicebron; and (5) that of Boethius. Such distinctions cannot be made by me in the present study. Neoplatonism became a myth, and the Middle Ages and the Renaissance and the Post-Renaissance were enticed by it.

[8] J. H. Randall, Jr., *The Role of Knowledge in Western Religion* (Boston, 1958), pp. 39–43; the quotation is from p. 42.

[9] Harbison, *op. cit.*, p. 23. We shall devote attention to some of these conflicts, e.g., Fortune-Fate-Providence, Free Will-Grace-Predestination, in the appropriate chapters of the second volume of this work. For the moment we may note that Petrarch (d. 1374) is the first European poet of the divided personality.

[10] W. T. Stace, *Time and Eternity* (Princeton, 1952), p. 122; see also p. 131.

[11] Armando Correia Pacheco, *Plato's Conception of Love* (Notre Dame, Indiana, 1942), p. 108.

[12] For a condemnation of the allegation that it was licit to wage war "to increase one's territory" or "for the honor of the prince," see Joseph Höffner, *La ética colonial española del siglo de oro: Cristianismo y dignidad humana*, trans. F. de Asís Caballero (Madrid, 1957), p. 434.

[13] See Randall, *op. cit.*, pp. 44–45.

[14] A whole book could be written on these paradoxes alone. One example: Alejo Venegas del Busto (d. 1554), in his *Agonía del tránsito de la muerte* (*NBAE*, XVI, 226b–27a), condemns Christian funeral customs: "From this one can infer the sin of those who feel and show excessive grief over the death of their relatives and friends. So greatly do they offend God in their demonstrations of weeping and sorrow that St. Cyprian declares . . . that he had a revelation from God commanding him to preach publicly that there should be no bewailing the death of the faithful who in answer to a divine summons depart this life."

[15] "Beaux seigneurs," said the dying Captain Bétissac (15c.) to his comrades, "I believe and say . . . that there is no such thing as a soul." J. Huizinga, who reports this (*The Waning of the Middle Ages* [London, 1924], p. 148), warns that "isolated cases of unbelief . . . should not be confounded with the literary and superficial paganism of the Renaissance, or with the Epicureanism of some aristocratic circles from the thirteenth century downward." We shall return to this point in a later chapter.

[16] Sidney Painter, *Medieval Society* (Ithaca, New York, 1953), p. 31.

[17] *The Great Chain of Being*, quoted in *The Tragic Vision and the Christian Faith*, Nathan A. Scott, Jr., ed. (New York, 1957), p. 48. "Petrarch's (d. 1374) *virtus* involves pagan and Christian ideas. *Virtus* itself is helpless against Fate, Nature, and Providence. . . . the existence of Fortune is both asserted and denied. Virtue resists; virtue yields. The 'affects' (joy, hope, fear, grief) are to be rooted out; they cannot be rooted out. Prosperity and adversity are real; they are only apparently real. . . . Part of the explanation is that Petrarch sometimes dealt with philosophical ideas but was not really a consistent philosopher. Sometimes he spoke as a pagan, sometimes as a Christian. His mood determined his attitude, and he was a man of many moods" (B. L. Ullman reviewing Klaus Heitmann, *Fortuna und Virtus: Eine Studie zu Petrarcas Lebensweisheit* in *Speculum*, XXXIV [1959], 661). Sir Thomas More (d. 1535) and his group of humanists held that the Aristotelization of theology had contributed to the contamination of the pure teachings and high moral standards of Christ. Erasmus (d. 1536) declared that the union of Aristotle and Christ is like a mixture of fire and water; yet he found that Christians hardly dared to deny a single doctrine of Aristotle and went to great lengths to twist his words to some sort of compatibility with Christ's principles. No less to blame was Roman law. Because of the civil law's appearance of justice, men twisted and stretched the teachings of the Gospel to make them agree with civil law, though the latter permitted the repulsion of force with force, approved of big business, legalized usury, and exalted war as a glorious thing, provided it be just. And what was a just war? The civil law defined it as one declared by the prince, no matter how stupid or puerile. See Edward L. Surtz, S.J., "Thomas More and Communism," *PMLA*, LXIV (1949), 555–56.

[18] E. E. Slaughter, *Virtue according to Love—in Chaucer* (New York, 1957), p. 197. See A. F. M. Gunn, *The Mirror of Love: A Reinterpretation of "The Romance of the Rose"* (Lubbock, Texas, 1952), pp. 446–48 and nn. 28, 29.

[19] E. K. Rand, *Founders of the Middle Ages* (New York, 1957), pp. 249–50.

[20] Francis Hermans, *Histoire doctrinale de l'humanisme chrétien* (Tournai-Paris, 1948), III, 121.

[21] E. R. Curtius, *European Literature and the Latin Middle Ages*, trans. Willard R. Trask (New York, 1953), pp. 520–21.

[22] María Rosa Lida de Malkiel, *La idea de la fama en la Edad Media castellana* (Mexico City, 1952), pp. 116–18.

[23] There can be no question that the feudal culture pattern acquired a special character in Spain because of the nature of the enemy—the Moor—that the Spaniard fought. The special quality of this struggle, and its spiritual effects, are studied by Américo Castro in *La realidad histórica de España* (Mexico City, 1954), and in supplementary articles and monographs. It is not the purpose of the present study to enter into the controversy stirred by these writings. See the review by J. E. Gillet of the first book in which Professor Castro's theory was formulated, *España en su historia* (Buenos Aires, 1948), in *HR*, XVIII (1950), 169–84; the review by A. A. Parker of the English edition of this book, *The Structure of Spanish History* (trans. Edmond L. King [Princeton, 1954]), *BHS*, XXXVI (1959), 54 ff.; and Peter Heintz, "Die Struktur der spanischen Persönlichkeit: Eine kulturanthropologische Einführung in das Werk Américo Castros," *Kölner Zeitschrift für Soziologie und Sozialpsychologie*, VII (1955), 101–18. Objections to Castro's thesis

that the Spanish nation had no existence as a nation until it came into contact with the Mohammedan enemy are listed by Carlos Clavería in his article, "Reflejos del 'goticismo' español en la fraseología del Siglo de Oro," in *Studia philologica: Homenaje ofrecido a Dámaso Alonso* (Madrid, 1960–1961), I, 359, n. 2. It will be necessary to touch on this subject again, especially in the chapter on medieval laughter.

[24] See R. Menéndez Pidal (ed.), *La leyenda de los Infantes de Lara*, 2d ed. (Madrid, 1934).

[25] See C. M. Bowra, *Heroic Poetry* (New York, 1952); P. Salinas, "La vuelta al esposo," BSS, XXIV (1947), 79 ff.; G. Correa, "El tema de la honra en el *Poema de Mio Cid*," HR, XX (1952). See also Américo Castro, "Poesía y realidad en el *Poema del Cid*," in *Semblanzas y estudios españoles* (Princeton, 1956).

[26] I call attention to the fact that Professor Castro sees here an Oriental influence: "For the rest . . . , the type of the fighting bishop in the medieval French epics should be included in this same current of Oriental influences, which it would be senseless to limit to Spain in those centuries." See his chapter on the Islamic-Christian institutions in *La realidad histórica de España*, pp. 202 ff.

[27] See E. Kullmann, "Die dichterische und sprachliche Gestalt des *Cantar de Mio Cid*," RF, XLV (1931), 6 ff.

[28] *El libro del Cauallero de Dios que auia por nombre Zifar . . .* , ed. C. P. Wagner (Ann Arbor, Michigan, 1929). I quote from the more convenient edition of F. Buendía, in *Libros de caballerías españoles* (Madrid, 1954), p. 51b.

[29] Hermann J. Weigand, *Three Chapters on Courtly Love in Arthurian France and Germany* (Chapel Hill, North Carolina, 1956), pp. 14–15.

[30] J. L. LaMonte, *The World of the Middle Ages: A Reorientation of Medieval History* (New York, 1949), p. 383.

[31] Dámaso Alonso, "*Tirant lo Blanc*, novela moderna," *Revista valenciana de filología*, I (1951), 26 ff.

[32] St. Augustine pointed out that if Christian doctrine regarded all war as sinful, Jesus could not have said to the soldiers (when they asked Him what they must do to achieve salvation), "Do violence to no man, and be content with your wages" (Luke 3:14). War, according to Augustine, was the punishment of injustice—a doctrine taken up by Gratian and Aquinas. Imperialistic wars of conquest were, of course, excluded; yet theologians could argue that a war of aggression could be "perfectly moral" and even necessary. See Höffner, *op. cit.*, pp. 74–77, 82, 358, 432, and Alfred Vanderpol, *La doctrine scolastique du droit de guerre* (Paris, 1925), especially p. 215.

[33] Madrid (1933), ed. La Sociedad de Bibliófilos Españoles (hereafter called Bibliófilos Españoles), I, 51.

[34] Ed. Barcelona, 1567, pp. 148–49 (1st ed. Coimbra, 1549).

[35] See Jerónimo de Urrea, *Diálogo de la verdadera honra militar, de cómo se ha de conformar la honra con la conciencia*, first published in Spanish at Venice in 1566. There were editions at Madrid in 1575 and Zaragoza, 1642 and 1661; Italian trans., 1569; French, 1585. See also F. R. Bryson, *The Point of Honor in Sixteenth Century Italy* (New York, 1935).

[36] In M. Menéndez y Pelayo, *Orígenes de la novela* (Madrid, 1905–1915), II, 537ab.

[37] This contradiction is clearly set forth in A. García Valdecasas' *El hidalgo y el honor* (Madrid, 1948), pp. 184–85.

[38] "Finalmente, todos aquellos que por salir con su honra posponen la honra de Dios, van despeñados por el derribadero de perdicion, que es camino ancho que lleuan [*sic*] al infierno" ([Salamanca, 1567], fol. 41v). There is an essay on Venegas in Julián Marías, *El oficio del pensamiento* (Madrid, 1958).

[39] "Todas la hidalguías se fundan en tiranías" (quoted in Américo Castro, "Lo hispánico y el erasmismo," RFH, II [1940], 21, n. 1).

[40] B. W. Wardropper, "Honor in the Sacramental Plays of Valdivielso and Lope de Vega," *MLN*, LXVI (1951), 81–83.

[41] Rom. 12:19; cf. Deut. 32:35, Heb. 10:30.

[42] Ed. P. Félix García (Madrid, 1947), II, 159.

[43] Francisco de Vitoria and Domingo de Soto made a distinction between vengeance and a related motive: the recuperation of one's personal honor. "To defend himself from ignominy and dishonor, one who has been slapped, for example, may kill the offender immediately with the sword." Hugo Grotius could not understand this Spanish way of thinking: "quod mihi a ratione et pietate valde alienum videtur" (*De jure belli ac pacis*, II, i, quoted in Höffner, *op. cit.*, p. 106 and note).

[44] "Este disparate sangriento, esta rabia facinorosa, esta furia delincuente en lo divino y humano, que se titula *Libro del duelo*, tiene la infamia de su descendencia tan antigua como el mundo" (*Obras en prosa*, ed. Luis Astrana Marín [Madrid, 1932], p. 1042a. See Mexía, *Silva . . .*, *ed. cit.*, Part IV, Ch. 9.

[45] *Epistolario*, ed. Narciso Alonso Cortés (Madrid, 1915), p. 72.

[46] Cited by C. A. Jones in "*Honour* in Spanish Golden-Age Drama: Its Relation to Real Life and to Morals," *BHS*, XXXV (1958), 202.

[47] *The Allegory of Love: A Study in Medieval Tradition* (Oxford, 1936), p. 29. The following material (cited by me in "Courtly Love in the Spanish *Cancioneros*," *PMLA*, LXIV [1949], 250) is extracted from pp. 21–22, 29 of Lewis.

[48] Ed. Agapito Rey in *Symposium*, IX (1955), 249.

[49] He cites fourteen moralists who uphold this view. See his "*Tirante el Blanco, Don Quijote* y los libros de caballerías," reprinted from the Prologue of the edition of *Tirante el Blanco* published by the Asociación de Bibliófilos de Barcelona, 1947–49, p. xlii.

[50] Quoted by Riquer, *op. cit.*, p. xl. See W. Krauss, "Die Kritik des Siglo de Oro am Ritter- und Schaeferroman," *Homenatge a Antoni Rubió i Lluch* (Barcelona, 1936), I, 225–46.

[51] "Por ventura deseando ser otra Oriana y verse servida de otro Amadís." This is quoted by Bartolomé José Gallardo, *Ensayo de una biblioteca españala de libros raros y curiosos* (Madrid, 1863–89), IV, cols. 49–50; hereafter these volumes will be cited as *Ensayo*.

[52] S. Montero Díaz, *Cervantes, compañero eterno* (Madrid, 1957), pp. 109–10.

[53] "No se pierde para con los hombres el [crédito] de christiano i cuerdo con salir [a un desafío]. Una culpa se comete contra la ley divina, es verdad; pero sin perder el crédito de christianos cometemos muchas contra ella cada día; pues ni por esso dudaremos de poner mil vezes la vida por la verdad de la ley, ni llega a dudar de que lo haremos, quando la ocasión lo pida, ninguno de los que nos ven salir" (Ed. E. Buceta [Madrid, 1935], p. 120).

[54] Esplandián, the son of Amadís and the hero of *Las sergas de Esplandián*, champions chastity and prefers crusades to adventures. The hero of the *Florisendo* (1510) is chaste, an enemy of magic, and a belittler of adventure-seeking as an unfortunate custom. See Maxime Chevalier, "Le roman de chevalerie morigéné: Le *Florisendo*," *BHi*, LX (1958), 444, 448.

[55] Henry Thomas, *Spanish and Portuguese Romances of Chivalry* (Cambridge, 1920), p. 83.

[56] See my article, "Sobre las dos Fortunas: de tejas arriba y de tejas abajo," *Studia Philologica. Homenaje ofrecido a Dámaso Alonso* (Madrid, 1960–61), II, 143–54.

[57] "Padre Ponce, hagan los frayles penitencia por todos, que los hijos dalgo armas y amores son su profesión.—Yo os prometo, señor de Montemayor . . . de con mi rusticidad y gruessa vena componer otra *Diana*, la qual con toscos garrotazos corra tras la vuestra" (Montemayor, *Los siete libros de la Diana*, ed. F. López Estrada [Madrid, 1946], p. xviii).

CHAPTER TWO

[1] Francesco Novati has indicated this in his *Studi critici e letterari* (Torino, 1889), pp. 200–202. Félix Lecoy, *Recherches sur le "Libro de buen amor"* (Paris, 1938), pp. 214–229, makes it clear that "nous avons à faire à une parodie joyeuse" (p. 216). Cf. Merker-Stammler, *Reallexikon der deutschen Literaturgeschichte* (Berlin, 1925–1931), II, 630 ff., s. v. *Parodie:* "Das Merkmal, das die P[arodie] von der gewöhnlichen Nach- und Umdichtung trennt, ist die bewusste Komik. . . . Die [rein komische Parodie] will nicht das ernste Vorbild der Lächerlichkeit preisgeben; ihr Endziel ist lediglich, eine sich selbst genügende Heiterkeit zu erregen. Der ursprüngliche Text bildet nur den neutralen Hintergrund, von dem sich die P. als selbständiges Gebilde abhebt." Elisha Kent Kane, in his verse translation of *The Book of Good Love*, privately printed, 1933, p. 76, n. 1, shows full awareness of the type of literary exercise involved: "Scriptural parodies, usually erotic as well as blasphemous, were popular pastimes for devout churchmen in the Dark Ages. By the twelfth century there are many complaints that bawdy tunes were being introduced into the church services to the increasing interest . . . of the congregation. With the Renaissance the gusto for malicious parodies increased, finally reaching its height in the seventeenth century. There is, in French, a 'Passion of Our Lady in Burlesque Verses' and a truly outrageous 'Lord's Prayer of the Syphylitics' beside which Juan Ruiz's parody seems inspired by piety itself." On the general subject of such parodies, see John G. Bourke, *Scatalogic Rites of All Nations* (Washington, 1891), and *Bibliographie des ouvrages relatifs à l'amour, aux femmes, au mariage, et des livres facétieux, pantagruéliques, scatalogiques, satiriques, etc.,* par M. le Cte. d'I. (Jules Gay), 4th ed., revised by J. Lemonnier, 3 vols. (Paris, 1894–1899).

[2] José María Aguado, *Vocabulario sobre Juan Ruiz* (Madrid, 1929), p. 186, says that Menéndez y Pelayo "n meditó o no pudo entender la escandalosa profanación," yet offers no interpretations himself, "pues el obscenísimo [sentido] . . . puede ya inferirlo del contexto todo lector del poema." The last part of this statement I deny. Kane's translation of 381d, "I'm like a bottle in the smoke from passionate despair!", is in no way adequate. On the other hand, Kane invents obscenities (as in 383c–d) which the Latin text neither provides nor suggests. María Brey Mariño, in her "versión" of the *Libro de buen amor* (Valencia, 1954), leaves the Latin in the text and translates in footnotes each of these phrases literally, with no attempt at an actual rendering of Juan Ruiz's *parody*. It would take a very knowing "general reader" to perceive the connections.

[3] Apud E. R. Curtius, *European Literature and the Latin Middle Ages* (New York, 1953), p. 421.

[4] C. S. Lewis, *English Literature in the Sixteenth Century* (Oxford, 1954), p. 70. Lewis refers to Bannatyne MS. 230, in his chapter "The Close of the Middle Ages in Scotland." Cf. J. Plattard, *François Rabelais* (Paris, 1932), pp. 159–160: "Elles [the religious ideas of Rabelais] ne sont pas . . . décelées par le ton familier ou bouffon qu'il prend lorsqu'il parle de l'Écriture Sainte, des mystères et des cérémonies du catholicisme: de telles facéties n'étaient pas tenues alors pour sacrilèges et l'on a montré qu'avant lui d'autres moines avaient commis de plus graves sans scandaliser personne. La guérison d'Epistémon, qui avait eu la tête coupée, contient des traits qui nous semblent une parodie des miracles de l'Evangile: ils n'impliquent pas une négation de ces miracles."

[5] Apud Carleton S. Coon, *A General Reader in Anthropology* (New York, 1948), p. 140b.

[6] *Papers of the Michigan Academy of Science, Arts and Letters,* XIV (1930), 187–207.

[7] An interesting parallel: the joyous "after-the-burying" dance-march, which may be observed among New Orleans Negroes today, was common to such

diverse places as Mexico, Italy, and the Scottish highlands. See Charles Edward Smith's review of *The Story of Jazz*, by Marshall W. Stearns, *New York Times Book Review*, Nov. 4, 1956, p. 6.

[8] E. R. Curtius, op. cit., p. 434. On laughter in early monasticism, see the bibliography listed in note 16, p. 422 of this book.

[9] Maurice Hélin, *A History of Medieval Latin Literature* (New York, 1949), p. 93.

[10] David Worcester, *The Art of Satire* (Cambridge, Mass., 1940), p. 150.

[11] "Le monologue dramatique dans l'ancien théâtre français," *Romania*, XV (1886), 359.

[12] Lecoy, op. cit., p. 361.

[13] "Si peu qu'on ait fréquenté familièrement quelques compagnies d'ecclésiastiques, parfaitement respectables dans leur vie et dignes de leurs fonctions—pour peu qu'on ait assisté à quelques 'dîners de curé' dans la vieille France—on s'aperçoit bien vite que l'esprit du moine Rabelais, du curé Rabelais, c'est pour une large part un esprit professionnel: un esprit d'homme d'église catholique, qui ne prend pas le rire pour un péché et qui parlant des choses du culte librement et familièrement, ignore certaines pudeurs circonspectes, certaines attitudes timorées qui sont le fait du réformé—ou du mécréant" (Lucien Febvre, *Le problème de l'incroyance au XVIe siècle* [Paris, 1947], p. 182).

[14] Américo Castro, *España en su historia* (Buenos Aires, 1948), p. 423. Cf. the second Spanish edition, *La realidad histórica de España* (México, 1954), pp. 404 f. The *Libro de buen amor* does indeed appear to be the earliest of known texts containing a parody of the canonical hours, but the point is of slight importance. Sacred parodies exist as early as the year 1182. For the year 1444, one year later than the second redaction of Juan Ruiz's book, fourteen years later than the first, there is a parody of *matins* recorded by P. Lacroix, in his *Sciences et lettres au moyen âge* (Paris, 1877), p. 266. This parody could scarcely have been influenced by Juan Ruiz, or by Mohammedan-Christian acculturation in Spain. It is also very possible that the parody of matins of 1444 itself was not the first one to be written in non-Spanish Europe.

[15] *Del Lazarillo a Quevedo* (Madrid, 1946), pp. 4–9.

[16] "Montoro y Mena 'blasfeman' no en tanto que cristianos nuevos sino en tanto que hombres de Castilla del siglo XV" (María Rosa Lida, "La hipérbole sagrada en la poesía castellana del siglo XV," *RFH*, VIII [1946], 130).

[17] "Here [i.e., in the opinion that what is fundamental in Juan Ruiz's art is 'la vitalización . . . de sus temas, lo cual le vino sin duda del Oriente'] many may differ and may continue to see in Ruiz fundamentally a Christian and a Western man, even though influenced by Arabic attitudes" (J. E. Gillet in his review of *España en su historia*, HR, XVIII [1950], 178). "Hay mucho camino por delante, antes de llegar a la anhelada síntesis. Anticipemos, sí, la opinión de que el europeísmo del *Libro de buen amor* no ha sido destruído por la apasionada y apasionante interpretación de Américo Castro" (Fernando Lázaro, "Los amores de don Melón y doña Endrina. Notas sobre el arte de Juan Ruiz," *Arbor*, no. 62, febrero de 1951, p. 212). I believe that the present article reenforces these two statements. See, however, *La realidad histórica de España*, pp. 378 and 404 ff.

[18] "Medieval parody is graceless, even blasphemous, delighting even more than the scorpion to sting the faces of men, and the *Beginning of the Gospel according to the Silver Mark* has blasted the entire Roman Curia with one triumphant breath" (Helen Waddell, *The Wandering Scholars* [London, 1927], p. 150). "M. Plattard a parfaitement vu que les plaisanteries rabelaisiennes, de tradition cléricale, ne différaient en rien de celles qui égaient cette littérature des Sermons Joyeux sur laquelle Emile Picot a naguère attiré l'attention" (L. Febvre, op. cit., pp. 161 ff.). For Picot, see n. 11, above. Cf. Eero Ilvonen, *Parodies de thèmes pieux dans la poésie française du moyen âge* (Paris, 1914) (*Pater, Credo,*

Ave Maria, and *Laetabundus* in critical edition with an introduction); Paul Lehmann, *Die Parodie im Mittelalter* (Munich, 1922); idem, *Parodistische Texte. Beispiele zur lateinischen Parodie im Mittelalter* (Munich, 1923); E. Gilson, "Rabelais franciscain," *Revue d'Histoire Franciscaine* (1924).

[19] *NRFH*, VI (1952), 313–315. Cf. the same author's article on "la hipérbole sagrada" referred to in n. 11, above.

[20] *RFH*, III (1941), 41. Italics mine.

[21] Eileen Power, *Medieval People* (London, 1924), Chap. I (note of María Rosa Lida).

[22] "Breve forma de confesar," *NBAE*, XVI, 10a.

[23] *Introducción a la sabiduría* (Madrid, 1944), p. 67.

[24] Marcel Bataillon, *Erasmo y España* (Mexico, 1950), II, 178.

[25] Sess. IV, Decret. "De editione et usu Sacrorum Librorum": "Post haec, temeritatem illam reprimere volens, qua ad profana quaeque convertuntur et torquentur verba et sententiae sacrae scripturae, ad scurrilia scilicet, fabulosa, vana, adulationes, detractiones, superstitiones, impias et diabolicas incantationes, divinationes, sortes, libellos etiam famosos; mandat et praecipit [Tridentina Synodus] ad tollendam huiusmodi irreverentiam et contemptum, ne de cetero quisquam quomodolibet verba scripturae sacrae ad haec et similia audeat usurpare, ut omnes huius generis homines temeratores et violatores verbi Dei iuris et arbitrii poenis per episcopos coerceantur."

[26] (Barcelona, 1567), pp. 117–118. Italics mine.

[27] Twenty-first ed., Oeniponte, 1932, II, 174–175.

[28] José María de Cossío, "Rodrigo de Reinosa y sus obras," *BBMP*, XXI (1945), 41.

[29] *Obras* (Lisboa, 1852), III, 300.

[30] B. Croce, *La Spagna nella vita italiana durante la Rinascenza* (Bari, 1917), p. 209.

[31] Bataillon, op. cit., pp. 300, 303.

[32] Ibid., p. 296.

[33] *Rituale Romanum* (Taurini, 1917), pp. 250. Cf. the *Oremus:* "Deus, qui . . . tribus Magis iter ad te stella duce pandisti. . . ."

[34] Cf. the prayer at the beginning of the *Libro de buen amor*, and F. Castro Guisasola's indication of its source, *RFE*, XVI (1929), 72.

[35] *NBAE*, II, 65b–66a.

[36] See Professor Gillet's treatment of the *Propalladia* and the Index, vol. I, pp. 64 ff. of his edition of *Propalladia and Other Works of Bartolomé de Torres Naharro* (Bryn Mawr, 1943), especially pp. 69–70.

[37] Specifically, the two works by Tirso de Molina cited below. Lupercio Leonardo de Argensola complains of this license in his *Memorial* to Philip II "contra la representación de las comedias": "Demás desto, las palabras sagradas y aun de la oración del *Ave María* y el *Kyrie eleyson* que usa la Iglesia con tanto respeto, las mezclan en canciones deshonestas en los teatros" (*Obras sueltas* de Lupercio y Bartolomé Leonardo de Argensola, ed. el Conde de la Viñaza, I [Madrid, 1889], 285).

[38] Ernest Mérimée, *Essai sur la vie et les oeuvres de Francisco de Quevedo* (Paris, 1886), p. 186, and note 2. Quevedo's *Sueños* apparently met with disfavor in this respect. In the 1629 edition Quevedo, "instruit par le scandale que causait le mélange des vérités et de la plaisanterie," made changes in the text in conformity with the decrees of the Council of Trent.

[39] Quevedo had indeed "denied" certain of his works. Sandoval's *Index* (1640), states (p. 425b): "todos los demas libros . . . que corren en nombre de dicho autor, se prohiben, lo qual ha pedido por su particular peticion, no reconociendolos por proprios."

[40] Mérimée remarks (p. 191): "La hardiesse des *Songes* aurait sans doute trouvé

grâce, même devant les inquisiteurs de Castille, si tous les ennemis de Quevedo ne s'étaient coalisés pour en montrer le danger."

[41] Gerhard Moldenhauer, "Spanische Zensur und Schelmenroman," *Estudios eruditos in memoriam de Adolfo Bonilla y San Martín* (Madrid, 1927), I, 325.

[42] Angel González Palencia, "Quevedo, Tirso y las comedias ante la Junta de Reformación," *Boletín de la R. Acad. Esp.,* XLIII (1946), 43–84.

[43] The phrase belongs to C. S. Lewis, in *The Allegory of Love. A Study in Medieval Tradition* (Oxford, 1936), p. 20.

[44] See above, the warning in this regard from the Nolden-Schmitt *Summa Theologiae Moralis.* "*Transeat a me calix iste*" appears in a *Mote de una dama* by Soria, *Cancionero castellano del siglo XV,* ed. R. Foulché-Delbosc (Madrid, 1912–1915), II, 269. Francis Hermans, *Histoire doctrinale de l'humanisme chrétien* (Tournai-Paris, 1948), II, 209, criticizes this in Rabelais: "Certes, il serait enfantin de considérer cela comme un crime irrémissible. Le clergé de tous les temps . . . s'est délecté à des jeux de mots inoffensifs sur les textes liturgiques. Rabelais est un clerc évadé du couvent, il en a conservé les habitudes, mais il a oublié que les clercs ne touchent pas aux paroles du Christ. . . ."

[45] *Cigarrales de Toledo* (Madrid, 1913), pp. 185–186.

[46] John Livingston Lowes, "The Lovers Maladye of Hereos," *MP,* XI (1913–1914), 18 ff., and William G. Meader, *Courtship in Shakespeare. Its Relation to the Tradition of Courtly Love* (New York, 1954), pp. 7 ff.

[47] *NBAE,* IV, 24b–26a.

[48] I copy from José de Onís, *The United States as seen by Spanish American Writers (1776–1890)* (New York, 1952), pp. 140–141. The poem was printed by Benjamín Vicuña Mackenna, in *Páginas de mi diario,* pp. 53–54.

[49] See José María Aguado, *Glosario sobre Juan Ruiz* (Madrid, 1929), pp. 186 ff.; Lecoy, op. cit., pp. 226 ff.; and Kane's translation of the coplas in question.

[50] *English Literature in the Sixteenth Century,* pp. 93–94.

[51] I follow the diplomatic ed. of J. Ducamin (Toulouse, 1901), sometimes preferring one manuscript reading to another, as any interpreter of the poem must do.

[52] It will be seen that my method obtains different results from that of Kane, who translates *copla* 374 as follows: "You have a rascal's breviary to pray with vagabonds,/ *With those who hate the ways of peace* your psaltry corresponds;/ *Behold how good* you signify with clack-dishes of bronze;/ Your rout *All night lift up their hands* to crime ere it absconds."

[53] Op. cit., pp. 423–424. *La realidad histórica de España,* pp. 404–405. In the latter place Professor Castro says: "Pero explicar los pasajes oscuros del *Libro* sale de mi plan, y me limito aquí a mostrar el entrelace del rezo abstracto con la experiencia del vivir terreno, ambos permutables y reversibles."

[54] *Mimesis* (Princeton, 1953), pp. 225–226.

[55] Cf. the heading of a poem in the *Cancionero de Sebastián de Horozco* (Sevilla, 1874), p. 34: "El Auctor a una dama por via de dialogo, y responde por ella por los mesmos consonantes, sobre que estando con ella un caballero no avia podido alçar. Es la respuesta bien del Palacio." Cf. also a line in a sonnet from the supposed *Obras del Reverendísimo Padre Cornejo* (MS), Gallardo, *Ensayo,* II, col. 583: "Alcé, llegué, toqué, besé, cubríla. . . ."

[56] *Obras en verso* (Madrid, Aguilar, 1932), p. 131b. Cf. p. 361b: "esforzóse en levantar."

[57] *Dictionnaire de l'ancienne langue française,* s. v. *instrument.*

[58] Compare Kane's rendering: "You rise up from your leman's bed; '*Thou shalt unseal my lips*'—/ You sing aloud to waken her, and utter wicked quips;/ '*Hear thou our prayers,*' while o'er a viol you thrum with finger tips/ Or chant '*In the beginning God* made women loose for slips.'"

[59] See J. E. Gillet in *HR,* XVIII (1950), 178, n. 4 and *MLN,* XXXIII (1918), 117–120; A. Castro, *La realidad histórica de España,* pp. 404–405.

[60] Lecoy (op. cit., p. 227) argues convincingly in favor of the reading of MS *G* (*legem pone*) as against *S* (*a longe pone*), which would have no connection with the liturgy.

[61] *Glosarios latino-españoles de la Edad Media* (Madrid, 1936), pp. 202b–203a. Castro finds *cutela* (i.e., *scutella*) defined in the Escorial Glossary as *comendón* and, after remarking on the difficulty of Juan Ruiz's *copla*, interprets its last line as follows: "El enamorado va a la iglesia para ver a su amiga; prefiere la misa de los desposorios, que por lo visto se decía sin cantar 'gloria in excelsis' y sin otros cánticos, es decir, en poco rato. Al ir a dar la ofrenda, el fiel distraído, iba de mala gana, cojeando; y cuando el cura rezaba el *comendón* (encomienda del alma de los difuntos), salía trotando, corriendo. Hay un refrán de Gonzalo Correas . . . 'Ni comendón bien cantado, ni hijo de clérigo bien criado.' Mientras el cura cantaba el comendón, se haría la colecta; y como resulta de nuestro glosario, la vasija con que se pedía se llamó también comendón; para no echar nada en ella, salía corriendo el enamorado a que se refiere el Arcipreste de Hita." The word *comendón* is known to occur only in the Escorial gloss, in Juan Ruiz, and in the *refrán*.

[62] Ed. Cejador (Madrid, 1913), I, 62.

[63] Kane's rendering of lines *c–d* is: "*Direct my goings in and out,*' you ardently implore./ '*Upright art though, oh Lord,*' says she, 'let's ring the bell some more!' "

[64] Alan M. F. Gunn, *The Mirror of Love. A Reinterpretation of the "Romance of the Rose"* (Lubbock, Texas, 1951), p. 225.

[65] Ibid., p. 229. See the discussion of *copla* 375, above.

[66] Op. cit., p. 190.

[67] Ibid., p. 191.

[68] Gunn, op. cit., p. 231, n. 8.

[69] *Guzmán de Alfarache*, ed. Clásicos Castellanos, IV (Madrid, 1929), 81.

[70] *España en su historia*, pp. 383 ff. Cf. J. S. P. Tatlock, "Mediaeval Laughter," *Speculum*, XXI (1946), 290–291; Curtius' excursus on "Jest and Earnest in Medieval Literature," op. cit., pp. 417 ff.

[71] *España en su historia*, p. 379; *La realidad histórica de España*, pp. 391 and 394 ff.

[72] *Mediaeval Studies*, XVII (1955), 173–184.

[73] *Cancionero de Baena* (Leipzig, 1860), I, 160.

[74] Ibid., II, 142.

[75] Op. cit., p. 449.

[76] "It is impossible to say with certainty what relationship exists between the play proper (*Diálogo del Nacimiento*) which is serious except for the prologue, and the humorous, indecent *Adición del Diálogo* which follows. Two shepherds, skilled in sophistry, ask the pilgrims absurd questions and riddles, engage in a contest of abuse and recite a sacrilegious farced version of the *Ave maris stella*, with which the play ends. It might appear that the new part was introduced before the singing of the *romance* three or four days after Christmas of the same year or later with the object of reproducing, at least, the burlesque spirit of the Boy Bishop revels" (J. P. Wickersham Crawford, *Spanish Drama before Lope de Vega* [Philadelphia, 1937], p. 38).

CHAPTER THREE

[1] ". . . coplas fútiles, coplas de *cancionero*, versos sin ningún género de pasión, devaneos tan insulsos que parecen imaginarios, conceptos sutiles y alambicados, agudezas de sarao palaciego tan pronto dichas como olvidadas, burlas y motejos que no sacan sangre: algo, en suma, que recrea agradablemente el oído sin dejar ninguna impresión en el alma"—*Juan Boscán* (Madrid, 1908), p. 240.

[2] *Les Obres* (Barcelona, 1909), p. 99. The extent to which March was read, ad-

mired, and imitated in Castile is well known. C. S. Lewis has shown the "unmistakable continuity" of the tradition of courtly love in English literature to the love poetry of the present day—*The Allegory of Love: A Study in Medieval Tradition* (Oxford, 1936), p. 3. Guillermo Díaz-Plaja, in his anthology *El sentimiento del amor a través de la poesía española* (Barcelona, n.d.), p. 8, is aware of the relationship here discussed. Menéndez y Pelayo, while properly stressing the fact that the *cancionero* poets did not imitate the Provençaux directly, creates the false impression that they retained only "la tradición métrica, más o menos degenerada" —*Antol. de poét. lír. cast.* (Santander, 1944), II, 24; cf. pp. 27, 114. A. R. Nykl has pointed out that the Portuguese *Cancioneiro da Ajuda* reflects the spirit of the poetry of the troubadours, and calls for further research in this connection— *Hispano-Arabic Poetry and its Relations with the Old Provençal Troubadours* (Baltimore, 1946), p. 395 ff.

This article was printed before I was able to see R. Lapesa, *La trayectoria poética Garcilaso* (Madrid, 1948) and P. Salinas, *Jorge Manrique o Tradición y originalidad* (Buenos Aires, 1947).

[3] It is well to quote here A. J. Denomy's definition of the *fin' amors* of the troubadours: "Far from differing in their idea of love, the so-called idealists and realists [among the early troubadours] concurred in teaching . . . a conception of pure love of desire arising from the contemplation of the beauty of the beloved and effecting a union of the minds and hearts of the lovers. It was a love that yearned for and, at times, was rewarded by the solace of every delight of the beloved except the physical possession of her by intercourse. Far from being pure in the accepted sense, or disinterested, it is sensual and carnal in that it allows, approves and encourages the delights of kissing and embracing, the sight of the beloved's nudity and the touching and lying beside her nude body,—in short, in all that provokes and fans desire. For it is the desire that is the essence of pure love. When possession puts an end to desire or . . . lessens it, then pure love ceases to be and is replaced by mixed love, if practiced by faithful lovers, or by false love if practiced by faithless lovers,—that is, by lust and sensuality practiced for their own sakes. Despite all the sensuality that such a love implies in our eyes, for the troubadours this love is pure, good and true. . . . It is spiritual in that it teaches the union of hearts and minds and not of bodies, and in its desire for the striving after ever closer union it ennobles him who loves to such an extent that it is the source of all good and all virtues. That is the only true love"—"*Fin' Amors: the Pure Love of the Troubadours, Its Amorality and Possible Source*," *Mediæval Studies*, VII (1945), 142-143. This article is reviewed, along with other recent studies on the subject, by H. I. Marrou, "Au dossier de l'amour courtois," *Revue du moyen âge latin*, III (1947), 81-89.

[4] Lewis, *op. cit.*, p. 113.

[5] *Ibid.*

[6] The nature of the alterations will become clear in the following pages. Suffice it to point out here that there is relatively little trace of the effort to enhance desire by the sight of, or by contact with, the nude body. Most of the poets would agree with Ausias March (*Cant* LV, iv): "Delit no sent la vostra carn tocant, / tant mon voler del vostr'es desijos." Sentiments like the following are rare: "El mucho deseo / habrá de matarme, / que tengo d' echarme / yo con vos / . . . / De morir sirviéndo's / cierta placermá, / si hacéis que duerma / yo con vos"—Anon., *Cancionero musical de los siglos XV y XVI*, ed. Asenjo Barbieri (Madrid, 1890), no. 14.

[7] *Laberinto de Fortuna*, cxv.

[8] Art. cit., p. 167.

[9] *Ibid.*, p. 155. Suero de Quiñones, as a sign of subjection to his lady, "llevaba todos los jueves al cuello una *cadena* de fierro"—Menéndez y Pelayo, *Antol.*, ed. cit., II, 208.

[10] "Poignant though that desire be, [the lover] is not to be pitied at its unfulfilment for it is an anguish healed by the very joy of desire" (art. cit., p. 164). "Once consummated, desire weakens and consequently growth in virtue and worth lessens" (p. 176). Cf. Santa Fe in *CPal*, p. 366: ". . . sepades / que si mercet denegades / *el gentil desseo gana*" (*CPal* = *El Cancionero de Palacio*, ed. Francisca Vendrell de Millás, Barcelona, 1945).

[11] Bartolomé de Torres Naharro, Romance II, *Propalladia and Other Works*, ed. Joseph E. Gillet (Bryn Mawr, 1943), I, 223.

[12] Lewis, p. 2. "Die Geliebte war . . . die Lehensherrin, und [der Dichter] diente ihr in der Erwartung, dass sie seine Dienste schliesslich durch eine rechtskräftige Anerkennung, ein Lehen, belohnen werde"—E. Wechssler, "Frauendienst und Vassalität," *Zeitsch. f. franz. Spr. u. Lit.*, XXIV (1902), 159. Cf. S. Pellegrini, "Intorno al vassallaggio d'amore nei primi trovatori," *Cultura neolatina*, Anni IV e V (1944-45), pp. 20-36.

[13] Denomy, p. 175, n. 35.

[14] *Ibid.*, p. 167.

[15] *Op. cit.*, p. 29. Lancelot is none the less made out by Chrétien to be a pious man.

[16] *Ibid.*, p. 21.

[17] *Ibid.*, pp. 21-22. E. Wechssler, *Das Kulturproblem des Minnesangs*, Band I, *Minnesang und Christentum* (Halle, 1909), p. 219, declares that ". . . der Sänger seinen Frauendienst unter der Einwirkung einer asketischen Zeitbildung mehr und mahr spiritualisierte und zu mystischer Andacht und Heiligenverehrung steigerte."

[18] Ed. Lesley Byrd Simpson (Berkeley, 1939), p. 32.

[19] In my article "The *Celestina* and the Inquisition," *Hispanic Review*, XV (1947), 213, I show that this deification of the *amiga* corresponds to a tradition firmly established in the *cancioneros*. To the evidence there adduced I am able to add the following: anonymous: "mi bien, mi dios y mi gloria" (*Questión de amor*, in Menéndez y Pelayo, *Orígenes de la novela*, [Madrid, 1907], II, 65a); Juan Alvarez Gato: "ado vistes aquel dios / cos dió la muerte y la vida" (*F-D*, I, 237); el Comendador Avila: "c'os adora como a dios" (*CG*, II, 12); Pedro de Cartagena: "y sin Dios porque creer / quiero en vos por mi querer" (*F-D*, II, 533); Diego López de Haro: "sabreys vos / si mi alma que allá está, / pues penando muere acá, / si en la gloria de su dios, / si biue allá" (*F-D*, II, 739); Juan de Mena: "non sé . . ./si vos ore por divina" (*CdeR*, II, 34); Sancho de Rojas, "este dios, dama d'altura" (*CG*, I, 628); el Comendador Román: "Vos, mi dios, por mi tristura" (*CG*, I, 449); Diego de Saldaña: "o dueña, mi solo dios" (*F-D*, II, 613); Diego de San Pedro: "y os tuue siempre por dios" (*CG*, I, 456); Fernando de la Torre: "pues que soys mi solo dios" (*CFT*, p. 137); Torres Naharro: "a la mi diosa y señora" (*op. cit.*, I, 182).

F-D = *Cancionero castellano del siglo XV*, ed. R. Foulché-Delbose, 2 vols. (Madrid, 1912-15); *CG* = *Cancionero General*, ed. Bibliófilos españoles, 2 vols. (Madrid, 1882); *CdeR* = *El cancionero de Roma*, ed. M. Canal Gómez, 2 vols. (Madrid, 1935); *CFT* = *Cancionero y obras en prosa de Fernando de la Torre*, ed. A. Paz y Melia, *Gesellschaft f. rom. Lit.*, Band 16 (Dresden, 1907).

[20] "Allá en la guerra Anibal, / en la paz acá Macías, / pues que yo sé que soys tal, / quiero que sepays mi mal" (Tapia, *F-D*, II, 449).

[21] "E aquel Macías, ýdolo de los amantes, del oluido porque le oluidaua, se quexaua"—*La Celestina*, ed. Cejador (Madrid, 1913), I, 117-118.

[22] "No sé que postremería / ayan buena los mis días / quando el gentil Maçías / priso muerte por tal vía"—*Obras* de Juan Rodríguez de la Cámara, ed. Bibliófilos españoles (Madrid, 1884), p. 79.

[23] "Yo hallo comigo trabajos tan juntos, / que hago ventajas al santo Macías"—El Comendador Estúñiga, *CG*, II, 205.

[24] *Op. cit.*, p. 64.

[25] Cf. the *Miserere* of Mosén Francisco de Villalpando, in *CPal*, pp. 184-189.

Other examples: "Amor, non puedo saber / yerro que a ti hiziese, / porque ya perder deuiese / tan en breue así plazer. / Bien harás en acorrer / a mí tuyo que padezco / el gran mal que non merezco, / pues en ti adoro e creo" (Juan Agraz, F-D, II, 209); "Dios de amor, a vos imploro / sy mi vida deseades, / Señor, que me proveades / de tan preçioso thesoro" (Ferrant Manuel de Lando, CB, p. 273); "Perdóname, amor, amor, / que mis días no son nada, / pues en fin de mi jornada / me tiene tu disfavor" (Garci Sánchez de Badajoz, F-D, II, 625).

CB = Cancionero de Baena, ed. P. J. Pidal (Madrid, 1851).

[26] Obras, ed. J. Amador de los Ríos (Madrid, 1852), p. 370.

[27] Ibid., p. 415.

[28] Cf. E. Panofsky, Studies in Iconology. Humanistic Trends in the Art of the Renaissance (New York, 1939), p. 142.

[29] See C. S. Lewis, op. cit., Index, sub vocibus Venus and Love, Psf. (= Amor, Cupid, God of Love, King of Love) and Paul Lehmann, Die Parodie im Mittelalter (München, 1925), treatment of Liebesleben, p. 142 ff., especially p. 156 ff.

[30] The Index of Quiroga (1583) condemns "Garci Sánchez de Badajoz, las lectiones de Iob, aplicadas a amor profano." Compositions of this sort, "en muchos Cancioneros fueron arrancadas de los folios, mientras que en otros casos . . . se limitaron a cruzar los versos de referencia con diversos trazos y garabatos que dificultan mucho su lectura." (Francisca Vendrell de Millás in CPal, p. 13.)

[31] (Barcelona, 1567), pp. 117–118.

[32] In Tirso de Molina's Cigarrales de Toledo (Madrid, 1913), pp. 185–186, a lackey draws a mildly amusing parallel between the sufferings of himself and his master while staying at an inn, and those of the Passion: even though Peter is not there to deny his Lord, cocks crow at midnight, and "no faltan moças tentadoras, que a fuer de la de Pilatos desatinan a los passageros. . . . Sólo falta que se ahorque Judas, que es el huésped que nos vendió, y oxalá lo haga, resucitando nosotros desta desdicha. . . . ¡Amén Jesús!" The relator of the tale remarks: "No bastaron cuydados para que no me riyese de la acomodada alegoría de mi desnudo impaciente."

[33] Op. cit., p. 83.

[34] Ibid., p. 75.

[35] CG, I, 371 ff. Cf. Menéndez y Pelayo, Antología, ed. cit., II, 208.

[36] Cf. Juan de Mena (F-D, I, 203–204): "Pues el tiempo es ya pasado, / y el año todo conplido, / desde que yo fuí entrado / en orden de enamorado, / y el hábito rreçebido; / y pues en tal rreligión / entiendo siempre durar. . . ." Cf. Jorge Manrique's coplas "de la profesión que hizo en la orden del Amor" (F-D, II, 238).

[37] "Las dos rricas tumbas" of the suicide lovers Ardanlyer and Lyessa were opened yearly "a las grandes compañas de los amadores que vienen de todas naçiones a la grand perdonança que en los tales días les otorga el alto Cupido, en visitación y memoria de aquéllos"—Rodríguez de la Cámara, El siervo libre de amor, ed. cit., p. 72.

[38] Cf. the Concilio Venerense of Bartolomé de Torres Nabharro, ed. cit., I, 242 ff. Here the treatment is burlesque, not serious.

[39] In Orígenes de la novela, II, 37a.

[40] "Si algo curioso hay en sus rimas [de D. Alvaro de Luna], como muestra del tono falso y convencional en que solían expresarse los afectos, es la extravagancia de las hipérboles amorosas, que no se detiene ni ante el sacrilegio"—Antol., ed. cit., II, 27; cf. pp. 237, 325–326.

[41] "Sur les origines et les fins du Service d'Amour," Mélanges de linguistique et de littérature offerts a M. Alfred Jeanroy (Paris, 1928), p. 223. On the relation of this article to earlier treatments of the subject by G. Paris, E. Wechssler, P. Rousselot, and K. Vossler, see pp. 223, n. 1; 226–227; 232; 241, n. 1.

[42] Lewis, p. 32. Cf. p. 191: "In the opinion of Chaucer's Troilus the bliss and pathos of a gravely conducted amour are the finest flower of human life."

[43] The word is Denomy's. See below.

[44] Lewis, p. 15.

[45] *Ibid.*

[46] *Ibid.*, pp. 15–16.

[47] *Ibid.*, p. 16.

[48] *Ibid.*, p. 17.

[49] *Ibid.*, p. 17. Cf. Wechssler's chapter, "Der Widerstreit zwischen Fraueminne und Gottesminne," *Das Kulturproblem*, I, 406–433.

[50] Art. cit. Cf. his earlier article, "An Inquiry into the Origins of Courtly Love," *Mediæval Studies*, VI (1944), 193–260.

[51] *Orígenes de la novela*, II, 38a.

[52] *Op. cit.*, p. 5. Francisca Vendrell de Millás is in error when she says in her *Prólogo* to CPal (p. 87; cf. p. 107): "Platónico era el amor y largo el esperar." No. 234 in CPal voices the poet's request for the sight of the beloved's naked body 'en el lugar que querría." If the poetry really were Platonic, the royal manuscript's *exornación* would not show "cierta libertad" (p. 9), which is obtrusively phallic. See Plates II (opp. p. 232), V (opp. p. 274), VII (opp. p. 364). This is apparent only in the zoomorphic figures; the nude human forms have been gently and discreetly blotted with ink. See also Plate VI (opp. p. 276).

[53] "Dante finds a *modus vivendi* with Christianity and produces a noble fusion of sexual and religious experience"—Lewis, p. 21.

[54] Ed. cit., p. 197.

[55] Cf. Mario Equicola, *Libro di natura d'amore* (Vinegia, 1531), fol. 81: "Non dicemo bello la soaue voluptà dell'odorato, la dolcezza del gusto, il giocondissimo moto venereo, per esser più il corpo che l'anima dilettare."

[56] Ed. cit., p. 198.

[57] *Ibid.*

[58] *Ibid.*

[59] *Op. cit.*, fols. 142^v, 144^v, 207. Even Castiglione permits the holding of hands, and the kiss. See *El Cortesano*, tr. Boscán, ed. M. Fabié (Madrid, 1873), pp. 502–503. Paul N. Siegel ascribes this condoning of sensual love in the young courtier to the mediæval chivalric tradition. See "The Petrarchan Sonneteers and Neo-Platonic Love," *SP*, XLII (1945), 176.

[60] The connection with the courtly tradition is especially clear in Villasandino's acrostic to a lady named Catalina (Catelyna): "*y* es otrossy la sesta, / que quiere dezir Ysseo, / a quien yo conparo esta / en bondat e en asseo" (F-D, II, 389). Cf. CPal, p. 166: "Ginebra, Reyna loada, / senyora de Camalote. . . ."

[61] See below. In discussing the problem of truancy we shall have occasion to refer again to this respected theologian.

[62] *Cancionero de Stúñiga*, ed. Fuensanta del Valle and Sancho Rayón (Madrid, 1872).

[63] Fernando de la Torre in *CFT*, p. 169. For a description by Juan Rodríguez del Padrón, see Menéndez y Pelayo, *Antología*, ed. cit., II, 209.

[64] This poem has been attributed to Alfonso Gonzalo de Castro. See Hugo A. Rennert, *Macías, o Namorado* (Philadelphia, 1900), p. 19.

[65] *Obras*, p. 409.

[66] "En este soneto el actor muestra quél, quando es delante aquella su señora, le paresçe que es en el monte Tabor, en el qual Nuestro Señor aparesçió a los tres discípulos suyos; e por quanto la estoria es muy vulgar, non cura de la escrivir" (*Obras*, p. 281). The following lines from Suárez (*CG*, I, 332) may or may not refer to *el amor angelical*: "Soys la luz que lumbre da / al nubloso coraçon; soys el bien mayor d'acá, soys el templo dond' está / todo nuestra deuoción: soys alas con que bolamos / en el mas alto desseo; / soys por do quiera que vamos / espejo con que afeytamos / lo que nos paresce feo." *El más alto desseo* might be interpreted as *fin' amors*.

[67] "L'amour lointain de Jaufré Rudel et la poésie des troubadours," *Univ. of North Carolina Studies in the Romance Languages and Literatures,* v (Chapel Hill, 1944), pp. 1–2.

[68] *Oríg. de la nov.,* II, 38a.

[69] Cf. Juan de Padilla, el cartuxano, in his *Retablo de la vida de Cristo* (F-D, I, 432): "Deben, por ende, juzgar sabiamente, / y no por la cara los sabios maridos; / a la deveces, los flacos sentidos / reciben engaño de poco accidente. / O crudo marido, que muy crudamente / degüellas tu dueña por sola sospecha, / ay de ti! ay, si tu mano derecha / derrama por suelo la sangre inocente!"

[70] Ed. Barcelona, 1847–48, I, 179.

[71] *Oríg. de la nov.,* II, 5b. The rejection however, was not absolute. Leriano's messenger returns another day: "En fin, pasado aquel día y otros muchos, hallaua en sus aparencias más causa para osar que razón para temer" (p. 6a).

[72] *Oríg. de la nov.,* II, 58a.

[73] Hernando de Ludueña, *Doctrinal de gentileza,* F-D, II, 731.

[74] Ed. cit., I, 229–30.

[75] *Oríg. de la nov.,* p. 37b.

[76] Hernando de Ludueña, F-D, II, 727.

[77] Diego del Castillo, F-D, II, 225.

[78] F-D, I, 204.

[79] Hernando de Ludueña, F-D, II, 727. Cf. Santa Fe, *CPal,* p. 332: "Pero si bien no sabredes / por la boca mi dolor / en mi gesto et color / muy claro lo conoçreedes."

[80] Soneto XI, *Obras,* p. 279. Cf. Contreras, *CPal,* p. 363: "el que sufre mal et calla / no deviera ser naçido."

[81] *Obras* de Juan Rodríguez de la Cámara, p. 98.

[82] Diego de San Pedro, *Sermón, Orígenes de la novela,* II, 39a.

[83] Soria, F-D, II, 268. Cf. Ludueña, F-D, II, 734.

[84] Santillana, *Obras,* p. 388. "Bernard de Ventadour, realizing his presumption in seeking the love of so elevated a lady, casts himself entirely on her mercy, making no claim of her whatever" (Denomy, art. cit., p. 167). Calisto's inferiority to Melibea "derives from the tradition of the sentimental novel, and this from the Dolce Stil Nuovo and the Provençaux"—Rachel Frank, "Four Paradoxes in the *Celestina*," *Romanic Review,* XXXVIII (1947), 58. When Gandalín suggests to Amadís that he could rightfully aspire to have Oriana or any other woman, no matter of what station, "Amadís que esto le oyó, fué sañudo, e dijo: Ve, loco sin sentido: ¿cómo osas decir tan gran desvarío? ¿Había yo de valer, ni otro alguno, tanto como aquella, en quien todo el bien del mundo es? E si otra vez lo dices, no irás conmigo un paso" (ed. cit., I, 113).

[85] "*Fin' amors* . . . is a love wherein desire is not the end in itself but a means to the end,—progress and growth in virtue, merit, and worth" (Denomy, p. 175). In the "mandamientos quel Dios de Amor vos a dado" contained in *El Sueño de Feliciano de Silva* (16th century) we read: "El quinto, que con sola pena / quieras ser galardonado." In this same *Sueño* the dreamer is received by Penelope and Lucrecia, who take him by the hand saying: "bien aventurado / amador, que mereciste / *en la pena* aver hallado / la gloria con que al presente / te hallas glorificado"—*Dos romances anónimos del siglo XVI. El Sueño de Feliciano de Silva. La muerte de Héctor,* ed. H. Thomas (Madrid, 1917), pp. 39, 42.

[86] "Mais, dès qu'on y touche, il s'évanouit, pareil à la fameuse espérance des Bretons: le retour du roi Arthur de l'île-fantôme, l'île des songes d'où nul ne revient"—Lot-Borodine, art. cit., p. 225.

[87] Cf. Guevara (F-D, II, 108): "En las cortes bien andantes / de nobles damas de estados / donde amores trihunfantes / son de sieruos bien constantes / con gentil gala tratados, / segund horden de cuidados, / los *pacientes* / de las nobles y eçelentes / son priuados."

[88] "Se (ceomo de Thraci e de Cretensi era costume) con pietre bianche e nere

felici ed infelici giorni li amanti notassero, non dubito seriano molto più li infelici: ͏a dico che uno solo e minimo instante del felice vale ed è di più efficacia che ͏ille hore e longo spatio di tempo del infelice. . . . Durate in le fatiche e passioni ͏'amore, che meglio è patirne che starne senza"—Equicola, *op. cit.*, fols. 87ᵛ, 88ᵛ.

[89] Diego de San Pedro, *Sermón, Orígs.*, ɪɪ, 38b. The expression of this thought is ͏xtremely widespread. One more example: "Cerca está ya mi morir, / muy lexos ͏oy de curar, / pues pregunto con llorar / y respondeys con reyr. / Por lo qual ͏uede dezir / mi obligado querer, / ni me daña el padecer, / ni me aprouecha el ͏:ruir. / Llamarme yo seruidor / de tal dama, avnque da mal, / es una victoria tal, / ͏:r vencido y vencedor: / que, avnque me falte el fauor, / es muy deuida razón / ͏ue auer dado el coraçón / haga ser bueno el dolor"—*Cancionera de don ͏'edro Manuel Ximénez de Urrea* (Zaragoza, 1878), p. 50. Cf. in the same ͏olume: "Mejor es tener tal mal / y padecer / que sin él placer tener" (p. 406). ͏ee also Gómez Manrique, *F-D*, ɪɪ, 124; Stúñiga, *ibid.*, p. 600; Santillana, *Obras*, ͏. 277; Santa Fe, *CPal*, p. 336.

[90] Pedro Manuel Ximénez de Urrea, *op. cit.*, p. 55.

[91] *Opúsculos literarios de los siglos XIV a XVI*, ed. A. Paz y Melia (Madrid, ͏892), p. 95.

[92] Alvarez Gato sounds a similar note in the volume cited, pp. 224–225, 240. Cf., ͏n similar vein, Hernando de Ludueña: "Por ende, quien me creyere / sirua bien ͏. quien bien quiere; / pero la dama no quiera / que el seruicio hecho muera /y el ͏eruidor desespere" (*F-D*, ɪɪ, 734); Perálvarez d'Ayllón: "y es razón / que quien ͏omo yo te quiere, / de tus mercedes espere / galardón" (*CG*, ɪɪ, 117).

[93] Stúñiga in *F-D*, ɪɪ, 596.

[94] *Op. cit.*, fol. 132.

[95] *Obras*, p. 287.

[96] Equicola, fols. 145ᵛ–146.

[97] *Questión de amor, Orígenes de la novela*, ɪɪ, 70b. Cf. Pero Messía, *CPal*, p. 310: ͏'Car no sé ygual tristura / ni más que ser amado." Mario Equicola remarks: "Le ͏agrime sono inditio de tenero animo e benigno" (*op. cit.*, fol. 148). On "das ͏Veinen als Tugend," see Wechssler, *Das Kulturproblem*, ɪ, 238 ff. Love = senti-͏mentality was "ein gegebenes Lebenselement der damaligen Christenheit" (p. 238).

[98] That love could produce death was recognized by serious writers in both the ͏5th and 16th centuries. El Tostado: "como dice Ipocras:—El amor es cobdicia ͏ʃue se face en el coraçón, por causa de la cual interviene(n) algunos accidentes ͏le que por ventura muere el enamorado" (*Tratctado que fizo . . . el Tostado . . . ͏:ómo al ome es necessario amar*, in *Opúsculos literarios de los siglos XIV a XVI*, ͏:d. cit., p. 228); Miguel Sabuco de Nantes (writing under the name of his daughter ͏Oliva): "Síguese ahora el afecto del amor y deseo. El amor ciega, convierte al ͏amante en la cosa amada, lo feo hace hermoso y lo falso perfecto, todo lo allana ͏y pone igual; lo dificultoso hace fácil, alivia todo trabajo, da salud cuando lo amado ͏:e goza. También mata en dos maneras: o perdiendo lo que se ama, o no pudiendo ͏ɪlcanzar lo que se ama y desea"—*apud*, Florencio M. Torner, *Doña Oliva Sabuco ͏Je Nantes, Siglo XVI* (Madrid, 1935), p. 101.

[99] Petrarch, Sonetto cɪx.

[100] *Question de amor*, p. 78b. Cf. Costana (*CG*, ɪ, 321): "yo que muero por ͏eruiros / sin vos mostraros seruida."

[101] *Obras* de Juan Fernández de Heredia (Valencia, 1913), pp. 29–31.

[102] Denomy, p. 167. Cf. Juan Luis Vives, *Tratado del alma* (Madrid, 1923), p. ͏226: "Juzgada por buena una cosa, y tan pronto como se ofrece a la voluntad, la ͏nueve ésta y atrae hacia sí mediante cierta conformidad natural como la que ͏:xiste entre la verdad y el entendimiento, entre la hermosura y los ojos. Este ͏novimiento de la voluntad que se manifiesta en una especia de alegría, en el ͏Jesarrugar la frente y sonreír, con lo cual significa que le gusta aquello por ser ͏Juen̄o, se llama agrado."

[103] Soria (*F-D*, ɪɪ, 260). Among the troubadours, Bernard de Ventadour, e.g.,

asks of his beloved only "that she know of his love, how purely he loves her" (Denomy, p. 166). In the *Cárcel de amor* the author addresses Laureola: "Si no crees que matar es virtud, no te suplica que le hagas otro bien sino que te pese de su mal, que cosa graue para ti no creas que te la pidirya: que por meior avrá é penar que serte a ti causa de pena" (p. 5b); and the Condestable de Portuga declares in his *Sátira de felice e infelice vida* (p. 85): "solamente movida a clemencia deseaba [yo] que de mi mal se doliese, e que mi desigualado pesar sintiese, pues non es alguna cosa más conuenible ni que más cara deua ser al gentil alto e virtuoso coraçón que haber merced, dolor e sentimiento de los triste infortunados." Cf. Vives, p. 233: "Todo amor que tiene su origen en la debida gracia es tanto más ardiente cuanto menos remunerados quedamos, o cuanto menos le deseó y esperaba aquel a quien aprovecha. . . . No es el amor puro y verdadero mientras no esté libre en absoluto de toda mira utilitaria. . . ."

[104] *Obras*, p. 100. For Jorge Manrique, cruelty consists in the refusal of the lady to grant such a boon: "Entiendo y sé lo que quiero, / mas no entiendo lo que quiera / quien quiere siempre que muera / sin querer creer que muero" (*F-D*, II, 240).

[105] The love of Amadís and Oriana was a true courtly love, as the author indicates by having Amadís pass successfully the test of the *arco de los leales amadores*, yet Oriana could say to her lover: ". . . mas como quiera que avenga, yo os prometo, que si la fortuna o mi juicio alguna vía de descanso no nos muestra, que la mi flaca osadía la hallará, que si de ella peligro nos ocurriese sea antes con desamor de mi padre y de mi madre y de otros que con el sobrado amor nuestro nos podría venir, estando como agora, suspensos padeciendo tan graves y crueles *deseos* como de cada día se nos aumentan y sobrevienen" (ed. cit., I, 240), and Amadís says to Oriana (p. 239) that his heart's great need "requiere mayor merced." Cf. Mario Equicola, fol. 135: "Perilchè essendo prossimi e propinqui a quella che amamo, il disio ne accende, lo amor ne infiamma, et al tatto solo delli suoi panni le nostri parti, che quiete si stauano, se essercitano, se irritano: ne si può contenere che non corran doue il disio del piacere le conduce, e da smisurato imaginato piacere concitati, non possemo acquietarne, ne poner fine a sospiri."

[106] Cf. Azpilcueta, *Manual de confesores y penitentes*, p. 30: ". . . y por consiguiente sumariamente deue preguntar [el confesor] los besos, abraços o otros tocamientos impúdicos, a los que no son casados. . . ."

[107] *Op. cit.*, fols. 75ᵛ-76. Caltraviessa's request to his beloved, "que vos viesse yo desnuda / en el lugar que querría" (*CPal*, p. 306), is most unusual, if not unique, in the Spanish *cancioneros*.

[108] "How can a woman, whose duty is to obey you, be the *midons* whose grace is the goal of all striving and whose displeasure is the restraining influence upon all uncourtly vices? You may love her in a sense; but that is not love, says Andreas, any more than the love of father and son is *amicitia*." (Lewis, p. 37; cf. Wechssler, *Das Kulturproblem*, I, 209).

[109] See below.

[110] This statement is too strong, as we shall see.

[111] Ed. Cejador (Madrid, 1913), II, 159. Cf. Cejador's note: "No es este dicho de barragana propio de la Melibea que nos pintó el autor," and Rachel Frank's article, "Four Paradoxes in the *Celestina*," *Romanic Review*, vol. cit.

[112] See, e.g., King Lisuarte's statement regarding Oriana: ". . . mas yo y la Reina hemos prometido a nuestra hija de no la casar contra su voluntad" (II, 71). Melibea's father was willing to grant to his daughter similar freedom, but her mother expresses shock at the thought that anyone so innocent as Melibea could think for herself in terms of marriage: ". . . piensas que sabe ella qué cosa sean hombres?" (*La Celestina*, II, 162-163).

[113] See the initial chapters of the novel.

[114] Cf. E. H. Templin, "The Exculpation of *Yerros por Amores* in the Spanish

Comedia," *Publications of the Univ. of California at Los Angeles in Languages and Literature*, I (1933), 1–50.

[115] Ed. cit., I, 277.

[116] Lewis, p. 104.

[117] *Op. cit.*, pp. 172, 104.

[118] The character of this truancy could not be put in clearer or stronger terms than by Denomy, p. 179. Cf. p. 183: "Courtly love is wholly divorced from Christian morality."

[119] *Apud* Denomy, p. 177, n. 42.

[120] Lewis, p. 183.

[121] *Obras*, p. 96. Cf. Juan de Torres (*CPal*, p. 244): "quien de linda s'enamora / atender deve perdón"; and Luna Condestable (*ibid.*, p. 283): "Senyor Dios, pues me causaste / sin comparaçión amar / tú me deves perdonar / si pasé lo que me mandaste."

[122] (Madrid, 1876), p. 12.

[123] Oriana says to Mabilia, referring to Amadís: "Esto me acontece siempre con vuestro primo, que mi captivo corazón nunca en al piensa, sino en complacer y seguir su voluntad, no guardando a Dios ni la ira de mi padre" (II, 195).

[124] Cf. no. 506: "... a una dueña, que era su ennamorada en León"; and 597: "... por amor e loores de una muy fermosa, que era su ennamorada en León."

[125] Lewis, p. 39.

[126] Denomy, p. 179. Cf. Wechssler's chapter, "Der Ausgleich zwischen Frauenminne und Gottesminne," *Das Kulturproblem*, I, 434–465.

[127] Lot-Borodine, p. 241.

[128] See his Canzone XXIX, *Vergine bella*. ...

[129] Lot-Borodine, pp. 241–242.

[130] Ed. cit., p. 98. Cf. p. 112: "Per sa bondat, prech la verge Maria / qu'en son servey cambïe mon voler, / mostrant me clar com han perdut carrer / los qu'en amor de les dones han via."

[131] *Oíras*, p. 33. Cf. Sancho Alfonso de Montoro: "Amores, amor, amores, camino de perdiçión, / ..., / quien en ti a confiança / a toda santidad yerra" (*CPal*, p. 424). The manuscript containing the poems of Juan Alvarez Gato is divided into two parts: "La meitad es de verdades, / la otra de vanidades." The latter are "coplas viciosas de amores, pecadoras y llenas de mocedades" (Menéndez y Pelayo, *Antología*, II, 324).

[132] *Coplas contra los pecados mortales*, his last work, continued by Gómez Manrique after his death (see p. 133). The lines here quoted are in *F-D*, I, 120–121.

[133] *Viage y peregrinación*, p. 8.

[134] "Mainte fois on s'est demandé pourquoi l'unique object chanté par les troubadours était la femme mariée, et, pour l'expliquer, on a toujours invoqué les conditions sociales qui ne permettaient pas à une jeune fille de ce temps d'être un centre d'attraction. Rien n'est moins exact. La noble demoiselle ... n'est nullement absente de la vie mondaine; gracieuse, fine et désirable, elle prend part, au contraire, à toutes les réunions et *caroles*, assiste aux joutes et tournois où plus d'une manche flotte, assurément, en son honneur. Elle est aussi l'héroine de toute une littérature du 'roman d'aventures' depuis ses origines. C'est même là la pierre de touche qui distingue ces deux types romanesques de l'amour courtois: d'une part, *la conquête de la fiancée*, où domine, malgré un certain verbiage élégant, l'égalité sentimentale des sexes; de l'autre, *la dévotion à la dame*, où éclate la supériorité, hautement proclamée, de l'aimée" (Lot-Borodine, p. 228).

[135] Cf. the heading of Juan Alvarez Gato's fragmentary poem, no. 106 in *F-D* (I, 251): "Auiendo conosçido el mundo y sentido en todos los estados y alcançado y gustado mucho de lo que se procura dél, y visto ques todo condenación del ánima ... deseando desnudarse de todas las vanidades ... y malos enxenplos que ha dado ... en las moçedades, así en el *trobar* como en los efetos de sus

obras liuianas, pensó de pelear connuestros tres contrarios [the world, the flesh and the devil] en cuyo poder se hallaua . . . [e] hizo esta copla al mundo . . tomando nueva vida espiritual debaxo de *la orden y ábito matrimonial y legal.* There has been preserved only one *copla* of 9 lines, followed by this notation "Daquí adelante no ay cosa trobada ni escrita, syno la deuoçión y buena dotrina.

[136] See Lewis, pp. 197, 339–344.

[137] The problem of the *doncella* in the novels of chivalry is very complex and requires a special study. The objective of love in the *Amadís* is usually marriage although there is a surprising amount of free and thoughtless *consummated* love to which no importance seems to be attached. Cf. ed. cit., I, 38: "Viendo ella este Lisuarte, y sabiendo sus buenas maneras, con él se casó, que por amores l servía." In the sentimental novel, *Questión de amor*, Vasquirán had asked fo Violina's hand in marriage, "lo qual no pudo alcançar por algún respeto que aqu no se escriue." He therefore took her boldly from her father's house and embarke with her for Italy, where they lived together until her death. There is no mentio of any ceremony, public or private. (Ed. cit., pp. 42–43.)

[138] The maiden's place in Spanish poetry is very different from the place sh occupies in the works of the troubadours: "Par sa nature propre, la jeune fill personnifie l'attente, l'avenir qui se noue, elle n'est que l'ébauche d'un être. Com ment aurait-elle pu combler les voeux de celui qui cherchait un astre fixe a firmament de ses amours? Il fallait à son attitude orante un object d'adoratio plus achevé, il lui fallait une femme dans la plénitude de sa maturité. Grâce elle, reine éphémère, mais combien adulée, grâce au rayonnement de sa beauté, la sagesse de son initiation, au sceptre de sa royauté, s'épanouit, au cœur du XII siècle, ce chef-d'œuvre du Moyen-Age poétique: *le service d'amour*" (Lot Borodine, p. 228).

[139] Similar references to *doncellas* may be found in CPal, pp. 171, 183, 226, 236 258, 264, 278, 285.

[140] "Mixtus vero amor dicitur ille, qui omni carnis delectationi suum praesta effectum et in extremo Veneris opere terminatur. . . . Hoc autem dico non quas mixtum amorem damnare intendens sed ostendere cupiens, quis ex illis alteri si preferendus. Nam et mixtus amor verus est amor atque laudandus et cunctorun dicitur origo bonorum" (Capellanus *apud* Denomy, p. 149, n. 43).

[141] Denomy, p. 177.

[142] "Der Spanische Cancionero des Brit. Museums," ed. Hugo Albert Rennert *Romanische Forschungen*, X (1899), 94.

[143] *Ibid.*, p. 45. Cf., in F-D, no. 603 (II, 315): "Esta cántiga fizo el dicho Alfonse Aluarez, por amor e loores de su esposa la postrimera que ouo, que auía nombre Mayor"; and no. 608: "Esta cántiga fizo Alfonso Aularez, por rruego del Conde don Pedro Niño, por amor e loores de doña Beatriz su muger."

[144] Lewis, pp. 339–344.

[145] Cf. Alfred Jeanroy, *La poésie lyrique des troubadours* (Toulouse, 1934), II 187.

[146] Mario Equicola, speaking of the *ingeniosissimi spagnoli*, sounds the following warning: "Ma se li serà vetato il lieto viuere, non li serà vetato il presto morire comenciò con amore, seguirà con fede, continuarà con seruire, perseuerà cor ostinatione, finirà con morte . . . : Et mille altre persuasioni, con le quali, o donne dal vostro proprio elemento che è la pudicità e honestà como del pesce l'acqua *tentano trarui a loro appetitti*" (*op. cit.*, fol. 213). In another place he says to the ladies: "Non vi moua l'altrui pallore che vi può esser poi causa de rosciore" (fol 212ᵛ). "The negative note," says Lewis, "is there because *Frauendienst* is not the whole of life, or even of love, and yet pretends to be the whole, and then suddenly remembers that it is not. The history of courtly love from beginning to end may be described as an 'amorous-odious sonnet,' a 'scholar's love or hatred' " (p. 145)

[147] *Juego de copas, apropiado a los amores de casadas*, CFT, p. 131.

[148] This theme of the falsity of the lover's protestations is developed at length in Gil Polo's *Diana Enamorada*, in *Orígenes de la novela*, II, 393b–394a and 396–396. This is but one of many instances of the continuation into the 16th century of 15th-century poetic practice.

[149] Vanegas, in *Canc. Brit. Mus.*, p. 100.

[150] Ed. Francisque-Michel (Leipzig, 1860), I, 102.

[151] *Tratado del alma*, p. 96.

[152] *Obras*, pp. 89–90.

[153] *Apud* Barbara Matulka, *The Novels of Juan de Flores and their European Diffusion* (New York, 1931), p. 334. Cf. Fray Luis de Granada, *Introducción del Símbolo de la Fe*, I, xxii, §2: ". . . la hermosura de alguna criatura . . . basta muchas veces para trastornar el seso de un hombre, y para hacerle caer en cama, y a veces perder la vida." Cf. Vives, *Tratado del alma*, pp. 230–231: "Así como por las obras juzgamos de la bondad interior, pensamos que es la cara imagen del alma, y por eso amamos naturalmente a quien es hermoso. . . . Es natural que la belleza de los cuerpos represente y en cierto modo ofrezca ante nuestra vida la de las almas en su cadencia, elegancia, proporción y armonía. . . . Por eso, nuestra alma tiende hacia la hermosure cual a cosa semejante; en ella ve expresado corporalment . . . lo que ya Dios la otorgó espiritualmente."

[154] Equicola, fol. 82ʳ. Cf. Wechssler, *Das Kulturproblem*, I, 373, and Fray Juan de Pineda, *Primera Parte de los treynta y cinco Diálogos familiares de la Agricultura christiana* (Salamanca, 1589), II, fol. 22: "Del amor común y sensual trahe Theodoreto [c. 396–458 A.D.] para dezir que el principio del amor es la vista, y que con esperança cresce, y con la memoria recibe nutrimento, y con el vso se conserua . . . y sin andar por enigmas entenderemos que el amor es efecto de la voluntad que se aficiona a lo bueno, y ésta tal afición y deseo de gozar de lo bueno llamamos amor. . . ." Cf. Frank G. Halstead, "The Optics of Love: Note on a Concept of Atomistic Philosophy in the Theatre of Tirso de Molina," *PMLA*, LVII (1943), 108–121.

[155] Ed. cit., p. 71a. In the *Cárcel de amor* (p. 2a) the allegorical figure *Deseo* carried with him an *ymagen* which is analogous to Cupid's arrows: "y con la hermosura desta ymagen causo las aficiones y con ellas quemo las vidas." Indeed, Laureano says to Laureola: "tu hermosura causó el afición, y el afición el deseo, y el deseo la pena" (p. 6b). It is beauty that causes the sudden surrender of Elisena in the *Amadís*, a surrender so overwhelming that she was ready to "caer en le peor y más baja parte de su deshonra" (I, 18.) Mario Equicola reports that Juvenal "como vn prodigio scriue di vn cieco inamorato" (fol. 182).

[156] Equicola says, addressing Fortuna: "nella tua occulta potentia si riserua che li indegni amanti amati ed odiati sian li degni" (fol. 119ʳ).

[157] *Obras*, p. 99. Of the stars Equicola says: "questa potentia si può con ragione vincere; e chi è più de ragione capace e participe, meglio la vince" (fol. 123ʳ). Cf. Vives, p. 155.

[158] *Id.*, *ibid.*, pp. 156–157. St. Thomas says: "Natura in sua operatione Dei operationem imitatur." See Leo Spitzer, "Zur 'Celestina,'" *Zeitsch. f. rom. Philologie*, L (1930), 239.

[159] "La favorable Fortuna / vos hizo muy generosa" (G. Manrique, F-D, no. 334); "Esta [i.e., Fortune] avos fizo más bella / de quantas yo vi jamás (G. Manrique, F-D, no. 359). Fortune and Nature work together: "Fortuna no discrepante, / y sabia naturaleza, / tales dos vuestro semblante / fabricaron sin pereza" (Santillana, CG, I, 93–94). God and Fortune cooperate: "pero Dios et la fortuna / en este tiempo dotaron / muchas de grant fermosura" (Luna Condestable, CPal, p. 284). God and Fate cooperate: "Bien veo que es locura /amar e non ser amado, / mas según Dios e ventura / nasce todo ombre fadado" (Alfonso Enríquez, *ibid.*, p. 184).

[160] Much remains to be said on Fortune and Fate in the *siglo XV*. The data

which I have collected are well summed up in these words of the 16th-century Antonio de Torquemada: "Tenía encima del arco de la puerta principal una letra que decía: 'Morada de la Fortuna,' a quien *por permisión divina* muchas de las cosas corporales son subjetas." (*Colloquios satíricos*, in *Orígenes de la novela*, p. 571a).

[161] *Obras*, p. 281. Cf. Santa Fe in *CPal*, pp. 336–337.

[162] Cf. Equicola, fol. 123ᵛ: "Molti e molte se han date ad arbitrio d'amore, lasciando de ragione il freno"; and fol. 213: "Sappiate che le passioni amorose vigor pigliano sempre, pongono sotto piedi senno e prudentia, e quanto più vigor piglia amore, tanto il senno vien meno, e l'intelletto manca." Cf. Lewis, p. 218: "Gower, as well as another, is faced with this necessity [of recantation]. For him, as for Chaucer, the love which he celebrates is a sin, and in the lover *Will* has usurped dominion over *Resoun*"; and pp. 121–122: "*Reason* is almost the only character in the poem who remains the same in Jean de Meun's continuation as she was in Guillaume's original. In both writers some of the best passages are put in her mouth and in both she speaks to rebuke the lover for the enterprise which he has undertaken. In Jean de Meun there is some confused struggle . . . to follow the poets of Chartres in their attempt to find a solution for the conflict between the courtly and the Christian ideals; but in Guillaume de Lorris there is no conflict. His hero has no reply to *Reason* beyond a wilful *sic volo sic iubeo*. . . . He gives to *Reason* exactly the function which she had in the *Lancelot*: to speak the truth and not be heard." See Vives's chapters on "La Razón," "El Juicio," "La Voluntad," and "De Ambos Géneros de Amor Indistintamente," and Alexo Vanegas, *Agonía del tránsito de la muerte, NBAE*, XVI, 120a, 224a; Francisco de Osuna, *Tercer abecedario espiritual, ibid.*, p. 321; Alonso de Madrid, *Arte para servir a Dios, ibid.*, pp. 598–599, 608–609. Wechssler says: "die Mittel zu diesem allem in der Schulpsychologie der Zeit erlernt worden sind" (*Das Kulturproblem*, I, 373).

[163] Gómez Manrique, *F-D*, II, 118.

[164] Pedro de Cartagena, *F-D*, II, 509. Mario Equicola, fol. 72ᵛ, divides human love into two classes: *naturale* (love of man toward God, love between the soul and the body, desire for what is good for self, children, etc.) and *accidentale*, or "quello che viene da *elettione e libero arbitrio*." The latter has two divisions: *honesto* ("amare quanto si deue e como"), and *inhonesto*, which is concerned only with the "sensitiua forma et voluptà." Errors in *amor accidentale* are: love of "il male in luogo del bene," excessive love of "quel che non deuemo," and insufficient love of "quel che sommamente amar deuemo."

[165] Cf. Vives, p. 104: "Pero el pecado cubrió nuestra mente de grandes y muy densas nieblas, por lo qual se malearon aquellas rectas normas." Through the Fall, man lost his "justicia primitiva." This can be restored in part through the intervention of Divine Grace. So in the *Amadís* (II, 234): "Y en esto . . . podéis ver a qué tampoco [*read* a qué tan poco] basta la fuerza del seso humano, cuando aquel alto Señor, aflojadas las riendas, alzada la mano, apartando su *gracia* permite que el juicio del hombre en su libre poder quede, por donde os será manifiesto si los grandes estados . . . pueden ganados y gobernados ser con la discreción y diligencia de los mortales; o si faltando su *divina gracia*, la gran soberbia, la gran codicia, la muchedumbre de las armadas gentes, son bastantes para le sostener."

[166] *Apud* Matulka, p. 335.

[167] *Sátira de felice e infelice vida*, p. 59.

[168] Juan del Encina, *CG*, II, 27.

[169] Hernando de Ludueña, *F-D*, II, 728. Cf. the *Tractado que fizo el Tostado . . . cómo al ome es necesario amar:* "Hermano, reprehendísteme porque amor de muger me turbó, o poco menos desterró de los términos de la razón" (*Opúsculos literarios*, p. 221).

[170] Cf. Calisto, *Cel.*, I, 122: "Pues sabe que esta mi pena e fluctuoso dolor no se rige por razón"; and Delicado, *La lozana Andaluza* [1528] (Buenos Aires, 1942),

p. 180: ". . . porque sé en qué caen estas cosas, porque no solamente el amor es mal que atormenta a las criaturas racionales, mas a las bestias priva de sí mismas; si no, veldo por esa gata, que há tres días que no me dexa dormir, que ni come ni bebe, ni tiene reposo."

[171] Fray Iñigo de Mendoza, *F-D*, I, 4. Cf. Amadís: "Señor . . . , mi juicio no puede resistir aquellos mortales deseos, de quien cruelmente es atormentado" (I, 127).

[172] Ed. cit., p. 4.

[173] Cf. Equicola (fol. 211): "Li *primi impeti* de natura in tutto vencersi dalla adolescentia non pur difficile, ma impossible credemo: Poscia chel *intelletto* dalla esperientia et vso confirmato piglia forza, lasciata la terra al ciel si può (como deue) inalzare, e qualunche a si sublime et alto volo non se apparecchia, quanto erre e quanto sia degno di reprensione si può comprendere." In other words, man lives by more than the *natural legge.* Both parts of this statement are in agreement with the teaching of St. Thomas. As for the second part: "Et, de cette manière, c'est l'intelligence qui meut la volontè; car le bien perçu par l'intelligence est l'objet de la volontè, qui la meut *par mode de fin.*" As for the first part: "Il s'ensuit que la volontè, *par mode d'agent,* doit mouvoir à leurs actes toutes les puissances de l'âme, sauf les forces naturelles de la partie végétative qui ne sont point soumises à notre libre arbitre"—Thomas Pègues, *Commentaire français littéral de la Somme Théologique de Saint Thomas d'Aquin,* IV, *Traité de l'homme* (Toulouse, 1909), p. 572. Cf. *Summa,* p. I, Q. 83, A. 4: "liberum arbitrium nihil aliud est quam voluntas," and Pègues, vol. cit., p. 602: "la volonté et le libre arbitre ne sont pas deux puissances, mais une seule."

[174] Fernán Pérez de Guzmán, *F-D*, I, 579. On the need for this struggle, cf. Gómez Manrique, *F-D*, II, 121, and Fray Iñigo de Mendoza, *F-D*, I, 93.

[175] "Estas" are *fe* and *esperanza.*

[176] The meaning is: Reason is reliable *only* through grace; man may otherwise use it to sin with.

[177] *La gran caridad divina* is divine grace.

[178] The *alano* is *la perfecta caridad* (see p. 15).

[179] *Monteria espiritual . . . en que la razón caza a la voluntad,* in Diego Sánchez de Badajoz, *Recopilación en metro* (Badajoz, 1910), I, 17. In the *Amadís* (I, 249–250), Angriote is married to his beloved after having shown great forbearance in not abusing her weakness at a time when it would have been impossible for her to resist him. So great was this forbearance, says the author, "que podemos decir que Dios . . . quiso que una tan gran resistencia *hecha por la razón contra su voluntad tan desordenada,* que sin aquel mérito que él merecía y tanto deseaba, no quedasse."

[180] Juan de Lucena, *Libro de Vida beata,* in *Opúsculos literarios,* p. 151.

[181] This is the doctrine of St. Thomas as well as of the Stoics. Cf. above, n. 47, and Pègues, pp. 553–554: "En fin, l'appétit sensible ne peut jamais mettre en branle la faculté motrice extérieure, si l'homme est dans son état normal et en parfaite possession de ses diverses facultés *sans que la volonté délibérée ait donné son consentement.*"

[182] Lucena, p. 188.

[183] Denomy, p. 206.

[184] Cf. Calderón: "Yo vi una hermosura, y yo / la amé, Don Juan, tan a un tiempo / todo, que entre ver y amar, / aun no sé cuál fué primero. / Rendido ostenté finezas, / constante sufrí desprecios, / fino merecí favores, / celoso lloré tormentos; / que éstas son las cuatro edades / de cualquier amor"—*Comedias de Calderón,* ed. Hartzenbusch (Madrid, 1925), II, 462.

CHAPTER FOUR

[1] *Francisco de los Cobos, Secretary to the Emperor Charles V* (Pittsburgh, ca. 1959), p. 36.

[2] Marcel Bataillon, "Plus Oultre: la cour découvre le Nouveau Monde," in Jean Jacquot (ed.), *Fêtes et cérémonies au temps de Charles Quint* (Paris, 1960), p. 13. Bataillon reviews the evidence suggesting that the device *Plus Oultre* was at first adopted by Charles without reference to the Indies, the meaning being simply that Charles had gone, or would go, beyond all others in knightly excellence and virtues. Bataillon observes, however, that the importance of the new discoveries in time came to give a geographical significance to *Plus Oultre*. I believe that it is possible to go farther: the presence of St. Christopher depicted on the sails of the fleet of 1517—*St. Christopher with his feet in the sea*—is an indication that already in 1517 the association of *Plus Oultre* with the idea of new realms beyond the Atlantic had taken place.

[3] Santiago was, of course, the sword-wielding patron saint of Spain. St. Nicholas (Pope Nicholas I) was a great defender of the rights of the church and a valiant protector of the weak. The former could suggest the Virgilian (and imperial) idea of "striking down the proud"; the latter, that of sparing and defending the humble (*Aeneid*, VI, 853: *parcere subiectis et debellare superbos*). In 1611, Covarrubias, in his *Tesoro de la lengua castellana*, gives a two-line entry under *Nicolas*: it means almost the same as Nicodemus, from νικος (*sic*) victory, and λαος (*sic*) people. Under *Nicodemus* the etyma given are νικος and δημος people, signifying "victory through the people." Similar associations may have helped to determine the choice of this saint along with St. Christopher. The other symbols—the Trinity, the holy Mother and Child—add to the general religious tone and correspond to the King's idea of his mission.

[4] *Le chevalier délibéré de Olivier de la Marche y sus versiones españolas del siglo XVI* (Zaragoza, 1950), p. 37.

[5] "Burgund: Eine Krise des romanisch-germanischen Verhältnisses," *Historische Zeitschrift*, CXLVIII (1933), 19 (cited by Clavería).

[6] Though I have learned much since I compiled it, I must refer—as a general and still useful survey of the problem of the Spanish Renaissance—to my article, "A Critical Survey of Scholarship in the Field of Spanish Renaissance Literature, 1914–1944," *SP*, XLIV (1947), 228–64.

[7] This stressing of the religious note, necessary as it is, does not imply that the Spanish (or European) Renaissance was all saintliness, or even all sweetness and light: Jules Michelet was excessively optimistic in his interpretation of history when he wrote of the budding Renaissance: "Un monde d'humanité commence, de sympathie universelle" (*Histoire de France*, IX: *La Renaissance* [Paris, 1879], 387). Although Ulrich von Hutten, just one year after Charles set sail from Middelburg, was inspired to write Willibald Pirckheimer (Oct. 25, 1518): O *seculum! o litterae! juvat vivere*—"Oh century! Oh flourishing studies! It is good to be alive"—the *seculum* was more cruel, more bloody, than golden, as the wars of religion became the *misère de ce temps* (Ronsard). Very soon after 1518 the Emperor Charles (Defender of the Faith) would have to bear the opprobrium caused by the sack of the Eternal City by his troops (1527), as well as the shock of finding himself branded a heretic by the Pope. In Spain, the bulwark of orthodoxy, the sixteenth century was, so to speak, "conceived in sin": very early (*ca.* 1507) the Inquisition was used to further political ends. See the section "Fray Hernando y los orígenes de la Inquisición" in the *Estudio Preliminar* by Francisco Márquez which prefaces the edition by Francisco Martín Hernández of Fray Hernando de Talavera's *Católica impugnación* . . . (Barcelona, 1961), pp. 17–22, especially p. 18, n. 16; for a more general view, see pp. 5–53.

[8] Metge's early use of Latinisms is in the medieval tradition in tone, style, and vocabulary (*Libre de fortuna e prudencia*, 1381); in *Lo somni* (1399) he uses Latinisms as a humanist. See Martín de Riquer's edition of his *Obras* (Barcelona, 1959), pp. 29, 164, of the *Prólogo*.

[9] Kenneth M. Setton, "The Byzantine Background to the Italian Renaissance,"

Notes 231

Proceedings of the American Philosophical Society, C (1956), 64–65; see also references in n. 19.

[10] *Obras, ed. cit.,* p. 159 (*Prólogo*).

[11] This is the title of a work by Alfonso García de Matamoros (Alcalá, 1553); see the modern edition with translation by J. López de Toro (Madrid, 1943).

[12] María Rosa Lida de Malkiel, *Juan de Mena: Poeta del prerrenacimiento español* (Mexico City, 1950); see also the review by J. E. Gillet, *HR,* XX (1952), 159–66.

[13] That this "culture" was like a candle casting its beams in a nonhumanistic environment has been apparent to any thoughtful reader of the sources. It has recently been proved by Nicolas G. Round in "Renaissance Culture and Its Opponents in Fifteenth-century Castile," *MLR,* LVII (1962), 204–15. I agree with his conclusions (p. 211): patrons and scholars of fifteenth-century Castile must have been aware of themselves as an isolated and untypical minority. Mena and his congeners were only pioneers. The concept of the inferiority of learning (compared to the warrior's prowess) persisted as a decisive cultural influence well into the reign of Ferdinand and Isabella.

[14] Mena's *Prohemio,* cited by Mrs. Malkiel, *op. cit.,* pp. 531–32.

[15] Cited in O. H. Green, "Juan de Mena in the Sixteenth Century: Additional Data," *HR, XXI* (1953), 138–39.

[16] See William J. Entwistle, "The Search for the Heroic Poem," in the University of Pennsylvania Bicentennial Conference volume, *Studies in Civilization* (Philadelphia, 1941), pp. 89–103.

[17] Green, "Juan de Mena . . . ," p. 139.

[18] See Michele Barba, *Della fortuna di Dante nel secolo XVI* (Pisa, 1890); Bernard Weinberg, *A History of Literary Criticism in the Italian Renaissance* (Chicago, 1961), II, chs. XVI, XVII: "The Quarrel over Dante."

[19] This was shown by Werner Krauss in "Wege der spanischen Renaissancelyrik," *RF,* XLIX (1935), 119–25 (cited by Rafael Lapesa, *La obra literaria del Marqués de Santillana* [Madrid, 1957], p. 253).

[20] On the persistence of the didactic aim, see Weinberg, *op. cit., passim.* On the poet as giver of fame, see Mrs. Malkiel, *La idea de la fama en la Edad Media castellana* (Mexico City-Buenos Aires, 1952), Index, *s. v.* Santillana.

[21] See Mario Schiff, *La bibliothèque du Marquis de Santillane* (Paris, 1905).

[22] In his *Carta Prohemio* he reserves the adjective "sublime" for those poets who composed in the Greek and Latin languages.

[23] See our Volume I, Index, *s. v.* Santillana.

[24] Many months after my section on Nebrija was written I received vol. XLIII (1960) of the *Revista de filología española,* dated "Madrid, 1962" but actually issued in late 1963 or early 1964. It contains a valuable article by Eugenio Asensio, "La lengua compañera del imperio: Historia de una idea de Nebrija en España y Portugal" (pp. 399–413).

[25] See Ignacio González Llubera's introduction to his edition of Nebrija's *Gramática de la lengua castellana* (Oxford, 1926); Cipriano Muñoz, Conde de la Viñaza, *Biblioteca histórica de la filología española* (Madrid, 1893); H. Keniston, "Notes on the *De liberis educandis* of Antonio de Lebrija," *Homenaje ofrecido a Menéndez Pidal* (Madrid, 1925), III, 127–41; F. de Onís, "El concepto del Renacimiento aplicado a la literatura española," in his *Ensayos sobre el sentido de la cultura española* (Madrid, 1932), pp. 195–223.

[26] The initial preoccupations of Renaissance criticism "are linguistic and philological even before they are rhetorical and stylistic." See Weinberg, *op. cit.,* II, 837–74.

[27] I. e., no scholar whose only ancient language is Latin. The quotation is from *The Portable Medieval Reader,* eds. J. B. Ross and Mary M. McLaughlin (New York, 1953), p. 604; see p. 613 for the similar position of Richard de Bury (d. 1345)

and the provision by Clement V at the Council of Vienne (1312) that courses in Hebrew, Greek, Arabic, and Aramaic be offered in the Universities of Paris, Oxford, Bologna, and Salamanca.

[28] M. Bataillon, *Erasmo y España* (Mexico City-Buenos Aires, 1950), I, 59. Loofs, in his *Dogmengeschichte*, quoted with approval by Harnack (*History of Dogma* [Boston, 1905], VII, 36, n. 2), enumerates among the conditions and tendencies in Catholicism prior to the Council of Trent (1545-63) the reorganization "in strict medieval sense" of the Spanish Church by the Crown under Ferdinand and Isabella; the zealous fostering by the mystics of Catholic piety; the humanistic efforts for reform; the ennobling of theology through humanism. The only inaccuracy here lies in the words *in strict medieval sense*, applied to the Spanish pre-Reformation. The Spanish theologian-humanists of the fifteenth and sixteenth centuries sought to ennoble theology by applying to the critical study of the Bible the methods and spirit of Renaissance philology.

[29] In his brief study, *The Erasmian Pronunciation of Greek and Its Precursors, Jerome Aleander, Aldus Manutius, Antonio of Lebrixa* (London, 1908).

[30] He obtained a scholarship at the Spanish College of St. Clement, which since the fourteenth century had been attached to the University of Bologna. For the intellectual climate there, see González Llubera's introduction (previously cited, note 25).

[31] A number of important Roman authors were born in Spain, among them Seneca, Lucan, and Martial.

[32] See Roger B. Merriman, *The Rise of the Spanish Empire in the Old World and the New* (New York, 1918-34). Spain's expansion to the fourth cardinal point—the north—will come later, when Charles I (Charles V of the Empire) incorporates the Low Countries into the possessions of the Spanish crown.

[33] He objects to the liberties taken by the authors of the novels of chivalry.

[34] He had earlier suffered the indignity of seeing some of his papers sequestered by the Inquisitor General. "The incident," writes Bataillon, "does not assume tragic proportions. In those happy days which precede Luther's excommunication, humanists have the right to laugh if they become convinced that 'official' science has made a *gaffe*. The ecclesiastical authorities do not resent the laughter, at least not when he who laughs is a man of the quality of Cisneros" (*Erasmo y España*, I, 44).

[35] Valla had died before Nebrija went to Italy, but the latter lived and studied there in the atmosphere that Valla had created. When, back in Spain, Nebrija found that his old teacher Pedro de Osma was condemned for expressing bold—almost Reformational—ideas concerning confession, Nebrija maintained silence regarding the condemnation, but he did praise Osma publicly in his *Dictionary*, and he ridiculed the theologians responsible for the denunciation (*ibid.*, pp. 30-31).

[36] On the shocking ignorance prevalent among the clergy, see the *Estudio Preliminar* of Francisco Márquez (see note 7 above), especially pp. 47-48 and nn. 38, 39; see also the principal source utilized by Márquez, Nicolás López Martínez, *Los judaizantes castellanos y la Inquisición en tiempos de Isabel la Católica* (Burgos, 1954). See also Bataillon, *Erasmo y Españo*, I, 12-26.

[37] See Emile Legrand, *Bibliographie hispano-grecque* (vols. XI-XIII in *Bibliographie hispanique*, comp. R. Foulché-Delbosc [New York-Paris, 1905-17]).

[38] Even the admirable Cisneros has his "negative side." In 1499 political forces became active which brought the blameless Fray Hernando de Talavera—the man who first raised the cross over the fortress of the Alhambra in 1492 and who served as the first archbishop of Granada—into serious trouble with the Inquisition. When the Court left Granada in 1499, Cisneros remained behind with full powers to deal with the problem of the newly converted Jews. Abandoning the policy of peaceful assimilation initiated by Talavera (and supported by the Queen), Cisneros preferred the swift harsh method of physical compulsion. A revolt followed. Besieged in his residence, Cisneros owed his life to the intervention of Talavera, who

promised to restore the status quo, only to be overruled later with ultimately tragic results. When Isabella died in 1504, Talavera was left without a protector and in 1505 was publicly arrested, charged with relapses into the practices of Judaism. Vindicated from the ridiculous charges in May, 1507, he died that same month. See Márquez's (previously cited) *Estudio preliminar* to Talavera's *Católica impugnación* . . . , pp. 13–16; see also p. 48.

[39] *La trayectoria poética de Garcilaso* (Madrid, 1948), ch. II: "The Assimilation of the New Art."

[40] *English Literature in the Sixteenth Century Excluding Drama* (Oxford, 1954), pp. 64–65.

[41] William C. Atkinson, "On Aristotle and the Concept of Lyric Poetry in Early Spanish Criticism," *Estudios dedicados a Menéndez Pidal*, VI (Madrid, 1956), p. 201.

[42] This famous quarrel was principally between Boileau and Charles Perrault, but the subject of the quarrel is everywhere. See William A. Nitze and E. Preston Dargan, *A History of French Literature* (New York, 1922), Part II (*Modern Times*), Bk. 1 (*The Transition from Classicism*), ch. I: "The Quarrel of the Ancients and Moderns: Results"; see also the *Petit Larousse illustré, s.v. anciens.*

[43] See pp. 208 ff. of Atkinson's article for the supporting quotations.

[44] See Oreste Marcí, *Fernando de Herrera* (Madrid, 1959), pp. 69 ff. ("Programa y teoría literaria").

[45] Alain Guy, *La pensée de Fray Luis de León: Contribution à l'étude de la philosophie espagnole au XVIe siècle* (Limoges, 1943), p. 203.

[46] Fray Luis seems not to have been satisfied with the efforts of his predecessors in these matters.

[47] I have followed the text as given by R. Menéndez Pidal, *Antología de prosistas castellanos* (Madrid, 1920), pp. 160–62.

[48] "¡Ah de la vida! ¡Nadie me responde!" This is the first line of one of his sonnets.

CHAPTER FIVE

[1] C. G. Osgood, *Boccaccio on Poetry* . . . , Princeton, 1930, p. 121 ff.

[2] Wallace K. Ferguson, *The Renaissance in Historical Thought. Five Centuries of Interpretation*, Boston, 1948, p. 20. Cf. C. R. Post, *Mediaeval Spanish Allegory*, Cambridge, Mass., 1915, p. 105 ff.; C. H. Grandgent, *Dante*, New York, 1921, pp. 260–261; and, especially, E. R. Curtius, *Europäische Literatur und lateinisches Mittelalter*, Bern, 1948, p. 243: ". . . Dante erhebt sich zu einer Freiheit und Weite, die das Mittelalter nicht kannte . . . Dantes Einzigkeit liegt darin, dass er sich solche Freiheit nimmt *innerhalb* des hierarchischen christlichen Geschichtskosmos."

[3] In the series *Storia dei generi letterari italiani*, vol. V. Milano, n. d., p. 328.

[4] Basel, 1920.

[5] Ferguson, *op. cit.*, p. 349. Cf. Ernst Cassirer, Paul Oskar Kristeller, John Herman Randall, Jr., and others, *The Renaissance Philosophy of Man*, Chicago, 1948, p. 149: ". . . the elaborate care with which the Scholastics, in particular Thomas Aquinas, had reconciled classical philosophy with Catholic doctrine had its influence in the fact that the Humanists, for the most part, simply took it for granted that there was no conflict between Catholicism and the classics; that the latter were pagan in form but Christian in content; that the Greek mythology and pantheon might legitimately be employed as a vehicle for expressing thoughts about Christian holy persons and saints. . . ."

[6] "Cette situation n'est paradoxale qu'en apparence; et ce serait une erreur de l'imputer uniquement au relâchement d'un clergé épicurien. . . . En réalité, la contradiction dure depuis les premiers siècles du christianisme: elle est dans la

234 Notes

culture même des hommes d'église . . . ; ils continuent d'aimer, comme humanistes, ce qu'ils condamnent—ou devraient condamner—comme théologiens. Qu'on se souvienne plutôt de Saint Augustin ou de Saint Jérôme, et de leurs tourments . . ." (Jean Seznec, *La survivance des dieux antiques. Essai sur le rôle de la tradition mythologique dans l'humanisme et dans l'art de la Renaissance,* London, 1940, p. 232).

[7] Oxford, 1936, p. 83.

[8] *Op. cit.,* pp. 83 and 75.

[9] *Italia e Spagna,* Torino, 1929, vol. I, pp. 99–100. Cf. Curtius, *op. cit.,* p. 249.

[10] Farinelli, *op. cit.,* vol. I, p. 391.

[11] See above, page 276, note 2.

[12] See Seznec, *op. cit.,* Livre I, Première Partie, Chapitre I, especially pp. 14, 16, 24.

[13] *Op. cit.,* pp. 41, 49, 230–231.

[14] *Op. cit.,* pp. 240–241. We have here the origin of the "versiones a lo divino" of literary works.

[15] *Op. cit.,* pp. 79, 242.

[16] See Anna Krause, *Jorge Manrique and the Cult of Death in the Cuatrocientos* (*Publications of the University of California at Los Angeles in Language and Literature,* vol. I, no. 3), Berkeley–Los Angeles, 1937, pp. 141–143 and note 154 (p. 173) and Pedro Salinas, *Jorge Manrique, o Tradición y originalidad,* Buenos Aires, 1947, p. 149 ff. Curtius (*op. cit.*) devotes all of Kapitel 13 to *Die Musen.* See his p. 241: "Die patristische Allegorese macht die Musen durch euhemeristische Erklärung harmlos und deutet sie in musiktheoretische Begriffe um (was in der Sequenzendichtung wieder auftaucht)," and the preceding page: "Die religiöse Bedeutung der Musen im untergehenden Heidentum ist wohl der tiefste Grund dafür, dass sie von der altchristlichen Dichtung ausdrücklich abgelehnt werden. Diese Ablehnung wird nun selbst ein poetischer tropos, der sich vom 4. bis zum 17. Jahrhundert verfolgen lässt. Er ist ein Index für das Anund Abschwellen des moralisch-dogmatischen Rigorismus. Oft verbindet er sich mit dem Bestreben, für die antike Muse einen christlichen Ersatz zu finden." In another place (pp. 244–245) Curtius says: "Die Abwehr der Musen durch den christlichen Dichter ist von Anfang an kaum etwas anderes als Kennmarke korrekter kirchlicher Gesinnung. Je pathetischer sie vorgetragen wird, umso weniger vermag sie zu überzeugen."

[17] That it is pseudo-pagan rather than pagan is shown by the quotation from Juan del Encina which appears farther on in this article.

[18] *Cancionero castellano del siglo XV,* ed. R. Foulché-Delbosc, vol. II, Madrid, 1915, p. 229. Manrique's lines are quoted by Curtius, *op. cit.,* p. 245.

[19] M. Menéndez y Pelayo, *Antología de poetas líricos castellanos* (*Obras completas,* Ed. Nacional, vol. XX), IV, p. 394.

[20] Menéndez y Pelayo, *Antología* (ed. cit., vol. XVIII), II, pp. 157–159.

[21] On the palinode in the love poetry of the *siglo XV* see O. H. Green, "Courtly Love in the Spanish *Cancioneros,*" in *Publications of the Modern Language Association of America,* 1949, LXIV, p. 273 ff., especially p. 278 ff. On what amounts to Boccaccio's palinode, see Curtius, *op. cit.,* p. 244, especially the reference to the "vier Hexametern, die Boccaccio als Abschluss für die *Commedia* verfasste. Gott und die Jungfrau Maria werden darin angerufen: sie mögen den leidenden Sterblichen nach dem Tode das Paradies gewähren. Der Dantekommentar ist in quälender Krankheit entstanden, nicht lange vor Boccaccios Tode. Er hat damals die Abfassung des *Decameron* in einem Brief bereut. . . ."

[22] Cf. the distinction made by Juan del Encina between poems treating sacred and profane subjects, in the quotation which will appear farther on in this article.

[23] *Pintamos* is in the preterit tense.

[24] *Canc. cast. del siglo XV,* ed. cit., vol. I, Madrid, 1912, p. 424.

[25] Vol. cit., p. 426.

[26] Mariano Puigdollers, *La filosofía española de Luis Vives,* Barcelona, 1940, p. 214.

[27] Américo Castro, *El pensamiento de Cervantes,* Madrid, 1925, p. 245, n. 2.

[28] Pedro Laín Entralgo, *La antropología en la obra de Fray Luis de Granada,* Madrid, 1946, p. 337.

[29] *Op. cit.,* pp. 336–340.

[30] Seznec, *op. cit.,* p. 242.

[31] See below.

[32] Ed. J. Quirós de los Ríos and F. Rodríguez Marín, Sevilla, 1896, p. 275.

[33] Castro, *op. cit.,* p. 27.

[34] "*El libro de la oración* dice: 'aprende a bien morir'; y el *Símbolo de la Fe:* 'aprende a bien vivir.' La quintaesencia de nuestro siglo XVI está constituída por la dramática coexistencia de esas dos reglas de vida, tan próximas y a la vez tan distantes entre sí" (Laín Entralgo, *op. cit.,* p. 340). On the "An- und Abschwellen des moralisch-dogmatischen Rigorismus," see page 278, note 3.

[35] Seznec finds in Isidore of Seville the most interesting application of euphemerism to history: "les dieux prennent un prestige nouveau" (*op. cit.,* pp. 16–17). Boccaccio, in his commentary on *Inferno* II, 7, "beruft sich auf Isidor, der ein so heiligmässiger Mann war (*christiano e santissimo uomo e pontefice*), auf Macrobius und Fulgentius. Die Musen sind Töchter des Zeus und der Mnemosyne, d. h., Gottvaters und des Gedächtnisses. . . . Also ein Rückfall in verstaubte Musenallegorese mit erbaulicher Tendenz" (Curtius, *op. cit.,* p. 244).

[36] In 1607, "pour figurer l'Eglise romaine invitant les protestants à rentrer dans son sein, on évoque la Nymphe Salmacis appelant Hermaphrodite!" (Seznec, *op. cit.,* p. 240).

[37] Ed. Francisca Vendrell de Millás, Barcelona, 1945. Cf. Curtius, *op. cit.,* pp. 242–243: "Einen Ausdruck des karolingischen Humanismus darf man darin erblicken, dass er die Musen wiederum zu Ehren bringt. . . . Bedeutugnsvoll ist das Auftreten der Musen in der südfranzösischen Sequenzendichtung, deren Mittelpunkte St. Martial in Limoges und Moissac sind. . . . Dass nun die Musen auch in liturgischen Sequenzen der ältesten Zeit angerufen werden, erklärt sich aus dem musikalischen Ursprung der Sequenz. Die Musen sind hier als Vertreterinnen der Tonkunst, nicht der Dichtkunst, aufzufassen; was durch die Patristik legitimiert war. Aus der Sequenz entstand die neue Lyrik des Abendlandes . . ."

[38] M. Herrero García, *Sermonario clásico,* Madrid, 1942, p. 10. Cf. Fray Pedro de Valderrama's *Sermón de San Agustín* (1612), *ibid.,* p. 90.

[39] Antwerp, 1552, pp. 616–617.

[40] Menéndez y Pelayo, *Orígenes de la novela,* II, Madrid, 1907, p. 207 *b.*

[41] *Biblioteca de Autores Españoles,* LXV, p. 389 *b.*

[42] *Comedieta de Ponça.* Miss Krause, *op. cit.,* n. 154, suggests that when Santillana, in stanza 3 of the *Comedieta,* speaks of the "estilo de los que fingían metáforas vanas con dulce loquela," he shows a "tendency to reject the classic mythology." I am not convinced. To me it seems that the Marqués is announcing that his *Comedieta* is to be composed in a more solemn style than such poems as his *Triunfete de amor, Infierno de los enamorados,* etc. In the latter poem Santillana invokes the Muses. His *El sueño* has an invocation to Mars.

[43] *Cancionero general,* no. 937.

[44] *Cancionero de Lope de Stúñiga,* Madrid, 1872, p. 194.

[45] *Arte de la poesía castellana,* in Menéndez y Pelayo, *Antología,* V, 1894, pp. 32–33. Curtius found this distinction between ordinary poems and poems of devotion to be characteristic "des karolingischen Humanismus." See *op. cit.,* p. 242: "Der Angelsachse Alcuin sah sich in einen höfischen Lebenskreis versezt, der in weltlicher Lob- und Freundschaftsdichtung erhöhten Ausdruck fand. In diesem Bereich gab er den antiken Musen Raum, während er sie aus der geistlichen Dichtung verbannte. Dieselbe Scheidung finden wir bei Angilbert, Theodulf,

Hrabanus Maurus, Modoin. Nur ein strenger Kirchenmann wir Florus von Lyon . . . vertritt den Rigorismus: wenn die Dichter Berge zur Inspiration brauchen, mögen sie Sinai, Carmel, Horeb, Zion wählen."

[46] *Cancionero*, ed. facsim. by Real Academia Española, 1928, fol. Aii *vuelto*.

[47] *Obras*, ed. Knapp, Madrid, 1875, pp. 451–452.

[48] Karl Vossler, *La soledad en la poesía española*, Madrid, 1941, p. 79.

[49] *Op. cit.*, p. 217.

[50] Frank Pierce, "The *Canto épico* of the Seventeenth and Eighteenth Centuries," *Hispanic Review*, 1947, XV, p. 8.

[51] Menéndez y Pelayo, *Calderón y su teatro* (*Obras completas*, Ed. Nacional, vol. VIII), Santander, 1941, p. 145. Cf. Curtius, *op. cit.*, p. 248 ff.

[52] Seznec, *op. cit.*, p. 285.

[53] Cf. fol. 12: "La mezcla de sagrado y prophano que pedís, escrita está por Salomón quando introduze al esposo dezir a la esposa que su vientre es como un muelo de trigo rodeado de açucenas: donde por el vientre se entiende la noticia que la Iglesia tiene de todas las doctrinas necesarias a la saluación figuradas en el trigo que es el verdadero pan y de más mantenimiento: y por las flores o açucenas que le cercan se entienden las doctrinas de los infieles *que ayudan*, bien trahidas, *a dar gracia a las verdades cathólicas* y mueuen el gusto de los estudiosos."

[54] Seznec, *op. cit.*, pp. 285–286. It was not until the eighteenth century that the function of mythology became purely decorative. Luzán criticizes Camoens for introducing Jupiter, Venus, Bacchus, etc., "en un poema de tal asunto y escrito para leerse entre cristianos"; but he asserts that poetry "se sostiene por la fábula y vive de la ficción," and concedes willingly to the poet the right to say, when describing a storm, that "Neptuno airado conmovió su reino" (Menéndez y Pelayo, *Historia de las ideas estéticas en España*, Ed. Nacional, vol. III, Madrid, 1947, p. 225).

[55] See above, page 277.

[56] Boccaccio is a case in point. See above, page 280, note 1.

[57] See above, page 278, n. 3.

CHAPTER SIX

[1] Erich Auerbach, *Mimesis* (Princeton, 1953), pp. 53, 57.

[2] Karl Vossler, *Introducción a la literatura española del siglo de oro* (Madrid, 1934), p. 124.

[3] "La voluntad de ser raro es quizá el único medio de relacionar los estados barrocos con lo que exista fuera de ellos." Américo Castro, "El Don Juan de Tirso y el de Molière," *Hommage à Ernest Martinenche* (Paris, n. d.), p. 104.

[4] Jean Rousset, *La littérature française de l'âge baroque en France. Circé et le Paon* (Paris, 1953), p. 9.

[5] "No society or no era is ever stabilized except in the pages of a book." Herschel Baker, *The Dignity of Man* (Cambridge, Mass., 1947), p. 123.

[6] *Diversas rimas* (Madrid, 1591), fol. 149v; 1587 is the date of the *aprobación*.

[7] Ed. Erasmo Buceta (Madrid, 1935), pp. 70, 73–74 et alibi.

[8] C. S. Lewis, *English Literature in the Sixteenth Century excluding Drama* (Oxford, 1954), p. 512.

[9] Ibid., pp. 271, 547. Cf. Castro, loc. cit.: "Para conseguir la rareza (estado de ánimo que no necesita ser consciente) se pueden utilizar además elementos preexistentes que no habían pretendido ser raros, lo mismo que otros, que, por cualquier caso, eran extraños y artificiosos (el estilo de Antonio de Guevara, por ejemplo)."

[10] I italicize *vulgares* looking forward to the discussion of the part played by the *vulgo* in determining the development of learned prose. See below.

[11] *Italics* anticipate the treatment (below) of the *dramatic* element in the new demands of the *vulgo*.

[12] From the Madrid, 1580 ed. (first ed. Anvers, 1555); copied by Gallardo, *Ensayo*, III, col. 96.

[13] Apud Francisco Terrones del Caño, *Instrucción de predicadores*, ed. Félix G. Olmedo (Madrid, 1946), p. lxxl. See above, note 11.

[14] This point will be stressed farther on in the present article.

[15] *El Doctor Huarte de San Juan y su Examen de Ingenios. Contribución a la historia de la psicología diferencial* (Madrid, 1948), pp. 213–214. See above, note 11 and below, note 36.

[16] Terrones del Caño, op. cit., ed. cit., p. ciii.

[17] See above, note 10.

[18] Aubrey F. G. Bell, *El renacimiento español* (Zaragoza, 1944), p. 132.

[19] Madrid, 1947, II, 136.

[20] Terrones de Caño, op. cit., ed. cit., p. cxxiii-cxxiv.

[21] Ibid., p. cxxxvii.

[22] *Apuntamientos de como se deben reformar las doctrinas y la manera de enseñallas*, ed. Madrid, 1769, pp. 32–33. See Margherita Morreale de Castro, *Pedro Simón Abril* (Madrid, 1949), Indice Analítico, s. v. Apuntamientos.

[23] Pedro Urbano González de la Calle, "Documentos inéditos acerca del uso de la lengua vulgar en libros espirituales," *BRAE*, XII (1925), 269.

[24] Ibid., pp. 266–267.

[25] Emilio Alarcos, "Los sermones de Paravicino," *RFE*, XXIV (1937), 185, 265, 279, 283, 318–319. See below, note 36.

[26] Ibid., p. 184, n. 1. See below, note 36.

[27] See above, note 1.

[28] Ed. cit., p. 125.

[29] Ibid., p. 58.

[30] Gallardo, *Ensayo*, III, cols. 934–935.

[31] "On the Attitude toward the *Vulgo* in the Spanish *Siglo de Oro*," *Studies in the Renaissance*, Publications of the Renaissance Society of America, IV (New York, 1957), 190–200.

[32] Alarcos, art. cit., pp. 279 f., 283 f., 319.

[33] See above, note 1.

[34] *RFE*, XXX (1946), 353–368.

[35] See above, note 11.

[36] Art. cit., p. 357–358.

[37] Ibid., p. 363. It is readily seen that *antiguos* and *modernos* placate the *auditorio* by providing *asombro*, in the one case by assuming the role of *farsantes a lo divino*, in the other by means of *agudeza*.

[38] Américo Castro, *El pensamiento de Cervantes* (Madrid, 1925), p. 211, n. 7. Cf. Edward M. Wilson, "Quevedo for the Masses," *Atlante*, III (1955), pp. 2–3: "Quevedo was perhaps as great a poet as Góngora or Lope de Vega. . . . To see how much of [his poetry] seeped down into the chap-books is not a useless investigation if it tells us which of Quevedo's poems could be appreciated by the man in the street . . . even if only a few examples of Quevedo's works can be shown to have been transmitted in this way, *the vulgar tradition is seen as something less debased than has often been assumed*." (Italics mine.) Cf. also p. 3: "In fact the seventeenth-century chap-books often transmitted a fair amount of poetry which would not shame a modern anthology." And p. 6: "This kind of *conceptismo* cannot be considered an aristocratic taste when it came within reach of ordinary working men and women."

CHAPTER SEVEN

[1] These were available from c. 1494 in the edition of Aldus. See Emile Le Grand, *Bibliographie hellénique* . . . , vol. I, Paris, n. d., pp. 20–22. Menéndez y

Pelayo (*Antol. de poet. lír. cast.*, vol. XIII, Madrid, 1913, p. 344) conjectures that Boscán used this poem for his "aprendizaje de la lengua [griega]." It was published, for purposes of instruction, by Demetrius Ducas at Alcalá c. 1514. See E. Le Grand, *Bibliographie hispano-grecque* in *Bibliographie hispanique*, New York, 1917, pp. 168–169.

[2] *Heroides*, XVIII and XIX. Martial's epigram *De Spectaculis* XXVb was also utilized, a fact not mentioned in A. A. Giulian, *Martial and the Epigram in Spain*, Philadelphia, 1930: "Mientras que voy, o aguas, amansaos! / Ahógame después quando volviere!" (*Las obras de Juan Boscán*, ed. W. I. Knapp, Madrid, 1875, p. 356; cf. p. 321).

[3] Menéndez y Pelayo (*op. cit.*, p. 347) regards it as very possible that Boscán and B. Tasso were personally acquainted. Cf. Francesco Flamini, *Studi di storia letteraria italiana e straniera*, Livorno, 1895, pp. 395–396.

[4] Menéndez y Pelayo, *op. cit.*, pp. 344–359.

[5] *Op. cit.*, pp. 345–346. Italics mine.

[6] The following description of Leandro (ed. cit., p. 312) gives in condensed form the outstanding characteristics of Castiglione's courtier:

> . . . un hombre tan noble,
> Un hombre que tan presto supo amalla,
> Un hombre tan hermoso y de tal casta,
> Que bien vió en él la alteza de su sangre,
> Un hombre que en su gesto señalaba
> En armas corazón, y en paz buen trato,
> Un hombre tal, en fin, que ella le amaba.

Ernesto Krebs, in his study "*El Cortesano* de Castiglione en España" (*Bol. de la Acad. Argentina de Letras*, 1940, VIII, 93–146 and 423–435; 1941, IX, 135–142 and 517–543; 1942, X, 53–118 and 689–748), does not consider the poetry of Boscán. Arturo Marasso ("Juan Boscán," *Bol. de la Acad. Argentina de Letras*, 1943, XI, 650–651) is aware of the importance of *El Cortesano*, but does not follow up the lead. The words "un no sé qué, no sé como nombrallo," which constitute for Marasso a "divergencia grave" between Boscán's *canción, Gentil señora mía* and Petrarch's *Gentil mia donna* are a reminiscence of Castiglione. See below. Adolphe Coster in his book *Fernando de Herrera (El Divino)*, 1534–1597, Paris, 1908, shows the important influence which *El Cortesano* had on Herrera. See pp. 124–127, 236–237, 244, 275, 281, 325. Juan Antonio Tamayo, "Castiglione y Boscán" (*Arriba*, December 19, 1943), does not touch on this point.

[7] Like Don Hermógenes, I cite the Latin text *para mayor claridad*. The text I use is Musaei grammatici *De Herone et Leandro Carmen* cum coniecturis ineditis Petri Francii, ex recensione Iohannis Schraderi. . . . Editionem novam auctiorem curavit Godofr. Henr. Schaefer. Lipsiae, MDCCCXXV.

[8] Ed. cit., p. 290. The only reference to intellectuality in Musaeus' poem is found in line 135: "Minerva post Minervam." I do not stress *hermosura*—an essential trait of *cortesano* and of *dama* and the moving force of Platonic love—because Musaeus' Hero is also beautiful.

[9] *El Cortesano*, ed. A. M. Fabié (Libros de Antaño), Madrid, 1873, p. 297.

[10] *Ibid*, p. 301. This insistence on intellectuality arises from the Socratic conviction that "siempre aquello por lo cual el apetito vence a la razón es inorancia, y la verdadera ciencia es imposible ser en ningún tiempo vencida por el deseo, el cual hace del cuerpo y no del alma; y si por la razón es bien corregido y gobernado, viene a hacerse virtud, y de otra manera hácese vicio; pero tanta fuerza tiene la razón, que se hace siempre obedecer de la sensualidad, y con maravillosas maneras y vías penetra hasta donde conviene, con tal que la inorancia no tenga ocupado aquello que ella debría tener de su mano" (*El Cortesano*, p. 429).

[11] Ed. cit., p. 291.

¹² *El Cortesano*, p. 431. Cf. p. 433.

¹³ Cf. *El Cortesano*, p. 495: ". . . puédese bien decir que lo bueno y lo hermoso en alguna manera son una misma cosa, en especial en los humanos, de la hermosura de los cuales la más cercana causa pienso yo que sea la hermosura del a ma, la cual como participante de aquella verdadera hermosura divina, hace resplandeciente y hermoso todo lo que toca. . . ."

¹⁴ Ed. cit., p. 294. Cf. *El Cortesano*, p. 378: "Gane ella hombres de bien por servidores que la amen verdaderamente, y gánelos no con las artes que hemos dicho de las otras, sino con su gentileza, con sus buenas costumbres, con su autoridad, con su gracia, *con un buen descuido*, y, en fin, con decir y hacer lo que debe."

¹⁵ *El Cortesano*, p. 293.

¹⁶ Ed. cit., p. 294. Cf., on *el estar queda*, *El Cortesano*, p. 293: "Mas sobre todo me parece que en la manera, en las palabras, en los ademanes y en el aire, debe la mujer ser muy diferente del hombre . . . en ella parece bien una delicadeza tierna y blanda, con una dulzura mujeril en su gesto, que la haga *en el andar, en el estar* y en el hablar, siempre parecer mujer, sin ninguna semejanza de hombre." On *un cierto no sé qué*, cf. above, n. 6, and *El Cortesano*, pp. 498-499: "Por eso cuando viere a alguna mujer hermosa . . . y . . . él [conociere] ser ella aparejada para enamoralle, luego a la hora que cayere en la cuenta . . . que sus ojos arrebatan aquella figura, y no paran hasta metella en las entrañas, y que el alma comienza a holgar de contemplalla, y sentir en sí *aquel no sé qué*, que la mueve, y poco a poco la enciende . . . luego debe proveer en ello con presto remedio, despertando la razón, . . . atajando de tal manera los pasos a la sensualidad."

¹⁷ This is an interesting development of his source: "Intuendo defessus sum, satietatem autem non inveni adspiciendi" (line 78). The *parte inmortal* is, of course, the *alma*, and the *manjar natural* is contemplation. Cf. *El Cortesano*, p. 445: "El fin de la vida activa debe ser la contemplación, como de la guerra es la paz, y de los trabajos el reposo." On *la parte inmortal*, cf. *ibid.*, p. 498: "Gran miseria y desventura sería de la naturaleza si nuestra alma, en la cual puede nacer fácilmente aquel tan encendido deseo que con el amor va mezclado, fuese forzada a mantenelle con solo aquello que a ella le es común con las bestias, y no pudiese volvelle hacia *la otra parte* que le es conforme y propia totalmente."

¹⁸ "Virginis autem bene olentem bonique coloris cervicem osculatus / Tale ver bum ait amoris ictus furore" (lines 133-134).

¹⁹ *El Cortesano*, p. 486. Cf. p. 380: ". . . porque si la hermosura, las buenas costumbres, el entendimiento, la bondad, el saber, la buena crianza, y otras muchas virtuosas calidades que a esta Dama hemos dado, son las cosas que han de enamorar al Cortesano, el fin deste tal amor de necesidad ha de ser virtuoso." Cf. Flamini, *op. cit.*, p. 400 for the Petrarchan traits which B. Tasso had given to Leander.

²⁰ Ed. cit., pp. 296-297. Cf. *El Cortesano*, p. 388: "Tras esto los ojos hacen mucho al caso, y son grandes solicitadores; son los diligentes y fieles mensajeros que a cada paso llevan fuertes mensajes de parte del corazón . . ." The "physics" of the visual process is fully developed on pp. 388-389. Cf. also the further treatment given it by Boscán, ed. cit., p. 297.

²¹ Ed. cit., p. 298.

²² *El Cortesano*, p. 483.

²³ *El Cortesano*, p. 504. Cf. p. 486: ". . . la sensualidad . . . , la cual en la mocedad puede mucho; porque la virtud del cuerpo en aquella sazón le da tanta fuerza, cuanta es la que quita a la razón, y por eso fácilmente derrueca al alma, y le hace que siga el apetito." And p. 516: ". . . no eran . . . viejas, sino . . . mozas . . . y de la edad en la cual él mismo ha dicho que se peude permitir a los hombres que amen sensualmente."

²⁴ Cf. on *blandamente*: "Desta manera será nuestro Cortesano muy aceto a su Dama, y así ella se conformará siempre con la voluntad dél, y le será dulce y *blanda* . . . y las voluntades de entrambas serán honestas y conformes, y por con-

siguiente vivirán vida bienaventurada" (pp. 500–550); on *vergüenza:* ". . . una *vergüenza natural* de mujer casta" (p. 300); on *cuerdo:* "Pero si este que la sirviere fuere discreto y le hablare con buena crianza y mansamente, y aun los amores que le dixere no fueren muy descubiertos . . . muestre [ella] entonces no entendelle . . . Y si los términos fueren tales que ella no pueda disimular, tomallo ha como burlando, o con una buena llaneza decille ha *cuerdamente* algunas palabras, de las cuales él ni pueda quedar desabrido, ni tampoco con asidero para quedar muy confiado . . . Si ella así lo hiciere, ternánla todos por avisada y *cuerda*" (p. 373); on *seso:* ". . . debe en este caso el Cortesano, sintiéndose preso, determinarse totalmente a huir toda vileza de amor vulgar y bajo, y a entrar con la guía de la *razón* en el camino alto y maravilloso de amar . . ." (p. 499).

[25] ". . . el verdadero amor ha de ser bueno, y siempre ha de producir efectos buenos en las almas de aquellos que con el freno de la razón corrigen la malicia del sentido, lo cual pueden hacer los viejos mucho más fácilmente que los mozos" (p. 486).

[26] "Con ninguna otra cosa puede Beatriz excusarse de culpa sino con haber errado por amor, el cual ya veis si se debe perdonar en los hombres como en las mujeres" (p. 276). Cf. pp. 276–277: ". . . las pasiones de amor gran desculpa traen consigo de cualquier yerro." Paul N. Siegel ascribes this to the medieval chivalric tradition: "Bembo [in *The Courtier*] goes so far in the acceptance of the chivalric tradition as to half condone the sensual love of the young courtier, provided that he conducts himself in the spirit of chivalry, acquires the chivalric virtues, and shuns sensual desire as he gains the knowledge and the rational control of his passions which comes with maturity" (*The Petrarchan Sonneteers and Neo-Platonic Love, Studies in Philology,* 1945, XLII, p. 176). On *la mano,* cf. *El Cortesano,* pp. 502–503: ". . . y así la Dama, por contentar a su servidor en este amor bueno, no solamente puede y debe estar con él muy familiarmente riendo y burlando, y tratar con el seso cosas sustanciales, diciéndole sus secretos y sus entrañas, y siendo con él tan conversable, *que le tome la mano y se la tenga;* mas aún puede llegar sin caer en culpa por este camino de la razón hasta besalle, lo cual en el amor vicioso, según las reglas del señor Manífico, no es lícito . . . el enamorado que ama, teniendo la razón por fundamento, . . . besándola . . . siente que aquel ayuntamiento es un abrir la puerta a las almas de entrambos. . . ." The situation of the two lovers excludes this type of *beso,* and Boscán makes no mention of any kiss.

[27] Cf. above, n. 24, and: "Y si él se pusiere en loalla, esté ella de manera en ello que ni lo recoja, ni tampoco lo deseche, sino que algunas veces parezca que lo *disimula,* y otras que lo toma llanamente."

[28] "Toda dama de precio se tiene por poco acatada, y casi recibe injuria de quien así livianamente se declara con ella por servidor, sin primero habella tratado y servido mucho por otra vía. Por eso, según mi opinión, el camino que el Cortesano ha de tener para descubrir su voluntad a su Dama ha de ser mostrársela más aína con un gesto, con un ademán, con *un no sé qué,* que con palabras" (p. 388).

[29] ". . . y creo yo que cualquier buen enamorado, si sufre tantas fatigas y tanto no poder dormir, si se aventura a tantos peligros, si derrama tantas lágrimas y usa tantas artes y maneras, como cada día vemos, por contentar a su dama, *no es principalmente por alcanzar el cuerpo,* sino por conquistar aquella gran fortaleza del alma, rompiendo aquellas duras peñas, y calentando aquellos cuajados hielos que en los tiernos corazones de las mujeres se hallan; y éste pienso yo que sea el mayor y más sustancial gusto, y el fin verdadero donde la intinción de un alto corazón tira" (p. 277).

[30] This appeal to the essential character of Venus is found also in Musaeus.

[31] On the part of *lágrimas* in Castiglione's conception of love, see above, n. 29, and *El Cortesano,* p. 505. There are no tears in Musaeus.

[32] Hero-Leander, Dido-Aeneas.

[33] On the "matrimonio clandestino" as against "el matrimonio solemne," see

A. Castro, *El pensamiento de Cervantes*, Madrid, 1925, p. 349, n. 1, and Joaquín Casalduero, *Sentido y forma de las 'Novelas Ejemplares,'* Buenos Aires, 1943, pp. 51 and 129.

[34] Cf. *El Cortesano*, p. 504: "Se le turba y trastorna hartas veces el verdadero juicio." See above, n. 23.

[35] "Septima nox agitur, spatium mihi longius anno" (*Heroides*, XVIII, 25).

[36] The act of suicide could receive no ecclesiastical condemnation, as it was committed by a pagan. But I do not wish to lay stress on the fact of suicide. The Inquisition never made objection to Melibea's self-destruction at the end of the *Celestina*. See my article, *The "Celestina" and the Inquisition, Hispanic Review*, 1947, XV, 211–216.

[37] *El Cortesano*, p. 453. Cf. p. 433: ". . . no os maravilléis . . . que os haya dicho que de la temperancia procedan muchas otras virtudes; que sabé, que así lo hacen; y cuando todas están juntas, si *el alma ayudada de la razón*, llega a estar templada y concorde con el armonía dellas, fácilmente después recibe aquel verdadero esfuerzo, con el cual se halla firme y constante en los peligros, y casi señora de todas las pasiones humanas." For Boscán's essential religiousness, see his *Conversión de Boscán (Después que por este suelo)*, and, *inter alia*, his Sonnets LXXXI and LXXXIII.

CHAPTER EIGHT

[1] Hugh Dalziel Duncan, *Language and Literature in Society* (Chicago, 1953), pp. 46–47.

[2] M. Cardenal Iracheta, "Algunos rasgos estéticos y morales de Quevedo," *Revista de ideas estéticas*, V (1947), 39.

[3] "De aquí infiero la mayor utilidad de esta obra sobre las demás; porque aunque el autor siempre se mostró desengaño, aun en los asuntos jocosos; pero allí el desengaño es como juego de cañas, en que las lanzas más divierten que penetran; aquí las tira de veras; y tan aceradas, que penetran hasta lo íntimo del corazón que las atiende, sin lisonjear" (*Obras en prosa*, ed. L. Astrana Marín [Madrid, 1932], p. 979a). It will be noted that there is a special emotional intensity even in this official document of authorization to publish. An historical study of all *aprobaciones* would be useful for the intellectual and social history of Spain.

[4] Ed. E. Buceta (Madrid, 1935), p. 70.

[5] Ed. Martín de Riquer (Barcelona, 1943), p. 458. An historical study of the semantics of this word is greatly needed.

[6] These two examples are taken from Rufino José Cuervo, *Diccionario de construcción y régimen* (Paris, 1886–93), II, 1057.

[7] Ed. J. A. de Balenchana (Madrid, 1874), pp. 378–79.

[8] Pierre Le Gentil, in volume I of his *La poésie lyrique espagnole et portugaise à la fin du moyen âge* (Rennes, 1949–53), makes much of the *desengaño* of the fifteenth-century poets, especially Bernardim Ribeiro (see pp. 150–51, 154, 234, 393–94 and n. 178, 416, 595). It is a question of one of the "romantic" aspects of the courtly love tradition rather than of the Stoic attitude of mind to which I have been referring. All the examples of the word *desengaño* (or its related verb) given by Le Gentil are Portuguese, not Castilian.

[9] See J. M. de Semprún Gurrea, "El desengaño en la historia del pensamiento español," *Cuadernos del Congreso por la libertad de la cultura*, núm. 10 (1955), 53–58. After bringing together literary texts to prove the importance of the word *desengaño*, this author sees it as one of the most profound characteristics of the inhabitants of Castile. See also Vicente Palacio Atard, *Derrota, agotamiento, decadencia en la España del siglo XVII (Un punto de enfoque para su interpretación)* (Madrid, 1949), especially chapters iv and v.

[10] See the modern edition published by La Sociedad de Bibliófilos Españoles (Madrid, 1882), II, 389–410.

[11] Authors of the books listed were, respectively, Martín del Barco Centenera, Jaime de Ruesta, Rodrigo Méndez Silva, Miguel Antonio Francés de Urrutigoyti (see *Bibliotheca Hispana Nova* [2 vols.; Madrid, 1738–88], II, 569–71).

[12] In volume I, cols. 3–4. Compare the title with that of the following book, issued at Murcia in 1652, by G. de Molina Lama: *How to Live in Opposition to Fortune: Political Schools Set up by Seneca to Enable One to Face the Vicissitudes, and to Be Comforted Amid the Miseries of our Time* (*Vivir contra Fortuna: Escuelas políticas de Séneca, para hazer rostro a los trabajos y estar consolados entre las miserias del tiempo*). See also Arnold Rothe, *Quevedo und Seneca: Untersuchungen zu den Frühschriften Quevedos* (Cologne–Geneva–Paris, 1965).

[13] It will be remembered that the year 1576 falls between the victory over the Turks at Lepanto in 1571, and the defeat of the Armada in 1588. In 1576 Melchor de Santa Cruz wrote in the dedication to Philip II of his *Book of a Hundred Treatises*: "The calm of the great and happy peace which exists in these blessed times of Your Majesty's reign has caused all good arts and honest exercises to flourish, so that not only learned men but ignorant persons like myself concern themselves with ingenious and erudite matters, each one according to his ability. I, most powerful Sir, have always been fond of spending my time in reading good books" (Gallardo, *Ensayo*, IV, col. 486).

[14] See Margaret J. Bates, *"Discreción" in the Works of Cervantes*, dissertation, The Catholic University of America (Washington, D. C., 1945).

[15] Ed. M. Romera-Navarro (Philadelphia, 1938–40), III, 149; my translation is an abbreviated paraphrase.

[16] Since Gracián is here concerned with happiness, it seems well to quote from Gonzalo Sobejano's "Nuevos estudios en torno a Gracián," *Clavileño*, V (1954), 27–28: "Happiness, *Ventura*, Fortune, contingency, vanity, death . . . are not words that serve as unshakable definitions, but are the names of certain foci of special functional perspectives. They vary in meaning and condemn to failure every attempt at systematization. The perspectivism of Gracián, exemplified in the multiple meanings of Fortune and of many other concepts, brings forward nothing new, but it signifies the complete dissolution of the old. (In Boethius, for example, Fortune has two aspects that amount to fixed definitions.) This perspectivism *is not a destructive procedure*, but rather a method of syncretic acceptance of tradition" (italics mine). I would add that the words "*he must seek them farther on*" signify that Gracián wants it known that he is not writing theology, or even a treatise on metaphysics. The actual finding of truth, happiness, and the other absolutes will carry the seeker farther out into the realms of speculation. That does not mean that those realms are unimportant to Gracián; he states the opposite: the guides that the seeker in those speculative realms will require are none other than the cardinal virtues of Catholic doctrine.

[17] *El Criticón*, ed. cit., I, 111.

[18] "Las bases antropológicas del pensamiento de Gracián," *Revista de la Universidad de Madrid*, VII (1958), 427.

[19] Maravall, *op. cit.*, p. 423; see *El Criticón*, ed. cit., I, 249 and 119.

[20] Maravall, *op. cit.*, pp. 423–45.

[21] The language is pithy, and I have taken care to bring out all the meanings. It seems well to repeat the Spanish text: "Consiguió con esto [i.e., el estudio] una noticiosa universalidad, de suerte que la filosofía moral le hizo prudente; la natural, sabio; la historia, avisado; la poesía, ingenioso; la retórica, elocuente; la humanidad, discreto; la cosmografía, noticioso; la sagrada lección, pío; y todo él en todo género de letras consumado" (*El Héroe. El Discreto* [Buenos Aires, 1939], p. 167).

[22] Ed. cit., III, 117–18; my translation is somewhat compressed.

[23] *Obras en verso*, ed. L. Astrana Marín (Madrid, 1932), p. 143a.

²⁴ "Tú responderás por mí / y dirás que no te temo: / que soy fuerte como España / por la falta de sustento" (*ibid.*, p. 996).

²⁵ "Veránse sumergidas mis mejillas, / la vista por dos urnas derramada / sobre el sepulcro de los dos Castillas" (*ibid.*, p. 136a). The reference is to Old and New Castile, the latter having been won from the Moors at a later date.

²⁶ "Las glorias de este mundo / llaman con luz para pagar con humo" (*Obras en verso, ed. cit.*, pp. 296a–97b).

²⁷ See *ibid., Letrillas* IX, X, XI (pp. 78b–79b).

²⁸ *La espera y la esperanza: Historia y teoría del esperar humano* (Madrid, 1957), pp. 136 and 146–49.

²⁹ "Fray Luis de Granada's *Introducción del Símbolo de la fe* belongs both to antiquity, to Christianity, and to the Renaissance (first edition, 1583). . . . It represents—along with the somewhat belated vital force of Lope de Vega—the apogee of the Christian and Renaissance optimism of our sixteenth century. Earlier than this book, we had the *Amadís*, Garcilaso, and Bernal Díaz del Castillo; contemporaneous with it, Herrera and Fray Luis de León; after it, the hour of out-and-out *desengaño*: Cervantes, Quevedo, Calderón" (Pedro Laín Entralgo, *La antropologia en la obra de Fray Luis de Granada* [Madrid, 1946], pp. 301–2).

³⁰ Alexander A. Parker, "Calderón, el dramaturgo de la escolástica," *Revista de estudios hispánicos*, III/IV (1935/36), núm. 3, pp. 273–85; and núm. 4, pp. 393–420.

³¹ "I easily touch the glass; / I touch not its inner soul," says Narciso in the *comedia* entitled *Eco y Narciso* (ed. C. V. Aubrun [Flers, 1961], lines 2589–90).

³² "Estas que fueron pompa y alegría / despertando al albor de la mañana, / a la tarde serán lástima vana, / durmiendo en brazos de la noche fría. / Este matiz que al cielo desafía, / iris listado de oro, nieve y grana, / será escarmiento de la vida humana: / ¡tanto se emprende en término de un día! / A florecer las rosas madrugaron / y para envejecerse florecieron: / cuna y sepulcro en un botón hallaron. / Tales los hombres sus fortunas vieron: / en un día nacieron y expiraron, / que pasados los siglos, horas fueron" (*Antología de la poesía lírica española*, comp. E. Moreno Báez [Madrid, 1952], p. 324).

³³ "Que toda la dicha humana / en fin pasa como un sueño" (from the last speech of the drama).

³⁴ "¿Quién por vanagloria humana / pierde una divina gloria?" (Act III, lines 779–80).

³⁵ "Acudamos a lo eterno" (*ibid.*, line 791).

³⁶ "donde ni duermen las dichas / ni las grandezas reposan" (*ibid.*, lines 793–94).

³⁷ "Realidad, voluntad y gracia en Cervantes," *Ibérida: Revista de filología*, III (1961), 113–28.

³⁸ *"Don Quichotte" de Cervantes: Etude et analyse* (Paris, n. d.), p. 111.

³⁹ E. C. Riley has demonstrated this brilliantly; see his *Cervantes's Theory of the Novel* (Oxford, 1962), pp. 209–10.

⁴⁰ See O. H. Green, "A Hispanist's Thoughts on *The Anatomy of Satire*" (by Gilbert Highet), *RPh*, XVII (1963), 131–32 and n. 14.

⁴¹ This has been shown by Irving A. Leonard. See his *Books of the Brave: Being an Account of Books and Men in the Spanish Conquest of the Sixteenth-century New World* (Cambridge, Massachusetts, 1949), especially chapters xviii, "*Don Quixote* Invades the Spanish Indies," and xix, "*Don Quixote* in the Land of the Incas."

⁴² I regret to state that I find that the chapter on Cervantes ("The Enchanted Dulcinea") in Erich Auerbach's *Mimesis* (trans. Willard R. Trask [Princeton, 1953]) represents a failure to understand Cervantes' intention.

⁴³ See my article, "El *ingenioso* Hidalgo," *HR*, XXV (1957), 175–93, especially 189–90 and 193.

⁴⁴ William J. Entwistle, "The Search for the Heroic Poem," in University of

Pennsylvania Bicentennial Conference, *Studies in Civilization* (Philadelphia, 1941), p. 97.

[45] In this and the next section I follow my article in *Ibérida*. . . . , cited in note 37 above.

[46] Of course, the father's will does not suppress reality here nor substitute his own interpretation for it. Rather, he rises above it. Américo Castro explains: "In the depths of our conscience . . . we think exactly as does the father of Leocadia; but we live in Toledo, a city in whose streets and squares there prevail plebeian concepts of honor which are the cause of pain and suffering. . . . Cervantes surmounts this plane of feeling and rises, in the last analysis, to the pure realm of the ought-to-be" (*El Pensamiento de Cervantes* [Madrid, 1925], pp. 364–65).

[47] In *RFE*, XXXII (1948), 287–305.

[48] In Nathan A. Scott, Jr. (ed.), *The Tragic Vision and the Christian Faith* (New York, 1957), pp. 84–85.

[49] See pages 120–21 of my *Ibérida* . . . article for a development of the idea of vainglory.

[50] See Edward Sarmiento, "Don Quixote and the Holy Images," *Dublin Review* (Autumn, 1947), 38–47, especially 42–43 and 46.

[51] Don Quijote is at times affected by omens, but he corrects himself or Cervantes corrects him; see the *Obras completas*, ed. A. Valbuena Prat (Madrid, 1956), pp. 1410b and 1349b.

[52] "Vi mi locura, vi mi desengaño, / mudable fuy entre tan firmes males, / y ser mudable yo, no fue tan poco; / q'entre tanta locura, tanto engaño, / entre desdichas, precipicios tales, / fuy por mudable venturoso loco" (ed. facsim. [Valencia, 1959], p. 34).

[53] Cambridge, Massachusetts (1952), pp. 50–78.

[54] Theodore Spencer, *Shakespeare and the Nature of Man* (New York–Cambridge, Massachusetts, 1945), p. 27.

[55] Marcel Bataillon, "Du nouveau sur Juan Luis Vives," *BHi*, XXXII (1930), 112–13.

[56] "Sur la composition des *Regrets*," *Mélanges Lefranc* (Paris, 1936), p. 348, n. 2. On the evening of October 18, 1534, six heretics were burned at Paris as a result of the *affaire des placards* (posters attacking the mass, etc.); twenty others perished at this time, some of those executed having their hands cut off first; more than two hundred were banished. From 1542 to 1546 at Geneva there were fifty-eight executions and seventy-six banishments. John Frith died at the stake praying for his enemies in 1533.

[57] *Le problème de l'incroyance au XVIᵉ siècle* (Paris, 1947), p. 361.

[58] Douglas Bush, "Seventeenth Century Poets and the Twentieth Century," *Annual Bulletin of the Modern Humanities Research Association*, No. 27 (1955), p. 24.

[59] Baker, *op. cit.*, p. 12. Don Cameron Allen has written with authority on this subject. He says of seventeenth-century thinkers: "The cosmological system in which they trusted was going to pieces; and with it, the neat sublunar organizations, which had brought stability and a sense of permanence to the Middle Ages and the early Renaissance, were likewise disintegrating and sinking from view in an echoless pit." See his *The Legend of Noah: Renaissance Rationalism in Art, Science, and Letters* (Urbana, Illinois, 1949), p. 30; see also *idem, Doubt's Boundless Sea: Skepticism and Faith in the Renaissance* (Baltimore, 1964).

[60] Francis Hermans, *Histoire doctrinale de l'humanisme chrétien* (Tournai–Paris, 1948), II, 210.

[61] C. S. Lewis, *De Descriptione Temporum* (Cambridge, 1955), pp. 10–11. The reference to the lion extends a symbol which the author introduced earlier (on page 10): "The sciences long remained like a lion-cub whose gambols delighted its master in private; it had not yet tasted man's blood."

⁶²See the long speech of Divine Love to Man in Calderón's *auto sacramental, El año santo de Roma* (*Obras completas,* eds. A. Valbuena Briones and A. Valbuena Prat [Madrid, 1952–59], III, 494–96).

CHAPTER NINE

¹ *El doctor Huarte de San Juan y su Examen de Ingenios. Contribución a la historia de la psicología diferencial,* tercera ed. corregida, Madrid, 1948 (first published in 1938 in *Span. Forschungen d. Görresgesellschaft* and in a second ed. "notablemente aumentada" in Madrid in 1939). In 1905 Unamuno in his *Vida de Don Quijote y Sancho*—apparently without knowledge of Salillas—cites Huarte on several occasions (2nd ed., Madrid, Renacimiento, n. d., pp. 15, 17, 126, 127, 233), but, though aware that Don Quijote was "de temperamento colérico, en el que predominan calor y sequedad" (p. 15), he sees no connection between this fact and the adjective in the book's title, and he fails to understand the interplay of humors, and hence of exaltation and depression, to which Don Quijote was subject: he does not realize that it is because *cólera* is yielding to *melancolía* that Don Quijote in II, 60 not merely allowed his squire to lay hands on his person but "prometió no tocarle en el pelo de la ropa"; that for the first time in his life "se deja vencer humildemente y sin defenderse siquiera; se deja vencer de su escudero" (p. 265). See the discussion of *melancolía* below. In 1906 Cejador, in the second vol. of *La lengua de Cervantes* writes s. v. *ingenio:* "Téngase en cuenta para entender el título de *Ingenioso Hidalgo* la doctrina de Huarte" and s. v. *ingenioso* refers to the study of Salillas. Also in 1906, W. W. Comfort reviewed Salillas' book in *MLN,* XXI, 30–32: "It deserves to be called to the attention of Cervantistas the world over." Comfort held that Cervantes obtained from Huarte his use of the adjective *ingenioso* in the sense of a man whose imagination has warped his judgment; he also accepted the parallels between the *Examen* of Huarte and the *Galatea* and the *Persiles.* In 1916 and in all subsequent editions of his critical edition of the *Quijote,* Rodríguez Marín gave no attention to this aspect of the word *ingenioso.* Castro disregards it in 1925 in *El pensamiento de Cervantes.* In 1936 A. Farinelli, in *Dos excéntricos: Cristóbal de Villalón.—El Dr. Juan Huarte* (Madrid), is skeptical: "también se ha tardado en reconocer su *afinidad espiritual* [italics mine] con Cervantes, que se observa por algunas derivaciones del *Examen,* muy singulares y convincentes." He refers to Salillas and to Father Iriarte, but without fully subscribing: "se consideró que. . . ." He concludes: "Muy leído, muy gustado y muy meditado fué este breviario de la vida, y es gran lástima que Cervantes se obstinara en no citarlo" (p. 98; cf. p. 88). For technical studies of the *Quijote* from the standpoint of abnormal psychology, see Dr. J. B. Ullersperger, *Historia de la psiquiatría y de la psicología en España* (Madrid, 1954), p. 79 and note. On Huarte, see the Indice de Nombres.

² For a general idea of the knowledge of psychiatric theories that a layman could be expected to have in Cervantes' time, see Covarrubias, *Tesoro de la lengua castellana* (1611), s. v. *loco:* "La etimología deste vocablo tornará loco a qualquier hombre cuerdo, porque no se halla cosa que hincha su vacío . . . puédese aver dicho . . . *a loquendo,* porque los tales suelen, con la *sequedad del cerebro,* hablar mucho y dar muchas voces; y si bien lo consideramos al hombre que está en su juyzio, si es muy hablador, dezimos comúnmente ser un loco. Entre loco, tonto y bovo ay mucha diferencia, por causarse estas enfermedades de diferentes principios y calidades. La una de la *cólera adusta,* y la otra de la abundancia de flema. *Vide verbo* bovo, y en esto me remito a los médicos." Throughout this article I underline freely words I wish to emphasize (such as *sequedad* and *cólera* in the present note) and shall not hereafter call attention to the fact that the italics are mine.

³ El Arcipreste de Talavera, *El Corbacho,* ed. L. B. Simpson (Berkeley, 1939), p. 208.

⁴"At the inception of a *hot* and *dry* passion, the gall pours forth *choler*." Lawrence Babb, *The Elizabethan Malady. A Study of Melancholia in English Literature from 1570 to 1642* (East Lansing, Michigan, 1951), p. 13. Prior to his first *salida* Don Quijote experiences both *hot* and *dry* passions: "The internal motions fall into two categories: *concupiscible* and *irascible*. Concupiscible passions arise when the *imagination* . . . perceives or conceives an object as *pleasing* . . . *pleasure* . . . desire . . . are '*hot and moist*' or '*sanguine*' passions. Accompanied by *dryness, heat* arouses combative passions—*boldness,* and anger, [which are] '*hot and dry*' or '*choleric*' passions." As he reads his tales of derring-do Alonso Quijano clearly experiences the *hot-moist* passion of *pleasure:* "aquellas intricadas razones le parecían de perlas." With the increase of cerebral dryness through lack of sleep the *hot-dry* passion of *boldness* becomes increasingly powerful: "ocasiones y peligros donde, acabándolos, cobrase eterno nombre y fama." See Babb, op. cit., pp. 4 and 12.

⁵"Demócrito Abderita fué uno de los mayores filósofos . . . que hubo en su tiempo; . . . el cual vino a tanta pujanza de *entendimiento* allá en la vejez, que se le perdió la *imaginativa,* por la cual razón comenzó a hacer y decir dichos y sentencias tan fuera de términos, que toda la ciudad . . . le tuvo por loco." Hippocrates was summoned to effect his cure. The physician, "haciéndole las preguntas que convenía para descubrir la falta que tenía en la parte *racional,* halló que era el hombre más sabio que había en el mundo. . . . Y fué la ventura que cuanto razonó Hipócrates en aquel breve tiempo fueron discursos del entendimiento y no de la *imaginativa,* donde tenía la lesión." Huarte apud Iriarte, op. cit., p. 317.

⁶Huarte says of St. Paul: ". . . haciéndole Dios de grande entendimiento y *mucha imaginativa,* forzosamente, guardando el orden natural, le sacó *colérico adusto*." Apud Iriarte, op. cit., p. 321.

⁷Don Quijote says to him, on two occasions: "Duerme tú, que naciste para dormir" (I, 20; II, 68). Helmut Hatzfeld, in *El Quijote como obra de arte del lenguaje* (Madrid, 1949), in the chapter on La Antítesis, discusses "el tema, que tan a menudo se repite, del descanso nocturno del caballero y el escudero," pp. 41–42, but without reference to typological physiology and psychology. Sancho remains throughout a *cachazudo,* although capable of anger which even his master is made to feel, and capable also of manifestations of *ingenio* which Cervantes finds it necessary to explain or at least to note with surprise: "el mayordomo ocupó lo que faltaba [de la noche] en escribir a sus señores lo que Sancho Panza hacía y decía, tan admirado de sus hechos como de sus dichos: porque andaban mezcladas sus palabras y acciones cono *asomos discretos y tontos*" (II, 51); "estoy admirado de ver que un hombre tan sin letras como vuesa merced . . . diga tales y tantas cosas llenas de sentencias y de avisos, tan fuera de todo aquello que del *ingenio* de vuesa merced esperaban los que nos enviaron. . . . Cada día se ven cosas nuevas en el mundo: las burlas se vuelven en veras y los burladores se hallan burlados" (II, 49). Cervantes does what he can to preserve verisimilitude. Don Quijote's advice to Sancho on the eve of this governorship is: "come poco y cena poco . . . , *sea moderado tu sueño*" (II, 43). Dr. Pedro Recio Aguado explains his dietary measures: "miro por su salud más que por la mía . . . , tanteando la *complexión* del Gobernador . . . , y así mandé quitar el plato de la fruta por ser *demasiadamente húmeda,* y el plato del otro manjar . . . por ser demasiadamente caliente y tener muchas especias, que *acrecientan la sed*" (II, 47). In spite of Sancho's fondness for *olla podria,* "le hicieron desayunar con un poco de conserva y cuatro tragos de agua . . . haciéndole creer [el médico] que los manjares pocos y delicados *avivaban el ingenio*" (II, 51). Both Sancho and Don Quijote follow an uneven line between the means and the extremes of their *complexión* or humoral temperament. Don Quijote's oscillations are no greater than those of Saul of Tarsus. See the *Addendum* at the end of this article.

[8] Patrick Cruttwell, "Physiology and Psychology in Shakespeare's Age," *Journ. of the Hist. of Ideas*, XII (1951), 75–89. See specifically, Francis Johnson, "Elizabethan Drama and the Elizabethan Science of Psychology," in C. L. Wrenn and G. Bullough, eds., *English Studies Today* (Oxford, 1951), p. 115.

[9] Johnson, op. cit., p. 116.

[10] Ed. cit., p. 212 ff.

[11] *Agonía del tránsito de la muerte*, NBAE, XVI, 185a. The reference is to Scot's *Physiognomia* (many eds. from 1477) and Indagine's *Introductiones apotelesmicae . . . in physiognomiam, astrologiam naturalem, complexiones hominum, naturas planetarum . . .* , Strasburg, 1522.

[12] Lucien Febvre, *Le problème de l'incroyance au seizième siècle* (Paris, 1947), p. 216.

[13] Babb, op. cit., p. 6.

[14] Ibid., p. 7 and note 1.

[15] Humors cause motions of the *heart*. Don Quijote, at this point in his life's trajectory, is suffering from the cold-dry passion of melancholy. Cold, in combination with dryness, provokes *contraction of the heart*. See Babb, op. cit., p. 12. Cf. E. M. W. Tillyard, *The Elizabethan World Picture* (London, 1948), p. 63: "The *natural* spirits are a vapor formed in the liver and carried with the humors along the veins . . . acted on in the *heart* by *heat* and air from the lungs, they assume a higher quality and become *vital* spirits. Accompanied by a nobler kind of blood, also refined in the *heart*, they carry life and heat through the arteries."

[16] "One of the oldest divisions of mental disorder is into melancholia and mania. In the former the dominant mood is depression; in the latter, exaltation." *Catholic Encyclopedia*, s. v. *Insanity*. It is natural that Don Quijote's mania—his mood of exaltation—should give way to its opposite as the end of his adventures, and of his life, approaches.

[17] On the effect of fever cf. Huarte apud Iriarte, p. 319: "Si el hombre cae en alguna enfermedad por la cual el *cerebro* de repente mude su *temperatura*, como es la manía y frenesí, en un momento acontece perder, si es prudente, cuanto sabe, y dice mil disparates, y si es necio [or *loco*, as in Don Quijote's case] adquiere más ingenio y habilidad que antes tenía."

[18] This of course is the antidote to the *lack of sleep* which was the original cause of Don Quijote's derangement. The cooling and humidifying effect of sleep has already been discussed. It will be discussed again in connection with Don Quijote's three *vueltas*. See below.

[19] Ed. cit., pp. 207–208.

[20] Cf. Alonso de Acevedo, *Creación del mundo*, BAE, XXIX, 266a: "El fiero Marte, *seco y encendido*, / Los inhumanos corazones prende / Con el ardor de su crueldad nacido, / Y por las venas llamas de ira extiende. . . ."

[21] Edward Sarmiento, "Don Quijote and the Holy Images," *Dublin Review*, Autumn, 1947, p. 35.

[22] That he read the *Corbacho* is also possible. There were four sixteenth-century editions.

[23] Ullersperger, op. cit., p. 80.

[24] Cf., below, the reference to the *loco* Luys López (note 53); the quotation from *La elección de los alcaldes de Daganzo;* and the parallel, established by Iriarte on pp. 318–319, between Antonio Moreno (the *caballero barcelonés* who protested that Sansón Carrasco had done great harm in depriving the public of the entertainment provided by Don Quijote in his derangement) and the *Grande de estos reinos* reported by Huarte as protesting the cure of his *paje* (a case that "sirvió . . . para la historia del . . . *paje* cervantino Tomás Rodaja" in *El Licenciado Vidriera*). Here is Huarte's text, closely paralleled by Cervantes: "Yo os doy mi palabra, señor doctor, de que ningún mal suceso he rescibido jamás de tanta pena como de ver a este paje sano; porque tan avisada locura no era razón trocarla

por un juicio tan torpe como a éste le queda en sanidad." On another analogue of the *Licenciado Vidriera*, see Alberto Escudero Ortuño, *Concepto de la melancolía en el siglo XVII* (Huesca, 1950) pp. 60–62, and note 4 on p. 62. But here there is a difficulty with respect to chronology which can, however, be explained away. See p. 62.

[25] Apud Iriarte, op. cit., p. 192.

[26] Ibid., pp. 208–209.

[27] Apud Cejador, *La lengua de Cervantes*, s. v. *ingenio*.

[28] *Tesoro de la lengua castellana*, s. v. *ingenio*.

[29] Iriarte, op. cit., p. 314.

[30] See the diagram of the four *complectiones* in Babb, op. cit., p. 11.

[31] Iriarte, op. cit., p. 316.

[32] See above, note 16.

[33] Iriarte, op. cit., pp. 316–317.

[34] Ibid., p. 318.

[35] Ibid., p. 320.

[36] Ibid., p. 321.

[37] Apud Iriarte, op. cit., p. 321.

[38] Apud Iriarte, op. cit., p. 320.

[39] Ibid., p. 324.

[40] Ibid., p. 325.

[41] Ibid.

[42] Throughout the *Quijote* there are many minor reflections of this concern with hot-dry and cold-moist. Even before Don Quijote's mission had taken clear shape in his mind, that is to say, before the heat and dryness of his brain had forced him to action, he felt the need of replenishing his bodily *moisture* and lowering his *temperature*: "Andaba a cuchilladas con las paredes; y cuando estaba muy cansado . . . bebíase un gran jarro de *agua fría* y quedaba *sano y sosegado* . . ." (I, v). In the final paragraph of the Second Part Cervantes says that his hero is his own creation, "a despecho y a pesar del escritor . . . tordesillesco que se atrevió . . . a escribir con pluma de avestruz grosera . . . las hazañas de mi valeroso caballero, porque no es cargo de sus hombres ni asunto de su *resfriado ingenio*."

[43] "The Renaissance term for digestion is *concoction*. The liver, being a hot organ, 'is to the stomake, as fyre vnder the pot.' The product of digestion in the stomach is a viscid, whitish fluid called *chyle*. This is conveyed to the liver, and there the nutrimental matter undergoes a second concoction, the products of which are the four primary humors" (Babb, op. cit., pp. 5–6). The *food* which Don Quijote demands will restore his humors; the *sleep* will supply *moisture* to his *brain* and reduce its temperature.

[44] Babb, op. cit., pp. 12–13.

[45] See above, note 15. Alberto Escudero Ortuño, in the study on melancholy already cited, pp. 41–42, says that Alfonso de Santa Cruz, in a work published in 1622, "da una pauta general que . . . dice así: "Un remedio universalmente aceptado se puede llevar a cabo al principio, bajo cinco aspectos: 1°. Buena alimentación de fácil asimilación; líquidos templados que induzcan al sueño . . . ; 5°. Fortificando el *cerebro* y el *corazón* que, según Avicena, es el más afectado. . . .""

[46] See above, note 16. The opposite of psychotic exaltation is psychotic depression. In II, 69 Don Quijote says: "Come Sancho, amigo, sustenta la vida, que más que a mí te importa, y déjame morir a manos de mis pensamientos y a fuerza de mis desgracias." Cf. Unamuno, op. cit., p. 262. Unamuno does not realize that cold-dry melancholy restores judgment at the expense of *la imaginativa*. He says: "Las *burlas* le abrieron los ojos para conocer a los animales inmundos y soeces" (p. 263). Dr. Andrés Velázquez, who published a *Libro de la melancolía* in 1585,

held that the persons most disposed to melancholy were, like Don Quijote, "flacos, morenos y vellosos." This was Galenic doctrine. Cf. Ullersperger, op. cit., p. 89.
[47] Cf. Sarmiento's article cited above in note 21. Unamuno, op. cit., p. 256 exclaims: ¡Abismático pasaje, henchido de suprema melancolía el del encuentro de los caballeros andantes a lo divino! Por buen agüero lo tuvo el Caballero, y era, en efecto, el agüero de sus próximas conversión y muerte. Pronto mejorada su aventura y adobado su juicio enderezará sus pasos por mejor camino, por camino de la muerte."
[48] "En ocasiones . . . la tristeza del ánimo, más que síntoma, es considerada como causa de la melancolía." Escudero Ortuño, op. cit., p. 48.
[49] "Melancholy is the humor most inimical to life." Babb, op. cit., pp. 11–12.
[50] Ibid., p. 21.
[51] This is common doctrine. "Pues en el cuerpo propio, muy claro es que puede la *triste* imaginación *matar* y la alegre también, con la violencia de la una y de la otra. La alegre echando fuera todos los espíritus y dejando el hombre sin vida, y la otra de los *apretar y ahogar* violentísimamente" (P. Mexía, *Silva de varia lección*, ed. Bibliófilos Españoles, Madrid, 1933, p. 316). Cf. Babb, op. cit., pp. 13–14: "When grief or a kindred passion *closes the heart,* the blood and vital spirits are locked within it and thus are denied to the rest of the body. The whole system is *cooled and dried* both by lack of blood and vital spirit and by the *melancholy humor* issuing from the spleen." Escudero Ortuño, op. cit., p. 29, quotes Ambroise Paré to the same effect: "el corazón está apretado y restringido . . . con frecuencia la muerte es consecuencia de ello." Cf. above, note 12.
[52] See above, note 17.
[53] Apud Iriarte, op. cit., p. 319. "Aquel famoso loco Luys López" is mentioned by Cervantes in the Prologue to his *Ocho comedias* as having been buried in the Cathedral of Cordoba, "entre los dos coros." It is obviously necessary to restudy in the light of these findings the problem of Cervantes' so-called "muerte *post errorem,*" which should be understood as "muerte *post melancholiam.*" Cervantes is not punishing his characters but rather is treating them in accordance with his understanding of psychological and physiological reality. The error is true enough; it has been committed. But the Celoso Extremeño and his congeners are not executed by Cervantes; they die of their own broken hearts. Even Camila, the guilty wife of the Curioso Impertinente, on learning of the death of her lover Lotario "acabó en breves días la vida, a las rigurosas manos de tristezas y melancolías" (I, 35).
[54] See Jorge Luis Borges, "Análisis del último capítulo del *Quijote,*" *Revista de la Universidad de Buenos Aires,* Quinta Epoca, I (1956), 28–36, especially p. 36: "El libro entero ha sido escrito para esta escena, para la muerte de don Quijote."
[55] B. Sanvisenti, "Il passo più oscuro del Chisciotte," *RFE,* IX (1922), 58–62. Cf. A. Centeno in *MLN,* L (1935), 375–378, and Margaret Bates, "Cervantes' Criticism of *Tirant lo Blanch,*" *HR,* XXI (1953), 142–144.

CHAPTER TEN

[1] Armand A. Singer, "The Sources, Meaning, and Use of the Madness Theme in Cervantes' *Licenciado Vidriera,*" *West Virginia University Bulletin: Philological Papers,* VI (1949), 31–53; see p. 41. In his conclusion Singer ". . . inclines to the belief that Cervantes included the whole matter of the insanity for no basic reason other than that *locos* were commonly depicted in books of his day and that he had an overweening interest in all phases of abnormality . . ." (p. 53).
[2] Idem, "Cervantes' *Licenciado Vidriera:* Its Form and Substance," in the same journal, VIII (1951), 4.
[3] "Casalduero has made what we believe is the first adequate attempt to give meaning to the structure of the *novela.* Applying his criterion of the baroque,

he finds a perfect balance and framework. The hero has three names . . . before, during, and after his madness. . . . Looked at another way, the story has four parts: travel, illness, madness, and cure and return to Flanders . . . Casalduero has supplied a neat framework. But what of the elements that it encloses? Why the travel; why the love potion . . . ; why the witty observations? . . . we must . . . not merely postulate a system of tonic and atonic rhythms" (Singer in his second art., 14–15).

⁴ "In order to communicate his sense of evil the artist must transform the fog of emotion into intelligible shapes and objectify the tangible forms of suffering . . . thus to clarify and project is to express himself well, and therefore to reveal a mastery of expression that excites admiring contemplation" (Melvin A. Rader, *A Modern Book of Esthetics* [New York, 1935], p. xix).

⁵ Susanne K. Langer, *Feeling and Form* (New York, 1953).

⁶ *Obras completas* (Madrid: Aguilar, 1956), p. 84.

⁷ Cf. Cervantes' insistence that "las cosas de Don Quijote" must be taken either with "admiracion" (*lo grave*) or with "risa" (*lo afable*).

⁸ On the long history of *preguntas y respuestas*, conspicuous in the sixteenth-century Torres Naharro and in the nineteenth-century *Martin Fierro*, see *Propalladia and Other Works of Bartolomé de Torres Naharro*, edited by Joseph E. Gillet, vol. IV: *Torres Naharro and the Drama of the Renaissance*, transcribed, edited and completed by Otis H. Green (Philadelphia, 1960), pp. 41, 299 ff., 558.

⁹ See note 2, above.

¹⁰ "The *pregunta* may well have developed out of the riddle, or parallel to it. Both are fundamentally a contest of ritualistic origin, the riddle predominantly a fertility rite, the *pregunta* traceable to a tradition mentioned in Sanskrit texts . . . A hymn in the Rig-Veda shows priests asking questions on various subjects, often cosmogony: I ask you where lies the navel of the earth? . . . Where do the halves of the moon go? . . . Why does the wind never rest? . . . Who are more in number, the living or the dead? . . . Which came first, night or day?" (Gillet-Green, op. cit., p. 301). The whole discussion is pages long and extends to Argentina, Chile, and Mexico.

¹¹ The humoral psychology of Don Quijote's aberrations is studied in my article, "El *ingenioso* hidalgo," *HR*, XXV (1957), 175–193.

¹² See O. H. Green, art. cit, p. 182, n. 24.

¹³ (East Lansing, Michigan, 1951), pp. 42–43.

¹⁴ See my article, "Realidad, Voluntad y gracia en Cervantes," *Ibérida. Revista de filologia*, III (1961), 113–128.

¹⁵ James Fitzmaurice-Kelly, *Chapters on Spanish Literature* (London, 1908), p. 140.

CHAPTER ELEVEN

¹ *Doña Clarines y Mañana de Sol*, ed. S. G. Morley (Boston, 1909), p. 23 and corresponding note (pp. 93–94).

² Composed, according to Rodríguez Marín, before Vera y Figueroa became Conde de la Roca (1628). He dates the MS as of the end of the sixteenth century or beginning of the seventeenth. I regard it as later than 1605 because of the apparent influence of Huarte (through *Don Quijote*).

³ "Un tema erasmiano en el *Quijote*, I, xxii," *Revista hispánica moderna*, XIX (1953), 88–93. See pp. 91 f.: "Mas si el sentido en ellas [ingeniosidades] no es erasmista, el gusto en recrearse con un género literario desusado hasta comienzos del 'quinientos' tiene sus raíces más directas en una modalidad que sólo pertenecía al libro de Erasmo."

⁴ When Don Quixote ceases speaking, the *alcahuete* expresses agreement and states that "en lo de hechicero, que no tuve la culpa." The pimping he readily

admits, "pero nunca pensé que hacía mal en ello." He then "tornó a su llanto como de primero," and Sancho pities him so greatly that "sacó un real de a cuatro del seno y se le dio de limosna."

⁵ In *El Licenciado Vidriera* the Licenciate is asked "qué le parecía de las alcahuetas. Respondió que no lo eran las apartadas, sino las vecinas." This is pure *ingenio*: "He replied that one should not worry about the bawds in the red-light district (*apartadas*) but should rather guard against those near at hand" (i.e. *vecinas*, neighbors, like the "señora de la casa de enfrente" complained about and condemned by Doña Clarines in the play by the Quintero brothers). See above, n. 1. For Cervantes' text, see his *Obras completas*, ed. A. Valbuena Prat (Madrid, 1956), p. 881.

⁶ Don Quijote "imposes his will on all he meets. . . . He addresses wantons as ladies, and they act as ladies for the nonce; an innkeeper, a barber, a peasant are forced into chivalrous rôles by the power of his enthusiasm. He compels country gentlemen, nobles, clergymen to reflect seriously upon great themes: public service, the function of culture, the principles of the arts, the duties of government" (William J. Entwistle, "The Search for the Heroic Poem," in University of Pennsylvania Bicentennial Conference, *Studies in Civilization* [Philadelphia, 1940], p. 97).

⁷ See my article, "El *ingenioso* hidalgo," *HR*, XXV (1957), 183.

⁸ Cervantes "was one of the first European writers—perhaps the very first—to have had a theory of the novel of any considerable scope at all" (E. C. Riley, *Cervantes's Theory of the Novel* [Oxford, 1962], p. 221).

⁹ On episodes, see Bernard Weinberg, *A History of Literary Criticism in the Italian Renaissance*, 2 vols. (Chicago, 1961), Index, s. v. Episode; William K. Wimsatt, Jr. and Cleanth Brooks, *Literary Criticism: A Short History* (New York, 1957), p. 177.

¹⁰ Riley, op. cit., pp. 130 f.

¹¹ "Quae homo perperam agit, an ordine agat. Mala in ordinem redacta faciunt ad decorem universi."

¹² *Patrologiae Cursus Completus. Series Prima.* Patrologiae Tomus XXXII, S. Agustini Tomus Primus (Paris, 1845; emphasis mine), cols. 999–1000: "Nam ea dicitis quae nec quomodo dicantur non visa, nec quomodo ea videatis intelligo; ita ea et vera et alta esse suspicor. Simile autem aliquod in istam sententiam tu fortasse unum requirebas. At mihi jam occurrunt innumerabilia, quae me ad consentiendum prorsus trahunt. Quid enim carnifice tetrius? quid illo animo truculentius atque dirius? At inter ipsas leges locum necessarium tenet, et in bene moderatae civitatis ordinem inseritur; estque suo animo nocens, ordine autem alieno poena nocentium. Quid sordidius, quid inanius decoris et turpitudinis plenius est meretricibus, lenonibus, caeterisque hoc genus pestibus dici potest? Aufer meretrices de rebus humanis, turbaveris omnia libidinibus: constitue matronarum loco, labe ac dedecore dehonestaveris. Sic igitur hoc genus hominum per suos mores impurissimum vita, per ordinis leges conditione vilissimum. Nonne in corporibus animantium quaedam membra, si sola attendas, non possis attendere? Tamen ea naturae ordo, nec quia necessaria sunt, deesse voluit, nec quia indecora, eminere permisit. Quae tamen deformia suos locos tenuerunt, meliorem locum concessere melioribus. Quid nobis suavius, quod agro villaeque spectaculum congruentius fuit pugna illa conflictuque gallinaceorum gallorum, cujus superiore libro fecimus mentionem (Cap. 8, n. 25). Quid abjectius tamen deformitate subjecti vidimus? Et per ipsam tamen ejusdem certaminis perfectior pulchritudo provenerat."

¹³ St. Thomas wrote in *Summa contra Gentiles*, Bk. III, chap. 71: "The good of the whole is more excellent than the good of the part. Accordingly, the prudent governor should disregard an occasional partial defect in order to increase—as a result—the good of the whole, just as the architect hides beneath the ground the foundations in order to give stability to the house. If the evil of certain parts of

the universe were to be suppressed, much of its perfection would be lost, because its beauty is revealed to us through the ordered balance of good and evil things. . ." (*Summa contra gentiles*, ed. bilingüe . . . con el texto de la leonina, traducción dirigida y revisada por el P. Fr. Jesús M. Pla Castellano, O. P., Biblioteca de Autores Cristianos [Madrid, 1953]. Vol. II, p. 272. Since both the Spanish and Latin texts are readily available in this edition, I do not quote the original).

[14] *Obras sueltas de Lupercio y Bartolomé Leonardo de Argensola*, ed. el Conde de la Viñaza, 2 vols. (Madrid, 1889), II, 241–253. Needless to say, Argensola's essay is an analogue, not a "source."

[15] Paris, 1543, and many later editions.

[16] *Enciclopedia* cit., art. cit., p. 1108.

[17] Cf. The Republic of Venice, *Volumen Statutorum, Legum, ac Iurium D. Venetorum, cum amplissimo indice omnium materiarum* (Venetiis, MDLVIIII); eadem, *Leggi e Memorie Venete sulla prostituzione fin alla caduta della Reppublica* (Venezia, 1870–1872).

CHAPTER TWELVE

[1] A propos of Charles Vincent Aubrun, *La comédie espagnole (1600–1681)* (Paris, 1966). See also E. C. Riley, *Cervantes's Theory of the Novel* (Oxford, 1962).

[2] For this and the following two quotations see Otis H. Green, *Spain and the Western Tradition*, 4 vols. (Madison-Milwaukee, 1963–66), III, 389.

[3] *Ibid.*, III, 393.

[4] *Ibid.*, III, 433 and note 112.

[5] Cited by Andrés Amorós, "El joven don Américo," *Insula*, núm. 245 (1967), p. 3.

[6] See Green, op. cit., IV, 207–08.

[7] "Incarnation in *Don Quixote*," in *Cervantes Across the Centuries* (New York, 1947), 136–78.

[8] On this interpretation of *Don Quixote* see Green, op. cit., IV, 60–73.

[9] We owe this concept of poetic justice in the *comedia* largely to the studies of A. A. Parker. See Green, op. cit., Vol. IV, Index, s.v. *Comedia, the Spanish*, and pp. 249–51 of the text. Ample bibliography is given in the notes to Gwynne Edwards' article, "Calderón's *La hija del aire* and the Classical Type of Tragedy," *BHS*, XLV (1967), 161–94. See also the earlier article of A. G. Reichenberger, "The Uniqueness of the *Comedia*," *HR*, XXVII (1959), 303–16.

[10] When Lope, late in his career, undertook to give literary form to a powerfully dramatic episode of his early emotional life, he turned his back on his own literary creation, the *comedia* in verse, and chose to write what he called an *acción en prosa: La Dorotea* (1632).

[11] Cervantes' idea of using the vagaries and the wisdom of a monomaniac (whose madness had intervals of marvellous lucidity) as so many prisms through which to contemplate the vagaries, the madness and the wisdom of human experience—this idea appealed to J. B. Priestly as "the best idea an author ever had." Because of the fruitfulness of this idea Cervantes "reached forward to inspire all the novelists who set their characters wandering, and gave godspeed to Gil Blas and Tom Jones and Wilhelm Meister and Mr. Pickwick and Sam Weller. He wrote, therefore, the best novel in the world. . . . He might be said to have pointed further forward still, beyond where his faith and hope could reach, towards Ibsen, Unamuno, Proust, Pirandello, Mann and Joyce. Of all our great novelists he is the youngest, because he is the first, and the oldest, because his tale of the mad knight is an old man's tale. He is also the wisest." See *Literature and Western Man* (New York, 1960), pp. 49–50.